The
Venerable English College
Rome

The
Venerable English College Rome

A History

SECOND EDITION

Michael E. Williams

GRACEWING

First published in Great Britain in 1979 on behalf of the Venerable
English College, Rome by Associated Catholic Publications Ltd,
London

Second edition 2008 published by

Gracewing
2 Southern Avenue
Leominster
Herefordshire HR6 0QF

ISBN 978 0 85244 048 3

Typesetting by
Action Publishing Technology Ltd, Gloucester, GL1 5SR

Printed in England by
Athenaeum Press Ltd, Gateshead NE11 0PZ

Contents

Foreword   ix
List of Plates   x
List of Illustrations   xi
Prologue   xv
Preface to Second Edition   xix
Abbreviations   xx

Chapter One   Beginnings   1
    The Hospice – Transition from Hospice to College –
    Early days of the College – Unique nature of the English
    colleges – Quarrels and dissensions – The visitation of
    1585 – The troubles of 1594–97

Chapter Two   Roma Barocca   34
    Exiles and strangers – The studies – Discipline –
    Decline or stability? – Fitzherbert – Roger Baines

Chapter Three   Cardinals Protector and Vicars Apostolic   60
    Cardinal Howard – The Stuarts – The rebuilding of the College –
    1739 visitation report – Student life in the mid-eighteenth century –
    Corsini and the finances – The suppression of the Jesuits –
    The English mission

Chapter Four   Dissolution, Interregnum and Restoration   92
    The College during the Interregnum – The English ecclesiastical
    scene – The restoration – The agency – Gradwell as agent –
    Gradwell as Rector

Chapter Five   The Wiseman Tradition   118
Character of Wiseman – Wiseman as Rector – Wiseman as agent –
Wiseman as bishop and cardinal – Baggs, Grant and the
continuance of the Wiseman tradition

Chapter Six   Mid-Century Problems of Ecclesiastical Training 141
Cornthwaite becomes Rector – Collegio Pio – Louis English as Rector –
The appointment of Frederick Neve – Talbot and the rebuilding of
the church – The Roman Association – Neve, Manning and Talbot

Chapter Seven   1870 and After   165
O'Callaghan – The occupation of Rome: 1870 – The College property
and the Duke of Norfolk – Edward Howard, Herbert Vaughan and
Henry O'Callaghan – William Giles – Burton and Roman theology –
Modernism

Chapter Eight   The Hinsley Tradition   192
The visitation under McIntyre – Hinsley's appointment –
The Hinsley spirit – Studies – The end of Hinsley's rule –
The rectorship of William Godfrey

Chapter Nine   The War, the Exile and the Return to Rome   220
Italian politics and the war – The exodus – Ambleside –
St Mary's Hall – The College property in Rome – The liberation of
Rome – The return

Chapter Ten   From Post-War to Post-Conciliar Rome   236
Post-war Rome – Macmillan hands on to Tickle – The Second
Vatican Council – Life after the Council

Appendices

I   The Buildings of the Venerable English College: 253
       An Historical Account by Jerome Bertram
II   The Bull of Foundation: Translation
       by Jerome Bertram   272
III   Statutes, Constitutions and Rules of the Venerable
       English College   281
IV   The College Martyrs and Year of Martyrdom   290
V   Cardinals Protector of the Venerable English College 292
VI   Rectors of the Venerable English College   295
VII   Episcopal Appointments of Former Students since 1818 298

VIII The Venerable English College Archives: 302
     General Description and Summary Catalogue

Select Bibliography and Reading List   330
Index   335

Foreword

'The Venerable English College is a great College,' Pope Benedict XVI told me when I brought him the seminarians' loyal greetings at the Mass for the Pontifical Universities recently. When Pope Benedict visited the Gregorian University in 2006, he singled out the *Venerabile* as having a special place in the origins of the university set up by the Jesuits to prepare secular priests for the Home Mission. The cover of this revised *History* shows the *Greg*'s founder, Pope Gregory XIII, blessing students of this College as they prepared to embark on that mission to the beleaguered Catholics of England and Wales four centuries ago.

Monsignor Michael Williams tells this whole story in a way which captures the unique place of this 'great College' in the history of the Church. I welcome his revised *History* enthusiastically. Michael Williams is quick to remind us that the *Venerabile* is the oldest British institution abroad. He helps us see why a recent Archbishop of Canterbury told an Anglican ordinand coming to stay in the College, 'You will be living on holy ground.' The tradition of welcoming Anglican Exchange students was initiated by Monsignor Murphy-O'Connor, the fourth Rector-alumnus to be appointed Cardinal Archbishop of Westminster, and whose Rectorship I am delighted to see included in this extended *History*.

Michael Williams draws largely for his account on documents to be found in the College Archive. We created recently a new Archive and have employed the services of an Archivist to care for it. Cardinal Tauran, the Vatican Archivist, came to open it; and captured the spirit of both that project and this revised *History* when he said, 'When you possess good Archives, it means you believe in your future!' This work of Michael Williams is most certainly an investment in the College and in the Church's future; and future generations of *Venerabilini* will remain deeply indebted to him for it.

Monsignor Nicholas Hudson
Rector
February 2008

List of Colour Plates

1 Martyrs' Picture, Durante Alberti
2 Ceiling fresco from Martyrs' Chapel
3 Ceiling fresco from Refectory
4 Painting of St Mary Magdalen anointing the feet of Christ
5 Fresco in College chapel tribune, Pope Gregory XIII praying with College students before their mission and martyrdom
6 St Edmund Campion, portrait
7 William Cardinal Allen, portrait
8 Ralph Sherwin window

List of Illustrations

1.1	Tomb of Christopher Cardinal Bainbridge	*page* xxii
1.2	Reginald Cardinal Pole	2
1.3	Owen Lewis, Bishop of Cassano	4
1.4	Remnants of Royal Coats of Arms in College	6
1.5	Fragment of stone relief from the Hospice church	6
1.6	Hospice church, from a woodcut, *c*.1580	9
1.7	Letter of Cardinal Charles Borromeo	10
1.8	St Ralph Sherwin	14
1.9	Frescoes in College chapel tribune	18
1.10	Plan of the centre of Rome (1576)	20
1.11	The first entries in the Liber Ruber	22
1.12	An engraving depicting Pope Gregory XIII with his foundations	25
2.1	The 'Seven Churches' of Rome, late sixteenth century	36
2.2	The Collegio Romano, the Jesuit house of studies	38
2.3	The piazza in front of the Collegio Romano	40
2.4	The Church of Sant' Ignazio	46
2.5	View of College and adjacent Mary Ward School (1593)	48
2.6	The Campo dei Fiori	50
2.7	La Magliana farm	52
2.8	View of Monte Porzio	54
3.1	Philip Cardinal Howard	61
3.2	Henry Cardinal Duke of York	64
3.3	Piazza Santissimi (Dodici) Apostoli lined with palaces	66
3.4	The Palazzo della Cancelleria	68

3.5	Requiem Mass of Queen Maria Clementina	70
3.6	Drawing of College from around 1685	72
3.7	The presently-named Martyrs' Chapel	74
3.8	Student dress in 1710	78
4.1	Robert Gradwell, Rector, 1818–28	96
5.1	Nicholas Wiseman, Rector 1828–40	120
5.2	Charles Baggs, Rector 1840–44	124
5.3	Thomas Cardinal Weld	128
5.4	Blessed Pope Pius IX	130
5.5	John Henry Newman and Ambrose St John in Rome, 1847	134
5.6	Nicholas Cardinal Wiseman	136
6.1	Design by E.W. Pugin for the new College chapel	148
6.2	The College church under construction in 1869	154
6.3	John Henry Cardinal Newman	156
6.4	Henry Cardinal Manning	158
6.5	Early photograph of the completed College church	159
6.6–9	Views of the new church opened in 1888	160
7.1	Julian Watts-Russell	169
7.2	Tusculum Cross (1883), erected by the students in 1864	173
7.3	Edward Cardinal Howard	176
7.4	Herbert Cardinal Vaughan	178
7.5	William Giles, Rector 1888–1913	179
7.6	The Rector, Mgr Giles, with students in 1890–1	182
7.7	Picnic at Tusculum, 1885	184
8.1	The College roofline after 1911	193
8.2	Arthur Hinsley, Rector 1913–29	197
8.3	Francis Cardinal Gasquet	198
8.4	An aerial view of Palazzola, the College summer residence	200
8.5	Palazzola cortile	200
8.6	Palazzola, the façade of the Church of Our Lady of the Snows	201
8.7	The College garden and *guardaroba*	202
8.8–10	Modernisation of College	204
8.11–12	The College library as refurbished in the 1920s	206
8.13	View of the new Gregorian University	210
9.1	The College as a hospital during the Second World War	221
9.2	St Mary's Hall, Stonyhurst, home to the College during the Second World War	226
9.3	Corpus Christi Procession, Stonyhurst	227
9.4	The walk between lectures at St Mary's Hall, Stonyhurst	228
9.5	Arthur Cardinal Hinsley	231

9.6	Bernard Cardinal Griffin	232
9.7	The bronze commemorative plaque at St Mary's Hall	233
10.1	Visiting St Peter's during the Jubilee on 12 December 1950	237
10.2–3	The *camerata* system and clerical street attire continued into the 1960s	238
10.4	Cardinal Godfrey visits Pope John XXIII with the College in attendance	239
10.5	Vatican II: Council Session in St Peter's	241
10.6	The College with Council Fathers: the English Bishops	243
10.7	William Cardinal Godfrey	244
10.8	William Cardinal Heard	245
10.9	Pope Paul VI visits Palazzola	247
10.10	Pope Paul VI with the students at Palazzola, 22 August 1963	248
10.11	Archbishop Ramsey visits the College	249

Prologue

It was on the occasion of the centenary of the reopening of the College in 1818 that Gasquet wrote *A History of the Venerable English College, Rome*. It was offered 'until something better is given to the public by one who can devote more time to the work than I have been able to do'. Since Gasquet's day not only has the College added more pages to its history, but further research into its past has helped to supplement and reinterpret the picture he presented. Some of this information is to be found in the pages of learned journals, a considerable contribution has appeared over the years in *The Venerabile* (1922–1974) and the careful work of succeeding generations of College archivists has made the task easier than it was for Gasquet. However, the more one researches the more material comes to light, and only when the available archives in the many sources to be found in Rome and England have been thoroughly examined, will it be possible to write a definitive history.

This, then, is only a provisional history. Like Gasquet's, it is written for an occasion – the fourth centenary of the Bull of Foundation in 1579. Because of its continuity with the English Hospice, the College can claim to be the oldest existing British institution abroad. But our concern here is only with the last four hundred years. A brief account of the Hospice is given in the opening chapter, but for a more scholarly record one must refer to *The English Hospice in Rome*, the sexcentenary number of *The Venerabile* (1962).

Some of the story is already familiar and well documented. This is particularly true of the early days of the College. For this part of the work there has been little new research so it is largely a restatement of other scholars' work. But other periods have been seriously neglected and it has been necessary to seek out further information on the late seventeenth and most of the eighteenth century. Much more attention has been given to the nineteenth century than was possible sixty years ago and a lot of the material in these chapters is presented for the first time. An attempt has also been made to throw some light on the Hinsley and Godfrey rectorships since they had some significance for the contemporary Church in England and Wales.

The varied nature of the sources brings its own problems. It is not so difficult to reach a detached historical viewpoint when one is dealing with past events that have been recorded and commented on before. But when one is working a relatively untilled field there is the risk of being so captivated by an individual piece of material that one falls into anecdote with subsequent loss of objectivity. This is especially true of the nineteenth century. It is sometimes assumed that this period's closeness to ourselves makes it more easily understandable. But there is the ever-present danger of projecting today's problems back into the previous age and this can result in an antipathy or sympathy towards some of the personages and events, often to the detriment of true historical judgment. This is a particular hazard for one writing in the ecclesiastical climate of the last quarter of the twentieth century.

Although at times one inevitably adopts a vocabulary and way of speech that is peculiar to the College or English Roman Catholicism, throughout the work the history of the College has been set against the backgrounds of both Rome and England. Not only is this essential for an understanding of what at first view might appear to be purely local domestic issues, but it can help to remind us of the part played by the College in the religious history of the last four hundred years – a period when English Catholics have had special links with Continental Catholicism.

After the narration, there is included a set of notes and appendices. As well as an English version of the Bull of Foundation, there is an account of the various Constitutions and Rules of the College which can give the reader an idea of the day-to-day routine of College life, which is assumed rather than stated in the main text. Some years ago *The Venerabile* (vols XXII–XXVI) began to publish a catalogue of the *libri* in the College archives. The catalogue is now complete but as it is too lengthy to publish in full, there is appended a general description of the archives and a summary catalogue. It is hoped that this account, brief as it may be, will be of use to scholars and provide an incentive for research and study for those who wish to examine further some of the issues raised in this book.

Perhaps something should be said here about the title 'venerable' and the name *Venerabile* that is given to the College. The first known document to refer to the College as *Venerabile Collegio degli Inglesi* is a 1580 broadsheet issued by papal authority granting indulgences to those visiting the College church and praying for the conversion of England to the Catholic faith. Since that time the title has been frequently used in official documents and although the English College, Rome is a Pontifical College, 'The Venerable English College' has been the preferred style and has been almost exclusively used since the nineteenth-century restoration. One tends to think of the name as being merited by the forty-one former students who suffered martyrdom, but even before their deaths the title was used and, indeed, since 1481 the Hospice had enjoyed the appellation of 'venerable'. The name *Venerabile* reminds us of the antiquity of the links between Englishmen and Rome, centred on the present site for over six hundred years but going back to that other English Hospice which King Alfred enfranchised and his predecessors founded. The pages that follow provide more recent examples of the rich and varied relationship between Englishmen, Rome and the Christian faith.

It remains to express my thanks to the very many people who have assisted me in this work. In the first place Cormac Murphy O'Connor whose idea it was that the fourth centenary should be marked by an up-to-date history of the College and whose successor as rector, George Hay, gave his full support and encouragement in seeing the work through to publication; the long line of College archivists present in the person of Jerome Bertram, whose own contribution is to be found in the appendices and the plans; the Cardinal Archbishop of Westminster (and Miss Elizabeth Poyser); the Bishop of Leeds (and Father George Bradley); the Abbot of Downside (and Father Philip Jebb OSB) for access, guidance and permission to quote from their archives; those who read some of the preliminary drafts and offered criticism and comments, Bishop Foley of Lancaster, John Allen, Godfrey Anstruther OP, Richard Ashton, Ronald Cueto, Francis Edwards SJ, Geoffrey Holt SJ, Anthony Kenny, Anthony Laird, Michael Sharratt, James Sullivan; and the whole body of friends old and new, *quorum fides cognita est et nota devotio,* who assisted and encouraged me and whom I gratefully used. They may perhaps recognise an odd piece of information or even a turn of phrase that is theirs. I hope they will accept its presence not as a theft but a tribute.

Michael Williams
Trinity and All Saints' Colleges
Horsforth
Leeds
Summer 1978

Preface to the Second Edition

It is nearly thirty years since this book first appeared and it has long been out of print. It is sometimes thought that in Rome time advances at a more leisurely pace than elsewhere but much has happened in recent years that has made it necessary to take a fresh look at the way the College history is unfolding. It is not only that changes have taken place in the life of the seminary but the view we have of our own English Catholic history has undergone some modification. This is not a new history; the original text has been preserved but there is a new chapter 'From Post-War to Post-Conciliar Rome' and the notes and appendices have been expanded to take account of some recent research and writings. A further addition has been made to the account of the College Archives although unfortunately it is not yet possible to publish a complete catalogue.

MEW
Easter 2007
Aston Hall
Aston-by-Stone

Abbreviations

AHSJ   Archivum Historicum Societatis Jesu

Anstruther   *The Seminary Priests. A Dictionary of the Secular Clergy of England and Wales* (4 vols)

CRS   Catholic Record Society Publications (Record Series)

ECA   English College Archives. Further specified according to series scr = scrittura, liber = book

Foley   *Records of the English Province of the Society of Jesus,* 7 vols

Gasquet   *A History of the Venerable English College Rome*

RH   *Recusant History. A Journal of Research in Reformation and Post Reformation Catholic History in the British Isles*

SCPF   Sacrae Congregationis de Propaganda Fide Memoria Rerum (ed. J. Metzler)

Venerabile   *The Venerabile,* Journal of the Venerable English College, Rome

Fig. 1.1 Tomb of Christopher Cardinal Bainbridge in the College church.

Chapter One

Beginnings

The story begins with the initiative of a group of Englishmen, most of them merchants, who bought a house on 27 January 1362 for the convenience and use 'of the poor, sick, needy and distressed people coming from England to the City'.[1] From early times inhabitants of these islands had visited Rome[2] but it was during the residence of the Popes at Avignon that Cola di Rienzo and Cardinal Gil de Albornoz[3] were sent by Innocent VI to restore order in Rome and it was in this period that hospices for Germans, Portuguese, Spanish, Swedish and English pilgrims were established. The English Hospice was a lay initiative, the work of a confraternity formed in the years following the 1350 Holy Year. By the time the papacy returned to Rome, the Hospice had become the spiritual centre of the English in the city and extensive rebuilding began in 1450. The membership of the confraternity was extended to students and scholars as well as royal envoys. Thomas Linacre, the classical scholar and founder of the Royal College of Physicians, was Warden of the Hospice in 1491, and amongst those who at one time or another were members of the confraternity one can number William Warham, future Archbishop of Canterbury, William Lily, the grammarian and teacher, and John Colet. By the time of Henry VII the Hospice was directly controlled by the English crown and became known as 'The King's Hospice'. Henry was anxious for it to make more provision for students and also to give hospitality to his ambassadors, one of the more famous of whom was Christopher Bainbridge, Archbishop of York and later Cardinal, whose tomb is still to be seen in the College church. The King personally

Fig. 1.2 Reginald Cardinal Pole.

appointed the Warden and there is further evidence of royal patronage in the records of Henry's famous warship, *Sovereign*, transporting revenue from England for the upkeep of the Hospice.

The sack of Rome in 1527 by Charles V's troops meant loss of plate and damage to the property. Henry VIII's breach with Rome marked a falling off in the number of pilgrims, so the Hospice now became a home for English exiles. The last royal Warden remained in office until 1538 when Paul III replaced him by appointing the English Cardinal Reginald Pole who was then resident in Rome. This was an attempt by the Pope to ensure that the Hospice confraternity would give its first loyalty to the papacy rather than the English crown. For a brief period in the reign of Mary Tudor, when Catholicism was re-established in England, the royal ambassador in Rome, Sir Edward Carne, became Warden of the Hospice. Pole had returned to England as Papal Legate and Archbishop of Canterbury.

With the accession of Elizabeth I in 1558, the royal connection was lost and the income from four vineyards and the rents of some thirty houses was no longer mainly spent on providing for pilgrims but for board and lodging for the exiles now resident there. These years of transition to a college have been investigated by A. J. Kenny[4] and an interesting picture emerges of the inmates. There were exiled pluralists in search of chaplaincies, scholars, dispossessed administrators – few of them saintly, although they had all suffered in some way for the Catholic faith. Some found other benefices in Rome and the more they were able to provide for themselves the less inclination they had to return to England. There was a small but distinguished Welsh contingent.[5] Gruffyd Robert, the grammarian, lived at the Hospice before becoming chaplain to St Charles Borromeo in 1565. Thomas Goldwell, although English by birth, had been made Bishop of St Asaph by Queen Mary and he was a resident. And there was Morus Clynnog.

Clynnog had had a more notable career than any of the other exiles. He had been twelve years at Oxford where he took the DD and BCL. He had lectured in civil law. For a further eight years he studied law at Louvain, Bologna and Padua. During Mary's reign he had held responsible positions with Cardinal Pole, frequently acting as his almoner and personal secretary. He had been nominated Bishop of Bangor but with the change of religion had decided not to be consecrated to an empty title. It was probably in 1563 that he returned to Rome and began to take an interest in the affairs of the Hospice.

One of the problems arising from the change of religion revolved

AVDVENVS VVDOVI
CVS EPVS CASSAN.

Fig. 1.3 Owen Lewis, Bishop of Cassano.

around the question of who now had supreme authority over the
Hospice. After the death of Pole, Giovanni Morone became
Cardinal Protector of England[6] and he claimed jurisdiction over its
affairs. These claims were not immediately accepted and it appears
that it was only when Clynnog became Warden that this position of
the Protector was acknowledged. In fact, Clynnog has the reputation of having sided with Morone against the Hospice confraternity.
In the light of future history this stand of the canon lawyer,
Clynnog, for the rights of the Protector is most interesting.

Life at the Hospice in those days was not very demanding. The
handful of priests circulated its offices and benefices among themselves.

> During the seventies the Hospice can have resembled nothing more
> than an Oxford Senior Common Room. The nine clerics resident
> there included two fellows of New College, one of All Souls, and an
> ex-president of Lincoln. The one Cambridge man concerned, Dr.
> Morton, steadily lost influence. It was not surprising that Sir Richard
> Shelley, English Grand Prior of the Knights of Malta, wrote to

complain to the Pope that the Hospice had become 'the exclusive preserve of Oxford men of plebeian origin ... who remain there for ten, twelve or even fourteen years, and are but benefice hunters.[7]

Liturgical commitments were not heavy and contemporary sources are scathing as to the behaviour of the chaplains, who spent their time card-playing, drinking, betting, entertaining dubious company and quarrelling among themselves. But Dr Morton and Dr Clynnog seem to have been innocent of these charges. They were scholars and Clynnog used his time to produce a simple introduction to Christian doctrine in Welsh, *Athravaeth Gristonogavl,* which was published in Milan in 1568. However, on the whole the exiles in Rome compared unfavourably with their compatriots in Flanders, who busied themselves with writings of a controversial nature.

However, they were interested in politics. The reconversion of England by force of arms was a constant theme and they welcomed the excommunication of Elizabeth and wished it to be made effectual by invasion.[8] It is here that another Welshman comes on the scene. Owen Lewis,[9] a former fellow of New College, a lawyer by training, had been professor of canon law at the new university at Douai and he came to Rome on legal business for the archdiocese of Cambrai in 1574. He soon acquired great influence in the Curia and was eventually to become vicar general to Charles Borromeo in Milan and then Bishop of Cassano in the Kingdom of Naples. He died in 1595 and was buried in the College church. It was as a by-product of the efforts of Lewis and Clynnog to plan an invasion of England, with the help of Spain, that the College in Rome was founded. In 1576 William Allen, another exile who had founded the college at Douai, was summoned to Rome to help draw up a plan of campaign. From this meeting came the decision to give effect to the scheme of turning the Hospice into a college to train men for the priesthood. Allen had already a full house at Douai and he seized the opportunity for establishing another college that would not only take the surplus numbers but also be situated in a place less liable to be affected by the war between England and Spain. The move was welcomed in Rome as a way of getting rid of the idle and quarrelsome chaplains at the Hospice and so Lewis persuaded Pope Gregory XIII to carry out a plan which had been proposed on several occasions before, as early as 1560 in fact. On 26 May 1576 Clynnog was elected Warden for the second time. Allen left Rome with instructions to send students from Douai to continue their studies in Rome and Cesare Spetiano,[10] acting on the instructions of the Cardinal Vice-Protector of England, conducted a

Fig. 1.4 Hospice and Crown: remnants of Royal Coats of Arms in the present College.

Fig. 1.5 Fragment of the finely-crafted stone relief from the Hospice church.

visitation of the Hospice. One of the objects of this was to enquire whether a greater number of persons could be maintained on the existing funds.

Transition from Hospice to College

The first students arrived from Douai in early 1577. They were John Shert,[11] Thomas Bell, John Gower, John Mush, John Askew and William Lowe. They were joined for a short time by Gregory Martin,[12] future translator of the Rheims New Testament, who was to supervise their studies. At Lewis's suggestion the Pope declared that the six scholars should live and study at the Hospice at the Hospice's expense. A new set of statutes was drawn up by Morone on 4 February 1577 which broadened the membership of the confraternity, placed restrictions on the hospitality expenses and forbade the chaplains to interfere in the scholars' affairs. Disciplinary rules were laid down for the scholars as to dress, religious duties and studies. Over the next few months the number of students increased and this created a serious accommodation problem so nearby and adjacent houses had to be rented. By May 1578 there were twenty-six scholars. Animosity developed between the old chaplains and some of the new students on the one hand, and Lewis and Clynnog on the other, because of alleged partiality towards the Welshmen. When Clynnog's tenure of office as Warden was prolonged for a year by Morone, the chaplains refused to re-elect him but chose Henry Henshaw in his place. Whereupon Morone separated the government of the College from that of the Hospice and Clynnog was appointed Rector of the scholars. In fact, he seems to have been the best qualified for this post and he had a close understanding with both Lewis and Morone as to future plans. Lewis used his considerable influence again to secure the services of two Jesuit fathers as spiritual director and prefect of studies. He also obtained a regular monthly subsidy from the Pope of one hundred crowns, equal to that given to Douai, a college four times the size. Tax concessions were also available from Philip of Spain, facilitating the import of wine from Naples.

Meanwhile the troubles in the Netherlands had meant that the college at Douai was forced to migrate into French territory at Rheims. More students arrived in Rome and this resulted in another Jesuit being co-opted on to the staff. By November 1578 there were about forty scholars resident. Despite further aid from the Pope the difficulties of sustaining so great a number increased daily. To provide room and funds for this influx Lewis persuaded the Pope to hand over the building entirely to Clynnog and the scholars. Henshaw the Warden and the other chaplains were given fifteen days' notice to depart and Clynnog was made perpetual governor of the Hospice and the Seminary. Resentment against him increased and the students rose in revolt against the Rector. The grounds of the revolt would seem to have been not only his partiality towards the Welsh students and the expulsion of chaplains but, in addition, the differing views as to the purpose of the new institution. There was agreement about the premises being used as a house of studies rather than a home for exiles, but there the similarities ended. Clynnog and Lewis belonged to an older generation and in their heart of hearts looked for the restoration of the old order. The Elizabethan schism was but a temporary setback and so the College was a place where men could be prepared for the days when England was once more reunited with Rome. There was no immediate prospect of return; in fact one of the early regulations lays it down that the students are to learn Italian to enable them, if need be, to take up posts in Italy. These views of Clynnog and Lewis seem to have been shared by Gregory XIII and Morone. Rome found it difficult to consider as normal any situation where the Church was not supported by a friendly civil authority. The students, however, for the most part belonged to a newer order. They were inspired by the more daring ideal of returning to England and ministering to those people who had remained loyal to the old religion. As this meant working against the establishment it would almost certainly involve their own arrest and even execution. The upshot of a long and acrimonious battle between the students and authority was that by the spring of 1579, after numerous petitions and memorials, Gregory XIII dismissed Clynnog and asked the Jesuits to take full charge of the College. So by the time the official Bull of Foundation reached the College, the Italian Jesuit, Agazzari, was firmly installed as Rector.

The Bull of Foundation is dated 1 May 1579[13] and hence this can be considered as the official birthday of the Venerable College of St Thomas de urbe. But there were events both sides of this date which makes its origins less able to be fixed to this particular moment. On the one hand, it was twenty months before the Bull reached the College, and on the other, as we have shown, there had long been an English presence on this site and indeed for several years the building had housed men who were preparing to be priests.

Fig. 1.6 The Hospice church, from a woodcut of *c*.1580.

Early days of the College

The new institution began on a sound basis. The Hospice funds and property were now to be directed to the maintenance of the College, but 'if for any reason the College be dissolved, the church, house and all properties must revert to their original status as a national hospice'.[14] The tradition of hospitality and receiving pilgrims did not disappear and from 1580 a record was kept of the visitors. This came to be known as the Pilgrim Book.[15] In addition, the College was endowed with a yearly grant and it was given property, including the Abbey of S. Sabino at Piacenza which alone brought in 3,000 ducats a year. The generosity of Gregory XIII to the new institutions in Rome is well known and the English College was particularly favoured. A contemporary source refers to the German College as the head of gold, the English College as the bust of silver, the Maronite College as the legs of iron and the Roman College, last of all, as the feet of clay.[16] The number of students was fixed at forty, the idea being that the College provided from its own funds for the maintenance and education of the alumni. This did not rule out the College accepting other students

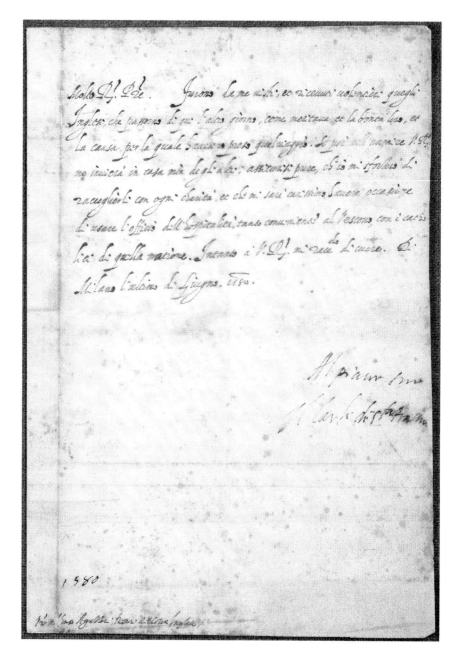

Fig. 1.7 Letter of Cardinal Charles Borromeo.

whose expenses were paid by themselves, relatives or friends; these were known as *convictores* or commoners.

Although later on there were to emerge rivalries and jealousies between some of the seculars and the Jesuits, one must not interpret this entrusting of the College to Jesuit superiors as anything sinister. From the beginning they had been a natural source to turn to for staffing and they had already been given the government of other enterprises in Rome. Moreover Robert Persons[17] was resident in Rome at this time and, as both a scholar and recent arrival from England, his advice was sought in the domestic quarrel at the English College. He understood the new mentality and in 1580 was to lead the first Jesuit mission to England with Edmund Campion and others. It was at his suggestion that the missionary oath was imposed. This was in addition to the initial oath the students took on admittance to the College, in which they swore to obey the rules and be loyal to the Pope. This further promise was to return after ordination and work in England. Ralph Sherwin was the first to be questioned and his reply 'potius hodie quam cras' (today rather than tomorrow) not only stands for his personal zeal, fitting for the canonised protomartyr of the English College, but also for the new spirit that marked the regime established in 1579.

Although the missionary priests were very much left to their own devices as to the arrangements for the journey home, the route taken by those travelling between Rome and England was dependent on the prevailing political situation. Between 1558 and 1578 the so called 'Imperial route' via Milan, the St Gotthard, the Rhine and the Netherlands was in common use. But after 1578 the 'French route' via the Mount Cenis pass, Lyons and Paris was used until the French civil war of 1589 occasioned a return to the Imperial route and the opening of a new 'Spanish route'. This latter involved a sea crossing from Italy to the east coast of Spain, then across land to Bilbao or another northern port for the journey to England.[18]

The early years of the College's history continued to be inspired by these missionary ideals and there was close co-operation between the College at Douai and the Jesuits at Rome, brought about by the efforts of Allen. Both colleges were now considered as missionary establishments for the education of those whose lives would be spent in unsettled and adverse conditions. Allen saw the two colleges as fired by the same ideal.[19] In his *Apologie and True Declaration*[20] he makes no distinction between them as to aim or recruitment. There is a similar course of studies; the kind of sermons preached, the exercises of religion and devotion are the same. Of course there is an obvious difference because of the importance of Rome.

> It pertaineth exceedingly to the general good and honour of our nation, that we may perpetually have a number of the most pregnant wits brought up in the principal seat, place and foundation of our christianity whither whatsoever is learned, wise, virtuous, of all the most famous universities, monasteries, societies and colleges through the world is recuiled[21] as to a continual mast of all kind of doctrine and prudence.[22]

The correspondence between the president of Douai, Dr Barrett, an English secular priest, and Agazzari, an Italian Jesuit, witnesses to the common interest of the two superiors, manifesting itself in such things as remarks on the Welsh character and an exchange of views on the suitability of students who had passed through both colleges.[23] A later president of Douai, Dr Worthington (1599–1613), fell into disfavour because he was so close to the Jesuits and was accused of wanting to hand over the College at Douai to their government.[24] It was only some years after the death of Allen that the two colleges began to drift apart. In origin they were two parts of the one enterprise.

The test of this missionary spirit was soon to be seen and the early 1580s were marked by severe persecutions of the Catholics in England. In 1581 Sherwin was the first student of the College to receive the martyr's crown.[25] The spirit of 'mission' was fostered in the College which trained students both to combat heresy and die a heroic death. Niccolò Circignani (Pomarancio) painted realistic frescoes of martyrdom on the walls of the College church. The originals have perished, but in the tribune of the present church there are copies.[26] A tradition dating from this time was that of preaching before the Pope every St Stephen's Day a sermon that glorified martyrdom. This practice continued up to 1870.[27] Alberti's altarpiece of the Holy Trinity was in position at this time.[28] The custom arose that on receipt of the news of the martyrdom of a former student, the community gathered before the picture in the church to sing a Te Deum. A similar tradition may have taken place at Douai[29] and although Gasquet says this was a privilege given by Gregory XIII[30] there is no documentary evidence for the granting of such a privilege. The College soon became known in Rome as the seminary of the martyrs, and St Philip Neri, when he was resident at S. Girolamo della Carità, opposite the College, used to greet the students with *Salvete flores martyrum*. Cardinal Baronius in his 1585 revision of the martyrology pays special tribute to the martyrs.[31]

Unique nature of the English colleges

These exceptional circumstances meant that although the colleges in Rome and at Douai had begun at a time when institutions for clergy training were opening up throughout the Catholic world as a result of the Council of Trent, they are not to be thought of as simply Tridentine seminaries. In its disciplinary decrees Trent was anxious to improve the standard of clergy education and at the same time make the priesthood available to those of more modest means who were unable to secure a university education.[32] But the Council visualised in its reforming decrees a stable situation for the Church quite unlike that which faced Allen and Persons.[33] In a letter of 1585 to Tolomeo Galli, Cardinal of Como and Secretary of State to Gregory XIII, Allen pointed out some of the unique features of the English colleges.[34] They were a different kind of institution from those which existed for no other purpose than the education of youth in countries where all was at peace. Because of the great need for priests in England Allen was accepting more students than were warranted by the income. There were travelling expenses to be paid and many had recourse to the College for spiritual instruction and consolation, in addition to those desirous of becoming priests.

Apart from these special financial considerations – 1585 was the year when the papacy made cuts in educational expenditure – there were other factors making for special treatment. Originally, Allen wanted to create at Douai a spiritual centre for Catholic exiles from England and to give English Catholics some sort of substitute for the universities at home that were now closed to them. He wished to provide his countrymen with an establishment for the instruction of Catholic youth. There began to develop a pattern of life very much modelled on that of the Oxford colleges and somewhat reactionary compared with the ideas of Persons. That such a college would include the education of future priests would be assumed quite naturally by Allen, who at the beginning did not seem to have the Tridentine notion of a separate institution for clergy training. The preparation for the ministry would be envisaged within the context of a general education.[35] But as far as Rome was concerned the visitation of 1585 raised the age of admission from fourteen to eighteen years and it was now stated quite clearly that students are *ii tantum, qui spiritualibus Angliae necessitatibus pro talento a Deo accepto possint opitulari* and so the only studies allowed were those in philosophy and theology. Thus there was ruled out the possibility of the College in Rome becoming a place for the study of the humanities and also

Fig. 1.8 St Ralph Sherwin.

any development 'downwards' into a school, which in fact took place at Douai.[36] Rome was to be a place for ecclesiastical studies.

Although in some respects Rome was nearer to the new spirit than Douai, the main reason why neither can be called Tridentine was because they lacked any clear relationship with a bishop or a diocese. Goldwell, the last survivor of the old Marian hierarchy, was resident in Rome but there was no one else in episcopal orders. Only Allen, who was not a bishop, could speak for the English Catholics. In 1581 a brief from Gregory XIII gave Allen faculties as 'Prefect of the English Mission' and for thirteen years he was, in effect, the ecclesiastical superior. But the unrealistic nature of the situation can be seen in the fact that at Douai students were still registered according to the pre-reformation dioceses.[37] Although this was sometimes also the case at Rome, for the most part the old dioceses were not mentioned but students were registered according to their county of origin. One of the stipulations of Trent[38] was that the diocese should provide financially for its seminary and the bishop should have a special relationship with those who were to assist him in the diocese. But the finances of the English colleges were provided by the Spanish crown in the case of Douai, and the revenue of the Hospice supplemented by papal grants at Rome.

The role of the bishop is more than that of financial guarantor. He has to 'call' or select candidates and give them their mission. In default of a hierarchy Allen and the College superiors had the decisive role here. In order to ensure that priests would return to labour in England, the 'missionary oath' was devised and this was administered by the Rector in Rome (a Jesuit) and at Douai by the president (a secular priest).[39] This gave the Rector of a seminary abroad a particular power which arose originally because there was no local hierarchy. But it also made him conscious of national needs – the mission was to the country at large and the College was to supply priests for national needs not diocesan. So the colleges were *de facto* assuming responsibility for the whole country. But the overall presence of Allen disguised the actual legal position. When he died, the Nuncio in Brussels was given complete jurisdiction over the English Catholic diaspora in the Low Countries, as well as the Catholics in England. He had episcopal powers as Vice-Protector of the English nation. He was the superior of Douai. But the College in Rome came directly under the Cardinal Protector. As will become clear from later events, both the Rector's and the College's reference to the episcopate was maintained by the link with the Cardinal Protector (or Nuncio in the case of Douai). The Rector was responsible to the Cardinal Protector. This was to cause difficulties later with the vicars apostolic, who sometimes thought of themselves as bishops with full canonical powers of jurisdiction.

It might be helpful if we contrasted the situation of Catholicism in England with that obtaining in Ireland at this time. Although under the same persecution, Ireland did retain its hierarchy and this meant that a large proportion of students in the colleges abroad catering for the Irish secular clergy had already been ordained priests before leaving their homeland. This practice persisted down to 1805. The fact that they were already priests enabled them to accept chaplaincies or foundations for masses and this income helped to defray the expenses of their ecclesiastical education which took place after their ordination.[40]

Clearly, then, the English colleges abroad were not normal Tridentine seminaries. Many years later when the hierarchy was re-established, responsibility for the upkeep of the colleges devolved on the episcopate of England and Wales as a body. This often had unfortunate results, it being left to individual dioceses to provide students with the result that the colleges abroad were 'national' in name only, the students coming from those dioceses that had the funds and inclination to send their future priests to Rome, Valladolid, or Lisbon.[41]

Quarrels and dissensions

One of the tragedies of English Catholicism, from early in the reign of Elizabeth I, was the way in which the upholders of the old religion were split by dissension. Groups of exiles often mirror the strains of life in the homeland and sometimes these seem to be intensified by the added tension of living in a small community abroad. The College in Rome reflected the English Catholic community in this respect as it did in the number of its martyrs and confessors. Although many hundreds of miles distant from England, it was by no means isolated from the conflicts at home.

Dubious characters were always liable to turn up in Rome: vagrants, criminals, and the merely curious, as well as genuine pilgrims and scholars. Granted that the authorities at home were anxious to discover all they could about the new establishment, it would be hardly surprising if they did not make use of every available source. One such adventurer was Anthony Munday[42] who visited the College in 1578. It would seem that he was accepted as a scholar, but he never took the missionary oath and did not stay very long. Several years later, however, in *The English Romayne Life*, he gave an account of the troubles he witnessed between the English and Welsh factions. The account is informative, amusing and partly fictitious. Munday became quite well known as a pamphleteer, chronicler and playwright and was particularly noted for his dramatic plots. His account of the College was welcome propaganda, yet it is hardly likely that Munday had been originally sent out to Rome as a spy. But he did turn informer and made use of his stay in Rome to give witness, some of it false, at the trial of Luke Kirby and John Shert. In 1595 there was the more spectacular incident which resulted in Walter Marsh, a former student, being burned alive in the Campo dei Fiori for an attack on the sacred host during a procession of the Blessed Sacrament. On 27 June 1595 Owen Lewis said a mass at the College in reparation for this sacrilege.[43] The College had to learn from experience how much care was needed in admitting guests and scholars and from time to time there were warnings as to who should be accepted and refused admittance. But within a few years serious disturbances arose in the College, first of all in 1585 and then in 1594–7. These took the form of a revolt by some of the students against the Jesuit superiors whom they themselves had petitioned for when Clynnog was removed from office. It would seem probable that an element of this trouble was due to agents provocateurs infiltrated into the College from outside.[44] But the issues are so complex that further treatment is necessary.

The visitation of 1585

1585 is an important date for the English clergy, for the papacy and for the history of the College. It was in this year that the name 'seminary priest' was coined in the Act of Parliament[45] which ordered all priests to leave the country within forty days, and condemned to death, as traitors, anyone remaining behind and all who harboured them. Students at seminaries abroad had to present themselves within six months to justices of the peace in England and all who supported priests educated abroad were to be punished.[46] In the same year Bishop Goldwell, the last of the Marian hierarchy, died in Rome and his passing could be interpreted as a symbol that the old order had now finally disappeared. Also in 1585, Gregory XIII died and his successor, the Franciscan Sixtus V, had a different set of priorities.[47] He reduced expenditure in his own household, made economies in the papal army and suspended the subsidies to the ecclesiastical colleges. Money was spent on the suppression of brigandage in the papal territories and in beautifying the city with public

Fig. 1.9 Frescoes in College chapel tribune (copies of the Pomarancio originals): Pope Gregory XIII praying with College students before they were sent to England and martyrdom. See also *Pl. 5*

monuments.[48] He also set afoot a reform of clerical life and ordered a visitation of all the churches and colleges in Rome. In addition to this general plan, his involvement in a dispute with the Jesuits, concerning their vows, resulted in his ordering an enquiry into the four seminaries in Rome under their direction, namely the German, English, Maronite and Roman colleges.[49] Neither Meyer nor Gasquet mentions this visitation of all the Jesuit colleges, but a knowledge of this does help to put the 1585 visitation of the English College into perspective. There were troubles in the College at this time but the 1585 visitation was not like that of 1595, which was ordered specifically because of internal troubles at the English College. Indeed, the acts of the 1585 visitation say of the students generally, 'putting on one side their spirit of independence, we have heard nothing grave against them, but have seen evidence of their modesty, continence and great piety'. This hardly indicates that the visitation was called because of a revolt. Neither is it true that Sixtus V withdrew the subsidy because he was disgusted by the divisions in the College, as Gasquet suggests. This economic measure was common to all colleges administered by the Jesuits.

However, the acts of the visitation do reveal that there were some matters for concern and many of these were, in fact, to develop into the serious troubles of 1594. One of the complaints of the students was that the Jesuits were enticing scholars into the Society, especially through the Sodality. Hicks[50] examines the whole case critically and finds little grounds for this accusation. A new and vigorous organisation was bound to attract many of the youth of the day and in 1579 there were positive grounds for a closer association with the Society, apart from the desire to be free from Clynnog's rule. However, it would hardly be surprising if there were not some who were against the new regime and the accusation of enticement could have been the cry of a disgruntled minority. But there was another side to this. Students were being supported in a college founded by papal funds[51] and after a probationary period they took the missionary oath to receive orders in due course and return to England. The other students who were paid for by parents or relatives, the convictors or commoners, did not take this oath and so they did not have the same obligations. Part of the purpose of the 1585 visitation was to check on papal expenditure. Once a person had taken the oath, and was *juratus* and an alumnus, he was provided for by the College funds. Any later decision to join the Society meant that the Jesuits were in effect getting the advantage of papal money. In fact, as Hicks shows, very few *jurati* did join the Jesuits.

Fig. 1.10 Plan of the centre of Rome (1576): the Hospice/College is No. 16.

Another grievance of the students was that they were being treated as children not as grown men, and they compared the discipline at Rome unfavourably with that at Douai. It is not clear whether there had been some tightening up in discipline, perhaps occasioned by the need to preserve clerics from violence in the streets of Rome, or whether it was an old complaint. In any case we get an indication of the sort of thing from a report that students coming from Douai were shocked to find that the priests and doctors of divinity were not given special marks of deference and did not enjoy special privileges in the more egalitarian college run by the Jesuits in Rome.[52]

However, despite the complaints of the students, the direction of the College was not changed. The Jesuits remained in control and there is no suggestion that at this date Allen had any desire to have them withdrawn. Agazzari was replaced by an English father, but within five years the Italian Jesuits were again Rectors and Agazzari was to enjoy a second term of office.

Perhaps the most important result of this visitation was the drawing up of the Constitution *Omnis Reipublicae Status*. This is a much more comprehensive document than the 1579 statutes and it puts in writing some of the implications of the decisions made then as to the missionary nature of the College. We have already referred to the raising of the age of admission from 14 to 18. The missionary oath introduced by Persons in 1580 now formed part of the Constitution. The disciplinary decrees were spelled out in great detail as was customary at this time[53] in an *ordo domus* which legislated for every hour of the day. This horarium continued into the eighteenth century and students from Douai often complained of its severity. The camerata system was firmly established. This was not just the rule that students had to go about the city in groups, not singly – originally for safety reasons – that survived until 1968,[54] but was an internal organisation whereby students were divided into groups and placed under the supervision of a prefect.[55] The prefect of camerata was not necessarily a student himself nor indeed even a member of the College, but he had charge over their discipline and studies.

The sodality was singled out for special mention in this visitation. 'Sodalitatem Assumptionis B.V. omnes venerentur uti decet, contraque sodales et eorum statuta obloqui murmurareve nemini liceat.' The sodality movement was begun by the Jesuits[56] and its main concern was apostolic works and personal perfection. It recruited from all walks of life and although there was no distinctive dress and its functions were of a private and spiritual nature it

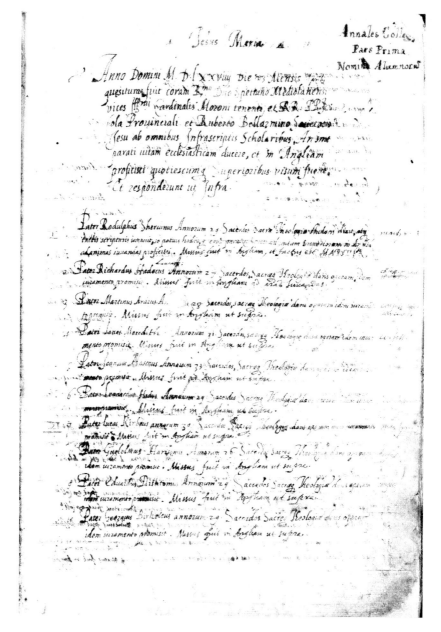

Fig. 1.11 The first entries in the earliest College diary, the Liber Ruber, with the name of Ralph Sherwin heading the list of students. His entry includes the words 'potius hodie quam cras' (better today than tomorrow) with which he dedicated himself to the mission in England.

was a potential power structure, as it provided the Society with lay support and often with new members.[57] Following the pattern of most Jesuit administered colleges, a sodality was set up at the English College in 1581.

Sodalists were expected to be a good influence, spreading peace, harmony and a respect for the rules. They were to concern themselves with the new and younger pupils to see that they imbibed the right attitudes, and they helped to foster progress in the studies by means of 'academies'. Admirable as these aims were, it was hardly surprising that they should not escape the charge of elitism, especially as there was careful selection before a student was accepted as a member of the sodality and one of the reasons for expulsion from the sodality 'si arcana sodalitatis enunciare soleat' could have an ominous ring. What exactly were the complaints against the sodality at the English College in 1585[58] is not clear, but two reasons can be suggested. Firstly, the officers of the sodality were encouraging submission and obedience to the prefects of camerata and so supporting a system that was not very popular. Secondly, it was feared that membership of the sodality was but a step away from membership of the Society. Of course, it could be that the sodality was encouraging loyalty to the Church as well as to the Society against attempts at subversion.

It remains unclear as to whether the 1585 visitation was occasioned by any special trouble at the College or whether it was only part of a much bigger enquiry of Sixtus V. We must try and avoid the temptation to read back into this year the beginning of the troubles that undoubtedly affected the College ten years later.

The troubles of 1594–7

A. J. Kenny[59] gives the fullest account of the troubles that arose at the College in 1594 and lasted until 1597. As he points out, they were related to the divisions and dissensions between Catholics at home. The issues were extremely complex, however, and cannot be reduced to simple pro- or anti-Jesuit feelings. They had much more to do with a policy for the survival of Catholicism. Some were prepared to trust the Elizabethan government, some were not. To prove themselves worthy of toleration Catholics often adopted violent anti-Spanish and anti-Jesuit attitudes and there were trouble-makers on both sides for whom politics clouded the religious issues. The College was to be caught up in this unfortunate turmoil.

As with the earlier troubles, much can be attributed to the natural exuberance of youth and the problems attendant on young Englishmen living abroad. On 28 May 1582 Allen had written to Agazzari: 'I know for certain from experience that it would be easier to guide to salvation a thousand souls in England than a hundred in this exile, which of itself breeds murmurings, complaining, contradictions and discontent. When Moses leads the peoples through the desert, he suffers much.'[60] But he could hardly have foreseen the graver troubles that were to beset his people when he had left the scene and the disunity could no longer be contained.

When Allen died, the Rector was an Italian Jesuit who exercised a benign rule over the students. However, below the surface the old grievances were still there and they were now sharpened by a growing anti-Spanish feeling that involved suspicion of such men as Persons, who had been associated with the College since its beginnings and who had indeed been Rector for a short time in 1588. Allen had been designated Prefect of the English Mission, subject to the Cardinal Protector. On his death, the Nuncio in Brussels assumed responsibility for both the Catholics in England and the exiles in the Low Countries. The management of the College in Rome was reserved to the Protector. Although its full effects only became noticeable later, this division of responsibilities was to weaken the link between the two colleges and also the link between the College in Rome and the Catholics in England. But whatever Rome might decide about the juridical position, Allen, from the point of view of his personality and connection with the beginning of the foreign colleges, was irreplaceable. No one had his unchallenged leadership among the exiles but it was not long before partisans began to put forward their candidates. The candidates themselves were often reluctant and there is little evidence that either Persons or Owen Lewis indulged in canvassing on a very large scale.[61]

The students at the College could not hold themselves aloof from these matters. They were shortly to return to England and were almost as much concerned with the administration of Catholic affairs at home as they were with the direction of the College. If there was an attempt from outside to recruit them to one side or another, it should not be thought of in simplistic terms, as if wickedly politically-minded people were corrupting the minds of saintly, dedicated missioners. Not surprisingly, because of his constant visiting of the College, it was the Lewis faction that was strongest among the students. But when Lewis died in 1595 the political activity took the form of an anti-Jesuit movement and

Fig. 1.12 An engraving issued at his death in 1585 depicting Pope Gregory XIII surrounded by the colleges and institutions he founded – the English College is at the top right hand corner; in the top centre is the Collegio Romano, where the Jesuits taught 'all sciences', see *Fig. 2.2–3*.

became associated with a rebellion against the superiors and the rules of the College. It was a serious disturbance and for two years the rebel students, Tempest and Hall, carried the majority of their companions with them and at the beginning succeeded in obtaining the removal of the Vice-Rector and a reduction in the number of Jesuits on the staff, their place being taken by student priests. To counter this and re-establish discipline, the Jesuits called in men from outside whom they paid to be prefects of camerata. On one occasion the military were called in to enforce the expulsion of some of the rebel students. The authorities decided to intervene and a visitation was ordered. This was to be presided over by Cardinal Sega, a well known trouble-shooter,[62] who had directed the previous visitation in 1585 to the English College and the other Jesuit-administered establishments.

The dispute was having its repercussions elsewhere. Many of the Roman students had originally come from Douai and they also returned to England via Douai so they were aware of the anti-Jesuit feeling in the Low Countries. This is one of the reasons why Sega's report made suggestions not only for the College in Rome but also for a reform in discipline at Douai.

Foley[63] gives Sega's report in full. Briefly one can say that the complaints against the Jesuits were listed and they were asked to reply to the accusations. Contrary to what was maintained, they said they had no ambitions to control the clergy in England. There is evidence to believe that the General of the Jesuits was prepared to withdraw his men from the administration of the College in Rome. In addition they strongly denied that they were enticing students or using the College as a novitiate. The discipline of the College was according to a system that the English felt to be quite alien. Students were expected to spy on their fellows and report rule breaking. But on the other hand the English wanted to retain certain laws of precedence and give privileges to student priests and to those with English university degrees; they did not appreciate a discipline that was intended to instil humility.[64]

Although there was exaggeration in the way the students presented their case, the temporal administration and provision of such things as food, clothing and accommodation was found to be defective, and to meet the costs of improvement it was recommended that the number of students be reduced. This last point is worthy of notice since it indicates financial difficulties less than twenty years after the Bull of Foundation.[65] The final decision was that the Jesuits should not be recalled from the English mission nor removed from their administration of the College, and the unruly students should be expelled or at least removed elsewhere. Any pleas that there should be participation in the government of the College were firmly rejected. 'The College must be governed on the despotic principle because the unripe age and studious pursuits of our scholars renders them unfit to take part in their own government.'[66]

As these 'stirs' of 1595 were not to be found in other colleges run by the Jesuits the blame was attached to the English character. In order to preserve the good name of the College and its superiors there were strong suggestions that the troubles were caused from outside, and the name and character of Lewis were blackened. To what extent Lewis was to blame has been discussed by Kenny,[67] and Anstruther[68] has suggested that Persons probably had a hand in the preparation of the official report. The real roots of the trouble would seem to be, as Kenny suggests, the faulty system. The superiors felt it was impossible to expel a student since he might apostatise and inform against the College and the missioners in England. Moreover in a college for the regular clergy administered by a secular order there were bound to be tensions, especially where the seculars had no hierarchy to whom they were responsible. The students either admired their superiors and were tempted to join the Society or they hated them and indulged in open revolt with no one to call them to order except their enemies.

Unhappily the visitation was not the end of the disturbances. Sega fell sick and the new Vice-Protector was Cardinal Toleto,[69] who was not at all favourable to the Jesuits and seems to have allowed, if not openly encouraged, the students from Rome to associate with the anti-Jesuit faction in the Low Countries and England. He ordered the 'extern' prefects to go and he succeeded in removing the Jesuit superiors from the jurisdiction of the General and placing them under his own control. Persons' pamphlet[70] concerning Spanish and other claims to the English throne further aggravated matters so that we find Agazzari, now in his second term as Rector, writing to Persons about the students' nationalism: 'I do not know whether they hate the Society because of the Spaniards, or the Spaniards because of the Society, or both because of the Scot or the Frenchman or something worse.' When Cardinal Toleto died in this same year the relief in Agazzari's mind is evident; to Persons he remarked,

> How providentially God removed all those who opposed the Society. While Cardinal Allen was faithful to it, God blessed and prospered him; as soon as he began to drift away, God cut him off. Then a more

dangerous enemy arose: Owen Lewis. He too was removed at the height of his power, followed closely by his henchman, Throckmorton. And now, Cardinal Toleto, the greatest hope the rebels had – he too is dead. Deus pugnat pro causa sua.[71]

After this brief but turbulent interlude some sort of peace was achieved. Camillo Borghese, the future Pope Paul V (1605–21) whose name is blazoned on the façade of St Peter's, became Vice-Protector. Persons was called in as peacemaker but his first efforts were only a temporary truce. There now occurred the famous incident of the English College students who passed themselves off as German College students when they were frequenting taverns.[72] Both the Rector and the Protector of the Germanicum were greatly disturbed, the police were summoned and soon they raided the Sign of the Rose near S. Marco and took a party of students into custody. The Pope was rather amused at the whole incident but he had a special envoy sent to the College, Don Acarizio Squarcione, papal fiscal and canon of the Lateran, who, under threat of torture, extracted confessions from the students of their visiting taverns and brothels and generally scandalous behaviour. There followed wholesale expulsions, but these were not as severe as might have been the case since many were simply transferred to Douai and most of those who were expelled behaved well in their new surroundings.

It was about this time that Persons became Rector once more. A new set of rules was drawn up and a new constitution.[73] This second rectorship of Persons was a period of twelve years of peace. The unruly element had been dismissed and the students accepted their Jesuit superiors. This was the time, 1598, that George Blackwell was appointed Archpriest with full ecclesiastical jurisdiction over the English clergy, but not himself in bishop's orders. The very internal harmony and stability of the English College during these years was to prove a mixed blessing since during the ensuing 'archpriest controversy', when Blackwell's authority was challenged, the College in Rome, united under Robert Persons, was considered by some disaffected Catholics to be in the hands of their enemies. It was accused of being partisan and unrepresentative of a body of Catholic opinion.[74] Paradoxically it was when the College was torn by dissension that it was most representative of affairs at home. But although to many in England the College in Rome was a hostile environment, there is need to say something more positive about the style of life and training under the regime established by Persons and carried on by the English Jesuits.

Notes

1 For the early history, see 'The English Hospice in Rome', *Venerabile*, XXI (Sexcentenary Issue, 1962); Margaret Harvey, *The English in Rome 1362–1420* (Cambridge, 1999).

2 W. J. Moore, *The Saxon Pilgrims to Rome and Schola Saxonum* (Freiburg, 1937).

3 Juan Beneyto Perez, *El Cardenal Albornoz Canciller y Caudillo de Castilla* (Madrid, 1950).

4 'From Hospice to College 1559–1579', *Venerabile*, XXI, 218–73.

5 This strong Welsh presence in Rome lasted from 1565 to 1590. See Tecwyn Lloyd, 'Dr. Gruffydd Robert and Morus Clynnog', *Venerabile*, XIV, 315–18; Tecwyn Lloyd, 'Alltudion o Gymru yn Rhufain (Welsh exiles in Rome)', *Ysgrifau Catholig*, 1961, pp. 23–35; Paul Bryant-Quinn, 'To Preserve our Language': Gruffydd Robert and Morys Clynnog, *The Journal of Welsh Religious History*, 8 (2000), 17–34.

6 W. E. Wilkie, *The Cardinal Protectors of England* (Cambridge, 1974) treats of the Protectors up to 1539 and pp. 5–10 has some general remarks on their position. In Appendix V of this volume can be found the names of the Protectors of the College from Morone to Heard.

7 Kenny, *Venerabile*, XXI, 224.

8 J. M. Cleary, 'Dr. Morys Clynnog's Invasion Projects of 1575–6', *RH*, 8, 300–22.

9 For Lewis, see D. Crowley, 'Owen Lewis and the Venerabile', *Venerabile*, II, 116–28; G. Anstruther, 'Owen Lewis', *Venerabile*, XXI, 274–94.

10 Cesare Spetiano was Bishop of Cremona, vicar general and friend of Charles Borromeo.

11 Shert, the future beatified martyr, was already a deacon when he arrived in Rome.

12 For Gregory Martin, see G. Anstruther, *The Seminary Priests*, vol. I. Martin's *Roma Sancta* is an early guide book to Rome giving an account of the churches and other sights. It also includes information on the seminaries there. It has been edited by G. B. Parkes (Rome, 1969).

13 Not the Feast of St George, 23 April. The Liber Ruber begins at this date when the College oath was first administered and contemporary copies of the Bull, ECA, liber 5, p. 289, read *septuagesimonono, 9 Kal Maii* but the original autograph in the Vatican is quite clear: *Datum Romae, Kalendiis Maii, anno pontificatus nostrae VII.*

14 Bull of Foundation, see Appendix II for text.

15 ECA, libri 282, 283, 292. Parts of this Book are printed in Foley, *Records*, VI.

16 Quoted by R. Garcia Villoslada, *Storia del Collegio Romano 1551–1773* (Rome, 1954), pp. 143–4.

17 A westcountryman, b. 1546, fellow and later Bursar at Balliol College, Persons left Oxford in 1575 and after a few months at Padua studying medicine, went on foot to Rome where he was received into the Society having previously been reconciled to the Catholic Church. He was ordained priest in 1578; cf. 'Letters and Memorials of Father Robert

Persons SJ', ed. L. Hicks SJ, *CRS,* 39 (1942); Francis Edwards SJ, *Robert Persons The Biography of an Elizabethan Jesuit* (St Louis, MO, nd.)

18 See J. Bossy, 'Rome and the Elizabethan Catholics. A Question of Geography', *Historical Journal,* VII (1964), 135–42.

19 Allen's slow conversion towards the ideal of a missionary college is treated by J. Bossy, *The English Catholic Community 1570–1850* (London, 1975), p. 18.

20 Published 1581.

21 Reciuled = gathered together.

22 The Bull of Foundation also makes special mention of the College's situation in Rome.

23 Correspondence, Allen to Agazzari, July and August 1580, *CRS, 9, 27, 29.*

24 P. Guilday, *The English Catholic Refugees on the Continent* (London, 1914), p. 108.

25 For a list of the College Martyrs see Appendix IV. Also, *The Forty Four: The Martyrs of the English College Rome* (Farnborough, 2000).

26 These paintings are mentioned with approval in the visitation report of 1585. Pomarancio had already done a similar work at S. Stefano Rotundo where they can still be seen. Engravings of the originals at the English College were published in *Ecclesiae Anglicanae Trophaea,* Rome 1584. A. Dillon, *The Construction of Martyrdom in the English Catholic Community 1535–1603* (2002), places these paintings in the wider context of the Counter-Reformation Church.

27 F. Rogers, 'St. Stephen's Day', *Venerabile,* VIII, 8–17. See also ECA, liber 281.

28 For Alberti's picture, see *Venerabile,* IV, 383–7; VI, 433–9.

29 Bede Camm, *Cardinal William Allen Founder of the seminaries* (London, 1908), p. 65.

30 Gasquet, *History,* p. 122.

31 *Venerabile,* XIV, 117–8.

32 Leon E. Hallin, 'La Formation du Clerge Catholique apres le Concile de Trente', *Bibliotheque de la Revue d'Histoire Ecclesiastique,* Fasc 50, iii (Louvain, 1970).

33 The part played by Englishmen in the development of seminaries is to be noted. Not only were Pole's ideas on clergy training influential at Trent, but Allen was consulted by Vanderville on behalf of the Spanish crown to advise on the setting up of seminaries in Spain, T. F. Knox (ed.), *1st and 2nd Douai Diaries* (London 1878), p. lv. Green in his account of Douai college, written *c.*1750 ('7th Douai Diary', *CRS,* 28, 328), argues that this college was the first transalpine seminary and owed much to Milan and we have already noted the Owen Lewis connection with Borromeo. Seminaries existed in Italy and Rome from the 1550s, but none seems to have actually been founded outside Italy before Douai.

34 T. F. Knox, *1st and 2nd Douai Diaries,* p. lxxvi.

35 For Allen's changing views on this matter, see J. Bossy, *The English Catholic Community,* pp. 18–19. For Pole's similar view, see A. Morey, *The Catholic Subjects of Elizabeth I* (London, 1978), p. 16.

36 For Allen's ideas on studies, see T. F. Taylor, 'The Douai Defence', *RH,* 10,

176–80; also J. Bossy, 'The Character of Elizabethan Catholicism', in *Crisis in Europe 1560-1660*, ed. T. Aston (London, 1965).

37 '1st Douai Diary', 193, gives a list of dioceses according to counties, which provides a sort of conversion table for those no longer familiar with the old diocesan boundaries. Jesuits, for administrative purposes, divided the English mission into 'colleges', each college being comprised of several counties. See Foley, *Records*, passim.

38 Session XXIII, Decrees concerning reformation, Chapter 18.

39 An ironical position was to arise in eighteenth-century Douai. Dismayed by the withdrawal of priests from the staff of the college for the English mission, the President, Witham, invoked the missionary oath. He claimed it was he, the President, who had the right to send men to England. The vicars apostolic could not recall them on their own initiative. They had not the power. '7th Douai Diary', *CRS*, 28, 79.

40 See Cathaldus Giblin OFM, 'The Irish Colleges on the Continent', in *The Irish French Connection 1578–1978*, ed. Liam Swords (Irish College, Paris, 1978).

41 When seminaries were established on English soil in the nineteenth century there was much discussion as to the advisability of diocesan as against regional seminaries, see D. Milburn, *A History of Ushaw College* (Ushaw, 1964), 183–93. In the mid-century there were changes of policy on the part of succeeding Archbishops of Westminster. M. E. Williams, 'Seminaries and Priestly Formation', in *From Without the Flaminian Gate*, ed. V. A. McClelland (London, 1999).

42 'The English Romayne Life', *Venerabile*, III, 252–61; C. Tumer, *Anthony Munday: An Elizabethan Man of Letters* (University of California, 1928); M. E. Williams, 'Anthony Munday', *Venerabile*, XIII, 36–44; A. J. Kenny, *Anthony Munday in Rome*, RH, 6, 158–62. D. B. Hamilton *Anthony Munday and the Catholics, 1560–1633* (Ashgate, 2005).

43 *Venerabile*, XVI, 265–6; *Venerabile*, XX, 16–18.

44 As Gasquet notes *(History,* 88) historians of the Society say that this was the real reason for the troubles. But see Kenny, *Venerabile*, XXI.

45 Eliz 27, c 2.

46 A. O. Meyer, *England and the Catholic Church under Queen Elizabeth* (1967 edn), p. 149.

47 See L. von Pastor, *History of the Popes*, XXI, pp. 127 and 173.

48 Amongst the more notable of his public works were the erection of the obelisk in St Peter's Square and the fountain Dell'Acqua Felice in the Piazza di S. Bernardo. His name is to be found inscribed at the very top of the interior of the dome of St Peter's. His own sumptuous tomb is in S. Maria Maggiore.

49 Sacchini, *Historia Societatis Jesu*, pt. V, tome 1, book 5, p. 23 refers to calumnies being spread at this time against all the Jesuit-run colleges.

50 L. Hicks SJ, 'The English College Rome and vocations to the Society of Jesus, March 1579–July 1595', *AHSJ*, III (1934), 1–36. A similar complaint of enticement was to arise in 1603 at Valladolid in Spain. But this time it was objected that the Benedictines were enticing students away from the Jesuits.

51 In addition to the Income from the Abbey at S. Sabino in Piacenza, the College received from Gregory XIII an annual income of 3,000 scudi in gold. This was paid by the Apostolic Datary. In 1585 Sixtus V stopped this. In 1590 Gregory XIV ordered an annual payment of 6oo gold scudi to be made and this continued until 1795. ECA, Document from Hinsley rectorship, scr. 86.

52 See T. F. Knox, *1st and 2nd Douai Diaries*, p. xxxii. For the difficult question of precedence at this period see *infra* in reference to the 1595 report.

53 Villoslada, *Storia del Collegio Romano 1551–1773*, p. 99.

54 The custom of English College men going out in fours was changed to twos in 1967 and then students were allowed out alone in 1968.

55 The number and composition of each camerata was fixed by the superiors and although at the English College it was sometimes a convenient means of detecting religious and political dissenters, its presence in the other national colleges indicates that it had further purposes too. It is interesting to read in the Vatican II *Decree on Training of Priests*, §7 (1965): 'In large seminaries, the students should be suitably organised in smaller groups, to enable more personal attention to be given to each student, while retaining unity of discipline and scientific training.' For a contemporary application see W. Steele, 'A College Group: After Two Years', *Ushaw Magazine* (1978) n. 251, vol. 89, 1–9.

56 E. Mullan SJ, *The Sodality of Our Lady Studied in the Documents* (London, 1912) (English translation of third edition).

57 A. P. Farrell, *The Jesuit Code of Liberal Education* (Milwaukee, 1938), p. 247, treats of complaints in the French province about the sodality. L. von Pastor, *History of the Popes*, XXIX, pp. 306–7, mentions the objections to the sodality in England. Richard Smith, a former student at the English College Rome and the vicar apostolic, was opposed to the sodality.

58 Hicks, *AHSJ*, III, 25. There do not seem to have been complaints about the sodality from other colleges and there is no mention of these objections in the 1595 visitation of the English College.

59 'The Inglorious Revolution 1594–1597', *Venerabile*, XVI, 240–58; XVII, 7–25, 77–94, 136–55. For Sega's report, see G. Anstruther, *Venerabile*, XX, 208–23.

60 *Letters and Memoirs of William Cardinal Allen*, ed. T. F. Knox (London, 1882), p. 136.

61 For Persons and the troubles at the English College 1594–97 see F. Edwards, *Robert Persons, The Biography of an English Jesuit*, pp. 198–214.

62 Sega was called in to arbitrate in the controversy about the Carmelite reform of Teresa of Avila and John of the Cross in Spain 1577.

63 Foley, *Records*, VI, 1–66.

64 The question of precedence and privilege was one that caused trouble in European society at this time. Catholics were not immune from it and it even lay behind the quarrels among the Catholic prisoners at Wisbech jail. See *The Wisbech Stirs*, ed. P. Renold, *CRS*, 51.

65 Perhaps due to the reduced papal subsidy.

66 Sega report quoted by Foley, VI, *Records*, p. 57.

67 Kenny, *Venerabile*, XVI and XVII.

68 *Venerabile*, XXI, 274–87.
69 Toleto, or Toledo, was himself a Jesuit, indeed the first member of the Society to be created Cardinal, but he disagreed on many points with Acquaviva, the General of the Order. Jerome Aixala SJ, *Black and Red SJ* (Bombay, 1968), pp. 191–7.
70 L. Hicks SJ, 'Father Robert Person S.J. and the Book of Succession', *RH*, 4, 104–37.
71 Letter of 25 September 1596, T. F. Knox, *1st and 2nd Douai Diaries*, p. 387.
72 The German college students wore their red cassocks *before* this incident, so it was not as a result of the tavern escapade that they had this distinguishing feature. See A. J. Kenny, *Venerabile*, XVII, 138–40.
73 ECA, scr. 4, 19. See Appendix III.
74 *Venerabile*, III 65–70. When Bishop and Charnock visited Rome in 1598 to lay before the Pope the appeal of the seculars against the Archpriest, Persons' attempts at being helpful were misconstrued. It was from now on that the rift with Douai grew, Douai being representative of the other point of view. In 1619 the Archpriest wrote to the Nuncio of Belgium: 'This College of Douai is the only source and seminary of our clergy because the rest, both in Italy and Spain, have been brought into the power of the Fathers of the Society and are now become seminaries not of the clergy (for which nevertheless they were intended) but of novices of the Society', '3rd Douai Diary', *CRS*, 10, 312. Douai continued to be something of a dumping ground for dissidents from Rome. In 1622 it was to receive students who had been dismissed by the Jesuits for dissuading fellow students from entering the Society in Rome.

Chapter Two

Roma Barocca

Because of the intrigues and jealousies involving many of the seculars and regulars in England, the historian has to proceed with caution in his examination of the records concerning the College.

First of all, the continual complaints[1] made throughout the seventeenth and eighteenth centuries were at least partially due to the seculars' dislike of the Jesuits who were superiors of the College. Moreover, the Rector of the seculars' College in Rome was at the same time the prefect of the English Jesuit mission. As a result one has to realise that the pertinent questions are: how far was the poor supply of priests coming from Rome solely due to the incompetence or malice of the Jesuits? Did Douai also experience financial difficulties? What was the standard of studies in Rome compared with Douai and the other foreign colleges? How far were the complaints about lack of pastoral training inevitable in a college on foreign soil?

Secondly, the difficulties that English Catholics experienced because they lacked a hierarchy have to be put into perspective. They have to be seen alongside the Jansenist and Gallican troubles in France. Both are aspects of the wider problem of the nature and powers of the episcopate that exercised the post-Tridentine Church in Europe.[2]

Exiles and strangers

Writing shortly after the troubles of 1594–7 Persons suggested that living in Rome could have an adverse effect on the students. He said it was a place which

> engendereth high spirits in them that are not well established in Almighty God's grace, for coming thither very young and finding themselves presently placed and provided for abundantly, and acquainted daily with sights and relations of popes, cardinals and princes' affairs, our youths that were bred up at home with much more simplicity ... than the Italian education doth comport, forgetteth easily themselves and breaketh out to liberty.[3]

Many of the students were country born and bred and later the authorities expressed a preference for candidates who had had some experience of town life.[4] However well motivated students may have been and however pious and desirous of leading an unworldly life, the Eternal City has never been a cloister and it could be a severe test of a vocation. Living and studying abroad has always had its hazards, whether it be in Rome, Douai, Valladolid or Lisbon. A strange climate, unusual food, an alien tongue and a remoteness from the constraints of family and home often lead the Englishman to lose his head and behave in an untypical manner. Rome furnished greater dangers both on account of its size and cosmopolitan character and also because, as well as being the centre of orthodoxy, it is also the last court of appeal and attracts the plaintiff of many an extravagant cause.

Measures were taken to immunise the students against possible infection. In the 1596 visitation Sega advised against more commoners being admitted. The disturbances raised fears that it was these students who were endangering the good order of the College.[5] In their complaints the rebels had asked to have 'English gentlemen admitted to conversation'. But, far from allowing this, the report suggested that the College should be isolated from the English community in Rome and that the local English residents should be given their own parish priest and organised into a sodality.[6] This was due to the conviction that one great contributory cause of the troubles since the foundation of the College in Rome, was 'the unchecked intercourse of the students with one another and with Englishmen not belonging to the College'. These regulations were to fall into abeyance within a few years, as we shall see, but from time to time in the history of the College, and indeed of other colleges, there have been attempts at similar arrangements

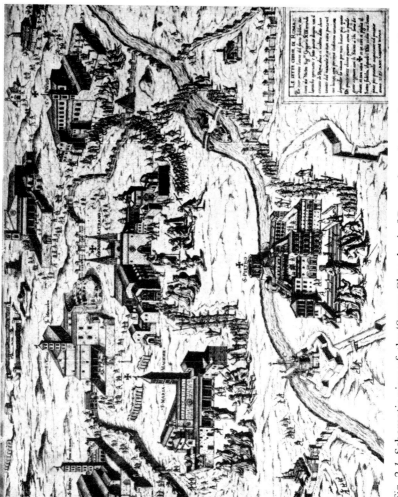

Fig. 2.1 Schematic view of the 'Seven Churches' of Rome, late sixteenth century, with the old church of St Peter in the foreground, the new dome under construction.

segregating clerical students from the laity.

Yet complete isolation was not possible. One cannot live abroad and remain entirely immune from foreign influences and in the seventeenth century something of the baroque quality of Roman life is to be found in the College. Moreover, however remote the institution might be geographically from England, the personnel was continually changing, with new students arriving and others leaving to work on the mission.

The studies

The intellectual and spiritual training of the future missioners to England was in the hands of the Jesuits. From early days the students attended the Roman College and took their part in the course of studies there. As early as October 1579 we learn of one of them being singled out for the honour of defending his doctoral thesis at a solemn public ceremony.

However, special consideration was given to students of the English and German Colleges in view of their need to be well instructed in controversies.[7] So what they learnt at the university was supplemented by lectures in the house; and although the College in Rome never matched the wealth of controversial literature that came from Louvain, Douai and Rheims, the College did have among its superiors distinguished controversialists like Persons, Holt and Fitzherbert. Indeed, many of Persons' own volumes found their way into the library and so augmented the existing collection bequeathed by Allen, Baines, Cope and Sheprey.[8] The *Opera Omnia* of John Fisher as well as an annotated copy of Foxe's *Book of Martyrs* would seem to have belonged originally to Persons. Cardinal Baronius, the Oratorian historian, presented a copy of his *Annales* and Luke Wadding his work on St Francis. Liturgical interests are indicated by the existence of a *sacerdotale* printed in Venice in 1587, a volume of 376 folios which was a *vade mecum* for the priest, providing him with guidance on the general rubrics of the new missal and breviary. There is also a Sarum Missal printed in Paris in 1555 and a Pontifical of 1563 which has Owen Lewis's autograph.

The students would have been pupils of Cardinal Robert Bellarmine at the Roman College and for a time Leonard Lessius, the Jesuit theologian, was *ripetitore* or tutor at the English College.[9] It would appear from the Sega report that the students were eager to take part in the full course of studies and disputations at the

Fig. 2.2 Pope Gregory XIII ordered the construction of the Collegio Romano in 1582 as the Jesuit house of studies. The piazza in front had earlier been enlarged and was now dominated by the Collegio and the Doria Pamphilj palace.

Roman College. But the Jesuit superiors of the College placed some restrictions on this in so far as they maintained that it would be a waste of time for some students to pursue a course in speculative scholastic theology. They were too dull for this and so they were directed to other fields such as casuistry and morals. There was resentment at this suggestion that a minor course was all that some students could manage, but Sega agreed with the practice and ruled that there had to be a rigorous examination each year which would assess the performance and capabilities of the scholars.[10]

The problem as to the exact kind of studies suitable for future missioners in England had occupied Allen's attention. Writing to Vanderville, regius professor at Douai and afterwards Bishop of Tournai, he said: 'Our students, being intended for the English harvest, are not required to excel or be great proficients in theological science, though their teachers ought to be as learned and prudent as possible.'[11]

In 1597 Clement VIII issued a decree[12] that placed restrictions on Englishmen taking degrees. Henceforth no one could proceed to a doctorate unless he had left the seminary four years previously. There were protests that this would mean the virtual abolition of the doctorate, as few would be able to keep up their studies or even have the inclination to resume study after four years on the mission. There were pleas that as some of the newly ordained were young and immature it would be an advantage to let them stay on and complete a doctorate before returning to England. But the brief seems to have been inspired by two things. First of all it wanted to prevent a repetition of the incident whereby Christopher Bagshaw,[13] no great scholar, managed to buy a degree for himself at Padua on his way home to England, paying for it with the money he had received for travelling expenses. Secondly there was an immediate need for priests in England and it was feared that some students might be deflected from their resolve to work in England by the attraction of further study. In 1609, when Richard Smith visited Rome on behalf of the Archpriest, part of his mission was to get the decree rescinded[14] but the arguments became lost in the complaints that the Archpriest's jurisdiction was being flouted by the Jesuit superiors of the College. It seemed to be forgotten that the decree also applied to Douai. The indications are that the concern of the seculars in this affair was political and not doctrinal.[15] Never once is complaint made about the Roman course as such being unsuitable for those destined to work in England. Surely if there had been any objections they would have been seized upon.

Fig. 2.3 An opposite view of the piazza, *c.* 1700, showing on the left the façade of the Collegio Romano and facing it the extensive Doria Pamphilj palace.

Of course the Roman College was little affected by all this. It seemed to presume that its students would proceed to degrees, although apart from the Jesuit students, few continued after their fourth year of theology.[16]

Discipline

After the death of Persons in 1610, we once again hear of disciplinary troubles within the College. These came to a head in 1623 and dragged on for more than a year. Some students were expelled and sent to Douai to complete their studies; others were disciplined.[17] We must remember that there were similar troubles about this time at Douai and both reflect the contentious nature of English Catholicism, the troubles in Rome being aggravated by the anti-Jesuit feelings, albeit of a vociferous minority.[18] In general the Jesuits accused the seculars of stirring up sedition among the students and the seculars accused the Jesuits of using the College to recruit for the Society. In fairness to the Society it should be borne in mind that the College in Rome was for the education of priests. There was nothing in the Bull of Foundation saying it was for seculars only. That it became necessary to legislate that students could not enter a religious order without the permission of the Holy See was not only a sad reflection on the disunity of the seculars and regulars but an indication of the precarious state of papal finances. The visitation of 1623 took place before the outbreak of trouble. It was, in fact, a result of the decree of Propaganda Fide of March 21 ordering a canonical visitation of all colleges. It began as an enquiry into the finances, but before long the visitor was drawn into the squabbles of the appellants[19] against the Jesuits. The missionary oath forbidding students to enter religion was, from the papal point of view, intended to protect the College and its papal funds from unnecessary expenses: it wanted a return for the money spent, i.e. missioners in England. As the Jesuits were to point out,[20] it was as much directed against the Benedictines as against the Society. Moreover it is highly unlikely that the Congregation of Propaganda would be anti-Jesuit. This congregation was set up in 1622 as part of the reorganisation of the Roman Curia. Its concern was to look after Church affairs in missionary countries and those places in Europe where Protestantism had reduced the Catholic community to a condition similar to those countries which Christianity had barely penetrated. The preliminary commission, from which Propaganda was to emerge, was in fact dominated by those who had been educated by the Jesuits and from the beginning there was a close understanding between the Society and Propaganda. Indeed, Propaganda took the missionary oath in use at the English College and used it as a model for oaths to be taken at other colleges.[21]

Decline or stability?

Several writers, including Gasquet,[22] speak of the seventeenth century as a period of decline for the English College and, as a place of preparation for priests to work on the English mission, it is compared unfavourably with Douai and Lisbon. There is a manuscript history of the Hospice and College dating from the early nineteenth century, possibly the work of Gradwell, which Gasquet seems to have known.[23] This work attributes the decline of the College after the death of Persons to two chief causes: (i) the number and character of the students, and (ii) the lack of efficacy in forming priests for the mission. Both these reasons need to be examined.

We are fortunate in possessing the *Responsa* for the whole of this period.[24] These give the replies of every student entering the College as to his age, parentage, education and previous religious history. One cannot but be struck by the great variety of backgrounds from which the students came. There are converts, those who have been imprisoned for their faith and schismatics (those who had attended Protestant services). Some speak openly of their religious difficulties, among which the existence of purgatory figures largely.[25] Their reasons for coming to the College are varied. Some have been attracted to the Roman seminary by its reputation (which hardly suggests that it was in decline). Some have come to learn Italian, to study letters or philosophy; some are well-seasoned travellers. What is important is that some state quite explicitly that they have no desire to be ecclesiastics. For example, in 1650, of eight admissions, four do not desire to become clerics. In 1651 four out of twelve have a similar opinion. In 1652 it is three out of eight. Now there are several ways of interpreting these facts. It could be argued that the College's acceptance of non-ecclesiastics was a retrograde step, a desire to fill up places in default of true vocations. If one's criterion of quality depends on commitment to the clerical state then this certainly was a period of decline.[26] But it could equally well be maintained that the College saw its role as a broadly educative one, as one of the continental colleges where

English Catholic laity could continue their eduction, and where they could be culturally open to the world. Such an openness is often easier and safer to the exile than to one in his own country; the very foreignness of the secular scene can act as a filter and make for a less involved viewing of 'the world'. A perusal of the Pilgrim Books of this period lends some support to the view that there had been a change in attitudes from those which were prevalent in the previous century. Past historians have referred to the visits to the College of John Milton in 1638, John Evelyn in 1644 and Richard Crashaw in 1646, and one can detect a mixture of surprise and self-gratification, implying that the reception of Protestants and men of letters must have called for an heroic effort to overcome the natural tendency in us all to hate our enemies. But if one attends to the *Responsa* and remembers the great variety of backgrounds of the students, such hospitality becomes a natural and obvious procedure. That future clergy should be trained in such a milieu certainly seems to fit in with what we know of conditions at home, which were far from the embattled community we are sometimes led to believe.[27]

Life at the English College in the seventeenth century provided plenty of opportunities for meeting people[28] and it seems as if the Sega regulations of 1595 had fallen into abeyance. In 1629 all the English residents in Rome were invited to dinner at the College, and it was customary to hold a banquet on the feast of St Thomas of Canterbury. Barberini in his visitation of 1630 was aware of this and the custom continued after his visit.[29] The studies and the reading of the future priests may have been closely supervised but at least one student had read his Luis de Granada[30] before entering.

This was the time when plays were frequently performed at the College[31] and the existence of a piece called 'Hierarchomachia or Antibishop' satirising the Archpriest controversy, enables us to see this dispute through eyes other than the bitter rival polemics of the controversialists. Although the regulations were that plays had to be on sacred subjects and contain no female characters, these rules were not always observed. Plays were usually performed during the final weeks of carnival[32] and the audiences were often large and were likely to include a few cardinals. Many of the plays had been first written and acted at St Omer, and Emmanuel Lobb SJ, who was to become Rector, 1647–50, was himself a playwright. The acting was undertaken by the students but professional musicians were sometimes hired.[33] The period 1612–48 was most prolific and the College continued to give plays at a time when the theatres were closed in England. But plays were also presented at the Collegio Romano, and it was usual for the Jesuits to mark academic feasts by stage productions.[34] Thus this period begins to emerge as one inspired by Jesuit humanism – not a dilettante humanism but a humanism motivated by apostolic and practical needs. Undoubtedly things had changed since the 1585 Constitution, but the state of affairs would at least have been understood by Allen in the early days of the College. The admission of students other than prospective priests was contrary to the guidelines laid down and the visitation of 1645 had something to say about the reception of pilgrims who were not Catholics and were unknown to the Rector. Henceforth, it was decreed that no one was to be admitted who was not sufficiently known to the Rector or his deputies to be a Catholic and a trustworthy pilgrim, not merely on business.

As for the second alleged reason for decline, namely the inefficacy of the College in forming priests for the mission, we have first of all to bear in mind what has just been said about the quality of the students accepted. Not all intended to take up the ecclesiastical state and one has to try and determine what exactly was the current need for priests. Bossy[35] suggests that one of the problems in the first part of the century was an over-supply of priests. There is no need to make the extravagant claim that the Jesuits in Rome were aware of this and so cut down the supply accordingly. Nevertheless, looking back at this period in the College's history, it need not necessarily be regarded a disaster for England that the College did not send more priests to the mission at this time. But the principal explanation as to why the numbers were few was a financial one. Europe was in the throes of inflation. The Douai Diaries[36] refer to the bad state of Douai and the 1612 visitation of that college recommended a cutting down of student numbers. In 1617 it was necessary to launch an appeal in England for the support of Douai. In 1623 the president, Kellison, went on a begging mission to England as no more money was forthcoming from Spain or from Rome. In all such emergencies the policy of Rome was always the same – cut down on the number of students.

Fitzherbert

If one wants a more positive view of the style of Catholicism found in the English College in Rome in those days, one could not do better than consider Thomas Fitzherbert, Rector from 1618 to

1640.[37] Born in 1552 at Swinnerton, Staffordshire, a student at Oxford, imprisoned for his faith in 1572, he was one of the laity who assisted Campion and Persons in 1580. After the death of his wife in 1588 he took up residence abroad. 'A great lover of books' and the author of several works of controversy, he acted as intelligencer for the Spanish king and was a close friend of the Duke of Feria. He travelled extensively in France, Spain and the Low Countries and was ordained priest in Rome in 1602. For some years he was agent for the Archpriest in Rome but his close association with Persons led him to give this up in 1609. He joined the Society in 1613 and then in 1618 became Rector of the English College in Rome, a post he held until a few months before his death in 1640 at the age of 88. The varied experience and life of such a man helps us to understand something of the calibre of the College in those days. His rectorate coincided with the pontificate of Maffeo Barberini, Urban VIII, 1623–44, the patron of Bernini, when, in spite of the financial gloom, Rome enjoyed a period of great splendour. It was now that baroque architecture reached its apogee in public and private monuments. In 1626 the new St Peter's was consecrated and in the same year the Pope purchased Castel Gandolfo. The Barberinis were distinguished patrons of learning and the English College in its own modest way reflected some of the glory. Sermons continued to be preached annually before the Pope on St Stephen's Day,[38] as they had been in the early days of the College, but now they are written out with more of a flourish and on at least one occasion the orator could not forbear to adorn his manuscript with the Barberini bees. When Cardinal Farnese, the Protector of the College, died in 1626, his funeral took place in the College church and sonnets in eight languages were addressed to his memory.[39]

In many ways the seventeenth century was a golden age for the Roman College too. A solemn papal visitation to the Church of the Gesù marked the centenary of the foundation of the Society in 1639. The building programme progressed with the commencement of the Church of S. Ignazio. The library was extended by donation and purchase, the Kircher museum of antiquities was set up and, although it was only completed after the Suppression, the Observatory was begun. The theology of the Roman College was not remarkable during this period[40] but scientific studies advanced and Galileo was given a very flattering reception in 1611, on account of his sensational telescopic discoveries. From about this time are to be dated treatises on sundials and the computation of the calendar, bound together and illustrated with a fine baroque

Fig. 2.4 Behind the Collegio Romano the Church of Sant' Ignazio was constructed in a flourish of baroque building during the middle of the seventeenth century.

pen and ink frontispiece,[41] still to be found in the archives. However, it was in the following century that the English College achieved a certain amount of notice through the work of Christopher Maire, Rector 1744–50, who collaborated with his fellow Jesuit, Roger Boscovitch, in studies on the meridian.[42]

It was during the Fitzherbert regime that the English College was indirectly connected with the beginnings of the Irish College, in so far as four Irish students were paid for at the College as commoners and were supported for three years by Cardinal Ludovico Ludovisi until the Irish College opened in 1628.[43] A few years previously the College had a connection with Mary Ward.[44] Her school was on an adjacent site, the angle of the present Via Montoro and Via Monserrato. Her sister, Barbara, who died of smallpox in 1621, was buried in the College church. A plaque commemorating the College's connection with the Institute has been placed over the door to the sacristy.

In 1622, at the request of Cardinal Mellini, co-protector of England, Fitzherbert presented a 'relatio dello stato del collegio inglese' to the newly established Propaganda Fide.[45] It states that the present income is not sufficient to support the fifty alumni required by the Bull of Foundation. These fifty alumni require another twenty persons to govern and look after them. In addition, there are expenses incurred in hospitality and *viaticum* (travelling expenses of new students and of those returning to England after ordination). Very often the commoners have to be aided as well as the alumni. Lest this way of life should appear extravagant the report adds that by order of the Pope, the College has been requested to put up supernumeraries. William Alabaster[46] stayed for a year; Dr Worthington, president of Douai College, and his servant stayed for two years and Dr Weston for three years. But the purpose of the College is not lost sight of and there is an account of the state of religion in England, the labours of past students, the conversions they have effected, the works of controversy and apologetics they have written, and those alumni who have been martyred or suffered for the faith. Eight years later, for the visitation of 1630, the *ragguaglio* adopts a similar tone.[47] The account of the visitation by Cardinal Barberini is interesting in that it bears out some of the observations we have made about the *Responsa*. We are informed that the majority of the alumni are 'nobili' and some of the best families of England are represented here. Some who were simply commoners and did not intend to become priests, nevertheless decided on a vocation while at the College. This same year saw the completion of an index to

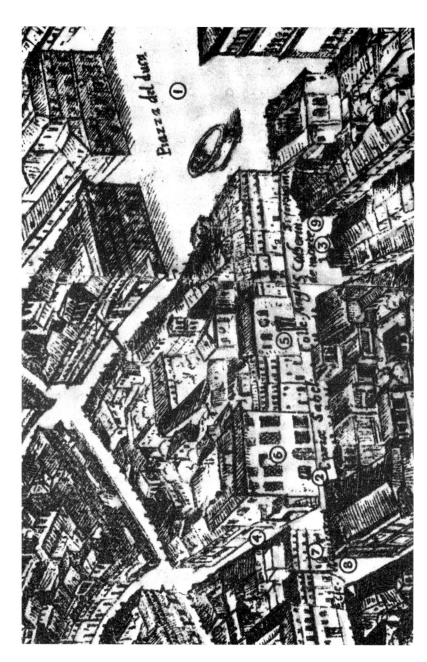

Fig. 2.5 View of College (5) and the adjacent Mary Ward school (6) in 1593.

the College archives[48] and Fitzherbert ordered a description of all the College property to be made.[49] This survey is not only valuable for its plan of the College, as it was before Cardinal Howard's rebuilding,[50] but also for a remarkable title page, illuminated in blue, gold and red with a rather full and rotund baroque version of the martyrs' picture, the Barberini bees, of course, and the inscription 'Franciscus Cardinalis Barberini Protector, R.P. Tomaso Fitzherberto Rettore, Sedente Urbano VIII'. Thus in the person of Fitzherbert the English gentry took its place alongside the Roman nobility.

Yet these glories are mingled with gloom. The Pilgrim Book for 1630 records, 'Hoc anno grassante peste per Italiam, pauci admodum venerunt Romam' and the Liber Ruber states, 'Non venerunt logici propter pesten quae per Italiam late grassatur.'[51] It was indeed an age of contrasts. Nearby, work was progressing on the church of S. Andrea della Valle which was soon to incorporate the chapel of the Barberini family, one of whose more distinguished members was Urban VIII. However, it was also the period when, as had happened with Giordano Bruno in 1600, executions took place regularly in the Campo dei Fiori and the cries of the prisoners under torture in the Corte Savella prison, next to the College, disturbed the students at their studies and devotions.[52]

There is another matter which illustrates Fitzherbert's management. It is a financial concern that is not mentioned in the 1630 visitation, which might mean that it had been cleared up by then. In the College archives[53] there are two copies of a document, 'Difficulties of account between the English College and the mission and the agreements of 1628'. The Rector, Fitzherbert, sets out these difficulties under fifteen headings. He took the opportunity of the presence in Rome of the procurators of the Society at their congregation, to call to the attention of the procurator of the English province some problems that had arisen from the close association between the finances of the College and those of the mission.[54] Of the fifteen cases, nine dated from the rectorship of Thomas Owen, Fitzherbert's predecessor. Persons, on his deathbed, recommended to Acquaviva, the General of the Society, that Owen should succeed him in the office of prefect of the English mission and Rector of the English College, and in fact, he held these offices from 1610 to 1618.[55] Whatever may have been the usual situation as regards keeping the mission funds separate from those of the continental institutions,[56] the combination of the two offices of Rector and prefect did create difficulties for Owen and for Fitzherbert who

Fig. 2.6 The Campo dei Fiori in the seventeenth century. As today, it was passed through almost daily by students on their way to the Collegio Romano. The market square was also used for public executions, including that of Giordano Bruno in 1600.

came after him. Some idea of the complications of the situation can be gained from the following cases:

(a) In 1612 Thomas Owen, Rector of the English College and prefect of the mission, sold a house belonging to the College, supposing the Pope's consent, for 300 crowns. With this money he paid off a College debt and bought some bonds. But the Pope refused to ratify this transaction and so Owen had to buy back the property. As the College was unable to raise money for this, mission funds were used. So the question was asked: how does the College stand in regard to the 300 crowns and does it own the bonds? If the initial purchase for the College were invalid, since it was bought with money that did not belong to the College, has the mission a right to it? Is one to consider that the said goods should be transferred to the mission? Fitzherbert's own particular concern was 'That the superiors of this house incur no suspicion of defrauding the College, nor the mission suffer any loss in case of a visitation, or change of superiors into seculars, or the dissolution of the College and its return to a hospice'. A clear case of divided loyalties and concern for a fair and just solution to a difficult case.

(b) Further problems arose concerning monies given to scholars going to the Jesuit noviciate at Liège. Is such money to be considered as alms and so part of the College account, or is the province to make good this payment to the College? Often it is necessary to help commoners pay their pension and sometimes this money was taken from the mission account. There was one case where it was uncertain whether property held by the Rector was on behalf of the College or of the mission. An architect was not only employed in the service of the College, but also on behalf of the mission. He was badly paid in any case and there was anxiety to make good for past injustices, but from which account?

The significance of this document is not merely that it shows a confusion between the accounts but it also manifests a sincere anxiety on the part of Fitzherbert, who drew it up, to put matters right. In most of the fifteen cases legal advice was sought and it would seem that such entanglements were not so common after this date.

Fig. 2.7 La Magliana farm, purchased in 1614 and used as a holiday home.

Roger Baines

A continual reminder of the complexity due to College interests being involved with those of the Society is seen in the case of Roger Baines's will.[57] Baines was born in 1546, converted from Protestantism, joined Allen at Rheims and came with him to Rome in 1579. In 1587 he was appointed *economus* by Holt having for many years served as Allen's secretary. When he died in 1623 he designated as his heir the Jesuit college at Louvain (later to be transferred to Liège) but there were instructions that the said College was to maintain an alumnus at the College in Rome on part of the income from the bequest. This alumnus was to be a relative, or failing that, to take the name 'Baines'. However, the bonds from which the income was to be derived both for Liège and the Roman burse were not yet complete. They were to be made up to the number of 100 by the publication and sale of ten volumes of Baines's own writings; only then would they yield the desired amount. A year after Baines's death permission was sought of the Pope to sell some of the bonds to solve some debts accruing to the mission. Despite this, the bonds were eventually brought up to the requisite number by the year 1626 and a dispensation was gained from the obligation of having Baines's works printed. In the 1628 document we have been referring to, it is asked from what date is the College entitled to its share in the income. It was decided that it should be from the time when the bonds were completed. Another document gives a list of Baines scholars and payment was made most years up to 1683, but when Cardinal Howard became Protector 'he would no more receive any such alumnus into the College'. In 1694, after the death of Howard, the college at Liège and the Rector of the College in Rome agreed that Liège had no longer any obligations to support the burse. They approached the procurator general who agreed that the payments should cease.[58] But nearly a century later[59] with the suppression of the Society, Cardinal Corsini reserved, from 1 December 1773, the Baines money for his own usage. The College asked legal advice as to whether the Cardinal ought to pay for a student or whether they must continue to support a student if he retains the money for purposes of the general administrative costs. The matter was discussed in 1788 at the meeting of the Congregation for the mission and on 27 June 1789 payment was resumed and it continued down to 1797.[60] It would seem that despite the decision of 1694 a scholar was maintained on the Baines legacy, and so there was a reminder of the days of Fitzherbert, until the closing of the College by the French in 1798.

These financial entanglements between the College and the Society were not always of a painful nature. The property at La Magliana, which the College used for many years as a weekly holiday home, was the result of a bequest to the Society by Tobie Mathew.[61] In the seventeenth century the Jesuits bought property at Monte Porzio and spent a great deal of money on the buildings. It was used as a place of *villeggiatura* (summer residence) by the English College for a small rent and later it was bought outright on behalf of the College.[62]

After the death of Fitzherbert, external events continued to have an adverse effect on the College economy. In 1645 there was a visitation under Cardinal Spada.[63] It was pointed out that rather than the English Catholics being unwilling to support a Jesuit establishment, it was a case of their being quite unable to provide any funds. The Civil War in England, the loss of College property in Italy – the Abbey at Piacenza had been ruined by war and plague – had meant that it was impossible to support more than thirty alumni.[64] The closure of the College was suggested, but a plea was made that the shortages were 'propter temporum calamitates'. By 1656 the situation had deteriorated further. There had been fires at the College in 1654,[65] there was the plague of 1655, further floods and war damage at Piacenza, the rents were no longer adequate and the problems of Catholics at home in England were increasing. It became difficult to provide a *viaticum* for those returning to England[66] and Pope Alexander VII refused to give money for this

Fig. 2.8 View of Monte Porzio, little changed from the seventeenth century when College students passed their *villeggiatura* at the house close to the parish church.

purpose. In the 1657[67] visitation Cardinal Barberini did not draw up any new constitution but was satisfied with making one or two observations and additions to the existing constitutions and rules. This was because the difficulties were almost entirely financial. The visitation of 1671 was mainly concerned with the property at Piacenza.[68]

The rather gloomy picture that emerges from a survey of the mid-seventeenth century has to be contrasted with the evidence provided by the *Responsa* and the Pilgrim Book, of the rich variety of visitors and residents at the College. It must also be remarked that although the number of students had fallen, the number of superiors was remarkably high. Even in mid-century when things were at their worst, there were usually a dozen fathers of the Society resident and presumably kept by the College out of mission funds.[69] For example, in 1646[70] the College could not support more than thirty alumni and yet there were also living in the house: a Rector, a minister, a confessor, a prefect of studies, a procurator, three ripetitori and three *coadjutores temporales* for the College administration, in addition to the father procurator of the English province and two *socii coadjutores*.

To sum up. The seventeenth century is portrayed as a period of decline, largely owing to the opposition in England to the Jesuits running a college for the secular clergy. Many of the sources we have are biased in favour of the seculars. But there is much to indicate that the Society adapted well to the changing situation, opening its doors to English people who were attracted to the College in Rome. As with the rest of Europe, the financial crisis hit the College badly. It was difficult for those involved to see where economies had to be made and with hindsight one can be critical of the style of life that was maintained. However, there was a complicated budget, arising from the fact that the Society was administering a college for the seculars in addition to their own colleges at Liège and St Omer, all of which establishments were concerned with the English mission, for which moneys and bequests as well as foundations had been left. The most effective and uncomplicated way to save money was to cut the number of students and this was Rome's policy also.[71]

Things were to change when Cardinal Philip Howard became Protector. A restoration of the buildings was to be undertaken and with the accession of James II and the appointment of vicars apostolic, after a long period of no English ecclesiastical government at all, it looked as if the troubles of the preceding years were to vanish. This was not to be and indeed the ecclesiastical, financial and political issues were to reappear in a different form.

Notes

1 Complaints were made about the scarcity of priests coming from Rome as early as 1609 in Richard Smith's mission on behalf of the Archpriest.

2 See L. von Pastor, *History of the Popes*, XXVII, p. 157 for the divergent views in Rome concerning the necessity of the episcopate for the maintenance of a particular church. The mission of Panzani to England (1634–6) was largely to determine whether there ought to be a bishop resident in the country. See Pastor, XXIX, pp. 312–3.

3 T. G. Law, 'The Archpriest Controversy', quoted by Kenny, *Venerabile*, XVII, 155.

4 J. Bossy *The English Catholic Community* pp. 198–202, gives an account of the social background of clerical students. A. Laird, 'The English College in Rome under Italian Secular Administration', *RH*, 14, 1977, 127–47, notes Corsini's views on this.

5 Foley, *Records*, VI, p. 60 gives a translation of the Sega report in full.

6 Foley, *Records*, VI, p. 66.

7 These measures were reinforced when Propaganda Fide was founded in 1622. Villoslada, *Storia del Collegio Romano 1551–1773*, pp. 72, 113–4, 224. 'Controversies' was the name given to a defensive, apologetic theology especially designed to meet Protestant objections to Catholicism. It made use of such writers as Bellarmine and Canisius.

 8 For a history of the Library, see L. W. Jones, 'The College Library', *Venerabile*, IV, 226–35; 329–39.

 9 'Il fut envoyé à Rome pour y repasser sa théologie, tout en remplissant les fonctions de répétiteur au collège anglais', Raoul de Scorraille, *François Suarez de la Compagnie de Jesus*, I (1912), p. 177. Suarez was Lessius' supervisor at this time. The date of Lessius' Roman stay is not given but it was between 1582 and 1584.

10 Foley, *Records*, VI, p. 62. For a fuller account of English College students at the University, see F. J. Shutt, 'Public Acts', *Venerabile*, XI, 40–4.

11 T. F. Knox, *The Letters and Memorials of William Cardinal Allen* (London, 1882), Letter XXV, pp. 52–67.

12 The 1597 Rules applied equally to Douai and in the 1612 visitation of Douai by Cesar Clement there were similar regulations about taking degrees. See '3rd Douai Diary', *CRS*, 10, 117–21, 357–63.

13 For Bagshaw, see G. Anstruther, *Seminary Priests*, I; see also *The Wisbech Stirs*, *CRS*, 51. Bagshaw played a prominent part in these disturbances as he had done in the troubles in Rome. A. Morey, *The Catholic Subjects of Elizabeth*, p. 202.

14 *The Letters of Thomas Fitzherbert*, *CRS*, 41, contains some of the documentation on the dispute and carries an important introduction and notes by L. Hicks SJ.

15 'If the very reverend archpriest of England should judge anyone fit to take such a degree, all he need do would be to notify the Cardinal Protector by letter and the letter would at once give the candidate permission to proceed. H. E. Cardinal Bianchetti told the agent, the reverend Dr. Smith, in the presence of Mr. Thomas More and Mr. Thomas Fitzherbert, English priests, that such was the mind of His Holiness', 'Letters and Memorials of Father Robert Persons SJ', ed. L. Hicks SJ, *CRS*, 39 (1942), 143.

16 Villoslada, *Storia del Collegio Romano 1551–1773*.

17 ECA, scr. 23, 6, 1, re 1624; 29, 5, 2, re 1625, Liber Ruber, nos. 595, 601, 603.

18 The seculars' case is given by M. A. Tierney (ed.), *Dodd's Church History of England* (1843), vol. 5 which makes use of William Bishop's account. The 1739 visitation report in its historical review of the College speaks of the 1623 revolt as being an attempt of the clergy of England to take away the government of the College from the Jesuits. It was their agents who stirred up the students, Liber 324, f 22. See also G. Swinburne, 'The Visitation of 1623', *Venerabile*, IX, 19–27; 138–47.

19 The appellants were those secular priests who appealed to Rome against the Archpriest Blackwell and asked for the appointment of a Bishop and also the removal of the Jesuits from the direction of the English College in Rome.

20 This interpretation of the oath of Alexander VII occurs in the preface to the 1739 visitation report. P. Guilday gives an account of the attraction to the Benedictines that was especially felt in Valladolid and Seville, *The English Catholic Refugees on the Continent*, p. 217. Maurus Lunn, 'Benedictine Opposition to Bishop Richard Smith 1625–1629', *RH*, 11, 1–20.

21 R. Wiltgen, 'Propaganda is placed in Charge of the Pontifical Colleges', in *SCPF*, 1/1 (1971), 483–505.

22 Gasquet, *History*, p. 107f, seems to be influenced by Dodd-Tierney.

23 ECA, liber 1292, *Breve ragguaglio dell'origine, progresso, e stato presente del Collegio Inglese existente in Roma.*

24 *CRS*, 54 and 55.

25 See D. P. Walker, *The Decline of Hell* (London 1964), for seventeenth century opinions on this matter. The College library still possesses a copy of a book from this period defending Catholic belief in purgatory, Jane Owen, *An Antidote against Purgatory* (1634). It bears the inscription in a seventeenth-century hand 'pro cubiculo Patris confessoris'. See H. E. G. Rope, 'A Forgotten Booklet', *Venerabile*, XVIII, 28–35.

26 It would be interesting to know why Propaganda was displeased with the College as is suggested in Liber 1291. Was it because it was acting against the 1585 Constitution?

27 J. Bossy, *The English Catholic Community 1570–1850*, p. 152 refers to the flexible religious views of the time.

28 F. J. Shutt, 'The English Romayne Life', *Venerabile*, VI, 172–8; 253–60.

29 ECA, scr. 30, 38. Panzani, whatever he may have thought of the Jesuits accepted an invitation to dine after his return from England. Blacklo also came to dinner at the College although not on the same day.

30 *CRS, Responsa*, 454.

31 ECA, liber 321 contains texts of plays and also words of music sung during intervals in the plays. S. Gossett, 'Drama in the English College Rome 1591–1660', *English Lit. Renaissance*, 1973, pp. 60–93. S. Gossett, 'English Plays in the English College Archives', *Venerabile*, XXVIII (1983), 23–33. S. Gossett, *Hierarchomachia or The Anti-Bishop* (London, 1982). R. L. Stewart, 'E. Lobb', *Venerabile*, XVII, 215–25. A. Shell, *Catholicism, Controversy and the English Literary Imagination 1558–1660* (Cambridge 1999), pp. 188–90, 211–17, 220–21. G. Dixon, 'Music in the English College during the Early Baroque Era', *Venerabile*, XXVIII (1984), 62–70.

32 The days immediately preceding Lent were those dedicated to carnival and were traditionally given over to licence. Clerics were forbidden on the streets and so had to provide their own innocuous entertainments at home.

33 *Venerabile*, I, 308.

34 Villoslada, *Storia del Collegio Romano 1551–1773*, pp. 162–6.

35 J. Bossy *The English Catholic Community*, pp. 220–1.

36 *CRS*, 10, xx–xxi.

37 *Letters of Thomas Fitzherbert*, *CRS*, 41. There is an important introduction to this by L. Hicks SJ. See also Foley, *Records*, II, series III.

38 F. Rogers, 'St. Stephen's Day', *Venerabile*, VII, 8–17. David Lewis the future martyr was one of those who preached before Urban VIII.

39 ECA, liber 274 (The Farnese Book) contains illustrations of the catafalque as well as the texts of sonnets in English, Irish, Welsh, Roman, Tuscan, French, Greek and Latin. See also *Venerabile*, III (1926), 35–6 and XXIII (1966), 329–30. D. Techwyn Lloyd, 'Dam o Farddomaeth, Gymraeg yn Rhufain (a Welsh poem in Rome)', *Ysgrifau Catholig*, 1961 pp. 36–8.

40 'Non si puo parlare di decadenza' says Villoslada, but he admits that there were no profound or original thinkers at this time, *Storia del Collegio Romano 1551–1773*, p. 214.

41 ECA, liber 1418: *De ratione temporum; Tractatus de horologiis; De horologiis solaribus.*

42 V. Hamilton, 'Thirtieth Meridian', *Venerabile*, XII, 129–37.

43 For a full account see Richard Ashton, 'The Venerabile and the Irish College', *Venerabile*, XXIII, 314.

44 Mary Ward, b. 1585, entered the Poor Clares at St Omer in 1606. In 1609, wanting a more active life, she founded with five other Englishwomen a religious congregation on the model of the Jesuits to provide for the education of women. After opening houses in Liège and elsewhere, she came to Rome in 1629 to secure papal approval. Her order was not approved for technical reasons, but her ideals live on in other institutes. L. Hicks, 'Mary Ward's Great Enterprise', *The Month*, CLI, 137–46; 317–26; CLII, 40–52; 231–8. Mary Oliver IBVM, *Mary Ward 1585–1645* (London 1959). Henriette Peters, *Mary Ward. A World in Contemplation* (English trans., Gracewing, Leominster 1994) especially pp. 332–6.

45 ECA, scr. 30, 37.

46 Born 1568, educated at Westminster School and Trinity College, Cambridge, Alabaster was a poet and after taking Anglican orders became a Catholic, spending the year 1598–9 at the English College; he returned to Rome in 1609 with the intention of seeking ordination, but was interested in 'cabalistic divinity' and later apostatised. His second stay at the College seems to be another example of a kindness to those in difficulty and under stress. An account of his conversion is in the College archives, Robert V. Caro SJ, 'William Alabaster: Rhetor Mediator, Devotional Poet', *RH*, 19, 62–79, 155–70.

47 'Ancora si ha da notare che essendo la maggior parte di questi alumni nobili, et alcuni di loro delle megliori famiglie d'Inghilterra si trovano sempre alcuni che potendo essere convittori, et studiare senza obligo di farsi sacerdoti et essere mandati in Inghilterra, si fanno alunni pigliando il giuramento dei Collegio per divotione, et ci sono altri ancora che essendo primogeniti, et heredi di buoni stati, l'hanno lasciati spontaneamente all fratelli minori per farsi sarcerdoti, et andare in Inghilterra al maryrio, si piacera a Dio ne farli degni.'

48 ECA, liber 227.

49 ECA, liber 240, 247, 248, 249.

50 See Appendix I.

51 Readers of Manzoni's *I Promessi Sposi* will be aware of the wars and plague that devastated Italy at this time.

52 ECA, scr. 8, 3d. Lionello Puppi, *Torment in Art: Pain, Violence and Martyrdom* (New York 1991) traces the route of the processions of criminals to public execution in 16th and 17th century Rome. They passed quite near to the English College.

53 ECA, scr. 6, 11, 4 and 5.

54 For a fuller treatment of the mission, see p. 69 and the visitation of 1739.

55 Foley, *Records*, VII/I, p. 562.
56 Bossy, *The English Catholic Community*, p. 231. Guilday, *The English Catholic Refugees on the Continent*, p. 156.
57 For Roger Baines, see *Venerabile*, I, 267. Also ECA, liber 227, 293; scr. 6, 14, 2:6, 11:3, 12:44, 2; Arch di Stato. Busta 723, n 2; B. M. add 48023 (Yelverton f 986); '1 & 2 Douai Diaries'; Strype. Ann IV. p. 386; A. C. Southern, *Elizabethan Recusant Prose 1559–1582* (1950), p. 352. Baines had two memorials, both of which survive. There was a monument on a pillar in the old church, now on the back wall of the new, and a slab on the floor over his grave, now on the wall of the passage opposite the main door of the present church. The martyr Edward Mico was a Baines scholar. See article by M. E. Williams, 'Baines, Roger', in *Oxford Dictionary of National Biography* (2004).
58 ECA, scr. 3, 12.
59 ECA, scr. 44, 2.
60 ECA, liber 517.
61 *Venerabile*, XV, 37–40. Tobie Mathew, Member of Parliament, son of the Archbishop of York, visited Rome in 1605 and met Persons, then Rector of the English College. He became a Catholic a year later, was imprisoned on his return to England and, after his release, travelled around Europe and after study at the Roman College was ordained priest in 1614. He gave money to the English Jesuits and from this donation the vineyard at La Magliana was purchased in 1614. See G. A. Hay, 'Magliana Revisited', *Venerabile*, XXVII (1979), 57.
62 In the early days the students used to go to Tivoli for a few days in the summer. From about 1614 the College rented or leased accommodation in Monte Porzio. The College bought the property there in 1708.
63 ECA, scr. 31, 1, 1.
64 The issue was always about the alumni, i.e. those for whom the College provided out of its own funds. For the story of the property at Piacenza see M. E. Williams, 'San Savino Abbey, Piacenza: A Forgotten Chapter of College History', *Venerabile*, XXX (1991), 9–15.
65 J. Cartmell, '1654 and the Fires', *Venerabile*, I, 306–34.
66 ECA, scr. 31, 2.
67 The date is 1657, not 1667 as Gasquet says, following the error of Brady, III, pp. 104–5. See ECA, liber 228.
68 ECA, scr. 31, 2.
69 One needs to remember that as far back as 1596 the students were complaining of the disproportion between students and superiors. Foley, *Records*, VI, p. 26.
70 ECA, scr. 31, 2.
71 See R. M. Wiltgen, 'Supervision of Pontifical Colleges by the Evangelization Congregation' in *SCPF*, 11 (1973), 237–8.

Chapter Three

Cardinals Protector and Vicars Apostolic

The fortunes of the English College in Rome were in a special way bound up with the person of the Cardinal Protector. It was Cardinal Morone who, at the beginning, prolonged Clynnog's tenure of office as Warden of the Hospice and then separated the government of the College from that of the Hospice. It was the Cardinal Protector who represented English interests to the Pope and advised on the government of the College. His name appeared alongside that of the Rector when the student's entry into the College was recorded in the Liber Ruber. However, his position was not always appreciated by the Catholics in England. When Richard Smith went on a mission to Rome in 1609 on behalf of the Archpriest it never seems to have occurred to the seculars that the Protector could be an arbiter in their dispute with the Jesuits. Even after 1622, when the Sacred Congregation of Propaganda Fide was set up, the Protector's word could be of the greatest importance. But whereas the colleges in the Low Countries and in France were directly answerable to the Nuncios of those places and through the Nuncio to the Cardinal Protector, the Rector of the College in Rome had to deal directly with the Protector.

In 1679 Cardinal Howard[1] was made Protector of England and Scotland at the request of Charles II. Philip Howard provides an occasion for treating of the College's attachment to the Stuart cause,[2] as well as describing the rebuilding of the College that took place in the late seventeenth century.

Fig. 3.1 Philip Cardinal Howard.

The Stuarts

The last English cardinal to be closely associated with the College had been William Allen. In the hundred years that had elapsed since his death the situation had changed to the extent that Howard, like Allen, was an exile but, unlike Allen, he was at home in court circles and enjoyed the good will of the reigning monarch. He had played a prominent part in promoting the Catholic marriage of Charles II and had been chaplain to the Queen, Catherine of Braganza, managing to combine this duty with his being prior of the English Dominicans in exile at Bornham. In 1670 he was nominated Vicar Apostolic of England by Propaganda Fide and after some two years' hesitation the Pope gave his consent. Whatever Howard's influence may have been in Rome and at the Stuart court, his appointment was not acceptable to the English secular clergy and he was opposed by those who wanted a true ordinary or no superior at all.[3] One may perhaps venture to ask how much of Howard's unacceptability as a vicar apostolic was due to his being a member of a religious order.[4] However, in 1679 he became Cardinal Protector of England and Scotland in succession to Barberini. Howard was by temperament a 'gradualist' and during the reign of James II he opposed the King's religious policy. Although his name had appeared at the trial of Titus Oates, there is no reason to suppose that he had anything to do with the so-called 'Popish Plot'. His influence in England ceased with the flight of James II in 1688, but he remained a loyal Stuart for the few remaining years of his life.

The colleges abroad shared his attachment to the Stuart cause and it is clear from the Douai Diaries that the happy events of the royal family were celebrated there,[5] just as Howard himself had given a great banquet in Rome on the birth of James Francis Edward, Prince of Wales, in June 1688. Among the Jacobite exiles in Rome at this time one can mention the Benedictine Philip Michael Ellis, former Vicar Apostolic of the Western District, chaplain to James II and secretary to Howard.[6] For a time he resided at the English College, but due to a quarrel between himself and the Rector, Ralph Postgate, he had to leave. There was a fear that he might be the centre of a faction in the College and in any case he could well afford to support himself and not rely on the College for sustenance. Eventually he became Bishop of the Italian diocese of Segni. Another exile was Sir Thomas Dereham, who died in Rome in 1739 and who left money for two burses to support convert clergymen to study for the priesthood in Rome. His magnificent tomb escaped the ravages of the French occupation and is still to be seen in the College church.[7] When the royal family left St Germain and took up residence at the Palazzo Muti, near the church of the Dodici Apostoli, the English College was able to attest its loyalty from close quarters.[8]

Social life in the eighteenth century was particularly splendid. Students at the English College could scarcely have been unaware of this aspect of Roman life. In 1745 for instance, when the Dauphin was betrothed to the Infanta Maria Teresa, dancing went on all night in front of the Farnese Palace with twenty cardinals looking on.[9] But the Stuarts were less extravagant and more pious. In the Pilgrim Book we read of people coming to Rome to be touched for the King's Evil by James III, the Old Pretender.[10] When James's wife, Maria Clementina, died in 1735 she was buried in St Peter's and members of the English College took part in the solemn funeral procession. When James himself died in 1766 there was a solemn funeral at the College.[11]

The papacy did not feel so well disposed to Charles Edward, the Young Pretender, as it had been to his father. This was partly due to his profligate life and his abjuration of the Catholic faith and partly for political reasons. There was clearly now no chance of the Stuarts regaining the throne and, for the sake of good relations with the reigning incumbent, the papacy ceased to support the new pretender. However, the various British religious communities in Rome remained attached to the Stuart cause and celebrated the accession of the new 'king' with a solemn Te Deum. Rumour reached the Pope that Charles had been 'crowned' at one of these ceremonies and as a result all four Rectors, i.e. of the English College, of the Scots College and of the Irish Franciscan and Irish Dominican houses, were removed from their posts.[12]

James's other son, Henry, Duke of York[13] took after his father. He was pious (known as 'the sacristan'), somewhat pompous, but much respected in Rome. He was created cardinal in 1747 and from 1749 it was his custom to celebrate each year the feast of St George with great pomp at the Church of the Dodici Apostoli. He became in turn, Archpriest of the Vatican Basilica, Camerlengo, and then in 1761 Cardinal Bishop of Frascati, a post held previously by Cardinal Howard.[14] When he became vice chancellor of the Holy Roman See in 1763 he spent much time at the Cancelleria near the College, but little is known of his relations with the College at this time. He remained discreetly neutral when the Jesuits were suppressed. On the death of his brother, the Young Pretender, he had the remains taken to his own

Fig. 3.2 Henry Cardinal Duke of York.

cathedral church at Frascati, since there was a ban on his being buried at St Peter's with other members of the family. Although he was now claimant to the British throne[15] the Cardinal York continued his old style of life. It is recorded that he joined in the celebrations when the news arrived in Rome of the repeal of the penal laws in 1791. He sold all the family jewels to help the Pope in his campaign against Napoleon, and, when, like many of the other cardinals, he found himself a refugee in Venice, he was offered a pension for life by George III. In 1803 he became Dean of the Sacred College and held the sees of Ostia and Velletri, but in fact continued to reside at Frascati. He never renounced his claim to the throne and when he died in 1807 he was buried in St Peter's with his mother and father, and the remains of his brother Charles Edward were now interred in the new family tomb. Pius VII commissioned the monument by Canova that is to be seen today. George III made a contribution to this memorial. The custom of English College students placing roses on the Stuart tomb on St George's day persisted until quite recently.

The rebuilding of the College

We must now return to Howard. As Cardinal Protector of England and Scotland, he spent much of his time in Rome. The monastery of SS John and Paul had been obtained in 1676 as a house for the English Dominicans, but he was more often than not resident at S. Sabina. However, for state occasions he wanted to make use of a more central site, namely the property next to the English College. As a member of Propaganda, his power and influence over the College was considerable and it was under his aegis that there took place an important rebuilding. Adjoining the College had been the notorious Corte Savella prison. When it was decided to rebuild this elsewhere, in the Via Giulia, the College bought the property in exchange for houses in other parts of the city, and alterations were carried out in the old buildings between 1658 and 1662. The reconstruction under Howard can be considered as a continuation of this work.[16] In the 1685 *status* there is a description of the College and its property and we can gather from this that the chief improvements were the removal of the library from above the church and the making of a new library and the new palace for Howard himself.[17] It was at this time that the ancient underground site was first discovered.[18] The work was completed in 1685 and, as will be seen from the plans, the College as it

Fig. 3.3 Piazza Santissimi (Dodici) Apostoli lined with palaces: Palazzo Colonna, *foreground right*, Palazzo Muti, *back left.*

appears today dates from this reconstruction. Howard's own apartments were in the newly acquired portion on the site of the old prison and part of the fine seventeenth-century ceiling can still be seen today in some of the rooms adjoining the *salone*. The designs of the new building were supposedly drawn up by Legenda and Carlo Fontana[19] and the result would have been even more spectacular had Andrea Pozzo's design for the church been carried out.[20] The rebuilding of churches and palaces on a grander scale was a characteristic of seventeenth- and eighteenth-century Rome and the efforts of Howard in this regard have to been seen within the context of the age. As Cardinal Protector he had to make public his care for the College and church over which he had charge. Howard thought in a grandiose way and this led some to think him prodigal and wasteful. He was not adverse to having a newly constructed piece pulled down and rebuilt if he did not like the look of it. He had a great gateway constructed and the campanile[21] resited. But this desire to live in style and make the College a building worthy of the English nation was misunderstood. During the actual rebuilding the Rector became anxious as to how the College would be able to pay the bills, especially as it was not clear what was Howard's gift and what was not. The demolition of houses for the construction of the new palace meant a loss of rent[22] and then the defeat and flight of James II put an end to this form of triumphalism among English Catholics.

There are other matters concerning Howard's rule that are deserving of mention. He had always been concerned about the poor quality of the English spoken by priests who had studied abroad. He therefore abolished the custom in the College of speaking Latin 'because these youths were beginning to forget their mother tongue'. Later the students petitioned for Latin to be restored. But the students were entirely on his side when he took the drastic step of banning the admission of commoners (convictors). These had been of considerable financial assistance, but there had been complaints about the arrogance and snobbery of a privileged class who were exempted from the common duties of the College. They were, however, reinstated immediately after Howard's death.[23]

The College was then involved in a protracted lawsuit. Howard's heir was the English Dominican province, but he had left one year's rent of his palace to the College[24] which, perhaps unreasonably, considered itself tricked and tried to secure from his heirs the cost of the rebuilding. It is interesting to note that in the account of the fabric in the 1739 visitation, there is reference to the extensive rebuilding, but the name Howard is not mentioned.

Fig. 3.4 The Palazzo della Cancelleria where Cardinal York spent much time when vice-chancellor. The exterior is largely unchanged today.

1739 visitation report

For the first time since its foundation, there now ensued two periods when the College had no Protector, 1694–1706 and 1711–17. These years were marked by continual complaints on the part of the seculars and the vicars apostolic against the English College in Rome and its Jesuit direction. Two things are worth remarking, namely the sameness of the charges to those raised in the early seventeenth century and the seeming disregard by the Roman authorities of anything that was said. This latter has sometimes been attributed to the strong pro-Jesuit lobby in papal circles but, be this as it may, the complaints fell on deaf ears because the Roman authorities looked at things from a different angle from that of the English vicars apostolic. It was a period when the popes were kindly but not very apostolic men and some of the issues were far too shrill for their liking. They trusted the Jesuit fathers to run the College and continued to maintain that responsibility for English College affairs was ultimately Rome's. Rather than generalise, it is best to relate these events to the visitation of 1737, which resulted in the report of 1739.

In 1699 a group of priests complained to the vicars apostolic about the English College.[25] They were dissatisfied with the character of the students, the studies, the spiritual formation and the small number of priests being sent to England. The Pope visited the College in person on 28 December 1701[26] and in 1702 a visitation was begun by Cardinal Francesco Barberini (a nephew of the other Francesco, who had been Protector and conducted visitations in the previous century). It became apparent that there was indeed internal trouble among the students, who objected to the camerata system and resented the employment of external Italian priests as prefects. To this effect they addressed a memorandum to the Pope and a letter to Barberini. The Cardinal took a strong line, insisting that it was against the Constitution of the College for each student to have his own room, and so the camerata system had to stay. Moreover he justified the external prefects by citing the previous history of the establishment, when much trouble had arisen because the prefects were internals. One can sympathise with the students because discipline was evidently strict, with an elaborate system of 'penances'.[27] However, the Rector in his report, prepared for the visitation, thought that the most pressing problem was that of the oath. He claimed that men were deterred from coming to Rome when they learnt that they had to swear an oath not to join a religious order.[28] The vicars apostolic could have got little consolation

Fig. 3.5 Requiem Mass of Queen Maria Clementina Stuart at the Basilica of the Santissimi Dodici Apostoli, 1735.

from the advice to the Rector that he should come to an arrangement with the Jesuit superiors in England to ensure that the College was well provided with suitable students. This would only confirm the bishops in their suspicions that the papacy considered the English mission to be entrusted to the Jesuits and that the seculars had little say in its affairs.

Gasquet tells us[29] that this visitation was suspended because there were rumours in Rome accusing the English seculars and the vicars apostolic of Jansenism. We know that Douai was suspected of Jansenism[30] but there is no indication of this being true of the College in Rome. At any rate the College in Rome ceased for a time to be the main centre of attraction. In 1707, however, a decision was made by Propaganda Fide to unite the Irish, Scots and English Colleges under one rule as the British College. Mary of Modena, the widow of James II and Regent for James III, protested and the plan was dropped.[31] Then in 1735 further letters of complaint arrived from the secular clergy and the vicars apostolic. Witham, the president of Douai, had openly expressed his dislike of the Jesuits' control of the College in Rome[32] and after the death of Bishop Giffard the seculars made a concerted effort to have them removed.[33] Laurence Mayes, the agent in Rome for the vicars apostolic, thought it would be quite impossible to dislodge the Society from the government of the College because of their great influence in Rome. All he could do by way of compromise was to suggest that Italian Jesuits should take over from English Jesuits.[34] The result of all this was that a visitation of the College began in 1737, the official report being published in 1739.

This report[35] is considered a model of its kind for its thoroughness and the way it sets out the findings. There was high praise for the fabric of the College. The rebuilding had made it an impressive place, airy and light. There was a description of the church which tells us that the tombs of Allen and Persons were situated in the middle of the nave. But when it came to speak of the economy, there was little good to say. The carelessness of this period contrasts strongly with Fitzherbert's day, and something of the financial attitude common in eighteenth-century papal Rome seems to have brushed off onto the College. There was complete disorder in the account books and the visitors treated the English superiors to a lecture on how to keep accounts and do elementary book keeping.[36] Moreover the finances of the College were tied up with those of the English mission and the colleges at Liège and St Omer.[37] The College was collecting rents from houses owned in Rome by the college at Liège.[38]

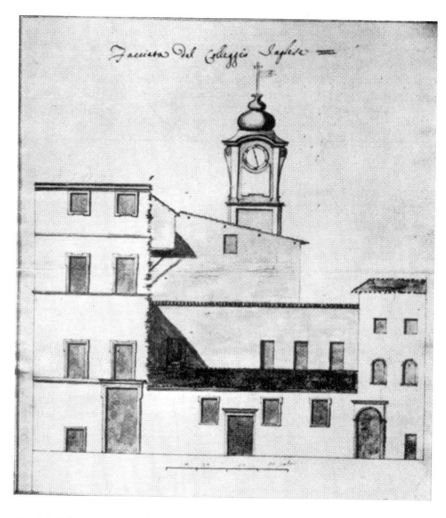

Fig. 3.6 A late seventeenth-century drawing shows the Howard reconstruction work, which left the Hospice church unaffected but confirms that the third storey 'Monserra' corridor with the 'Captain's Bridge' date from around 1685.

The visitation report gives the annual number of students from 1700 to 1739 and what became of them all.[39] Rome compares unfavourably with Douai, even allowing for the fact that not all of the one hundred students that Douai averaged were seniors or indeed destined for the clerical state. At Rome over these years the average number of students was twenty-four, about the same as the number of senior clerical students at Douai, but this figure disguises a decline from thirty-eight in 1700 to sixteen in 1739. As there were quite a few losses before ordination this meant that the actual numbers of those returning to England as ordained priests were very few indeed. For example, in 1718 there was only one for the English mission. The following year, 1719, there was only one new student admitted. This shows a definite decline since the previous century and explains the anxieties of the vicars as to the viability of the College.[40] Neither does the paucity of students from Rome seem to have been compensated for by quality. In fact when one assesses the men who were the formative influences on Catholic life in the seventeenth and eighteenth century, be they vicars apostolic or writers like Gother, Godden, Sargeant, Blacklo and Challoner, none of them were from Rome, but from Douai or Lisbon.

The result of the visitation was a new set of constitutions, based on the Barberini rules of 1658, and there was appended a whole series of points for discussion and deliberation. They ask radical questions and, although they include the complaints of the vicars apostolic, some of them go much further and show that Rome was well aware of the issues. They have an interest that far outstrips the century in which they were written. They could apply to almost any period of history, since they raise such matters as the desirability of a College in Rome at all, and who is the most fitted to run it. It is not the answers that matter much, in fact some of the questions posed are not answered at all, or at best evasively. The most important queries are: should the direction of the College be changed, i.e. from the control of the Jesuits of the English province? Should there be an Italian Rector? Should the annual accounts be under the care of Propaganda Fide? Should there be a reduction in the number of mouths fed? Should the number of alumni be reduced? Should the method of study be changed and schools opened in the College? Should young men who are not fully English but who have English mothers be admitted? Should alumni be received if they are too young to begin the philosophy course? How should alumni be recruited and dismissed? Should those who have just completed their course and been ordained remain on as tutors? Can the travelling expenses back to England be fixed at some agreed sum? Is it in

Fig. 3.7 The presently-named Martyrs' Chapel was built in the reconstruction years 1680–85 for the Jesuit Confraternity of Our Lady of the Assumption chapel. It served as College chapel during the nineteenth-century rebuilding of the main church.

keeping with the purpose of the College for alumni to proceed not to England but to Flanders to act as chaplains to English monks and nuns resident there? The *dubia* take up eleven pages of the book, the replies only two.

The visitation report has a message for the vicars apostolic too. Their original complaints had been taken up and were seen to be, to some extent, justified, but there was need to state what the role of the Protector was. This statement is of importance as it not only calls on precedent, as the Constitutions demand, but it provides guidelines that are to be followed later, especially with Gradwell in 1818 and Hinsley in 1918. Referring to the brief of Clement VIII, *In Supremo,* in 1600, the report reminds its readers that the Protector is in complete charge of England and the dependent islands. Moreover, he is in charge of the College with all the faculties, jurisdiction and privileges which are to be found in the Bull of creation of the College, *Quoniam Divinis Benefacti,* Paul V's *Personalis Officii Cura* of 1605 and Clement VIII's *In Supremo.* Moreover he has the same authority over other seminaries and residences of the English nation. Clement VIII gave this to Cardinal Henry Caetani

in 1599 and to Edward Farnese in 1600. It is the Protector who
designates the president of Douai and who can appoint a visitor
and lay down rules for the College. It is he who assigns two feast
days in honour of English saints to be kept by the above-named
seminaries. He can delegate his government of these institutions
and revoke any such delegation. As to the English mission, the
Protector is the prefect and head of the mission to England,
Scotland, Ireland and the other islands and dependencies. It is he
who gives faculties to secular and regular priests, as laid down in
the motu proprio *Inter maximos* of Gregory XIV and the brief *In
Supremo* of Clement VIII. The Protector is the *judex ordinarius* to
whom should be referred all controversial doubts and difficulties
arising for missioners, whether secular or regular. All business with
the Pope should be conducted through the Protector. This section
of the document ends with details of the faculties of the Protector as
regards dismissorial letters to ordinations from tonsure to priesthood, faculties for confession, celebration of mass, saying the divine
office, vows, oaths, marriages, feast days and fasts, the prohibition
of books, the granting of indulgences and so on. For each claim,
documentation and precedent is given.

Such extensive powers were not likely to be accepted by the vicars
apostolic at this period of Catholicism in England and, in fact, in
the College's copy of this visitation report there is a remark at the
end, in another hand, to the effect that these faculties are not yet in
force. But the claim shows that Rome considered the affairs of the
English College to be her concern just as she considered the affairs
in England her concern and there could be no question of an independent church there. The references in Gregory XIV's *motu
proprio* to Allen shed light on his position. English Catholics looked
on him as their natural leader and inspiration, but this decree
makes it clear that for Rome he was important because he had been
delegated to this post of leader. Succession to Allen was to be found
neither in Persons and the Jesuits, nor in the Archpriest or the first
vicars apostolic, but in those who had received a delegation similar
to Allen's, in effect the Cardinals Protector, Borghese, Farnese,
Barberini, Howard. The real gap in the succession was not the one
from 1655–85 when there was no vicar apostolic,[41] but the time
from the death of Howard in 1694 until the appointment of
Caprara as Protector in 1706. These were the uncertain years for
English Catholicism, from the Roman point of view. It was then that
there were suspicions of Jansenism among the seculars and reliance
had to be placed on the Jesuits, who could be trusted to follow the
Roman line.

The crucial point was that of jurisdiction and power; pastoral matters were in second place. Back in 1627 Bishop Richard Smith, the Vicar Apostolic, claimed that the regulars had to receive their jurisdiction and faculties from him, but this view was not supported by Urban VIII. Smith was not the ordinary in England but simply one delegated by the Holy See. In the decree of 5 October 1696 Innocent XIII gave jurisdiction to the vicars apostolic, but the regulars did not readily accept this and the matter was still contested at the time of the 1739 visitation. The vicars apostolic made formal demands for their position to be recognised but Propaganda favoured the view of the regulars. Changes came under Benedict XIV and there was support for episcopal government in the brief *Emanavit Nuper* of 1745 and the Bull *Apostolicum Ministerium* of 1753 which placed the regulars under the vicars apostolic and so was contrary to the view expressed in the 1739 report.[42] But whatever joy the vicars apostolic gained from this decision it did not alter the position of the College in Rome. This was placed under the special charge of Cardinal Monti,[43] who was appointed Protector *pro tempore* and given instructions to see that the regulations of Clement XII issued in 1739 were carried out. Although the vicars apostolic had won the day against the regulars, their position was no better as regards the College in Rome, and the power of the Protector meant that they felt as if the College were not really theirs at all. They tended to blame the Jesuits for this state of affairs, and thought that if the English seculars took over the administration all their troubles would be over. In fact, they failed to see the Roman position. It held control of what was a pontifical college and not a Tridentine seminary dependent on the bishops. The powers of the ordinary were to be found in the person of the Protector.[44]

The whole of this dispute had a disastrous effect on recruitment to the College in Rome. The vicars apostolic and Challoner in particular tried to provide students.[45] Not only was there a general lack of enthusiasm for the College under its present management, but there was a lack of vocations. The Jesuits could always rely on a supply coming to Rome from their own college at St Omer, but when the Society was suppressed in France in 1763 that source dried up. Moreover, as part of the growing unpopularity of the Society, the College property at Piacenza was seized by the Duke of Parma in 1768. So even if there had been students it is doubtful if the College's finances would have been able to support many more than were in fact in residence. Between 1768 and 1773 no new students were admitted, and when John Kirk, the future English Church historian, arrived in 1773 there were only seven students and three superiors.[46]

But it was now no longer merely a matter of the English seculars being opposed to the Society; there was a massive build-up of opposition, which was eventually to win over even the papacy. That the College did not fall with the Jesuits is due to the legal position of the Protector. Once more Rome had to exercise control directly and had at hand someone who was capable of administering the establishment both efficiently and according to the rules – Andrew Corsini.

Student life in the mid-eighteenth century

Before we speak of the achievement of Corsini, in many ways the greatest of the eighteenth-century Protectors, mention should be made of some aspects of student life during this period of the College's history. There are student diaries that cover the last years of the Jesuit rule,[47] and from these it appears that although students were few in number the general pattern of life was little changed. There were plays, visits to the gardens at Pamfilj and late summer holidays at Monte Porzio. The customary complaints and grouses were perhaps more frequent than before, but this is not surprising as at this time very young boys were accepted. The age of admission had dropped to 14 because of scarcity of vocations and also the closure of St Omer. The standard of studies in the eighteenth century requires mention.

One of the complaints voiced by Bishop Stonor in 1736[48] had been that the studies in Rome were useless and impracticable, the three-year philosophy course served no useful purpose, and there was far too much indulgence in scholastic and theological subtleties. He said there was no pastoral theology whatever and the students left Rome with hardly any knowledge of their own native tongue. One has to allow for some prejudice here and also, in passing, it can be remarked that there have been periods in the College history when the complaint was that the students seemed to have no knowledge of the Italian language, after spending seven years in the city. Rome was likely to be sceptical of Englishmen like Stonor trying to tell her what was useful or practical theology, as it was only twenty years previously that she had had to step in and investigate complaints about the unorthodoxy and Jansenistic tendencies of the English clergy.

The 1739 visitation report makes some mention of studies. It speaks of scripture, controversies, moral theology and other studies being specially accommodated to the needs of the English mission. This was the tradition dating back to the early days of the College.

Fig. 3.8 Student dress in 1710. It remained almost unchanged from the earliest days of the College until the 1960s.

The students not only attended the Roman College, where they took their turn in the public theological debates, but they also had daily tutorial sessions in the house from two masters who cared for the particular needs of the students and who took note of the place where they would eventually be exercising their mission. Up to the suppression of the Society this procedure continued, and, although information is scanty, there are one or two notebooks which give us hints of what was studied.

The *ripetitore*'s book runs from 1642–1739,[49] but it proves something of a disappointment, since it is for the most part simply a calendar, giving the lecture days and holidays and little information as to the content of the courses. In the seventeenth century the *Summa Theologica* of St Thomas Aquinas was the *liber textus* and the College possesses the notes of Henry Morse, the future martyr, taken from the lectures of Fr Terence Aliciati on *De Beatitudine*. There are also twenty *conclusiones* on *De Beatitudine* and *De Actibus Humanis* that were disputed at the German-Hungarian College in 1622.[50] Perhaps this indicates that there was some sort of co-operation between the German and English Colleges, who were preparing for a similar pastoral situation. But as the seventeenth century progressed, the plan of the *Summa* of St Thomas was left and the treatises on grace, sacraments, the Incarnation etc. began to develop as separate entities. Surprising, by modem standards, is the fact that it was not until the time of Benedict XIV that there were Chairs in Church History (1742) and Liturgy (1748). One of the texts used in the English College was a work of Richard Arsdekin or Archdeacon. Archdeacon was an Irish Jesuit from Kilkenny,[51] who taught theology at Louvain and Antwerp, and who died in 1693. In 1671 he produced a work[52] on 'controversies' that was especially suited for the use of priests in missionary countries.[53] It was in the tradition of Canisius. After revision, it eventually become *Theologia Tripartita*, the three elements being polemics, speculative and practical theology. Finally, when a full bibliography was added, it was called *Theologia Tripartita Universa*. The work was much praised, but in 1700 it fell under a ban and was prohibited until it could be corrected. Some of the replies in the section of *casus conscientiae* had to be amended, especially those concerning the possibility of 'philosophical sin' – wrong-doing that offended reason but not necessarily God. Archdeacon became suspect during the disputes about probabilism, when the Jesuits were often accused of 'laxism'. A new and corrected version of the work came out in 1718. The College possesses the 1700 edition and also a series of annotations and corrections which seems to indicate that Fr John

Thorpe,[54] who taught moral theology, was aware of the need for a sound causuistry.[55] Other fragments from this period are notes on the philosophy of John Locke and theological theses on the Church, including 'Sola Romana Ecclesia est vera Christi ecclesia', which provides a suitable opportuntity for returning to the subject of the Cardinal Protector.

Corsini and the finances

Corsini's nomination on 13 March 1773 as Protector of England and the English College was welcomed by the vicars apostolic. He was congratulated by T. Blount, the president of Douai, on 5 April 1773 and a week later by Challoner and his co-adjutor and the two Midland District bishops. Before the summer was over he had received grateful notices from the Northern and Western Districts, the superior of the English seminary in Paris and finally from Philip Perry, the Rector of Valladolid.[56] Doubtless all were expecting decisive action from this nephew of Pope Clement XII and his position vis-à-vis the Society was seen as hopeful for the cause of the seculars in England and the government of the College in Rome. In the event they were to be bitterly disappointed, not because he was not decisive – they formed a right judgement as to his character – but because their view was clouded by their anti-Jesuit prejudices; they misread the Roman attitude towards the College. Decisive as it was, Corsini's action was not high-handed, since all he did was to exercise the power to which he was legally entitled. His policy concerning the College was set out in his reply to Walmesley, Vicar Apostolic of the Western District. The disorder in the account books, found in the 1739 visitation, had not been rectified, silver plate was in pawn at the Monte di Pietà and the archives were in disorder. One of the first things Corsini commanded was a complete inventory, and to facilitate this the library and archives were temporarily closed and sealed. Soon a complete index to the archives was drawn up.[57] To ensure that he had full financial control, an appeal was made to the Pope.[58] This request was granted, at least as far as the affairs of the English College at Rome were concerned. The reply betrays the hesitation of the Curia at the time and no direct reference was made to Corsini's claim over the English clerical establishments on the continent. Since the time of *Apostolicum Ministerium* we can detect a weakening of the Protector's powers in favour of the vicars apostolic.[59]

The two areas singled out for reform, finance and discipline, were closely connected, since it was Rome's supposition that the College had to be a going concern and pay for itself. In Corsini's mind the quality and recruitment of students were related to the economic health of the establishment. The financial mismanagement was not to be attributed to the fact that the superiors were Jesuits, but rather that they were Englishmen who were just not capable of managing their affairs, which involved property held in Rome and other parts of Italy.[60] Rome was sick of the bickerings of the English among themselves. Italian secular clergy would have a neutral cooling effect, as well as being better equipped to deal with the finances. The appointment of an Italian Rector in place of the English Jesuit, deposed when the Society was suppressed, ought to have been foreseen by anyone who had read the 1739 report carefully. Even Bishop Stonor's remark of 1738[61] that things might be worse if the Italian seculars were in charge, could be taken as a shrewd intimation of what might easily happen. But the sequence of events in the Protector's assumption of full powers is important if we wish to avoid interpreting the events from 1773 onwards as simply indications of an anti-Jesuit policy. Corsini is in fact an example of an efficient administrator of the Enlightenment.

On 5 April 1773 (the day that Blount wrote his letter of congratulation) Corsini held the first *congregazione* or meeting, to deal with College affairs.[62] This was before the suppression of the Society in Rome, and the Jesuit Rector, Hothersall, was present. From this day forward regular monthly meetings were held dealing with College financial affairs such as rents, property and burses. After Corsini's death, the new Protector, Romualdo Braschi, continued this custom and on almost every occasion the Protector presided in person and signed the minutes.[63] On the suppression of the Society in August, a second series of meetings began to be held – usually on the same day. These dealt with mission affairs. Here too, the Protector presided and signed the minutes. During these years an efficient administration was built up and the two books of account were scrupulously kept separate. We shall have to return to the subject of the mission funds later.[64]

The suppression of the Jesuits

Kirk[65] gives a graphic account of how the suppression appeared to those who were students at the College in those days. On 16 August 1773 the Bull *Dominus ac Redemptor* was read in the College by Pier Francesco Foggini. The Jesuit superiors were placed under arrest by Corsican soldiers and after three days were allowed to depart, but only after they had given full information concerning the College funds. Foggini was placed in overall charge as 'Procurator'. The Vice-Rector was a man named Giovanucci; no Rector was nominated. The College also played host to the General of the Jesuits, Father Ricci. He was brought there under armed escort and imprisoned for a time until he was taken to the Castel S. Angelo.

It is important to realise that in these new conditions of College administration Corsini did not obtain money from the papacy to restore the College fortunes; it was not a matter of the College being bailed out. He simply saw to an efficient use of what was already there.[66] In 1768 all Jesuit property in the Duchy of Parma had been confiscated and this included the extensive College properties at Piacenza. It proved extremely difficult to show that this belonged to the College and that this was not in fact a Jesuit foundation. Yet by 1781 Corsini had succeeded in getting the Piacenza property restored to the College, the Duke allowing the alienation of the property and the reinvestment of money in the Papal States. This meant, as Laird observes,[67] that the College could now meet the costs of students' travel to Italy from England and this seems to have been a decisive factor in the steady improvement in student numbers towards the end of the century.

But this sense of priorities was not appreciated by the vicars apostolic. They continued to press for English superiors, as did the students, and this was construed by Rome as a desire for the lax administration of the past. Both the Protector and the vicars apostolic were anxious that the College would recruit a good class of student, but they differed sharply on how this was best achieved. Corsini, the man on the spot, wanted, as new rulers have often wanted, a clean break with the old regime, and to this purpose he negotiated for the transfer of students elsewhere, being careful to approach Douai through the Nuncio in Brussels.[68] However, to obtain new students was even more difficult than it had been in the past. The former Jesuit college of St Omer continued under the control of Douai and the vicars apostolic. But the English vicars were rather suspicious of the new regime in Rome, not only because the College was being directed by Italians but also because they felt their own power or influence being threatened by the Protector. Complaints reached them from those students who had survived the change over, whether still in Rome or now at Douai. Some of these student complaints were of a very trivial nature and one cannot but agree with Laird that, however amusing in a schoolboyish sort of way, they have been given an undue importance by some writers. Not sufficient attention has been paid to the more favourable reports and to the dubious character of some of the plaintiffs. It is small wonder that the arguments of the vicars apostolic for English superiors cut little ice with Corsini and however hard Bishop Talbot pressed the case,[69] after he succeeded Challoner as Bishop of the London District, he could not alter the situation. It is doubtful if they even succeeded in getting the promise of an English superior when next the post of Rector fell vacant.[70]

From the beginning Corsini exercised full protectorial rights and only used the Italian procurator or Vice-Rector as an executive. Only when Felici succeeded Magnani does the title 'Rector' reappear in the College minute book; presumably the Protector then considered the emergency was over and there could be a Rector once more. But the number of students dropped considerably and young boys not yet in their teens were admitted. This was not out of policy but from necessity. It meant that for the most part the College was little more than a school.[71] Lectures were held in the house and there still survive themes and exercises from these days. There are translations into Latin from Italian originals, dictations, precis, together with one or two reports on students' progress written by their Italian masters.[72] But in 1789 Corsini ordered Felici to send students once more to the Collegio Romano because there was a severe shortage of students there,[73] and under the aegis of Felici, confidence in the College began to be restored. There were now more students studying philosophy and theology, and more were reaching ordination. The College was no longer a financial drain on the vicars apostolic as it could now afford to accommodate more alumni.

The English mission

Corsini's problems were not diminished by the suppression of the Society of Jesus. His position regarding the College had been clarified since he assumed complete control in March, but there was now the complication arising from the fact that the Rector of the College was prefect of the mission and so administered the mission funds as well. At the suppression, these funds devolved on the Holy See, but there was still the distinction between the College business, formerly administered by the Jesuits and now by Corsini, and the Jesuits' own funds, now administered by the Holy See in the person of Corsini. Difficulties were to arise with certain bequests which had been made to the mission rather than to the College in Rome. Whatever may have been the case before 1773, from then on we have a series of account books pertaining to mission funds; these are almost complete until the French occupation.[74] As with the College affairs, there can be little doubt as to the efficiency of the administration of this business by Corsini and his successors. There is the same regular book-keeping and personal supervision.[75] From the mission fund a pension was paid regularly to the ex-Jesuits who had been superiors of the College. The Baines scholarship[76] was resumed in 1789 and was paid for from this fund. Travelling expenses for the students were accounted for and this sometimes involved dealings with Robert Smelt, the agent of the vicars apostolic.[77] On the other hand the mission fund received payment from the College account for items such as the produce of the farms and vineyards at Monte Porzio and La Magliana.

But the matter of the mission fund was made even more complex by the fact that the mission was responsible for institutions and property outside Italy, and the decree of suppression of the Society was not equally enforced throughout Europe. As these events have a bearing on the attitude of the English vicars apostolic to the Jesuit rule of the College, it is well to relate them here.

Owing to the patronage of the Prince Bishop of Liège, the College there and its Jesuit staff had escaped some of the fiercer penalties of the suppression of the Society in the Low Countries. Although it was now nominally a different establishment, an 'academy', the same staff of former Jesuits was in control. In 1789 William Strickland, the Rector, sent a memorandum to Pius VI complaining of the maladministration of the Liège funds at Rome after the suppression.[78] The Pope referred the matter to Propaganda Fide and Propaganda passed it on to Corsini for action to be taken, telling him to look into the matter and forward his suggestions. Corsini approached the Rector, Felici, and after some delay and with the complaint that he had to give up his holiday to work on it, Felici produced a long historical account of the relationship between the mission, the College in Rome and the College at Liège, which he sent on to the Protector. He argued that once the College at Liège was opened, the English mission and Liège College became identical. In the account books, the terms 'the Jesuit mission', 'the Jesuit College at Liège', 'the English College Liège' are interchangeable. Hence the property and monies held in Rome on behalf of Liège were in fact nothing more than the mission fund.[79]

Meanwhile Mgr Stonor, the agent in Rome for the vicars apostolic, had been in touch with Felici, supporting him against the claims of Liège and the accusations of the former Jesuits. Thus, we have one more instance of the College in Rome becoming involved in the politics and fears of the vicars apostolic, suspicious lest the Liège community should be trying to regain some measure of control in Rome, when all they wanted was to secure some of the property that was theirs. When Corsini received news from Felici he informed the Pope and Cardinal Zurla, the Secretary of State. A decision was made that, in the circumstances, no reply was advisable to these claims. But in 1794, Liège, this time in the person of James Connel, presented a new memorandum to the Pope[80] and this resulted in a congregation of four cardinals being set up to enquire into the case. The Rector was asked for a new report. Felici, having received no thanks for the previous document, was reluctant to go to the trouble of writing another, so a copy of the 1789 letter was made out in 1794.[81] But then came the French invasion and the Liège Academy removed itself to England. The matter did not end there since Fr Marmeduke Stone, the last president of the Academy at Liège, became the first president (later Rector) of Stonyhurst and his desire to continue the Liège tradition on English soil involved him in a dispute with both the vicars apostolic and Rome. A letter was written to Pius VI in the name of 'The President and professors of the Catholic seminary of Stonehurst [*sic*] in England'. It was pointed out that, thanks to the kindness of Signor Weld, who had helped establish it on his feudal estate in Lancashire, this was the first seminary on English soil. Although they had lost their goods, including the library and mathematical and scientific instruments, the Liège community was now settled at Stonyhurst and there were about 80 alumni, many of whom were destined for the ecclesiastical state. They asked the Pope for his apostolic protection and the same privileges they had enjoyed at Liège. In an audience of 14 February 1796 His Holiness granted these and here begins yet another saga, namely Stonyhurst's claim to be a pontifical college and so exempt from the rule of the vicars apostolic.[82] The threat to the jurisdiction of the vicars apostolic presented formerly by the Jesuit administration of the College in Rome, was now transferred to an establishment in England. The College in Rome was freed from its complicated system of two accounts, for although the fund of the mission and the College were kept separate until 1797, when the books resume again after the brief interlude of the Roman Republic, no distinction is made between what belongs to the College and what belongs to the mission.

So, at the end of the eighteenth century, despite the many

changes in the condition of Catholics in England, and the alteration in the administration of the College in Rome, the leading parts were still played by the vicars apostolic, the Cardinals Protector and the Society of Jesus.

Notes

1 Born 1629, grandson of the Earl of Arundel Earl Marshal of England, Philip Howard was solemnly professed as a Dominican friar in Rome in 1646. He was made Cardinal in 1674, died in 1694 and was buried in S. Maria sopra Minerva in Rome. W. M. Brady, *The Episcopal Succession*, III (1877), pp. 110–14, 118–21, 127–39. P. Guilday, *The English Catholic Refugees on the Continent* (1914), p. 403. G. Anstruther wrote a life of Howard which was never published. I am indebted to him for some of the information in this account. Judith F. Champ, 'Cardinal Philip Howard OP. Rome and English Recusancy', *Venerabile*, XXX (1995), 34–45.

2 It should be noted that during the Civil War the College was royalist in sympathy and holidays were given for royal victories. This was in striking contrast to the previous generation when the oath of loyalty to James I had been a matter of such contention to English Catholics. For further background concerning the Stuarts, see G. Albion, *Charles I and the Court of Rome. A study in Seventeenth Century Diplomacy* (Louvain 1935).

3 Opposition came from the 'Old Chapter'. This was a self perpetuating body that traced its ancestry back to the chapter appointed in 1623 by William Bishop, the first Vicar Apostolic. His successor Richard Smith confirmed their position, but they were not formally recognised by Rome nor by Douai College. When there was no vicar apostolic between 1655 and 1685 they virtually ruled the church in England (or at least the secular clergy). At one time they were associated with a form of Gallicanism. See Gordon Albion, 'The Old Chapter and Brotherhood 1623–1973', *Clergy Review*, LVIII (1973), 679–88; J. C. H. Aveling, *The Handle and the Axe* (1976), p. 120; J. Bossy, *The English Catholic Community*, pp. 60–9.

4 Gasquet implies that the objections of the seculars were to the idea of a vicar apostolic and not to Howard personally (p. 169). But for Howard's connection with monarchy, gentry, papacy and the religious orders, see Bossy, *The English Catholic Community*, p. 60.

5 For example: attitudes towards the 1715 rising, the marriage by proxy of James to Clementina Sobieski 1719, the births of Charles Edward in 1721 and of Henry of York in 1725, the prayers offered for the success of the 1745 rising. See 'Douai Diaries'. This might be a suitable place to record that not only did Father E. Lobb SJ, a future Rector of the Venerabile, receive James II into the Catholic Church, but Father Huddleston, a former student of the College in Rome, attended Charles II on his deathbed.

6 B. Novarro, *Filippo Michele Ellis* (Centro Studi di Lazio 1973). G. A. Hay,

'An English Bishop in the Volscians', *Venerabile*, XIX, 398–405. J. A. Williams, 'Bishops Gifford and Ellis and the Western Vicariate 1688–1715', *Journal of Ecclesiastical History*, XV/2 (1964), 218–28.

7 'Sir Thomas Dereham', *Venerabile*, IX, 156–9.

8 There seems to be nothing in Rome corresponding to the controversy at Douai after 1716 about the oath of loyalty to King George.

9 M. Andrieux, *Daily Life in Papal Rome in the Eighteenth Century* (Eng. trans., London 1968), p. 137.

10 The King's Evil. A form of scrofula that was thought to be curable by the royal touch according to a power of healing handed down from Edward the Confessor. Keith Thomas, *Religion and the Decline of Magic* (London 1971), especially pp. 192–8.

11 B. Ward maintains that the Duke of York had promised to pay the expenses of this function, but did not in fact do so, to the financial embarrassment of the College, *The Dawn of the Catholic Revival* (London 1909), p. 60.

12 R. L. Stewart, '1766 and All That', *Venerabile*, XV, 266–70. See also *Venerabile*, XXIII, 347–8. It is interesting to observe how at times the attachment of English Catholics to the Stuart cause proved embarrassing to Rome. The Roman agent of the vicars apostolic, Stonor, and his friend Strickland were in fact favourable to the Hanoverians.

13 B. Tucker, 'The Cardinal King of England', *Venerabile*, XVIII, 135–48.

14 One of Henry's acts as bishop was to build a Passionist monastery on Monte Cavo, on the site of the ruins of the Temple of Jupiter for his friend Paul of the Cross.

15 He had a medal struck inscribed 'Dei gratia sed non voluntate hominum'.

16 For the Corte Savella prison, see *Venerabile*, XIII, 83–7. Also Nicholas Schofield, 'Beatrice Cenci: Fact or Fiction', *Venerabile*, XXXII (2000), 22–35.

17 ECA, scr. 31, 5, 7, 13, 1. See also Appendix I on the College Buildings.

18 J. Fox, 'The Stable Barracks of the "Blues"', *Venerabile*, XXIII, 27–31. J. Fox, 'The Ancient Site, Fresh Discoveries, A Final Analysis', *Venerabile*, XXIII, 175–81.

19 There is some doubt about the part of these architects in the design. See Appendix I on the College Buildings.

20 J. Cartmell, 'The Chapel of St. Thomas of the English', *Venerabile*, III, 31–40. Pozzo was responsible for the ceiling of the 'Sodality' chapel and the fresco of St George in the refectory was probably originally by one of his pupils.

21 Like many clerics of his day, Howard seems to have had an interest in clocks. In his will he left a collection of clocks to be distributed among his friends.

22 Howard had to destroy property left to the College by a certain Bernadino Pippi. The rents from this were now no longer able to provide a free burse for a student.

23 I am indebted to Godfrey Anstruther OP for this information. See Vatican Archives, Barb. Lat. 2606.

24 *CRS*, 25, 89–92. One survival of the Howard legacy would seem to be the large painting of the pharisee's supper in the refectory, given to Howard originally by his mother in her will. See Brigitte Kuhn, 'An Unknown Painting by Andrea Pozzo in Rome', *Venerabile*, XXX (1993), 17–24.

25 P. Moakler, 'The Visitation of 1702', *Venerabile*, XVIII, 67–78.

26 A memorial slab to this visit is to be seen over the sodality chapel door.
SODALITIUM HOC CLEMENS XI P.O.M.
PRAESENTIAE SUAE MAIESTATE ILLUSTRAVIT
ET POST SACRORUM PEDUM OSCULA
ALUMNOS AD OMNEM PIETATEM
ALLOQIO INFLAMMAVIT
XXVIII DECEMBER MDCCI

27 J. Garvin, 'The Fault is told', *Venerabile*, IV, 10–19; 145–52; 'Fracas', *Venerabile*, XVIII, 179. It would seem that eighteenth-century seminarians were very like their secular contemporaries as regards drunkenness and fighting. Rules had to be made to combat this.

28 According to the acts of the 1739 visitation, the oath of Alexander VII was interpreted as prohibiting entry into the *cloister* and so not directed specifically against the Jesuits.

29 Gasquet, *History*, p. 171.

30 Eamon Duffy, 'A rubb-up for old soares: Jesuits, Jansenists and the English Secular Clergy 1705–15', *Journal of Ecclesiastical History*, XXVIII/3 (July 1977).

31 *SCPF*, II, 627. For a fuller account see M. E. Williams, 'A British College in Rome', in R. McCluskey (ed.), *The Scots College Rome 1600-2000* (Edinburgh 2000).

32 'Seventh Douai Diary', *CRS*, 28, 107.

33 ECA, scr. 45, 7 and B. Hemphill, *The Early Vicars Apostolic of England 1685–1750* (1954), pp. 135–48. There was a petition to Rome from the two Vicars Apostolic Petre and Stonor, complaining of lack of priests and bad administration. No priests were coming from Seville, Valladolid or Rome. Only a poor quality of student went from St Omer to Rome and so they asked for the College to be handed over to the seculars. Edward Dicconson, former vice president of Douai and vicar general to Bishop Stonor, was sent out to Rome to assist L. Mayes. While in Rome he was appointed vicar apostolic of the Northern District.

34 ECA, scr. 45, 7: Letter of Stonor against this suggestion of Mayes.

35 ECA, scr. 31, 1 and liber 324.

36 The justness of their complaint is instanced by a document in ECA, scr. 31, 8 in reference to the year 1723: 'Introitus annus est incertus, annis communibus aestimari potest circa 6000'.

37 ECA, scr. 31, 8 for 1720; 31, 9 for 1735.

38 ECA, Liège papers, scr. 42, 11–13; 42, 3; 42, 6.

39 Gasquet gives a breakdown for these years which he has taken from the visitation report, *History*, p. 173. See also ECA, scr. 31, 6; 31, 8; 31, 9.

40 There were similar low figures for the Scots College, cf. *SCPF*, II, 627. It was during this period that special arrangements were made to provide

places in Douai and at Rome for ordinands from the Western District, *SCPF*, II, 616. There was indeed a legacy left to the Jesuits for setting up a college in Cornwall.

41 Or indeed from 1631 when Richard Smith left England to live abroad.

42 Fenning, 'The Three Kingdoms: England, Ireland and Scotland', in *SCPF*, II, 620. E. H. Burton, *The Life and Times of Bishop Challoner* (1909), 250ff.

43 This was part of the new legislation that was finalised in 1741, whereby a congregation was set up with extensive and unrestricted supervision and control over each and every pontifical college and seminary. M. Wiltgen, 'Supervision of Pontifical Colleges by the Evangelisation Congregation', *SCPF*, II, 236–47.

44 This dispute is part of that bigger controversy in the post Tridentine church on the nature of the episcopate. When petitions were made to Rome for the consecration of bishops for the English mission it was often on the grounds that someone was needed to consecrate the oils for baptism and the anointing of the sick ('First and Second Douai Diaries', Intro., lxvi) or for someone to confirm. The episcopate was seen in terms of order rather than jurisdiction. Some high placed people in Rome were against bishops being appointed. Cardinal Mellini thought bishops were not necessary for the maintenance of a particular Church (Pastor, 27, 157). See also the reasons adduced for the episcopate in the Barrett-Parsons correspondence, *CRS*, 41, 98. One should also remember that many considered that only the dogmatic decrees of Trent were operative in England. The disciplinary decrees were in suspense. See J. Bossy, *The English Catholic Community*, p. 53.

45 For Challoner's views on the College and his efforts to help, see Burton, *The Life and Times of Bishop Challoner*, pp. 10–11.

46 V. Lloyd, 'Decline and Fall 1. The Last Years of Jesuit Rule 1770–1773', *Venerabile*, XV, 245–582; 'The Bad Boy's Diary 1773–1779', *Venerabile*, XVI, 2–16.

47 S. Weetman, 'An Eighteenth Century Diary (Casemore)', *Venerabile*, VIII, 18–27; 123–39. Kirk's Diary is at Oscott. Liber 815 is a transcript.

48 ECA, scr. 46; Gasquet, *History*, p. 175. Birmingham Diocesan Archives, A953 for Stonor's complaints to Rome in 1740.

49 ECA, liber 320.

50 ECA, liber 1417: *Scripta Patris Terentii Aliciati in 1a 2ae S. T. accepta* Henrici Claxton a. 1622. Claxton was Morse's alias. For Morse's days in Rome, see P. Caraman, *Henry Morse, Priest of the Plague* (London 1957), especially 19ff.

51 H. Hurter, *Nomenclator* and C. Sommervogel, *Bibliothèque de la Compagnie de Jesus*, I, c, 515–21.

52 The original title was 'Praecipuae controversiae fidei ad facilem methodum redactae ac resolutiones theologiae ad omnia sacerdotis munia; praesertim in missionibus accomodatae cum apparatu ad doctrinam sacram cui accessit summa doctrinae christianae (Canisii) selectis exemplis elucidata'.

53 There is a section giving examples of heroic constancy under persecution taken from the recent history of Belgium, England and Ireland and this includes a life of Oliver Plunkett.

54 For John Thorpe, see Kirk, 'Biographies of English Catholics', Foley, *Records*, VII/2; G. Holt, 'The English Jesuits 1650–1829', *CRS*, 70, 246. Born 1726, after teaching at St Omer he was tutor in Rome, English penitentiary at St Peter's and agent for the English province of the Jesuits. After the suppression of the Jesuits he was given a pension and died in Rome in 1792.

55 See ECA, scr. 46, 6 which includes 'Syllabus earum quae addita sunt in novissima editione Theologiae Tripartitae Richardi Arsdekin'.

56 ECA, scr. 50, 3. For this period in the College history see R. A. Laird, 'The English College Rome under Italian Secular Administration 1773–1798', *RH*, 14, 127–47.

57 ECA, Inventorio 1773–4, libri 1593–1603.

58 ECA, scr. 50, 3, 14 and 45, 1; 45, 2; 45, 7–10.

59 One should recall that the Rector in Rome was directly responsible to the Protector. The President at Douai dealt through the Nuncio in Brussels. By 1791 Rome was considering the vicars apostolic as at least indirectly responsible for the conduct of the English College at Douai. But what was already taking place at Douai in the 1790s was not yet the case at Rome. B. Ward, *The Dawn of the Catholic Revival in England 1781–1803*, II, pp. 70–1.

60 The new situation was by no means peculiar to the English College in Rome. Other foreign colleges there had Italian superiors, if not the Rector then bursar or administrator. A parallel case was that of the colleges in Spain. J. H. Pollen, 'St Alban's Seminary Valladolid 1602–1608', *The Month*, XCIV, 348–65 speaks of the fundamental difficulties of the Spanish seminaries, namely the difficulty of combining Spanish and English management of the colleges. Only Douai and Lisbon had English superiors throughout their history.

61 ECA, scr 45 7: Stonor Correspondence.

62 ECA, liber 217.

63 ECA, liber 217 1773–88; liber 218a 1789–97. Congregazione del Ven. Collegio Inglese. Liber 218 1773–97 Congregazione del Missione Inglese.

64 See page 84 above on mission funds.

65 Diary, see V. Lloyd, 'Decline and Fall II, The Bad Boy's Diary 1773–1779', *Venerabile*, XVI, 2–16.

66 In this respect the dismissal of Rector Magnani, in 1787, is significant, as Corsini told Stonor this was for financial mismanagement. For details of this negligence see ECA, scr. 46, 1, 5. There had been student complaints by Kirk and Kennedy against Magnani in 1779 and the vicars apostolic had asked for an English Rector, but there is no evidence that Corsini paid any attention to their complaints, cf. Laird, 'The English College Rome under Italian Secular Administration 1773–1798', *RH*, 14.

67 *RH*, 14, 139.

68 ECA, scr. 50, 3; 50, 4 for the correspondence between Corsini and the Nuncio at Brussels on the recruitment and exchange of students between Douai and Rome. It is to be noted that Douai too was in difficulties; cf. Milburn, *History of Ushaw*, pp. 12ff.

69 ECA, scr. 50, 12. Talbot to Corsini 21 December 1781.

70 It would appear that Corsini realised that there was need for some Englishman to be on the staff to give language tuition and for this purpose Stephen Green was appointed. But there seems little evidence that he undertook to nominate an English Rector. When negotiations were being made for the reopening of the College in 1817 it was argued that such a promise had been made. See Laird, 'The English College Rome under Italian Secular Administration 1773–1798', *RH*, 14.

71 John Kirk was only thirteen years old when he began to write his famous diary. The Venerabile was not the only place where there were unruly schoolboys in the late eighteenth century; cf. *Venerabile*, XIX, 497.

72 ECA, scr. 44, 8 contains an account of the examinations held in the College in 1789, 1790 and 1791 during the months of August and September and in the presence of the Cardinal Protector. They were held in the chapel on the second floor (the present students' common room).

73 With the suppression, the Roman College was taken out of the hands of the Jesuits. It is not certain when exactly the English College students ceased to attend lectures there.

74 ECA, liber 461 gives the *entrata & uscita* of the mission fund 1773–83. Liber 514 is the register of holdings on behalf of the mission in the Monte di Pietà 1773–1797. Liber 521 gives the deposits in the Monte on behalf of the mission 1783–95. In addition to the above we have the account books of the vice prefect of the mission; liber 464 Magnani 1784–7, Felici 1787–98.

75 Aveling, *The Handle and the Axe* (London 1976), p. 312, tells us that most English institutions abroad were in severe financial trouble in the 1780s. The Venerabile would seem to be better off than most, thanks to Corsini.

76 For Baines, see Chapter 2, p. 52 above.

77 e.g. 21 June 1791, ECA, liber 521.

78 ECA, scr. 41, 1, 1 (iii) and (iv).

79 This identification is borne out by the account books that are in Rome. Very little money in fact passed between Liège and Rome. The practice was to reinvest any income or profit arising from the Roman property so as to hold a credit account in Rome.

80 The draft of this is in ECA, scr. 42, 4.

81 ECA, scr. 42, 3.

82 See B. Ward, *The Dawn of the Catholic Revival in England 1781–1803*, II, Chap. 24, esp. pp. 103–4; *The Eve of Catholic Emancipation*, I, Chap. 14.

Chapter Four

Dissolution, Interregnum and Restoration

Just when the College seemed to be once more a going concern under Felici[1] and when the number of students was beginning to increase, external events struck at its prosperity. In the long history of Rome the first two hundred years of the College's existence were remarkable for the immunity of the city from the foreign invader, but in 1796 Bonaparte invaded Italy. Despite the 1797 treaty between the French and the papacy, there were fears for the future of Rome. So, although sudden, it was not entirely unexpected when, on 10 February 1798, General Berthier entered Rome and took possession of the Castel Sant' Angelo and the French soldiers were billeted all over the town.[2] There was considerable pillaging and other acts to avenge the murder of the French general Duphot by Italian patriots.[3] The Tree of Liberty was erected in various parts of the city and the Pope left Rome early on the morning of Ash Wednesday for Siena, soon to be taken into custody by the French. On 23 February the English and Scots Colleges were sequestered in the name of the French Republic. All priests secular and regular who had not been born in the area of the 'Roman Republic' were ordered to give in their names and their employment. There was a general exodus from the city. The English and Scots students received passports and left for England on 31 March under the guidance of 'the Abbé Macpherson', who was agent for the Scots bishops.[4] Like the English, the Scots had an Italian Rector and he had to leave the city, being a native of Calabria. The Rector of the English College remained for a time in a Rome where the papal court was reduced to two infirm Cardinals and a few prelates of Roman birth, who soon secularised themselves and found other employment. Of the College property, some of the furniture was sold but no one offered to buy the property at the price the French authorities were prepared to recognise. Felici and the remaining professors and servants stayed on, although they now had no income and there is no record of them receiving mass offerings after the beginning of April. Smelt, the agent for the English vicars apostolic, left Rome for Tuscany in March and eventually settled in Pisa. He wrote to Bishop Douglass from there in April: 'I have desired a person in Rome to purchase the archivium of the College; another who understands English is to examine and separate what regards our concerns from papers of no value. The ex-Rector promised to secure for me the book containing an account of all the students since the foundation.'[5] A small part of the College lands was sold off and parts of the house in Rome were let to various families. Smelt tried, as far as he could from the distance of Pisa, to look after College interests and he reported to Douglass in December 1799 that Mr Fagan, His Britannic Majesty's agent in Rome, had the property of the English, Scots and Irish Colleges under his care.

It is remarkable how the College, although without staff or students, managed to survive. In a document[6] headed 'Libertà, Egualianza Anno Primo della Repubblica Romana' there is the official declaration of the suppression of the College on 19 Ventoso (March) 1798. This is accompanied by an account of the College, its foundation and its purpose. It is sympathetically written and is probably the work of Cini, the *essatore* – it seems to be in his hand. Although this and similar documents were signed by the French 'agents des finances', it appears that the affairs of the College, during these eighteen months, were managed by Signor Cini, who now bore the title 'Cittadino Cini essatore dell'ex collegio inglese'.[7] Cini had held this position for some years before the dissolution and whatever the legal position of the College now was, suppressed or not, it did remain a moral entity and was administered by the resident Italian and Roman officials who had not been compelled to leave the city as they were not ecclesiastics. Smelt was not at all happy about the activities of the *essatore* in respect of the College property and suspected him of double dealing.[8] One document from these times is of particular note as it reveals something of the true state of affairs under the French occupation. It is a receipt and runs:

Ho ricevato dalla Repubblica Francese per le mani del Cittadino Vincenzo Cini scudi 40 quali sono per la pensione di mesi sei, cioè

dal primo luglio fin a tutto dicembre dell' anno scorso 1798 che io
avevo sopra il Collegio Inglese di Roma già sopresso.

Cittadino Nicola Porter
Roma 1 Marzo 1799.

Citizen Nicholas Porter was an ex-Jesuit and a former member of
the staff when the Society was expelled in 1773. Yet even under the
French 'Roman Republic' his pension was paid from the mission
funds. Evidently it was only a pittance as he was near starvation
later on in the year, but thanks to the good offices of Smelt and
others he was able to survive until he died in August 1802 over
eighty years of age.[9]

These were difficult years when the College lay empty, yet the
account books were faithfully kept so that when the new Pope, Pius
VII, entered Rome in July 1800, although there had been losses,
much of the property survived.[10] The Concordat between Pius VII
and Napoleon meant the end of the Roman Republic and the
removal of the threat to carry out the decree of dissolution of the
College. Camillo Branchini became *essatore* in 1801 and continued
in this office right into Gradwell's rectorship in 1818.[11] With the
Pope and cardinals returned to Rome, Braschi, the Cardinal
Protector, was now able to countersign the account books.[12]

However, the peace with Napoleon was an insecure thing and in
1809 Pius VII, like his predecessor, was taken into captivity. By a
decree of 17 May the Papal States were annexed and this time the
College property again suffered heavily and was ransacked by the
French soldiers, as much because it was English as because it was
ecclesiastical. There is a gap in the records for 1809 yet during the
second papal absence from Rome College affairs continued. We
have records[13] of the meetings of the *congregazione* for College and
mission affairs for the years 1810 and 1811. These were no longer
presided over by the Cardinal Protector but by the Mayor of Rome.
However, this is not so inauspicious as it may appear since the
Mayor at this time was Duke Braschi, a nephew of the late Pius VI
and a relative of the Cardinal Protector.

The unsettled affairs in the city did not entirely prevent foundation masses being said.[14] Neither is this surprising as these were an
important source of income, as well as an obligation in justice.
There is a gap from April 1798 and any unfulfilled obligations were
later absolved, but in 1803 the registers resume. However, the
masses were no longer said in the College but at other churches: S.
Giacomo degli Incurabili, SS. Trinità dei Pellegrini, SS. Ambrogio e
Carlo, S. Andrea degli Scozzesi. This situation obtained until 9

March 1818 when Gradwell said the first foundation mass in the College again.[15]

With the defeat of Napoleon the European powers set their minds at the Congress of Vienna to a restoration of the order that had been so violently upset. A similar mood is detectable in Rome. On 24 May 1814 the Pope returned and almost immediately, 2 June 1814, English College affairs were taken in hand by Braschi, the Protector. On his orders a meeting was held at the house of Parisotti, the procurator of the College, and there were present the College solicitor, the accountant and the *essatore*. The legal and economic condition of the College was scrutinised. A list of debtors was compiled and the solicitor was charged with the task of securing the restitution of the furniture and other moveables that had been taken elsewhere by the French. Braschi was present in person and signed the minutes. From this day forward the *congregazione* resumed and was held every month, at first in Parisotti's house and then from September 1814 in the College itself. Right up to the time of his last illness (February 1816) Braschi took an active part in these meetings. When Braschi fell ill his place was taken by Pietro Francesco Galeffi and then in 1817, after Braschi's death, when Galeffi in consequence lost his legal standing as deputy, Ercole Consalvi, the Secretary of State, took over the temporary administration of College affairs.

The one lesson that stands out clearly from these years of the interregnum is that with English Catholics unable to translate their concern for the College into effectual action, Rome took special care of the College and its property. The fact that during this time the material fabric of the College deteriorated must not lead us to forget that the very continuance of the College as an entity was due to the support of the Holy See, either directly through the Braschi family or indirectly through the loyalty of the Italian lay officials. That this should be so is to a large extent attributable to the legal standing of the Cardinal Protector.

At the customary monthly meeting of the *congregazione* on 17 November 1817, Consalvi, the acting Protector, asked the accountant to assess the income of the College for the coming year 1818 and also

> di presentare all'eminenza sua un altro approximativo delle spese occorenti per il mantenimento di una determinata quantità di giovani Inglesi, Rettore, Prefetto, inservienti e tutto altro occorente per l'esercito e la repristinazione del nostro Venerabile Collegio.

Fig. 4.1 Robert Gradwell, Rector, 1818–28.

Gradwell was already in Rome at this time, officially as agent for the English vicars apostolic, but anxiously waiting to be appointed Rector. But it was only four months later, when it was seen that the College funds were able to support a staff and students, that the College was allowed to reopen. That decision lay with the Protector and the *congregazione*. That such an economic requirement was primary for Rome is quite in keeping with the visitation of 1739 and Corsini's actions from 1773 onwards. Moreover, in the Constitutions of 1818[16] the number of alumni is limited to those that can be financially supported, namely eight students. The College had to pay its own way; there was no question of the vicars apostolic having to raise fees. The alumni owed the College everything; she was truly *alma mater*.[17]

The English ecclesiastical scene

With the flight of the students to England in 1798 and their subsequent dispersal, the College ceased to exist as a community. As we have seen, the material fabric was preserved and was being kept ready for a new community, but the nature of that community would depend on the situation obtaining in England. The College was originally founded to fulfil a particular need. The Church in England wanted priests who would carry on 'the old religion' and these men could no longer be educated at home. Recruitment was determined by this factor and the success or failure of the College was measured by its production of such priests. Changes and shifts of emphasis had been taking place all through its history. In the early days it was quickly realised that new conditions had arisen in England and there was no question of a return to the old Marian regime. Then, when the persecution ceased, different qualities were required of the missioners. There soon appeared a divergence of outlook between the vicars apostolic and Rome. Rome saw the Jesuits as faithful executives on behalf of the Church. The vicars apostolic saw them as a rebellious element that limited their own power. Rome considered Italian superiors as being the only really efficient administrators for a pontifical college in Rome; in England this government was not at all appreciated and there were demands for a greater independence. If the College were to reopen, at the beginning of the nineteenth century, then it would have to be to fulfil a need of the Catholic community as it now was. After all, it was this English Catholic community that had to provide the students and, it was hoped, the superiors. Several changes had been taking place in England and this was an opportunity to re-assess and see what need, if any, there was to have a College in Rome.

All the English colleges on the continent of Europe had suffered during the Napoleonic wars. Those in the Iberian peninsula had survived and were still functioning. To close them would have required a definite move on the part of the bishops. Those in France and the Low Countries had ceased to exist. The property had been confiscated and the students dispersed. Attempts were made to get the British government, the victor in the wars, to press their claims for restitution against the defeated French.[18] But the loss of these establishments was sweetened by the hopes of being able to set up seminaries on English soil. In 1791 the Relief Act had given Catholics a measure of freedom to practise their religion and although there was a special provision forbidding the foundation of colleges and convents in England,[19] it was hoped that Catholics, by a prudent use of their newly acquired liberty, might earn a mitigation here. In fact Catholic colleges had been established, despite the illegality, at Sedgley Park and Standon Lordship, and as recently as 1794 a school for ecclesiastical and lay students was set up at Maryvale (Old Oscott). From 1794 a foreign education for the clergy was no longer necessary because the Douai tradition, modified to meet the new circumstances, had resumed in England at Ushaw and Old Hall. It took some years to settle the nature of these colleges and their relationship to Rome, whether they were to be considered as pontifical or not. There was also a dispute among the bishops concerning jurisdiction;[20] but there were colleges in England before the English College was forced to close. Neither must we forget that the Liège Academy, formerly run by the Jesuits, was now on English soil and the 'gentlemen of Stonyhurst' were preparing men for ordination.

The students from Rome were the last of the exiles to reach England; their College was the last to close. But were there any special reasons why, now that the structure of anti-Catholic legislation was being dismantled in Great Britain, the College in Rome should be re-established?

There were those in England who were not enthusiastic for such a college.[21] In the 1790s a 'liberal' Catholic movement had been growing apace. This was characterised by a coolness towards certain forms of Catholic piety which were branded as superstitious, and also by a critical attitude towards the papacy and rule from Rome. A desire was expressed for a more native form of Catholicism which would be more acceptable to the government. This would end some of the isolation experienced by Catholics. Meetings were held to promote these ideas and the Catholic Committee emerged. This was soon to become the Cisalpine Club and a strong anti-papal line was adopted. Lay participation in the government of the Church was envisaged as a check on clerical rule which would be conducted by the bishops with minimal interference from Rome. These currents of thought were part of a general feeling that could be found on the continent as well.

As a result of the events in France, the Revolution and the Terror, there was a turning away from extreme liberal ideas. The misfortunes of Pope Pius VII at the hands of the French began a reaction the other way and a popular wave of sympathy was felt towards the papacy. Politically England was drawing closer to an alliance with the Papal States. An indication of this rapprochement can be seen in the visit of Cardinal Consalvi, the Secretary of State, to England in 1815.[22] How far the papacy was prepared to go to gain English support for the recovery of the Papal States can be gauged by the so called 'Quarantotti Report' of 16 February 1814. On the advice of the Scottish bishops' agent Macpherson, Mgr Quarantotti, the Secretary of Propaganda and in complete charge at a time when all the cardinals were outside Rome and the Pope was still at Fontainbleau, conceded that the king of England might be permitted to approve or reject a Catholic subject that was proposed for episcopal office. Thus at this time Propaganda was not adverse to a royal veto on appointments to the Catholic episcopate.[23] In addition to the above considerations, England was important to the papacy on account of her role in respect to the many Catholic communities that were now being incorporated into her expanding empire. It was the London and the Western Districts that had the most to do with the colonies and these vicars apostolic often had to deal with Propaganda Fide on overseas ecclesiastical matters through their agent in Rome.

In 1784, Dr Carroll became Prefect Apostolic of the Catholics of the thirteen states and so America became ecclesiastically independent of England. The links remained since Carroll was consecrated Bishop of Baltimore by Bishop Walmesley at Lulworth in 1790 and he often found it convenient to use the same agent in Rome for his affairs as the one used by the English vicars apostolic. The gradual spread of British influence over the West Indies raised the question of the extent of the jurisdiction of the vicar apostolic of the London district. The victory over France had meant that some of the former French possessions in Canada and the Caribbean were now under British rule. Moreover, the opening up of the new territories far distant from Quebec meant that somebody had to concern himself with the interests of the Church in those parts. So, the papacy's interest in England was a much more complex issue than was sometimes appreciated back at home. Rome saw that the role of England, both at the Congress of Vienna and as the ruler of a rapidly expanding empire, was very much involved with the interests of the Church.

It is against this background that one has to see the restoration of the English College in Rome. As English and Roman, political and ecclesiastical, interests began to converge, so did the suitability of a restored presence of English Catholicism in Rome.

The restoration

The re-opening of the College had been considered soon after Pius VII's entrance into Rome in the summer of 1800.[24] The vicars apostolic and their agent were most anxious to have English superiors in charge of its affairs, but this created a special difficulty, as Smelt wrote to Douglass on 13 January 1801:

> Cardinal Consalvi, Secretary of State, about five weeks ago wrote a note to the Cardinal of York, by order of His Holiness, to inform him that he had decided the house should be given up to national superiors, but for certain prudential reflections, it could not be done at present ... these prudential reasons are because the Pope is cautious of shewing any favour to our nation whilst the French army is on the confines of his dominions.

Cardinal Braschi, the Protector, was concerned that all debts should be paid off and the fabric fully restored before it was occupied again. Smelt wrote in December 1801:

> I shall therefore only repeat Cardinal Braschi's views of the subject – that so far from wishing any human to live in the house, he would not even send a brute animal into it. A surveyor was sent by him to examine the premises and form an estimate of what sum of money will be necessary to repair the damage: from his report it appears that between eight and nine thousand crowns will be required to render the house habitable – however the Cardinal hopes at the end of two years to open the College again ... it looks like some houses in London destroyed by Gordon's mob in 1780.

To help defray costs, the vineyards at Monte Porzio were let out on a twelve-year lease and by 1804 work was able to start on repairing the College. However, the political situation deteriorated and so it was only when the Pope returned to Rome from exile a second time that the re-establishment of the College in Rome was once more requested by the English bishops.[25]

To understand the actual restoration of the College in 1818 one has to appreciate the events that immediately preceded Gradwell's arrival in Rome. The re-opening was more than just the re-establishment of an old and venerable institution. There were involved such matters as: who should be in charge of the administration? If there were to be national superiors, would they be secular clergy? If secular clergy, who precisely would be Rector? What sort of a college was acceptable to the vicars apostolic? When in 1813 plans were being mooted for a combined British (English, Scots and Irish) college in France, Dr Poynter, Bishop of the London District, in a letter to Castlereagh, said it was not intended to re-establish English Catholic colleges in France. In future the English Catholic clergy would be educated in England.[26] However, the following year he visited Rome and he made a request to Litta that the College there should be reopened. Bishop Milner was also in Rome at this time and he too, quite independently, petitioned Litta, the Cardinal Prefect of Propaganda, for the reopening.[27] Milner was in fact offered the post of Rector but he refused.[28] It has been suggested that the rectorship of the College in Rome was a way of tempting Milner to leave the English scene. That such an offer should have been made creates the impression that the rectorship was a pawn in a political game. This view is strengthened by the bid that Gandolphy[29] made for the post. Moreover, had not the Pope refused his consent, Litta would have attached the College to Propaganda Fide in 1817.[30] So while there is evidence that the vicars apostolic did put in a strong plea for the re-opening of the College,[31] one has to bear in mind the motives behind such a request. The vicars apostolic had no romantic feelings about the English College in Rome. For the most part they were Douai men and could not be expected to have warmth towards a College that had been administered by the Jesuits and then by the Italian seculars. Glorious as Rome's past may have been, Douai had its martyrs too. Although the Jesuits had been ousted at the suppression, the vicars apostolic felt that they had been cheated when Corsini brought in the Italians. On the negative side they did not want the pre-1798 situation to re-occur nor did they wish the Jesuits, restored in Italy but not yet in England, to be given charge. From the more positive point of view it would be very advantageous to them to have an establishment of their own in Rome, a base from which their agent might work.[32]

The agency

In their dealings with Propaganda Fide and other congregations
the vicars apostolic employed agents. From 1748–90 Christopher
Stonor had acted as agent for the English bishops and he received a
pension from the Cardinal Duke of York. His agency covered the
years of the suppression of the Society and the Corsini regime, and
he had by no means an easy task to perform. He was involved in
English College affairs at a time when there was great discontent
among the vicars apostolic concerning the government of the
College. When he died in 1795 (his memorial slab can still be seen
in the church of S. Caterina opposite the College) he left his own
small personal income for the support of the English agent. In 1790
he was succeeded by Robert Smelt, whose dealings with the English
College included negotiations for the travel out from England to
Rome of the new students. For this he received payment from the
Italian seculars in the last years of their rule, when the finances
were improving. But about 1810/11 he had to return to England
for health reasons and he continued to draw the agency money.[33]
Pressing business arose in 1812[34] and Paul Macpherson, who was
agent for the Scottish bishops, was commissioned to act on behalf of
the English bishops. Macpherson, 'The Abbé' as he was known, has
already appeared in these pages as the one who accompanied the
English and Scots students out of Rome and Italy when the French
took over in 1798. But Macpherson found it difficult to work for
the English bishops and he resigned his post in 1817. As Smelt had
by now died, the post was open. The agent for the vicars apostolic
had never resided at the English College, which was understandable granted the attitude of the vicars apostolic to the Jesuits. The
office was an anomalous one as the agent was never part of the legal
or political structure officially recognised by Rome. During the
1830s, in fact, Rome was to request the bishops to deal directly with
Propaganda and not through the agent. It was the position of the
Cardinal Protector that made the role of the agent unnecessary in
Rome's eyes, except as a carrier of messages. Christopher Stonor's
long period of office was successful because his family background
and personal qualities made him the embodiment of an important
section of opinion both among the vicars apostolic and the Catholic
laity in England. Now, in the early nineteenth century, the English
bishops were confronted with new problems that disturbed the
domestic scene and threatened to divide the community. It was
important to secure the favourable ear of Rome. For its part, Rome
had certain interests in England as the centre of an Empire and the

vicars apostolic were ecclesiastical superiors of some of the colonies. If this last fact was of secondary importance to English opinion, it was not necessarily so unimportant to Rome.

Braschi had been in failing health for some time and matters came to a head when he died in April 1817. The power struggle was now no longer simply a matter of whether the English seculars should administer the restored establishment but who would succeed Braschi as Protector. Among the contenders for the office were Litta, the Prefect of Propaganda, and Consalvi, who was Secretary of State and who had assumed the temporary management of the College in the vacancy.[35] It is at this point that the Society of Jesus once more enters into College history.

Litta, in a communication of 2 December 1816, expressed the view that however much he might wish to see the Jesuits once more recognised in England, this would not be possible if the civil powers were opposed to the idea. But opposition to the Society came from another quarter too. Poynter was adopting the line that the restoration of the Society in England would be injurious to the cause of Catholic emancipation,[36] and, as Pollen says,[37] it was 'unfortunate for the padri that Dr. Poynter, the least friendly of the vicars apostolic was also the most popular in Rome'. This would seem to be because Consalvi understood Poynter's view. In such a game of cat and mouse the first move is often the most crucial and so it was now. Walsh, an elderly ex-Jesuit, was visiting Rome *ex devotione* and he approached Grassi,[38] the head of the Italian Jesuits, and suggested that the English College should be restored to the Society. This, as Pollen notes, was a tactical error; the English fathers did not wish to take it over at this moment: they had too few members to staff it, their status was not yet recognised in England and to assume such a responsibility would only aggravate their position and lead them into future controversy with the vicars apostolic. However, Macpherson saw the danger and he had the interests of the English vicars apostolic at heart. They were in danger of being out manoeuvred and should the Jesuit claim be upheld, it would not augur well for the outcome of their dispute with the 'gentlemen of Stonyhurst' at home. It now became urgent that the bishops took the re-opening of the College seriously. Lingard was in Rome at the time and wrote to Poynter on 5 June[39] appraising him of the situation and asking for the appointment of an agent who would 'get the English College for him [i.e. Poynter] from Cardinal Consalvi'. Robert Gradwell's name was suggested. Two further letters followed from Lingard and in the one of 24 July Lingard expressed the fear that Dr Milner or the Jesuits would thwart them. Lingard's own reputation in Rome was not safe, as there had been accusations against him as being a notorious Jansenist and he was treated with suspicion by Litta.[40] Several years later Lingard was to give a brief account of his part in a letter to Husenbeth.[41]

> I am much pleased with the account of the Roman College in the last number [Catholic Magazine] but not with that for June p. 360. It is said 'After 20 years, at the repeated representations and earnest entreaties of the bishops in England his holiness Pius VII restored it to the English clergy.' Now this is not at all the fact. Representations had formerly been made by the bishops but to no effect. But the bishops had no more to do with the restoration of the College than the man in the moon. On the death of Cardinal Braschi, the Protector, who had kept possession as long as he lived, Mr. Walsh applied to the Pope through Cardinal Litta, to obtain it for the gentlemen of Stonyhurst. He met with a refusal and left Rome. I accidentally heard of this, consulted Macpherson, and waited with Mr. Macpherson on Cardinal Consalvi, to whom as Secretary of State in the absence of any Cardinal Protector the care of the College belonged. From him we obtained a promise that, if the bishops would propose to him a clergyman for Rector, *he* would appoint him, provided no Protector were appointed in the meantime, and would take care that the property of the College should be devoted to its original purposes. Dr. Gradwell was proposed by the bishops and appointed by Cardinal Consalvi, as Secretary of State. That appointment was afterwards confirmed by Pope Pius. The care of Cardinal Consalvi to recover whatever had originally belonged to the College, was deserving of the highest praise. He may be called the second founder.

Lingard's suggestion that Gradwell should be chosen was supported by Poynter in a letter to Macpherson of 25 July and on 30 August Robert Gradwell was nominated as agent for the vicars apostolic.

Why were Poynter and Lingard so keen on appointing Gradwell for this difficult task? What was his background? Gradwell was educated at Douai and had never been to Rome. As he himself confessed, he was both ignorant of the Italian language and without a single acquaintance in the City.[42] But when a student at Douai, he had been a contemporary of Poynter and was imprisoned with him when the French occupied the town. He then taught at Ushaw and became known to Gibson, Vicar Apostolic of the Northern District, but ill-health compelled him to retire and take on light duties as chaplain to the Fitzherbert-Brockholes at Claughton in Lancashire. He kept up his intellectual interests and was friendly with John

Lingard. His suitability was to be found in the fact that not only was he known to Poynter, Gibson and Lingard but he was also known to share their views on events in England, which in these days were overshadowed by the independent conduct of Bishop Milner and the efforts of the Jesuits to re-establish themselves. Such a one would be amenable to being initiated into the Roman scene by Macpherson and would be able to maintain the support of Consalvi, who was of the opinion that it would be a political mistake to recognise the English Jesuits.[43]

So it was that Gradwell was sent out as agent. 'Mr. Gradwell will set off about the end of next week with powers of agent and I hope to take immediate possession of the College as Rector. We shall not send students with him, as we wish to know for certain that the College is given to us before we send them.'[44] That Gradwell's mission was basically an anti-Jesuit one is indicated by a passage later on in the same letter, where reference is made to the writings of Gandolphy, the Stonyhurst priest who was causing anxiety to the vicars apostolic: 'Sir John Coxe Hippisley leaves London for Rome on Monday. He will be of great service to us for the recovery of the College and I hope in other respects. I shall send by Mr. Gradwell an extract of some propositions out of Gandolphy's works.'

After some delay, Gradwell eventually arrived in Rome on 2 November 1817, but not before Macpherson had received a note from Consalvi expressing displeasure at the haste with which Gradwell had been dispatched.[45] On arrival, Gradwell took up residence with Macpherson at the Scots College and on 13 November he registered as agent. According to Ward,[46] Consalvi introduced Gradwell as the new Rector on his arrival in Rome in the autumn, but this seems highly unlikely given Consalvi's caution and Gradwell's own official standing at this time. It is more likely that he introduced him as agent.[47] This was the only definite thing about his position. He had the backing of Poynter and Gibson but the Roman authorities were an unknown quantity. Macpherson was initiating him into the new job and while Consalvi was considered favourable, Litta and Propaganda Fide were thought to be on the side of 'the Jesuits'. In January 1818 Macpherson wrote to Gradwell expressing his hope that he would soon be Rector[48] and in full possession of the College. In those days of uncertainty as far as the rectorship was concerned, Gradwell devoted his time to agency work and in February he drafted a memorial on the state of the English mission, followed in March by a memorial on the 'parties that disturb the mission'.[49] The tone of both these writings is strongly anti-Jesuit, and, after an historical survey, he spends much time in giving an account of the Plowden, Gandolphy and Stonyhurst affairs and the activities of Bishop Milner.[50] It is so blatantly on Poynter's side that one can quite understand why Milner wrote, on 2 February of the following year, to the effect that he refused to consider Gradwell as his agent, since it would be impossible for him to represent Milner and the other bishops simultaneously, as their views conflicted so much. Moreover, he said he did not intend to send any students to the English College; all hopes for his students were centred on Oscott.[51]

On 8 March Gradwell received notification that he was indeed appointed Rector.[52] There followed many congratulatory letters and in a letter from Lingard there occurs a startling story of an attempt by the Jesuits to seize the College. Lingard's letter is dated 29 May 1818[53] and runs: 'A short time ago while he was in the Vatican with Consalvi, Grassi entered the College, took formal possession, and turned out Gradwell's servant, telling him that his master might go to an inn. Gradwell on his return took possession again, and wrote an account of all to Consalvi, who immediately sent for Grassi and reprimanded him most severely. All this shews that Gradwell is safe while Consalvi reigns, but he will have hard work afterwards.'

There is also a letter from Coxe Hippisley[54] at the end of May which refers to Jesuit manoeuvres against the College.[55] Gradwell, writing to Consalvi on 18 April, does indeed mention an incident in which he returned to the College one day to find his cook had been dismissed. But according to his version this was due to an action perpetrated by the *computista* and *essatore*. There is no mention of the Jesuits being responsible.[56]

Gradwell had much to contend with in those days preceding his installation. A certain Father P. O'Handley, an Irish Augustinian, set himself up as Rector of the Venerable British College at S. Eusebio and spent freely on entertaining and rebuilding the church premises. The new college, he claimed, was for English, Welsh, Irish and Scots and his intention was to accept Protestants as well as Catholics. Gradwell and Macpherson were branded as imposters. O'Handley was arrested by the papal police in May 1818, on a charge of fraud.[57]

Gradwell's installation took place on 11 June. He attended the *congregazione* on that day, the College was declared open, two deputies were appointed, one for finance and one for discipline, and eight students were expected from England for the coming October. The new constitutions were also published on that date.[58] In September letters of gratitude were addressed to the Pope and

Consalvi on behalf of the vicars apostolic, for the restitution of the English College to the secular clergy. The first alumni arrived on 18 December, six Ushaw men: Henry Gillow, Nicholas Wiseman, James Fleetwood, William Kavanagh, James Sharples and George Heptonstall. Heptonstall was for rudiments and the rest were for philosophy. The next day four more students arrived from Old Hall: Richard Alberry, Richard Crosby, Daniel Rock and John Kearns. On Christmas Eve Gradwell presented to the Pope, in a special audience, as many students as could be suitably dressed for such an occasion.[59]

Gradwell as agent

Before going on to say something of Gradwell's rectorship, we must give an account of his activities as agent, since these situate the College and its Rector within the policy of the vicars apostolic.

In his early years as agent Gradwell not only kept the journal that is to be found in the Westminster archives, but also a scrapbook and diary.[60] In these he speaks of being engaged on agency business two or three times a week.[61] Pollen's contention[62] that he saw his mission as being anti-Jesuit and anti-Milner is borne out by his memorials about the English mission. His appointment as Rector was considered by his friends as a victory over the Jesuits. Joe Hodgson, vicar general of the London District, wrote:[63] 'I congratulate you on the restoration of the English College to its *old* masters [italics mine]. When will the Index publish the decree on the golden works of Mr. Gandolphy?' In the Gandolphy papers[64] there are to be found paginal references to the doubtful passages in his work on prayer and the sacraments. Gradwell was evidently presenting the case for a condemnation. He was also concerned with the 'catechism' of another 'gentleman of Stonyhurst', R. Plowden, and this brought him into conflict with Milner, who alone of the vicars apostolic was prepared to defend Gandolphy and Plowden. This led to Gradwell classifying Milner as belonging to 'the Jesuit party'. In agency work that called for special pleading from his friends and against their Jesuit enemies, Gradwell felt most at home.[65] But he was reluctant to take on agency work for Canada and he doubted his qualifications for acting as agent to the Archbishop of Baltimore in 1821.[66] Wiseman took over some of these foreign agencies when he eventually became Vice-Rector and seemed to thrive on them.

Gradwell as Rector

As Rector of the College, Gradwell proved a success despite his previous inexperience of the College in Rome. It has to be remembered, however, that he had to rule according to the new Constitution of 1818 and this meant that the *congregazione* presided over by Consalvi continued and, on one occasion at least, he had to be reminded of where the ultimate power lay.[67]

Despite the good administration of the College funds and the financial health of the place, Gradwell found the state of the buildings to be very neglected. He described it thus in a letter to Lingard.[68]

> When I first came to the College, I found a great cartload of dusty and rotting papers on the library floor. The greater part were rubbish but several were very valuable. There were letters of Cardinal Pole, which perhaps have been printed, some in Latin some in Italian: letters and other things in the handwriting of Fr. Persons, Garnet, Fitzherbert, Southwell, Blond etc ... I selected all the valuable papers and carried them carefully to my own room, where I filled three drawers with them. I read them with curiosity. Though many of them are published, referred to, or abridged by Dodd etc., there were many quite new to me. Unfortunately two of my drawers did not lock. A superannuated servant had used these valuable papers as waste paper before I found out.

Who this superannuated servant was we do not know, but we do know that there were many personal links with the old days. In *Recollections of the Last Four Popes*, Wiseman described Vincenzo who had served the College faithfully for 40 years and who greeted the returning students, 'he stood to attention, from the wagging appendage of his grey head to the large silver buckles on his shoes'. Then there was Benedetto Girolamo, who was both cook and tailor. To his sister Gradwell wrote 'I can testify that he is a better tailor than cook'. Gradwell found himself very much impeded in his direction of the College by the actions of the *essatore* and *computista* who resented his presence.[69] However, shamefully as he was treated, he did not realise that his position as Rector was much less autonomous than he supposed. It was not a matter of the *congregazione* handing back powers which they had assumed temporarily while the College was unoccupied. Since the time of Corsini it was they who held the power and, according to the new Constitution, the Rector was the administrator.[70]

It is not easy to assess how far the decay of the buildings was due to culpable neglect and how far to the depredations of the French troops. Gradwell tells us that the College was used as Murat's headquarters, Wiseman that the coffins in the church were dug up for lead, but, as Laird notes,[71] there is no contemporary document confirming this statement. But on 27 July 1819 the ruins of the old church began to be demolished and on 16 August there were discovered, under the church, the remains of an ancient Roman street.[72]

The first students had arrived in December 1818 and on 8 January 1819 it was decided that schools were to take place in the College for the rest of the current academic year. Two professors came from the Gregorian to teach logic and mathematics. After the examinations, which took place in the presence of the Vice-Protector and the professors, the College went to Monte Porzio for a month. The summer *villeggiatura* began on 29 September and on 8 November the students began to attend the Roman College. This late summer holiday, which meant that the students were in Rome for the whole of August, was the custom for many years. In November Gradwell requested the Pope for the privilege of preaching before his Holiness each St Stephen's Day. This ancient tradition dated from the time of the martyrs and permission for its renewal was granted. The first of these annual sermons after the restoration took place at the Quirinal Palace and it was preached by Nicholas Wiseman. The practice continued each year until 1870.[73] On St Thomas's Day, 29 December 1819, nine cardinals were present to celebrate the feast in the College chapel.[74]

One of Gradwell's early troubles with the running of the College was the health of the students. In his scrapbook[75] he states that he does not think Rome is harmful to health, but this may have been with the intention of not frightening off the vicars apostolic from sending out students. However, the diet was necessarily meagre in those days[76] and he records that on 15 March 1819 Alberry began to spit blood. Many other illnesses are recorded and on 19 September 1820 Kavanagh died of a fever. Most of the first intake of students seem to have suffered from some sickness or other, but Wiseman is the only one whose indisposition is attributed to overwork.

It was not long before Gradwell had another problem to deal with, that of the studies. All the students except one were going to lectures at the Roman College and the Rector noted who were the lecturers there and what each student was studying.[77] But on 26 May 1820, he wrote, 'I studenti poco contenti del lento andamento delle scuole al Collegio Romano.' Despite these complaints the students carried off prizes after their first year and earned praise for their studies from the Vice-Protector. But the following spring there were more complaints from the students. These coincided with another problem that had its effect on student discipline. On 16 May Gradwell drafted a letter to Consalvi concerning the *economo,* Sig. Tosti, in which he complained that when he was away in England on business, Tosti had contracted debts, had 'embellishments' undertaken which were quite unnecessary and concealed these expenses by creating fictitious credit. Moreover, by his personal behaviour he had offended the students.[78] The congregation held on 15 June was severe. This much we gather, both from Gradwell's diary and from ECA, liber 614, where he speaks of 'Molte nuovi regolamenti sul governo futuro del collegio'. The power of the *congregazione* was reasserted and special responsibilities were given to a Mgr Nicolai. There was ordered an inventory to be made of all the property, furniture, etc. All of this is very reminiscent of the days of Corsini. Then, during the summer, Gradwell took up the case of the students who were complaining about the studies. On 19 July he wrote to Poynter suggesting classes at home, indicating his anxiety about the students' health, endangered by their attendance at classes in all kinds of weather and having to sustain the unhygienic conditions at the Roman College.[79] It is not impossible that this dissatisfaction with the Roman College might have been prompted by the fact that the Jesuits were at this time trying to regain control in place of the seculars who had run the College since the suppression. On 30 July 1821 he drafted a letter to Consalvi advocating classes at home. This document deserves quoting as it is an eloquent representation of the case against attending lectures at the Gregorian.

> Hence it is plain that the life of an English missioner requires a peculiar mode of education, more extensive and more active than the education of those who aspire only to one object, for example to the altar or to the confessional, or to the pulpit, or to the study alone. It is for this reason principally that all the other English seminaries, which persecution at home caused to be established on the continent, although established in towns where there existed an university, abandoned the public schools about 200 years ago, to institute schools at home, under the direction of experienced missioners and able professors, for instance at Douai, Rheims, Louvain, Valladolid and Lisbon. The only exception besides the English College at Rome, was the small seminary kept up at Paris for graduating a few members of the clergy in sacred theology. This change was adopted not because the schools in the different universities of France, Spain,

Portugal and the Low Countries were bad or contemptible but because they were found by experience to be not so well adapted for the formation of English missionaries as schools at home. Some were too scholastic and minute. All of them too limited and too slow.

He then goes on to contrast what he calls the missionary system with that of the university.

The great advantage of the former system [missionary] is in saving and good use of time. There are no journeys to schools, no attachments to tedious and obsolete forms, no spending disproportionate time to minor questions, no reducing of all scholars to one uniform standard and pace. The master in the upper school talks less but makes the scholars talk more. Each student is under the necessity of learning every question in his treatises well. The dull are helped forward and the clever not retarded. The upper students are entrusted with authority over the lower.

Here we have someone brought up in the Douai tradition expressing his doubts about the system obtaining in Rome. Although at Rome there were both lessons at home under a *ripetitore*, or tutor, and lessons in the public schools under the professors, after two years' experience he found the two institutions frequently clashed, and considered that lessons at home were most suitable for future missionaries. To the complaint that such a change would isolate the English students from other nationalities and so deprive them of one of the benefits of living in Rome, Gradwell suggests that such intercourse was already precluded by the strict discipline in force. 'The seclusion of our students from all society, good or bad, is at present carried to excess. Even the higher students are under restraints more monastic than the friars themselves and little suitable either to their past or future kind of life.'[80] Poynter, however, was not convinced by Gradwell's letter and replied that 'most of the advantages of a Roman training would have been lost had they ceased to attend the public lectures'.[81]

When the *congregazione* met in November, Consalvi was present and Gradwell's views were discussed.[82] Naturally, they turned down the request and decreed that all alumni of the English College without exception, whether grammarians, humanists, rhetoricians, philosophers or theologians should study at the Roman College. They should adapt themselves to the method of study of the university and behave as all other collegians. The custom of the time (which was not confined to the Roman College but had been the practice at Douai and Lisbon also) was for each student to copy up their lesson dictates each day. A concession was made whereby not every student was obliged to do this, provided sufficient copies were circulated. It was stressed that students needed to study the matter of the treatises, not just the thesis headings. If they read books other than the text book these were to be considered as secondary and supplementary reading and not to replace the texts. Detailed regulations were also made about what examinations the students should take at the university. Finally the camerata rules were reiterated. On this last matter Gradwell wrote[83]

> They would wish to have the privilege of strolling two by two in the metropolis as they would in the lanes and fields at Ushaw and Old Hall. This is impossible: it is quite contrary to all ideas of propriety in Rome, and for reasons not very obvious perhaps to good lads, would be the road to ruin. But instead of walking out with one or two Italian priests as prefects, two of the oldest are dressed *da abate* and they go out in two bodies every afternoon, and on some days in the morning, where they will.

So it was that the typical English College university routine was established. When the Roman College was handed back to the Jesuits in 1824, the English College students followed their secular masters and transferred to the *Apollinare,* the seminary for the diocese of Rome. This was nearer to the English College and had better appointed premises. It was here that in 1824 Wiseman defended his doctorate by public act. The defence lasted all day, two-and-a-half hours in the morning before eight doctors and one-and-a-half hours in the afternoon before two doctors and in the presence of 32 prelates. No less distinguished was Errington's performance three years later.[84] Gradwell became converted to the system and when many years later his successor as Rector, Wiseman, wrote to him as Bishop in the London District, making a similar petition to have schools in the house, Gradwell replied: 'The petition of the students to have schools at home is mischievous as well as unwise. I, for one, on many accounts never will consent to your students abandoning the Roman public schools to have private schools at home.'[85]

The rest of Gradwell's rectorate can be briefly told. In 1823 Pius VII died. It was nearly fifty years since a Pope had died in Rome and since a conclave had been held there. Gradwell was in England at the time, but the Vice-Rector, William White, left an account of the ceremonies at the Quirinal Palace.[86] Consalvi, who had done so much for the reopening of the College, died in 1824.[87] But the College seems to have found a new friend in Pope Leo XII who visited Monte Porzio in 1827 and who occasioned great surprise, on Holy Saturday of 1828, by presenting a calf to the College.

On 18 June 1828 we find, under item ten of the agenda for the meeting of the *congregazione*, a reference to the Rector's promotion to the episcopate. Gradwell's rectorship ended as it had begun, with official recognition by the governing body. Wiseman, who was at the time Vice-Rector, was asked to exercise the office of Rector 'fintanto che giungerà dall'Inghilterra al Trono Pontificio la debita formale petizione dei vescovi vicarii apostolici di quel regno per la nomina statute di Rettore nel suddeto personal.'[88] The new regime began under the same auspices as the old. On 24 June Gradwell was consecrated bishop in the College chapel by Cardinal Zurla,[89] the Protector.

Notes

1 See B. Ward, *The Dawn of the Catholic Revival in England*, I, p. 65, for Stonor's favourable reports about Felici.

2 B. Ward, *The Dawn of the Catholic Revival in England*, II, pp. 176–93 gives a graphic account of these days, using as his source the letters of Smelt the bishops' agent to Bishop Douglass. These can be found in the Westminster Archives.

3 It is interesting to compare the summary vengeance of the French on the Italians for the assassination of their soldiery, with the vengeance of the Germans in 1944 at the Ardeatine caves.

4 D. McRoberts, *Abbe Paul Macpherson 1756–1846* (Glasgow, 1946). R. McCluskey, *The Scots College Rome 1600–2000*, especially pp. 67–76.

5 This is a reference to the Liber Ruber.

6 ECA, scr. 111, 13.

7 In the official documents, the term 'citizen' is used as well as the new republican calendar, but in the bills of account the old dates, titles and days of month and years are still found.

8 See letters of Smelt to Douglass, 6 December 1799, to Horrabin, 27 January 1800 and 21 March 1800, Westminster Archives.

9 Smelt to Douglass, 6 September 1802, Westminster Archives.

10 ECA, liber 545, *Bilanci degli anni 1798 & 1799 del ritratto e spese della vigna de La Magliana a pertinenza del Ven Collegio Inglese amministrata dal Sig. Giuseppe Cini.*
   ECA, liber 546, *Ricevute diverse che appartengono all'entrata ed uscite del Sig. Giuseppe Cini dall 19 Nov 1799–21 Ap 1801.*
   ECA, liber 547, *Ricevute ed altri documenti appart. al conto di casso di Sig. Guiseppe Cini 1 Magg 1801–Dic 1801.*
   ECA, liber 548, *Ricevute ed altri documenti appart. al conto di casso di Sig. Giuseppe Cini Genn–Dic 1802* (This is signed by Braschi).

ECA, liber 522, *Entrata ed uscita dei danari spettanti al collegio e missione inglese di Roma in potere del Sig. Giuseppe Cini depositario di detti duo luogi 1 Magg 1801–Dic 1802.*

11 The Cini family did not relinquish their connection with the College. The old servant whom Wiseman mentions in *Recollections of the Last Four Popes* as greeting the new students in 1818, was probably Vincenzo Cini whose name occurred in the document cited above about Nicholas Porter. The Branchinis were also to serve the College for many years. Giovanni Branchini, the son of Camillo, did a portrait of Gradwell and visited England in search of artistic commissions from the clergy. A Branchini was gentiluomo to Wiseman when he became Archbishop of Westminster. Pietro was *essatore* in 1875 and some of the family occupied an apartment in the College cortile, at the beginning of the present century.

12 ECA, liber 525–8 are of Branchini's accounts from 1801–1813. The Libro Mastro Provisorio runs from 1800–1805 (liber 538).

13 ECA, liber 612.

14 R. A. Laird, 'The College Church', *Venerabile*, XXIV, 34.

15 ECA, liber 665–78 and 680–94. Gradwell had in fact celebrated mass on the Feast of St Thomas, 29 December 1817, but this was by leave of Consalvi as he was not yet Rector of the College (Gradwell's Journal, Westminster Archives).

16 See Appendix III for full text.

17 At the time of writing, of the overseas colleges it is only the English and Scots Colleges in Spain that carry on this policy of relieving the bishops of some of the financial burden of educating students for the priesthood. This is possible by the wise investment and administration of recent Rectors. However, as financial independence implies a certain measure of power, it is not always considered an unmitigated advantage.

18 B. Ward, *The Eve of Catholic Emancipation* (London 1911), I, chapter 14, pp. 202ff.

19 B. Ward, *The Dawn of the Catholic Revival in England*, II, p. 70. In 1813 there was a petition to the Pope concerning the seminaries in England. The colleges at Ushaw and Old Hall wanted the power to confer the doctorate of divinity.

20 D. Milburn, *A History of Ushaw College*, especially pp. 350–2.

21 See H. Aveling, *The Handle and the Axe*, pp. 329–45 and J. Bossy, *The English Catholic Community*, pp. 330–5.

22 Consalvi's portrait hangs in Windsor Castle and the Lawrence portrait of George IV is to be seen in the Vatican Galleries. For the background to England's relationship to the Papacy see G. Mooney SJ, 'British Diplomatic Relations with the Holy See 1793–1830', *RH*, 14, 193–210.

23 H. Fenning, 'The Three Kingdoms England, Ireland and Scotland', in *SCPF*, II, 604–19, especially 622–3. B. Ward, *The Eve of Catholic Emancipation*, II, pp. 71ff.

24 See Smelt's Agency papers, Westminster Archives.

25 Poynter's petition of 4 November 1815 is to be found in ECA, liber 649.

26 B. Ward, *The Eve of Catholic Emancipation*, II, Chapter 31, pp. 255–69.

27 Ibid., III, Chapter 34.

28 Ibid., II, pp. 112–3.

29 Peter Gandolphy, of Italian descent, was one of the 'gentleman of Stonyhurst'. His views caused concern to the vicars apostolic and his book on liturgical matters was put on the Roman Index of prohibited books. See ECA, liber 649, letter of Macpherson n. 81, 1 June 1816; also Leeds Diocesan archives, Smith correspondence, 11 Jan 1807.

30 Lingard to Poynter, n. 183, 5 June 1817, vol. II, Ushaw transcript.

31 ECA, scr. 55, 5.

32 It is in the light of the above that one has to see the 'discovery' made at this time by Macpherson of a document from 1783, purporting to grant the secular clergy control of the College. This was a valuable piece of evidence to support the claim of the vicars apostolic to the College.

33 B. Ward, *The Eve of Catholic Emancipation*, II, p. 72.

34 This was concerning the Quarantotti rescript, see above p. 74.

35 Galeffi, who had been for a time deputy to Braschi, was interested, but Macpherson considered him as pro-Jesuit. Quarantotti's name was also suggested.

36 See J. H. Pollen, *The Month*, CXV, 1910, 449ff, 585ff and CXVI, 1910, 23–36.

37 J. H. Pollen, *The Month*, CXV, 593.

38 Grassi had not only spent some time in England at Stonyhurst, but had also become a naturalised US citizen in 1815 and was presently on a mission to Rome on behalf of Archbishop Leonard Neale of Baltimore.

39 Ushaw transcript, Lingard Letters, vol. II, n. 183.

40 Ibid., n. 185.

41 Ibid., n. 171, Letter written in July 1832. The last number of the Catholic Magazine was that of May 1832.

42 For Gradwell and the Venerabile see R. P. Redmond, 'Robert Gradwell', *Venerabile*, III, 345–53; D. J. Leahy, 'Robert Gradwell', *Venerabile*, VI, 123–40; also B. Ward, *The Eve of Catholic Emancipation*, III, p. 198. It is interesting to note that as early as 1813, enquiries were being made as to the suitability of Gradwell. Macpherson to Poynter, 30 August 1813, Westminster Archives.

43 For Gradwell's relations with the Jesuits see D. J. Leahy, 'Robert Gradwell', *Venerabile*, VI, 123–40. Also J. H. Pollen, *The Month*, CXV, 499 and 585.

44 ECA, scr. 55, 8, Letter 102 from Poynter to Macpherson, 5 September 1817.

45 For an account of Gradwell's journey and the perils at sea, *Venerabile*, III, 346–7. In his journal Gradwell describes his first days in Rome and his efforts to learn Italian, Westminster Archives.

46 B. Ward, *The Eve of Catholic Emancipation*, III, p. 7.

47 This is borne out by Gradwell's own entry in his journal for 10 November, 'Presented to Consalvi. Immediately acknowledged me as agent but seemed dubious about the College saying there was no revenue.'

48 ECA, scr. 66, 5.

49 ECA, liber 650.

50 A further instance of Gradwell's sympathies is to be found in his journal entry for 14 January 1818, 'Reading Dodd to refresh my memory'.

51 ECA, scr. 54, 3, 7. Milner to Gradwell, 2 February 1819.

52 ECA, scr. 56, 1.

53 Ushaw transcripts. Letter 217.

54 Sir John Coxe Hippisley, MP for Somerset, was Pitt's secret agent in Rome from 1792–96. He served as an official go-between in several transactions with Rome.

55 ECA, scr. 54, 6.

56 Quoted in *Venerabile*, XXIV, 291–3. Neither is there any mention of the Jesuits in Gradwell's Journal entry for this date.

57 Fr O'Handley is mentioned in Gradwell's journal for 11 March and 20 May 1818.

58 ECA, scr. 56, 1 and liber 614. The 1818 Constitution is to be found in Appendix IV.

59 Wilfrid Ward, *The Life and Times of Cardinal Wiseman* (London 1897), I, p. 26.

60 ECA, Scrapbook liber 650; Diary, scr. 59, 1.

61 See *Venerabile*, IV, 120.

62 *The Month*, CXVI, 23, where Pollen speaks of 'a touch of Josephism' in the opposition to Milner.

63 ECA, scr. 59, 1.

64 Ibid.

65 Gradwell was in fact accused of making mis-statements (a) concerning the offence that would be given to the British Government if the Jesuits were restored and (b) saying that the petition from the laity contained forged signatures, B. Ward, *The Eve of Catholic Emancipation*, III, pp. 39, 46.

66 ECA, Canadian Agency, scr. 63. Also Baltimore papers.

67 ECA, liber 614. In June 1821 the congregation asserted its powers vis-à-vis the Rector.

68 Quoted in *Venerabile*, VI, 125.

69 See Gradwell's Journal for 13 April, 2 May, 9 May, 5 June, Westminster archives.

70 A. Laird, 'The English College under Italian Secular Administration 1773–1798', *RH*, 14, 147, quoting Archives of Propaganda Fide Congresso, Collegio Inglese F461 – 'Qui tamen Rector praesit alumnis in iis, quae ad mores pertinent, nec ullo modo administrationi se immisceat; contrariis quibuscumqve non obstantibus.'

71 'The College Church', *Venerabile*, XXIV, 35.

72 See Appendix I for a full account of the buildings.

73 ECA, liber 630.

74 B. Ward, *The Eve of Catholic Emancipation*, II, p. 13, gives a description of this day.

75 Quoted in *Venerabile*, XVIII, 87–9.

76 See Constitutions in Appendix III.

77 ECA, liber 650; also scr. 56, 4.

78 ECA, scr. 56, 2, 4b and 4c; also *Venerabile*, VI, 134.

79 ECA, scr. 56, 2; also Archiv di Stato di Roma Arch generale 2046.
80 ECA, scr. 56, 2. Similar views on the studies in Rome are to be found in Gradwell's letter to Smith, 6 December 1821, Leeds Diocesan Archives, Smith correspondence, 124.
81 See *Venerabile*, III, 350.
82 ECA, liber 614.
83 Quoted in *Venerabile*, III, 349.
84 Gradwell's pride in his students is evident from his letters to Smith of 16 October 1826 and 14 November 1827, Leeds Diocesan Archives, Smith correspondence, 224, 251.
85 Quoted in *Venerabile*, VI, 133.
86 B. Ward, *The Eve of Catholic Emancipation*, III, pp. 105–6.
87 See Gradwell to Smith, 1 March 1824, Leeds Diocesan Archives, 161.
88 ECA, liber 616, 132. There was some objection to Gradwell's appointment as coadjutor to the London district. This was due to his anti-Jesuit views. *Venerabile*, III, 351.
89 For a sketch of Cardinal Zurla see G. Swinburne, *Venerabile*, VII, 23–31.

Chapter Five

The Wiseman Tradition

The figure of Wiseman dominates the history of the English College in the early years of the nineteenth century. He was one of the first students to come to the re-established College in 1818, his brilliance as a scholar made an impression in Rome, and as Vice-Rector and then Rector at the age of 27, he made the College a centre of intellectual and social life. When he eventually left Rome after 22 years continual residence, he was to impress his particular brand of the Roman spirit on Catholic life in England and in this Manning and Vaughan were his heirs, as well as his successors, at Westminster.

Wiseman was an exceptional person and so, in one sense, he was greater than the College. Not many students have commenced their studies in Rome with his background. Born in Seville[1] of Anglo-Irish parents, his training at Ushaw revealed not only an exceptional talent but an interest in history and the classics that would give him an immediate sense of homecoming on his arrival in Rome. Rome was the place where his natural talents and tastes were able to grow and develop. He arrived in the city at a time when the papacy was re-establishing itself after the Napoleonic exile of Pius VII. He witnessed Leo XII's re-organisation of ecclesiastical studies in the Papal States and it was due to the opening up of professorships to public competition that Wiseman was to apply successfully for the chair of Syriac at the Sapienza, the University of Rome.[2] Gregory XVI's patronage towards the Vatican museums and the excavation of the forum ruins found a natural response in Wiseman, who as a boy at Ushaw had been instrumental in the founding of a classical society. The spirit of papal Rome is well described in his *Recollections of the Last Four Popes*. This was a work of his later years, but time only deepened first impressions. His first letter home to his mother contains the following passage:

> On Easter Sunday we went to St. Peter's and heard a mass celebrated in the presence of His Holiness by Cardinal Mattei, and after the ceremony, secured places to see the Pope give his benediction. He was carried on a sumptuous chair of crimson velvet and gold, and in a rich cape, and his tiara with a triple crown, surrounded by Bishops and Cardinals he appeared in the grand balcony over the front door. It was something above earthly to see an Emperor and Empress, a Queen, Dukes and Princes of the highest blood kneeling before the Sovereign Vicar of Christ, with thousands of people of all nations.[3]

A period of hope and optimism had been ushered in by the re-establishment of papal Rome and the re-opening of the English College.

The *villeggiatura* at Monte Porzio gave him a lasting appreciation not only of the Italian countryside, which he shared with many of his 'romantic' contemporaries, but also of the Italian country people and their piety. He was able to understand the frail boundaries between age-old pre-Christian country ritual and Christian devotions. Grace built on nature. He had little of the built-in resistance to such forms of piety that the older Catholics of the Challoner/Douai school had, or for that matter the new converts. Yet he could understand the old Catholic view; his years at Ushaw saw to that, as did his association as student and Vice-Rector with Gradwell.[4] But he felt an instinctive *rapport* with the Latin world, something that was not acquired, as in the case of Faber, but born into him in Seville amidst the sights and scents and sounds of Andalucia.[5]

His varied background gave Wiseman an openness to the world of Rome and he seized every opportunity to learn. Curiosity and pleasure in the arcane and exotic led him to oriental studies and to friendships with scholars and antiquarians, men like Mgr Angelo Mai at the Vatican Library, Fea, and Cancellieri, the author of such works as *The practice of kissing the Pope's foot antecedently to the embroidering of the cross on his shoe*; *On the country houses of the Popes* and *The bite of the tarantula spider*.[6] Wiseman was attracted by the new and the strange; he fell under the spell of Lamennais and Lacordaire in France, of Dollinger in Munich. Liberal ideas intrigued him and he took note of political events in Ireland and in Europe. His flair for languages (Mezzofanti[7] was his contemporary) can be explained not

Fig. 5.1 Nicholas Wiseman, Rector 1828–40.

only by his quick intelligence, but by his desire to speak and communicate and adopt another 'persona'. He has left a large foreign correspondence with his many scholarly and ecclesiastical friends in Rome. He could easily identify with other people and places, and his energies were so channelled that he adorned what he put his hand to, whether it was public speaking, writing or music. In many ways he was an actor and he needed a backdrop and a supporting cast. He found them easily provided in Rome. In England he gathered supporters around him, but he had to create his own stage sets and often the part he played was not in the local idiom.

Rome took note of his scholarship and took for granted his piety and pastoral concern, but it understood him in a way it never understood Newman. Although not himself a master of gesture in the Italian way[8] he had a Roman sense of extravagance if not arrogance. This meant that he could be trusted. He was predictable. He made mistakes. He chose friends who would support him. There was nothing hidden. He seemed the ideal man to identify with the various factions in England, the old Catholics, the older converts and Tractarians. He would be able to cope enthusiastically with any new situation that might arise.

But Wiseman was not only a 'Roman', he was representative of many contemporary Northern Europeans. We must not forget that Stendhal was resident in Rome during Wiseman's rectorship and Wiseman himself was in many ways but another romantic Englishman visiting Italy and ready to be impressed by the classical sites. Macaulay was two years his senior and John Keats arrived in Rome only two years after Wiseman. Wiseman was also an English Catholic returning to his roots, to a land where religion and culture were no longer in opposition but in close harmony. These two factors, his romanticism and his Catholicism, can help us understand his enthusiasm for the papacy and also his vision of Catholic emancipation and a restored hierarchy. But, for all his apparent Latinity, Wiseman's reactions were much more emotional that rational. He did not understand the rational objections of those in England to a Roman-style religion and this put him at variance with a considerable body of Catholic opinion. Neither did he appreciate that the Rome of the *Last Four Popes* was indeed the last age of papal Rome. He was witnessing a peculiar form of Roman Catholicism that was shortly to disappear, a Catholicism that some of his less enthusiastic contemporaries considered decadent.

Wiseman's Roman days ended in 1840, before the movement towards the unification of Italy had gathered its full momentum.

However, the impressions made by those early times lasted throughout his life and his successors at the English College, especially Baggs, Grant and Cornthwaite, persisted in a picture of Rome that became more distorted with the passage of time. As the patrimony of St Peter dwindled year by year, so the Popes clung to the old ways. The hours of the day were still reckoned to begin in the evening with the sound of the 'Ave', when most of Italy had adopted the 'French' system we use today. The response to acts of political violence and the frequent outbreaks of cholera took the form of processions, novenas and exposition of relics. Not that prayer is to be underestimated or despised, but when it is unaccompanied by effective action in the secular or political field it only encourages the growth of secularism and unbelief. It was these forms of devotion proliferating in the besieged citadel of Gregory XVI's Rome that Wiseman wanted to transplant to England. Somewhat ironically it was those in England who opposed such an Italianisation of the Church there, that were branded as reactionaries.

Recent historical writing has shown a more sympathetic understanding of the problems facing the papacy and the conservative position in general, and there is less of the uncritical acceptance of the ideals of the Risorgimento, that was the custom until quite recently.[9] However, it remains a fact that the undoubtedly positive aspects of the Risorgimento, its attempts at social reform and the restoration of a dignity to the Italian people, so long exploited by foreign powers, were never appreciated by Wiseman, or indeed by the English College in the nineteenth century. Their wholehearted acceptance of the papacy blinded them to the inefficiency and less enlightened aspects of papal rule.[10] They accepted the whole package and so reaped the opprobrium of the anti-clericals, who could not distinguish between the English clergy and the Roman clergy; indeed, in much, there was no difference. But if Wiseman could not distinguish between the papacy in its essence and the way it was exercised under his last four Popes, neither could the papacy itself. In a state of siege everything is used in defence and the extreme sensitivity of Rome to any criticism of the status quo became understandable. In such circumstances, it is very easy to be found guilty of lacking in respect to the Holy See, just as it is easier to commit treason in wartime than in times of peace.

Wiseman's version of the Roman spirit was for many years the only one acceptable in Rome and anyone desirous of holding office in the Church had to share it, but this attitude cannot be entirely identified with the English College. Neither Manning, Vaughan nor Talbot were ever students at the College yet they were all in the Wiseman mould. On the other hand many of those who opposed his policies at one time or another – Daniel Rock, George Errington, Edward Cox, Thomas Grant – were either his contemporaries or pupils in Rome. The history of the College is more subtle and nuanced than just the story of its most illustrious student, Vice-Rector and Rector. The College was in another way greater than Wiseman. One begins to see this as one moves from a consideration of the person to his achievement as Rector.

Wiseman as Rector

As Rector, what did Wiseman do for the College? Certainly he brought it renewed fame in Rome. However, the trust that he established by personal contact and friendships,[11] not hindered by a language barrier, did not mean that there was no interference in the running of the College. Wiseman's regime was by no means perfect or free from complaint, nor did he feel secure, despite his reputation. He left the day-to-day administration to other people, first to Errington, his Vice-Rector, who worked with Signor Branchini according to a system 'which is sound, honest and accurate'.[12] He did some lecturing to the students on scriptural matters and English controversy, as well as acting as tutor in theology for a time.[13] But much of his time was spent outside the College on business in Rome or elsewhere, and the students saw him as a kindly and understanding, but rather remote figure.[14] Although he tried to communicate his own tastes in architecture and antiquities, accompanying them on walks through the city, such concerns were not to everybody's liking. It is interesting to discover that the same style of life was adopted by him when he was later the Rector at Oscott. He was much away from the college, visiting the great houses, both Protestant and Catholic, and, as one of the students remarked, 'We had a feeling that Oscott, next to Pekin, was the centre of the world.'[15] When Ignatius Spencer[16] arrived as a student in Rome, there took place that change in Wiseman whereby his interests became less academic and more pastoral. The idea of the conversion of England made him rather restless and he visited England in 1835 with a view to exploring the possibilities of Bishop Baines's scheme for the establishment of a college at Prior Park, near Bath. During the last years of his rectorship Wiseman's attention turned more and more towards England and the idea grew that it was there that his future lay.

Fig 5.2 Charles Baggs, Rector 1840–44.

Perhaps these thoughts were encouraged by the trials of being Rector. Because of the threat of cholera then sweeping Italy, Thomas Weld, the Cardinal Protector, had advised that no new students be sent from England for the time being. The epidemic reached its peak in the summer of 1837, when we learn that at least 12,000 died in six weeks. The College buildings in Rome were put at the disposal of the authorities as a hospital. The students were sent to Monte Porzio and they organised a committee of health in the village, which in fact escaped the epidemic.[17] But besides the cholera there were other anxieties. There are indications that Cardinal Weld wished to make changes in the administration and consulted Bishop Briggs to this end.[18] There were rumours in Rome that the Jesuits were going to be put in charge. Grant[19] writes: 'many reports to the disadvantage of the English College have circulated and it is also reported that this College is to be placed in their hands'. In the same letter he records Pope Gregory XVI's visit to the College and how he burst into tears when he heard of the antipathy towards the Society in England. It is not easy to ascertain how far these moves were directed against Wiseman personally, but it is perhaps worth recalling that it was at this time that the Jesuits were given charge of the administration of Propaganda Fide College and in 1838 a sensation was caused in Rome when Odescalchi, the Viceregent, resigned his office and joined the Society.

Wiseman as agent

Wiseman, of course, was not only Rector of the English College, he was also agent in Rome for the vicars apostolic. We have seen how Gradwell looked upon this charge as largely a commission to further Poynter's policies against the Jesuits. Wiseman however considered himself much more as the interpreter of Rome to the vicars apostolic than their advocate in Rome. This is clear from the attitude he was to adopt on the matter of the restoration of the hierarchy,[20] where he helped to switch this from a possible national and anti-Roman move to a blatant assertion of ultramontanism. But already in his agency days there are indications of friction between himself and certain vicars apostolic. When the Pope complained to him about the lack of respect shown by the English bishops, Wiseman attributed this to the bishops' ignorance of the forms and etiquette of the Roman court. Already at this time there was a growing suspicion about Wiseman's critical views towards the older secular clergy and his bias in favour of the religious orders,[21] and when their lordships gathered for their annual meeting in April 1838, it was resolved 'that the future agent of the bishops in Rome be unconnected with the English College and not employed in any other office'.[22] In fact this never came to pass as Baggs, who succeeded Wiseman as Rector, acted as agent for most of the vicars apostolic. Writing to Briggs on 28 February 1839[23] Wiseman told of the difficulties of his position as agent in Rome and of the strained relationships which had developed over the past six months between Rome and the vicars apostolic. He said he could not be blamed for this state of affairs, as the vicars apostolic had kept him in the dark concerning the questions at issue. So it seems as if there was some sort of boycott of Wiseman in the bishops' dealings with Rome. One must not magnify these difficulties that Wiseman encountered as Rector and agent, but at least they serve to show that his early career was not one long story of effortless success.

Wiseman as bishop and cardinal

In May 1840 Wiseman was made coadjutor to Bishop Walsh of the Midland or Central District and he took up residence as Rector of St Mary's Oscott. His subsequent work in England, in the Midlands and later in Westminster, involved him in many journeys to Rome. On one of his visits, in March 1854, we are told that after lunch he finished carving his name on the marble pillar in the garden, which he had begun as a student.[24] He did not always stay at the English College although he rarely missed paying a visit to Monte Porzio. When he had news of his promotion to the cardinalate he thought that this might mean that he would have to leave England for good and take up residence in Rome. The announcement of the restoration of the hierarchy came after the news of the red hat. For the brief time between the two announcements he seriously considered buying a villa at Monte Porzio, so as to be able to escape at times to a less formal atmosphere than that of the Curia. It was on one of his visits to Monte Porzio that he composed much of his novel, *Fabiola*.

As a bishop in England, his attitude to the English College was subject to the same constraints as affected the other bishops. There were demands on him to support the colleges and seminaries at home and this sometimes led to his being considered disloyal to his former College. But although the English College was now part of Wiseman's past history, Rome remained an ever-living present. Both at Oscott and later at Old Hall he saw that 'Romans' were appointed to the staff, if not English College men then those who had a similar outlook to his own, such as Vaughan and W. G. Ward. In 1860 he set up an institution, which was aimed at keeping Catholics abreast of the sciences and literature of the day. It was modelled on the pattern of the Roman 'Academia' to which he had belonged in his youth, and it was to arouse the suspicion of liberal Catholics.[25] Roman ideas proliferated in his schemes. The Oblates of St Charles were his idea and so was the suggestion that Newman should consider joining the Oratory of St Philip Neri. Both suggestions are connected with the history of the English College. St Philip used to greet the students from his house opposite the College, 'Salvete flores martyrum', and on their way back to England there grew up the custom of calling on St Charles Borromeo when they passed through Milan. If, in later life, Wiseman valued Rome itself higher than the College, this was because the College owed all it had to its position in Rome. That he considered Rome as an ideal place for the formation of the clergy can hardly be doubted, but the reasons do not depend solely on the way of life of a particular college. No doubt recalling his days as a student and professor he wrote:

> He knows that every professor whose lectures he hears has been directly and immediately appointed, after careful selection, by the Pope himself, and that every class-book which he reads has the same supreme sanction; he feels himself almost under the direct tuition of the Holy See; however pure and sparkling the rills at which others drink, he puts his lips to the very rock which a divine word has struck, and he sucks in its waters as they gush forth living.[26]

It was the safeness of the Roman training and its theology that Wiseman found valuable and it was this aspect that made him recommend Rome. Manning and Vaughan proved to be loyal disciples. But Newman? He too was sent to Rome, not to the Venerabile but to the College of Propaganda Fide. Here he had an opportunity of meeting and discussing theology with the Jesuit professors of the Roman College. This would hardly have been possible at the English College, since at this time the students were attending the Apollinare, the non-Jesuit seminary, for their lectures. However, Newman did visit the English College for theological disputations on Thursdays in early 1847.[27] It was his stay in Rome that convinced Newman that he could not become a professor of theology.

> Now the conviction has now and then come on me that it is very inexpedient for a person like me, a convert, and a writer (and so pledged

Fig 5.3 Thomas Cardinal Weld.

in a way to certain opinions) to be a theological professor or the like. Mr. Brownson, Fr. Passaglia and Dr. Grant[28] all together are a great difficulty in the way of a person coming forward as a theologian. It is all in addition to the jealousy in England. I say I cannot work without support against England. I come to Rome and find no support if I undertake theology.[29]

It would seem that those virtues extolled by Wiseman in his *Recollections* were the obstacles to Newman's acceptance of Roman theology. Ward's remark about Wiseman is extremely penetrating:[30] 'It is interesting to observe that scholars, or linguists, or historians or artists or antiquarians interested him far more than thinkers or theologians.' It is perhaps fitting to recall that in his last illness Wiseman is reported to have said of himself, 'As people in the world go to a ball for their recreation, so I have enjoyed a great function.'

Baggs, Grant and the continuance of the Wiseman tradition

When the names for the new vicars apostolic were being considered in early 1840, Wiseman, Rector of the English College, was at the head of the list. Second to his was the name of Charles Baggs, his Vice-Rector.[31] Despite some objections, Wiseman was appointed. However, it was thought that Baggs, who lacked pastoral experience and was quite unknown in England, would not be suitable for such a task.[32] Yet after three years as Rector (he succeeded Wiseman) and as agent for the vicars apostolic, these objections no longer debarred him, and in 1843 he was appointed to succeed Baines in the Western District.[33] Such rapid promotion need not surprise us, since the Rectorship of the English College was now being looked upon as a suitable first post for a promising young man. It was a good testing ground since it entailed administrative and disciplinary responsibilities in the College and involved relationships with the bishops at home and the authorities in Rome.

Baggs's short rectorate was marked by economic difficulties. When the College reopened in 1817 it received fifty scudos a month from the Apostolic Datary, but in 1838 this payment ceased. This was due to the financial straits of the papacy. It still depended for its supply of gold on Spanish sources, and the political situation there had meant that these supplies were interrupted. Through the good offices of the Protector, Giacomo Giustiniani (whose candidature, incidentally, in the 1831 papal election, had been vetoed by Spain), a grant of twenty-five scudos a month was obtained in 1840.

Fig 5.4 Blessed Pope Pius IX, elected Pope in 1864, laid the foundation stone of the new College church in 1866.

Although an improvement, this was still only half of what the College had been accustomed to receive. In a letter to Briggs the Rector wrote, 'Dr. Wiseman therefore intended to beg the bishops not to send any new students for a short time. May I therefore beg your lordship to wait till those of your students have finished, the more so as your number is filled by the six students you already have here.'[34] So it was that a system of rationing was introduced, whereby names were to be sent to the Cardinal Protector by the vicars apostolic and he selected those who were to be admitted as students. The College could not afford to support more than twenty, so these had to be fairly distributed among the Districts. This was not an entirely new departure since selection and nomination by the Protector would seem to have been an ancient custom and quite in keeping with what we know about his powers over College affairs. However, the new circumstances called attention to it once more and when such control became something more than a formality it was bound to raise the question in the mind of the bishops: 'To whom does the College really belong?' In this case, selection was required in order to restrict numbers. A later Rector was to complain that this system restricted both his and the bishops' powers.[35] Later still, in 1871, the Bishop of Shrewsbury complained, at the Low Week meeting of the bishops, that the new rules of the College (under O'Callaghan) took away the bishops' power of nominating students. But it would seem that the bishops' powers in this regard were slighter than they imagined.

Baggs continued the Wiseman tradition in so far as he inherited the same responsibilities and problems as Rector of the College and agent of the bishops. He also qualified himself for high office. This same process was to be continued by Thomas Grant, but not without some initial difficulties.

Grant's career has some similarities with Wiseman's. He was born in France of Irish parents and, his father being a serving soldier, he received his early education at Chester, under the patronage of the local priest, Dr Briggs (later to become Bishop of the Northern District), who encouraged him in his vocation. He was sent to Ushaw and then to Rome. We can follow his career, from his student days to the time he was appointed first bishop of Southwark, in the letters he wrote from Rome to Briggs. Over sixty of these are extant.[36] We learn of his journey out to Rome as a student, across the channel, through France overland, as far as Chalon-sur-Saône, then by river to Marseilles and by sea to Cività Vecchia. On arrival there the students were forced to spend some time in quarantine before being allowed to proceed by road to

Rome. We can follow Grant's developing interests in liturgical and canonical matters. While still a student he felt close enough to Briggs to report on 'your lordship's subjects', their health and behaviour. He also seems to have been on close terms with the Rector, Wiseman. After taking his doctorate by public act and after his ordination to the priesthood, his interest and ability in canon law led to his being asked to stay on in Rome as secretary to Cardinal Charles Acton.[37] In 1842, Acton became Cardinal Protector of the College, Giustiniani resigning in his favour. In the following year Baggs asked Grant to succeed Eyre as Vice-Rector of the College. Grant replied: 'The Vice-Rectorship of the English College, which implies a compound of the duties of vice-president, prefect, procurator, and superior, offers no temptations.'[38] When Baggs was appointed to the Western District in 1844, there was a three-month discussion among the vicars apostolic as to the suitability of Grant as Rector.[39] Wiseman and Acton supported his case but Baggs wanted Errington, and this view was seconded by Griffiths and Briggs. Writing to Briggs on 13 February 1844,[40] Acton says of Grant: 'The presidency of the English College might serve as a means of his acquiring gently and by degree more experience. His delicacy of conscience will serve to keep up the discipline of the College.' He then goes on to suggest that he himself will keep an eye on College affairs and from time to time bring in theologians of the city to talk to the students. He will also ensure that missionary cases from England will be discussed. But these intentions of Acton only served to enkindle that deep suspicion of Rome that was only a little below the surface. Bishop Brown, who was in Rome at the time, expressed the fear that Acton really meant to instal an Italian assistant and so he and Griffiths set about proposing alternative names to that of Grant. This did not prove to be easy. Dr Weedal of Oscott had to be ruled out on health grounds, and Dr Rock, who was approached, declared that the climate in Rome was dangerous for him. Eventually it was decided that Grant should be nominated pro-rector, 'that he may have a trial whether he would be likely to succeed as Rector and agent'.[41] Very soon the opposition ceased, but perhaps this was as much due to confidence in Acton as to Grant's abilities. Griffiths, writing to Briggs on 27 March, expressed gratitude to Acton 'for protecting the College against the attempt lately made by Lambruschini, at the wish of the French ambassador'.[42] Grant accepted the rectorship with diffidence, saying that he would have preferred a subordinate role at Ushaw.

In his life of Manning[43] Purcell remarks that in the 1840s the English College was anything but Roman. It is hard to understand what exactly this can mean. Both Baggs and Grant followed in the Wiseman tradition. They were very much involved in the affairs of the Holy See and they were on good terms with the Cardinal Protector. It might refer to the students being left too much to their own devices, the Rectors being concerned with external affairs. It might even refer to the lack of an Italian piosity in their devotions and prayers. But more likely, this anti-Roman accusation is something thought-up long after the event to 'explain' Grant's opposition to Wiseman's policies.

Grant's rectorship was marked by important outside events. There were the final negotiations for the restoration of the hierarchy and this added burden to his agency work meant that he had to ask for help, as he felt at one time that he could not continue as both agent and Rector. This was one of the reasons why Bishop Ullathorne, Vicar Apostolic to the Western District, went out to Rome in 1848.[44] It was a time of important visitors to Rome. Wiseman, of course, was frequently in the city. Newman spent a year at Propaganda Fide and Manning, still an Anglican, visited Rome.

Equally important for the College were the political events in Italy. Gregory XVI died in 1846 and great hopes were entertained for his successor, Pius IX – at any rate it would be difficult for him to be any worse than the late Pope. There were scenes of enthusiasm during the first months of the new reign. The new Pope did not seem to have such a closed mind to the world as did his Camaldolese predecessor. A Turkish ambassador arrived in Rome, the noble guard were now officially allowed to wear moustaches, it was decided to allow the railway into the Papal States[45] and on 1 January 1847, the clocks on Monte Citorio and the Roman College began to record 'French' time. But such measures were not sufficient to stop the mounting wave of revolt and revolution that was affecting the Papal States, as much as the rest of Europe. The Pope was unwilling to meet the demands for a constitutional government of the Papal States, he refused to declare war on Austria and, amidst a wave of unpopularity, he had to flee to Neapolitan territory at Gaeta. Even before he left Rome there had been a decline in public order and this, coupled with the financial chaos, put the College and its students at considerable risk. Writing to Briggs the Rector remarked, 'All these political questions are important in a religious sense, because in the present state of uncertainty and transition, men's minds are agitated and unwilling to settle down quietly to the duties of everyday life and least of all to the exercise of piety and religion for which Rome is so remarkable.'[46] A more

Fig. 5.5 John Henry Newman and Ambrose St John in Rome, 1847.

lengthy quotation from the same letter shows how this affected student life at the College.

> Last year (scholastically speaking) nothing was done in the public schools. The University closed early, and upon the departure of the Jesuits,[47] the number of those who frequented the Roman College, taught by their professors, was much diminished and those who did frequent the schools broke up early in the year. Next to the Roman College and the University, the chief establishment for theological courses was the Roman Seminary, whose school was taught by the secular clergy. After the dispersion of the Jesuits, His Holiness desired the latter to assume the care of the Roman College, which had been held by them from the suppression until 1825 and subsequently by those fathers. The schools went on languidly, and I judged the wisest course to be that our students should remain at home to attend such lectures as I could manage to give them myself, and thus we went on until the beginning of August, when rumours of fresh troubles induced me to remove them to our usual country residence. One of our duties here is to write dissertations upon subjects proposed by the Rector and for this year I have given them some canonical theses in order to accustom them to discussing the questions which are most likely to be familiar in England.

The foreign colleges in Rome at this time were recognised by the papacy as national property,[48] and the British government accepted its responsibilities. In 1849, Palmerston directed the chargé d'affaires to look to the safety of all British property that belonged to religious establishments and this seems to have staved off trouble for a time.[49] Later in the year a unit of the Royal Navy prepared plans for the evacuation of British subjects. Such a comforting presence doubtlessly influenced Grant in his choice of words when he wrote to Briggs, 'It is my duty as Rector to stand by my ship, and be the last man to fear danger.'

The bishops in England had their preoccupations too. For their own reasons they wanted Grant back in England. Not only was he an able Church lawyer and consultant, but Wiseman had the idea of exchanging him for Errington. Errington, not yet a bishop, was working in the North and Wiseman thought he would be a good man to succeed Grant in Rome. Ushaw was also interested in Grant and wanted him as a professor at the college. Amidst all the worries of the Italian situation Grant was now asked to decide about his own future. He asked Briggs's advice, but he was acute enough to realise that, should he accept, there would be problems for the College in Rome. As there was at present no Vice-Rector he wrote requesting that one should be appointed. He made it clear that, in

Fig. 5.6 Nicholas Cardinal Wiseman, first Cardinal Archbishop of Westminster.

the circumstances, were the Rector to be removed for any cause, including death or sickness, then if there were no Vice-Rector there would be a danger of the College falling into Italian hands, since the Cardinal Protector would know of no English priest to appoint. The future Rector has to have some experience of 'learning how to manage property according to the peculiarities of Roman law' or else 'a pretext would be given for placing Italian counsellors to direct him. Hence it is important to have the future Rector as vice for a time in order that he may acquire this kind of knowledge'. For the post of Vice-Rector he suggested Louis English, who was one of the senior students at the College.

Despite a difficult winter, the spring of 1850 brought better days. The Pope returned to the city in April and so did the General of the Jesuits. Student numbers were expected to be back at the maximum figure of twenty and Grant's own father was able to visit his son in Rome. The hierarchy was re-established in England and Wales, Wiseman was created Cardinal and the following year Grant, as a reward for his labours and endurance, became the first Bishop of Southwark. Wiseman considered Southwark, the south bank of the river, to be a hotbed of Anglo-Gallican sentiment. Grant, with his Roman experience, his organising abilities and knowledge of canon law, would be a valuable asset to the bench of bishops. Although his later history does not belong to these pages, we must record that he returned to Rome in 1869 for the Vatican Council. He was already a sick man and was taken ill in the Council chamber. He died in the College in Rome and was visited on his deathbed by Pius IX in person.

Notes

1 For Wiseman's connection with Seville see B. Linares and B. Trevett, 'Wiseman and Seville', *Venerabile*, XIV, 264–73, 354–61.
2 Nicolas Cardinal Wiseman, *Recollections of the Last Four Popes*, Chapter VI, Leo XII.
3 ECA, scr. 75.11.1, Letter dated 13 April 1819. Printed in *Venerabile*, IV, 154.
4 As B. Fothergill notes (*Nicholas Wiseman*, London 1963, p. 240), this is the great difference between Wiseman and Manning. Manning's version of the Roman spirit was not tempered by an appreciation of the old tradition of English Catholic piety perilously guarded in penal times and hallowed by the blood of martyrs.
5 We are told that with Spaniards and Latins Wiseman lost the stiffness and shyness he had with Englishmen especially the 'old' Catholics. See W. Ward, *The Life and Times of Cardinal Wiseman*, II, p. 175.

6 W. Ward, *The Life and Times of Cardinal Wiseman*, I, p. 29.

7 Cardinal Mezzofanti (1774–1849) learnt Latin, Greek, Spanish and Swedish as a boy. In the seminary he added to these Hebrew, Arabic and a number of other eastern languages. He taught Arabic, Hebrew and Greek at Bologna and in later life learnt Chinese. He was reputed to speak forty languages well and to have a fair knowledge of another thirty.

8 W. Ward, *The Life and Times of Cardinal Wiseman*, I, p. 78.

9 A. J. Reinerman, 'Papacy and Papal State in the Restoration (1814–1846)', *Catholic Historical Review*, LXIV (1978), 36–46.

10 Wiseman's recollections of these days brought a counterblast: *My Recollections of the Last Four Popes and of Rome in their Times. An Answer to Dr. Wiseman*, Alessandro Gavazzi (London 1858). Gavazzi was an ex-priest and although his work lacks the urbanity of Wiseman and is at times crudely polemical, it at least shows that there was another interpretation.

11 Among his friends can be numbered St Vincent Pallotti, who probably acted as spiritual director at the English College for a time. C. Johnson, 'St Vincent Pallotti and the College', *Venerabile*, XXII, 168–71.

12 Gasquet, *History*, pp. 254–5.

13 Leeds Diocesan Archives, Briggs Correspondence 723, Grant to Briggs, 8 May 1840.

14 W. Ward in *The Life and Times of Cardinal Wiseman*, I, p. 232, tells of the remark made to Wiseman by a priest whom he met in Paris, 'Président d'un college à Rome? Et voyageant partout, loin de vos élèves. Mon fils, je tremble pour vous.' For Wiseman's absences from the College and the remarks they occasioned in Rome see B. Ward, *Sequel to Catholic Emancipation*, I, pp. 13–14.

15 See D. Matthew, *Acton*, p. 35. Wiseman also boasted that St Mary's College, Oscott 'is the best in Europe and the whole world', Leeds Diocesan Archives, Briggs Correspondence, 817, Hogarth to Briggs.

16 George Spencer, youngest son of the second Earl Spencer of Althorp, after six years ministry in the Church of England, became a Catholic, greatly influenced by Ambrose Philips de Lisle. When he came to the English College in Rome he was some years older than Wiseman and after a course of two years' study under Wiseman and Errington, he was ordained and went to England to work in the Birmingham diocese. When he was Rector at Oscott Wiseman obtained his services as spiritual director. Some years later, in 1845, Spencer became a Passionist and took the name Fr Ignatius of St Paul. He associated with Dominic Barberi. His cause has been introduced. See Urban Young, *Life of Fr. Ignatius Spencer C.P.* (London 1933); Fr. Pius a Spiritu Sancto, *Life of Fr. Ignatius of St. Paul* (Dublin 1866). See also Anna Maria Reynolds, 'Loss and Gain: A Tale of 2 Converts', *Clergy Review*, August 1977, vol. 62, 308–17; J. Vanden Bussche CP, 'The Hon and Revd George Spencer at the English College Rome. His Correspondence (1830–32)', *The Downside Review*, no. 412 (2000), 173–98.

17 Nicholas Cardinal Wiseman, *Recollections of the Last Four Popes*, Gregory XVI, Chapter III; also *Il Tempo del Papa Re. Diario del Principe Don Agostino Chigi 1800–55* (Edizioni del Borghese Milano, 1966).

18 Leeds Diocesan Archives, Briggs Correspondence, 166, 175, 188.

19 Ibid., 222.

20 B. Ward, *The Sequel to Catholic Emancipation*, I pp. 135–51; W. Ward, *The Life and Times of Cardinal Wiseman*, II, p. 55. J. D. Holmes, *More Roman than Rome* (London 1978) notes (p. 85) that in 1843 Wiseman had opposed a movement in favour of the restoration of the hierarchy organised by Daniel Rock (who had been a classmate of his at Rome).

21 Pope Gregory XVI, himself a regular, considered the religious orders to be more loyal to the Holy See than the seculars. R. J. Schiefen, 'Anglo-Gallicanism in Nineteenth Century England', *Catholic Historical Review*, LXIII, January 1977, 14–44. For Wiseman's association with St Vincent Pallotti, see Clyde Johnson, 'St Vincent Pallotti and the College', *Venerabile*, XXII, 168–71.

22 B. Fothergill, *Nicholas Wiseman*, p. 90; see also Acta of Hierarchy meetings, Westminster Archives.

23 Leeds Diocesan Archives, Briggs Correspondence, 495.

24 ECA, liber 822, G. Johnson's Diary.

25 From 1830 Wiseman was a member of the Accademia di Religione Cattolica, as was Alexander Grant, Rector of the Scots College as well as Bishops Gradwell and Poynter. A. Piolanti, *L'Accademia di Religione Cattolica* (Rome 1977).

26 Nicholas Cardinal Wiseman, *Recollections of the Last Four Popes*, Pius VII, Chapter 2.

27 *Letters and Diaries of John Henry Newman*, ed. C. S. Dessain, vol. XII.

28 This Grant was not Thomas, the Rector of the English College, but his namesake, Alexander, who was Rector of the Scots College.

29 *Letters and Diaries of John Henry Newman*, ed. C. S. Dessain, vol. XII, pp. 41–2.

30 W. Ward, *The Life and Times of Cardinal Wiseman*, I, p. 29.

31 Leeds Diocesan Archives, Briggs Correspondence 647, letter from Fransoni to Briggs, 29 January 1840.

32 Leeds Diocesan Archives, Briggs Correspondence, 648, unsigned letter in Latin.

33 Baggs was bishop for only two years; he died prematurely in 1845. A. Burton, 'College Rectors II, Charles Michael Baggs', *Venerabile*, IV, 112–16. M. E. Williams, 'Baggs', in *Oxford Dictionary of National Biography*, 2004.

34 Leeds Diocesan Archives, Briggs Correspondence, 813, 1029.

35 English wished to change the system, but Wiseman did not accept these proposals. J. Campbell, 'College Rectors VI, Louis English', *Venerabile*, V, 29.

36 To be found among the Briggs papers in the Leeds Diocesan Archives.

37 In his notes on the practical consequences of the restoration of the hierarchy in 1851, Grant stresses the importance of a Roman education for canonists. For Grant see M. Clifton, *The Quiet Negotiator* (1992).

38 Leeds Diocesan Archives, Briggs Correspondence, 1339.

39 Ibid., 1451, 1458, 1461, 1468.

40 Ibid., 1474.

41 Ibid., 1475.

42 It is not clear to what incident this refers.

43 E. S. Purcell, *Life of Cardinal Manning, Archbishop of Westminster,* II, p. 307.

44 'The English College and the Restoration of the Hierarchy', *Venerabile,* XV, 40–5.

45 Some years later, in 1856, the line from Rome to Frascati was inaugurated. The Pope, accompanied by Cardinals Antonelli, Altieri, Canziani and Roberti travelled in the first train, which was composed of three coaches, a *camera, salotto,* and *capella.* The journey only lasted a little over half an hour! For those interested, Pius IX's train can be seen in the Museo di Roma (Palazzo Braschi).

46 Leeds Diocesan Archives, Briggs Correspondence, 1796.

47 Under revolutionary pressure, it was the papal government that ordered the Jesuits out of the Roman College several months before the Pope left Rome. The seminary (Apollinare) moved in and their students made use of the church of S. Ignazio. The Gesù was taken over by the German College, upon the departure of the Jesuits.

48 ECA, scr. 78, 2.

49 During a short period English College students were forced to wear lay clothes to protect themselves from possible assault, *Venerabile,* XX, 43.

Chapter Six

Mid-Century Problems of Ecclesiastical Training

The problems that were to confront the English College in the mid-nineteenth century were clearly related to Catholic life in England, following the Oxford Movement and the restoration of the hierarchy. The Oxford Movement resulted in an influx of a new style of candidate for the priesthood, for which special provision had to be made, and the establishment of the hierarchy meant that, for the first time in the College's history, there were bishops in ordinary, and it was to be seen whether this would effect any changes in the position of the Cardinal Protector.

For some years now the Protector of the English College had been someone with British connections: Weld, Giustiniani (he had Scottish blood on his mother's side) and Acton. Their links with England had not necessarily meant that they were more favourable to the vicars apostolic than Italians would have been – Acton in fact had opposed the restoration of the hierarchy – but at least the fear of an Italian take-over of the College was somewhat allayed and Rome herself could feel that there was someone in the city who could express the English point of view. But Mgr George Talbot was to prove far more influential than any of the English cardinals in Curia. Talbot was a member of the Wiseman circle, being a friend of Edmund Stonor[1] and a school-fellow of Edward Howard at Oscott when Wiseman was Rector. Rather reluctantly he consented to leave parish work in Southwark and go to Rome in 1850 as Wiseman's representative. However, he quickly achieved a position of influence in Rome, much of it due to the personal friendship he developed with Pope Pius IX. It is not at all clear why Wiseman thought it necessary to have his own representative in

Rome when he was then but vicar apostolic of the London District. It is not very likely that he was going back on his principles that the Rector of the English College should also be agent of the bishops, since at this period he had every confidence in Grant. Perhaps he felt the need for a personal friend to be stationed in Rome. What is clear, however, is that from the College's point of view the arrival of Talbot in July 1850 marked the beginning of a new chapter in its affairs. When he arrived, Cardinal Ferretti, a cousin of Pius IX, was Protector, but from this date Talbot had more and more to do with College matters, long before he became the official Pro-Protector Delegatus in August 1860.

Cornthwaite becomes Rector

Grant had never been given a Vice-Rector as he had requested, and so when he left Rome in 1851 to take up his duties as Bishop of Southwark, he had little choice but to leave in charge for the *villeggiatura* the senior student, Louis English, who was already ordained and pursuing further studies. When Robert Cornthwaite, the new Rector, arrived, he immediately appointed English Vice-Rector. It is not clear why Cornthwaite was nominated to succeed Grant, but, judging from his early correspondence with the president of Ushaw, it was not entirely unconnected with the efforts being made to raise Ushaw to the rank of a pontifical college. Cornthwaite supported these claims.[2]

Cornthwaite's rectorship is remarkable for two things: the provision of new facilities for the training of converts for the priesthood and the re-establishment of the link between the English College and the Jesuits of the Roman College. Let us consider the matter of studies first.[3]

When the Jesuit order was re-established in Rome, after the suppression, it resumed control of the Roman College. The English College continued to frequent the lectures at the Roman Seminary, run by the seculars, which was now known as the Apollinare. Twenty-four years later, in 1848, the Jesuits were once more expelled from the Roman College and the studies were entrusted again to the seculars of the seminary. As we have seen in our account of Grant's rectorship, the English College withdrew its students for a time from all public lectures, but in 1850, when the Jesuits returned, the English continued with lectures at the Apollinare. This meant that since 1773 there had been no contact with Jesuit theology and so the College was not yet directly influenced by the revival that had begun in the 1840s and was the work of such men as Perrone, Passaglia, Taparelli and Liberatore. On 31 August 1854 Cornthwaite wrote to Briggs:[4]

> The schools of the Roman Seminary which they now attend have had most excellent professors as all who remember Professor Graziosi[5] and the late Cardinal Fornari in their prime can testify. Now, however, and for some time past, I have felt very serious dissatisfaction with the state of all the schools there, except one. On the other hand, the Jesuit schools at the Roman College are at the present moment probably the best in Europe.

He goes on to say that the English students would benefit from the higher standards and that the only real objection that occurs is 'the fear that it may be injurious to expose students for the secular clergy to the influence of religious'. But after pointing out that a change to the Roman College would mean that the Jesuits were simply professors and not superiors, Cornthwaite adds: 'I may add, as a proof that I am alive to the danger of the students becoming discontented with the state to which they are bound by oath, that I have myself substituted a secular for a regular confessor for the College.' Thus, even in the middle of the nineteenth century the secular fear of the regulars, and of the Jesuits in particular, still persisted. Grant, in his letters to Briggs, had admitted to being afraid that the College would be taken over by the Jesuits at the time of Wiseman and Baggs. Now we have his successor considering it necessary to clear himself of any pro-Jesuit sympathies by making changes in the spiritual direction of the students. Perhaps it should be mentioned that John Morris was Vice-Rector of the English College at this time and it may be that he had an influence on Cornthwaite in re-establishing the links with the Society.[6] At any rate, later in life, after being secretary to Manning, Morris himself joined the Jesuits.

Collegio Pio

We must now turn to the question of a training for the priesthood more suited to those who offered themselves later in life. The age of the students admitted to the English College had increased over the past few years. All were over twenty and most were over twenty-five years old. The new influx of converts to the English Catholic community, many of them Protestant clergy wishing to continue as ministers but now in union with Rome, led to much discussion as to what was the most suitable training. Wiseman considered Rome as the ideal setting. Mgr Talbot, himself a convert, put forward a scheme for setting up a special college for older converts and also for those more mature Catholics who, as part of the religious movement of the 1840s and 1850s, had given up professional prosperity in order to offer themselves as candidates for the priesthood. Grant had indeed already raised this matter in a letter to Briggs[7] in 1849. Wiseman looked upon this favourably as it would be a way of 'Romanising' the converts. However, the age and experience of these men called for a different sort of training and discipline from that provided in the normal seminary, and there were particular difficulties in Rome, as students there were expected to go about in camerata, which in practice meant in groups of no less than six. This would be especially irksome to older men. Talbot attracted the interest and help of Pius IX, and property in the Piazza Scozzacavalli in the Borgo, within sight of St Peter's, was obtained. It was indeed historic ground for Englishmen, not only because of its association with the Schola Saxonum, originally in this locality, but also because it was reputed that the property had been at least partly built with English money by Sir Thomas Dereham, the Jacobite exile whose tomb is in the church of the English College. In 1852 the Collegio Ecclesiastico began its existence[8] with an Italian as its first Rector, but it was Talbot who presented the first six students of the new college to the Holy Father in a private audience. In February 1853 Dr Louis English, Vice-Rector of the English College, was made Rector of the new Collegio Ecclesiastico, which soon became known as the Collegio Pio, as a tribute to the Pope who had ratified the foundation. Despite the apparent need for such an institution and the official blessings it received, there were problems. How was it to be supported financially, and what were the implications of now having two English colleges in Rome? An appeal to English Catholics for funds was launched in early 1854, but it was not long before it was decided that it would be of mutual advantage if the Collegio Pio were to move and take up residence in an unused part of the English College. Cornthwaite arranged for old rooms to be refurbished and new ones built on the terrace overlooking the College garden. The Collegio Pio was to have its own corridor, staircase and common room, but it was to share the chapel, library and refectory with the English College. Wiseman, who had been in favour of the original venture, was against the union of the two colleges under one roof that was decreed on 29 March 1855.[9] It was not so much the physical sharing of one building that was objectionable; it was the constitution whereby the English College only catered for those under the age of twenty-four. The Pio not only accepted older students but anyone reaching the age of twenty-four during his course was expected to transfer to the Pio, with its less demanding discipline. Moreover, Cornthwaite was made the one Rector of the two colleges, but he was not allowed to interfere in any way with the direction of the Pio, which was the concern of Louis English.

The scheme did not work at all. To the problems of administering a college in the conditions of financial and political instability of Rome in the 1850s, Cornthwaite now had the extra complication of being in overall charge of two establishments but with no effective governing power in one of them. The English College found it difficult enough to provide for its own students, but it was now expected to furnish accommodation and subsidise the new institution. In addition there was something of a personality clash between English and Cornthwaite. As we have seen, English had been in effective charge of the English College before Cornthwaite arrived. He was then Vice-Rector and after that Rector of a new and independent college. In this latter capacity English had had close dealings with Talbot, whose brainchild the Pio was, and who, in the early days, dealt directly with that College's affairs, there being no Cardinal Protector. There had grown up a friendship with English which lasted many years and spread to other members of his family. His elder brother Ferdinand, who had been Vice-Rector of the English College for a period under Grant, became agent in England for Pio affairs and was later to become Bishop of Port of Spain, Trinidad, in the West Indies.[10] When Louis English died, Talbot kept in touch with his sister Isabella, who inherited her brother's belongings, and he obtained for her the honour of Papal Countess. Talbot's genuine kindness to the English family must be recorded, but it did not help Cornthwaite much.

Things came to a head in 1857. Cornthwaite and English exchanged aggrieved letters in March; they were evidently not on speaking terms. Then Cornthwaite left for a holiday in England and it was not expected that he would return. He formally resigned his post in early summer 1857, giving as his reasons to Briggs[11] financial worries and the whole idea of the union of the two colleges. Four years later he became Bishop of Beverley.[12]

During Cornthwaite's absence English kept Talbot informed of the state of the English College. The Vice-Rector, Dr Banns, was ill and at Monte Porzio, so in effect the College was without any government. English's position made him hesitant to intervene in the affairs of another college. Of course, the proper person who ought to be referred to was the Cardinal Protector. But Ferretti was of little help; he was timid and afraid of offending the bishops and he excused himself on the grounds of being too busy about more important matters. This meant in effect that it all depended on Talbot.

From a reading of the correspondence to Talbot from such men as Wiseman, English and Morris, who all had the interests of the College at heart, I think it is clear that rather than interfering in College affairs Talbot was trying to do his best to help by taking decisions when Ferretti's policy was to let things be. That Talbot rather enjoyed his position, with his friends in the Curia and his easy access to the Pope, cannot be doubted. But that could be an argument in his favour. He did get things done and had it not been for Talbot and English the College might have had Italian superiors again or have been closed altogether for lack of suitable superiors. One needs to bear this in mind even in the late part of the story and the Neve rectorship.[13]

Cornthwaite's regime was not a happy one. From his letters he appears as a somewhat rigid and unsympathetic figure. His later dealings with the College, his ready acceptance of Neve as Rector and equally ready acceptance of his dismissal, indicate that he was a man prepared to accept decisions that had been made by others. He was worn down by the responsibility of being in charge of two establishments, a task which would indeed have been daunting for anyone.

Problems of administration and finance affect students very little. Even political events in a foreign country can be ignored by the insular exile. Writing many years later one such remarked:

> Red-shirted Garibaldians might fill open places with riotous rows, chauvinists might send cannon and grape shot through the very walls, but English College men without a flicker of an eyelid continued with their Avancinus, and sanctified with *spaghetti al burro* the Fridays and lean days of the Church.[14]

Fortunately not everybody was as insensitive as that, and G. Johnson in his diary[15] not only records internal College affairs but sometimes tells of the riots, the bomb attempts and the anti-clerical demonstrations, including the public execution by guillotine of criminals and revolutionaries.

> 25 January 1854. The three men were all executed, blaspheming God and cursing the priests all the way to execution. The drums beat to drown their voices, all died impenitent and the last man danced on

the scaffold. The executions took place near the Bocca della Verita near the gasworks. The holes are still left in the middle of the road where the scaffold was erected. Paid a visit to the church in which prayers are always offered for the condemned before executions.

We must remember that the Rome of the year when the Immaculate Conception was defined and the restored Basilica of St Paul outside the walls was solemnly consecrated was also the Rome that lived in fear of revolution. But the Italian public did not find their drama only on the streets. The 1850s also saw the first performances of Verdi's *Rigoletto, La Traviata* and *Il Trovatore*.

Louis English as Rector

Writing to Talbot, while Cornthwaite was in England, English said of the Rector, 'I hope indeed that he has done with the College, although truly I dread the increase in responsibility; still anything is more bearable than such dire mis-management and all the evils in every direction of which the poor good man is the innocent parent.' English's candidature for the rectorship was very strong. He was already in Rome, he had had plenty of experience, he was friendly with Talbot and in his capacity of administrator of the Pio he had had dealings with many of the bishops. Moreover, as he said in a letter of 8 July 1857 to Talbot, 'I look on Dr Manning as our best and most powerful friend.'[16] But, of all the bishops, it was Wiseman who was most hesitant about English's suitability. This was on grounds of his health. At this time Wiseman himself was not at all well and he probably appreciated the strains that responsibility could place on a person's constitution. But there may have been other reasons. However frail English's body may have been, he had a mind of his own and his plans to reform the administration of the College soon brought him into conflict with Wiseman. One of the reasons why past Rectors had been unable to give undivided attention to College affairs was because they were burdened with agency work for the bishops. Grant had complained about this and for a time Ullathorne had resided in Rome to negotiate the restoration of the hierarchy. English now proposed that some other person should become the bishops' agent. This brought an immediate response from Wiseman, who argued that if English were no longer bishops' agent, then all correspondence would cease between the bishops and the Rector, except for purely College matters.[17] Thus the Rector would be in ignorance of the relationship between the

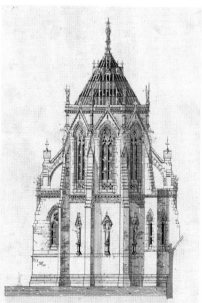

Fig. 6.1 Design by E.W. Pugin for the proposed new College chapel, side and east end elevations.

bishops and Propaganda Fide and so would know little of the problems of England, as seen from the official Roman point of view. There would be a return to the situation obtaining in the previous century, when the bishop dealt with an agent who had nothing to do with the College.[18] This, according to Wiseman, had resulted in a decline in the number of students sent by the bishops. Moreover, should such a custom be restored, then the agent would have to have his own private means or seek some ecclesiastical provision for his support. He would also have to be someone who could keep the confidences of the bishops. In Wiseman's mind, the confidence of the bishops in the English College was bound up with this added function of the Rector. The bishops would send students to Rome if the Rector looked after their diocesan interests. So he was adamant against any change to a system that had begun under Pius VII and Consalvi, in spite of powerful opposition in Rome. 'For I have the minute history of the efforts made to keep Dr. Gradwell out of the rectorship and to disjoin the offices ... The arrangement has not worked at all ill for every Rector has been found worthy of the episcopate.' It is difficult to follow Wiseman's argument. Gradwell came to Rome originally as agent. There was no problem here since this was exclusively a matter for the vicars apostolic and the agent held no official position. But the rectorship was not within the competence of the bishops to bestow; it belonged to the Protector. As things worked out Gradwell and his successors did combine the two offices and it did result in a supply of students to the College from those bishops who had confidence in the Rector. But if there had been a distinct agent, what was to prevent the bishops, if they wished to support the College, from opening up a correspondence with the Rector – their own convenience or laziness? In any case the bishops did not have all that much freedom; even if they did send students, the final nomination came from the Protector, a practice which in fact English did wish to change but Wiseman refused.[19]

The result of all this was that English had to keep on the agency[20] and his health grew worse. He was an efficient Rector. He reaped the benefits of Cornthwaite's move of the studies to the Roman College, and his 'hunger for medals' led to the accusation that he let students endanger their health by excessive study. His demands for only the best students met with a reply from Wiseman that Rectors have often had to face: 'You urge: send us your very best men, and they will be returned to you first rate scholars, professors etc. I send them and they never return. What better is my College for anything sent there. On the contrary they are a loss.'[21]

English had great plans for expansion and development. He

firmly believed in the principle that the College should educate students at its own expense and not be a financial burden on the bishops. He spoke of the need for money so that an even greater number of priests could be provided for England, free of charge. The College at this time had only room for twenty-three students and he planned to adapt and take over rooms that were at the moment let out to lodgers. He estimated £1,000 as being sufficient to make up for the loss of rent such a conversion would involve, and a further £500 to £1,000 for the necessary alterations. Moreover, he did succeed in raising money whereby ten more students were able to be received on the funds of the College. This expansion has to be placed in the context of Rome in the 1860s. It was not merely Wiseman's view that a Roman education was beneficial to Englishmen; this was a time when the papacy was encouraging the foundation of other national seminaries in Rome as part of Pius IX's policy of centralisation. The Pope had, at great expense, founded and endowed a seminary for 60 or 70 students from the Papal States. The French College, the North American and South American Colleges, as well as the Lombard College, were all part of this movement, as indeed was the Collegio Pio. Dr English's expansionist ideas were in perfect keeping with the Rome of his day.

Unfortunately his health deteriorated. He was compelled to spend several months a year in England and during these absences the College was governed by Talbot, now Pro-Protector Delegatus. Wiseman was worried about the succession and mentioned to Talbot that the choice of the next Rector would be a very important decision. While on holiday at Torquay, English took a turn for the worse and he wrote, a dying man, to Talbot thanking him for his great kindness and support during his life and added: 'A word about the succession to the rectorship to you, the Protector of the College. Resist the overwhelming influence of Cardinal Wiseman; at least let the bishops give the Holy See a chance.'[22]

The appointment of Frederick Neve[23]

On the death of the Rector, while on holiday in England, 18 July 1863, College affairs were managed by Edmund Stonor, acting on behalf of Talbot. The rectorship of English had been somewhat unsatisfactory to Wiseman and some of the bishops. They had felt that they had not been given sufficient say in his promotion from the Collegio Pio to the rectorship of the Venerabile. They did not approve of his attempt to separate the rectorship from the agency. Great care was taken in submitting the *terna* of names to the Pope. Crookall, professor of philosophy and Vice-Rector at St Edmund's, Ware, headed the list. However, Drinkwater, English's Vice-Rector, did not think Crookall suitable and in a letter to Talbot he remarked: 'Dr. Crookall would hand the College over to the Branchinis with great ease and delight.'[24] The second name on the *terna* was Bamber, a canon of Southwark, and the third the vicar general of Clifton, Frederick Neve. The appointment of Neve was a courageous one and marked a new departure. Since Gradwell, the Rector had been a young man usually in his thirties. Neve was 57. Moreover, he was one of the converts of 1845 and so brought another point of view to the College and to Rome. He had been a student at the College, but his association was of the briefest. Ten years older than his Rector, Grant, and already having had pastoral experience as an Anglican, he was ordained after a course of only two years. This meant that he was 'not particularly skilled in scholastic Latin' and his knowledge of Italian was negligible. But to make up for these disadvantages he brought to the rectorship considerable missionary experience and a knowledge of English literature, and was considered to be 'a man of sound common sense, a holy man and possessed of a thoroughly ecclesiastical spirit'.[25] Moreover he had never had any difficulties with Wiseman or the other bishops.

The first years of his rule were very successful. The number of students increased from 24 to 44, though much of this was no doubt due to the efforts of the previous Rector. Foreigners were admitted to the Collegio Pio.[26] The Pope paid a personal visit to the College at Monte Porzio.

Talbot and the rebuilding of the church

Talbot now began another scheme. This was to rebuild the church, which had fallen into disrepair since the time of the French occupation.[27] He proposed to make the Church of St Thomas of Canterbury both a chapel for the College and the English national church in Rome. To this end an appeal was launched. The plan has several interesting features, which throw light on some of the currents in English Catholic life at this time. Originally the design for the building was a neo-gothic edifice by Edward Welby Pugin, but this was discarded for the more 'Roman' design of Vespignani, on the lines of a minor basilica with plenty of marble and gold. But the Roman theme is to be seen at a deeper level, in the actual appeal itself, where Talbot suggested among the motives for contributing, loyalty to Rome and the Holy See. On a visit to Rome in 1863, Manning preached a sermon at S. Carlo in which he extolled St Thomas as a martyr for the ecclesiastical immunities. His contemporary significance was to be found in the need to harden resistance to Gallicanism, Josephism, Leopoldism, Anglicanism and other manifestations of the national spirit. Not surprisingly, in Wiseman's hands the appeal took on a European dimension, and he suggested to Talbot that the appeal should be extended to France and Germany. Wiseman saw contribution to the new church as a gesture of defiance to the revolutionary spirit, an act of reparation for the damage done by the French revolution to the old Church and a reminder of the welcome extended by England to the French emigré clergy.[28] The ultramontane nature of the undertaking was further underlined by the fact that it was Pope Pius IX, in person, who came to lay the foundation stone in 1866, and from this date all the published subscription lists were headed by the Pope's donation of £100.[29] Writing later to O'Callaghan, Talbot expressed his hopes for the effect that such a building would have on the students: 'It is impossible to put the Roman spirit into the students without a church in which they can have their Quarant'ore, their altar of the Blessed Virgin and St Joseph, and other Roman devotions.'[30] As we shall see later, the demands on English Catholics for enterprises nearer home meant that funds did not come in as rapidly as had been hoped and for a time work was suspended on the rebuilding.

The Roman Association

At this time too, there was founded in England the Association of the Venerable College of St Thomas *de urbe* (The Roman Association). This was set up to foster a love for Alma Mater; to keep up old College friendships; to assist the bishops in carrying out the oft-expressed desire of the Holy Father, namely to send to the College of St Thomas in Rome such students from the colleges in England as shall be fully competent to avail themselves of the great advantages offered by the theological school in the Eternal City. Although there is no indication that Neve had any part in its establishment, such a spirit among past alumni would be of great encouragement to the Rector.

Neve, Manning and Talbot

When Wiseman died in 1865, Neve's position suddenly became insecure. Several issues seem to have been involved which had lain dormant as long as Wiseman lived, but with the accession of Manning to Westminster they now came to the fore. Neve was not finding the support he needed from Drinkwater, the Vice-Rector he had inherited from English. So, taking advantage of Drinkwater's frequent absences in England appealing for the church fund, Neve had him replaced by Giles,[31] who moved over from being Vice-Rector of the Pio to Vice-Rector of the Venerabile.

There was also Neve's own position in the events of 1865–7 concerning Newman. In 1864 or early 1865 Neve had informed Clifford that Newman was very unpopular in Rome. The Jesuits thought him too liberal, Stonor was against him, and Talbot had objections to the *Apologia*.[32] In December 1866, Neve wrote to Ullathorne telling of the attempt to denounce Newman's sermon on the Pope and the Revolution, which was preached in response to a pastoral of Ullathorne on the trials of Pius IX. Neve was anxious that what Newman had actually said should be available on the continent and in translation in Rome. Neve indicated that the 'prejudice against Newman is strong and disgraceful. It all comes from England. To save themselves trouble Propaganda take the word of a few people only, and enquire no further'. When Ambrose St John came to Rome on Newman's behalf, although he did not stay at the College, Neve helped him in his defence of Newman.[33]

In addition to this, Manning, the new Cardinal Archbishop of Westminster, had his own ideas on the education and training of the clergy, and the English College was included in his schemes. He found great faults with the administration and discipline. This was not so much an objection to Neve, but to what he called the 'whole bad tradition'. There was some justice in this remark,[34] since the College had been governed with a fairly loose rein under Wiseman. English had complained about Cornthwaite, and English himself seems to have realised that part of the trouble was that the Rector was engaged in so much agency work outside the College walls that the internal discipline tended to be neglected. Manning's criticism of the English College was that 'the Rector was too weak to resist the tradition of liberty and laxity. The mixture of men from so many colleges will always make for confusion, till a strong discipline is introduced ... we have a false notion that Englishmen must be treated *altogether* differently. Somewhat perhaps, but *in the main* the same discipline ought to be imposed'.[35]

Fig. 6.2 The College church under construction in 1869. Surveying the work are Henry O' Callaghan, Rector 1867–88, and George Talbot, Pro-Protector Delegatus of the College.

There was nothing new in such criticisms; in fact they bear a striking similarity to those used by the Italian seculars in the late eighteenth century, as a reply to the complaints from the students and vicars apostolic about the harshness of their regime. Even before that, the most common complaint against the English Jesuit fathers was that they were too lax. Not that Manning would have been in favour of non-English superiors, but the complaints he was voicing would at least be understandable to the Roman authorities. John Morris, Cornthwaite's old Vice-Rector and now secretary to

Manning, was also interested in the state of the College. He wrote to Talbot and said that English College men were not making sufficient impact on England. This was because the best men were not looking to Rome 'for the men to fill their chief professorships'. Some months later when O'Callaghan was finally installed as Rector, Manning pursued this line and said that the Venerabile ought to produce professors, vicars general and bishops and not mere missioners. It is now that there becomes more explicitly articulated the idea, derived from Wiseman, that the value of the College in Rome is to train men in the Roman spirit, so that they may control the administration and education of the clergy. In practice, Wiseman had made use of 'Romans' in this way often because he knew them personally. Now it was being advocated as policy. It was no mere chance that this development began to take place in the late 1860s, the last days of Papal Rome. It was to continue for many years and this idea of Manning becomes reincarnate in the twentieth century with the rectorship, delegacy and cardinalate of William Godfrey.

The desire which Morris expresses, to cream off the best students and send them to Rome, had serious implications. It threatened possible conflict with the colleges at home. 'It would be necessary to make students desire to go to Rome in spite of the wish of their own college in England to keep them' and he goes on, 'Could not this be done by keeping them in Rome for some years, say three, after their ordination. The secular clergy suffers badly by the shortness of its course.' When one recalls the past history of the College, one sees that a new departure is being suggested here. The missionary oath was often interpreted not merely as returning to work in England as a secular priest, but also 'potius hodie quam cras' (today rather than tomorrow). Post-ordination studies were rather the exception than the rule and the lure of academic success was regarded as a risk that could divert a person from the role of missioner. When the Jesuits were in charge there was a clear choice: home to the mission or stay on in Rome and join the Society. But in recent years the possibility of a career beginning in Rome was greater. Grant had been a case in point. He secured permission from Briggs to stay on as Acton's secretary and in the event this proved a suitable training for his future work in England as a bishop. The idea of staying on after ordination would, if put into practice, have to be undertaken with the consent of the bishop and also financed from the College funds, since at this time the majority of students were still alumni.

On one point at least Manning's criticism of the College was

Fig. 6.3 John Henry Cardinal Newman.

sound. He desired a system independent of personalities that would allow the Rector time to devote to agency work. In his appreciation of the importance of a constitution and rules, he was no doubt thinking of the Tridentine seminary system, which he was trying to introduce into England at this time. But the English College had never been a diocesan seminary and what he might achieve at home, in his own diocese, would not be feasible in the national college in Rome. So his thought went to a religious order. He considered the Sulpicians. Talbot suggested the Jesuits, but Manning knew the past history of the College. 'I have a great penchant for the body you name. They have been in Rome my friends, teachers, directors. But I should see with anxiety for the secular clergy in England the change we speak of. The reaction upon us here would be unfavourable and would weaken not strengthen us.'[36] In the same letter he remarked 'Moreover, what is wanted is three good rulers like O'Callaghan' – O'Callaghan was the superior of S. Chiara, the Roman house of the Oblates of St Charles – and he continued, 'If there were a system like the discipline of S. Chiara introduced, the Rector, even a common man, would be able to work it.' Talbot took this as a hint and began to work to have O'Callaghan installed. The bishops visited Rome for the eighteenth centenary of the martyrdom of St Peter in 1867 and it was only after they had returned to England that Talbot made his move to force Neve's resignation.[37]

In July 1866 Neve had come up against problems of discipline and felt that Talbot was not supporting him sufficiently. Students appealed to the Protector, as was their right, but it was never quite clear what Talbot's views were, and they spread the story that he agreed with them against the Rector. A lot of the trouble came from those students who, on reaching the age of twenty-four, automatically passed on from the English College to the Pio. The arrangements between the two colleges were proving as unsatisfactory to Neve as they had to Cornthwaite and English. Neve asked for a visitation of the colleges. Talbot refused this request and threatened to resign as Protector if Neve continued to press for a visitation. Neve's correspondence with Talbot the next year, in July 1867, indicates that he was ready to give up the rectorship and suggests that 'it might be better for the College if it were put into other hands than mine'. In a later letter (to Ullathorne), Neve tells us that Talbot regarded him as an unsuitable Rector because 'he was too recently at Eton and Oxford and did not understand Catholic young men'. To this Neve had replied that Talbot himself was 'fresher from both places by many years than I am'. Talbot's

Fig. 6.4 Henry Cardinal Manning.

Fig. 6.5 Early photograph of the completed College church. The benches are arranged for a community smaller than in later years.

threat of resignation was no longer mentioned and as relations between the two had broken down completely, Neve had an audience with the Pope, where he asked leave to resign. But the Pope replied that he would have a talk with Talbot first.

When his resignation was accepted, Neve asked that Mr Smith, the Vice-Rector of the College Pio, should be nominated as pro-rector. The *villeggiatura* was 'a difficult time' and Mr Smith 'a very accurate man who would stick to any rule you gave him'. But on 31 July he wrote, 'The students go out to Monte Porzio tomorrow under the care of Mr. Smith. I had intended to inform them of the changes at dinner tomorrow before we went out, but to my surprise I find that Mgr. Stonor has already related all to them, so that the servants of the house have known it all for several days ... I was at Monte Porzio yesterday, I found him in complete control giving orders to everyone, to me among the rest.' Neve asked Talbot either to inform him officially that Stonor was his superior, as Talbot's *sostituto,* or to request Stonor to leave the house and take up his quarters elsewhere.

So Stonor, Talbot's friend, who ran College affairs after the death

Fig. 6.6–9 Views of the new church, opened in 1888: *top left* – the high altar, without the canopy seen in the earlier photograph (p. 159); *top right* – a view from the tribune; *bottom left* – outer wall alongside the Via Monserrato; *bottom right* – the main entrance door used only for special celebrations.

of English, was once more in charge. By this time it was clear that Talbot intended O'Callaghan to succeed. Yet Neve was expected to continue to fulfil certain duties until O'Callaghan had completed his leave in England and was ready to assume control. On 13 November O'Callaghan arrived at Monte Porzio and two days later Neve moved out into lodgings. After a few months acting as agent for the English bishops (except Cornthwaite, Roskell and Grant) he returned to England in the early summer of 1868. He became Provost of the Clifton Chapter and died in 1886, at the age of 80.

Neve was convinced that he had been dismissed for disagreeing with the Pro-Protector. This was the real cause, not laxity in discipline nor inefficiency in administration. The incident certainly shows the power of Talbot. Other Protectors enjoyed power over the Rector and College affairs but in Talbot's case it seems to have been associated with a personal friendship with the Pope and a shrewd estimate of likely reactions on the part of the English hierarchy.

Talbot deemed it wise to justify his actions publicly. He wrote to Manning on 1 October 1867:[38] 'Some of the English bishops are displeased at the manner in which Fr. O'Callaghan has been nominated Rector of the English College ... I am much grieved if I have offended them, as I never intended to do anything that might give them offence.' He then goes on to give his account of the appointment. This contains complaints about internal discipline under Neve, and Neve's own anxiety to resign, as he was proving incompetent in a task that was far beyond his powers. When the Pope conferred with Talbot and accepted his recommendation to accept Neve's resignation, the conversation then turned to a successor. 'I suggested Fr. O'Callaghan as the only English priest in Rome fit for the post. Instantly, he approved of the choice and I asked him to authorise me to send the *biglietto,* which he accordingly did.' In another letter[39] Talbot stated that a *coup d'état* was absolutely necessary. 'If I had written to your grace asking you to *interpellare* the English bishops about a fit person, they would have recommended some respectable old priest whom they want to get rid of, and if they proposed him it would be difficult to reject him, as was the case with Dr. Neve, of whom Dr. Clifford had become tired. If I had asked you to name one yourself, all the odium would have fallen on your shoulders whereas it has fallen on mine.'

Although it does not excuse Talbot, his actions become a little more understandable if we remember that he himself was under some pressure during this summer. There is little doubt but that he was devoted to the English College and the Pio and for some years the new College church had been the centre of his attentions. But despite the appeals for money, the project was running into financial difficulties and work had been ordered to be stopped. In some distress Talbot had written to Neve. Neve, now no longer in charge, replied: 'I suppose that your threat of resigning means nothing. Now that I have no interest in the matter, I will give my opinion viz. that you should get yourself named a cardinal. It is an injury to the College that you are not one. In property questions and litigation, you want a secretary and a lawyer to study the matter and answer opponents ... if you are serious and will not be made a cardinal, you might recommend Cardinal di Luca. He speaks English and as far as I know is not biassed any way in English ecclesiastical politics.' It would appear that the building of the church had run into difficulties because of compensation to a tenant of a house that had been demolished and this tenant had access to several cardinals and sometimes to the Pope himself.[40]

Talbot was very pleased with the conclusion of the Neve affair and in the autumn he sent glowing reports to Manning of O'Callaghan's progress.[41] As for the reasons why he suggested O'Callaghan as a suitable Rector, he lists these as follows: O'Callaghan had spent eighteen years at St Edmund's College, so he was acquainted with life in a college; he had been successful in ruling the Oblates at S. Nicola in Rome; he had a knowledge of Italian; he was well thought of by the Pope and got on well with the authorities in Rome. He felt above all that he had full confidence in him and that he would be most attentive to the commissions entrusted to him by the bishops.[42]

We shall never know how close O'Callaghan and Talbot really were and whether the alliance would be any more durable than that of Talbot and Neve. Talbot had a breakdown in health and had to leave Rome in 1869, to die in a mental home at Passy, near Paris, on 16 October 1886.

Notes

1 Edmund Stonor, third son of the third Lord Camoys, studied at Oscott and was ordained by Cardinal Wiseman. For two years, 1861–2, he was a student at the Collegio Pio. He spent the rest of his life in Rome, was close to Cardinal Edward Howard and Mgr George Talbot, acted as chaplain to the English Zouaves and was engaged in several diplomatic missions. In 1889 he was made titular Archbishop of Trebizond. He died in Rome in 1912. See H. E. G. Rope, 'Archbishop Stonor: A belated tribute', *Venerabile*, VIII, 320–33.
2 ECA, scr. 77, 8. D. Milburn, *A History of Ushaw College*, especially p. 238.

3 J. Slater, 'The English College and the University', *Venerabile*, V, 4–16; 134–48.

4 Leeds Diocesan Archives, Briggs Correspondence, 1876B.

5 Graziosi was a close friend of Pius IX and one of the leading Thomists of the day.

6 John Morris, a convert, came out to the College in Rome as a student with Frederick Neve in 1846. He was a contemporary of Cornthwaite and after returning to England as a priest came back to Rome to take up the duties of Vice-Rector, when Louis English moved to the Collegio Pio. The author of several books, he was later secretary to Manning and he attended Wiseman in his last illness. J. H. Pollen, *Life and Letters of Fr. John Morris of the Society of Jesus* (London 1898).

7 Leeds Diocesan Archives, Briggs Correspondence, 1804.

8 H. K. A. Mann, *Brief Sketch of the History of the College of the Venerable Bede in Rome* (London 1918). Michael J. McConnon, 'The Pontifical Beda College. A History 1852– 1985', *The Beda Review* 1985, 2–10.

9 Two former English College students, Bishops Goss and Grant seem to have been in favour of the union.

10 This see had been previously offered by Talbot to Errington. J. D. Holmes, *More Roman than Rome*, pp. 92–3.

11 Leeds Diocesan Archives, Briggs Correspondence, 1929.

12 This appointment was much to the satisfaction of G. Talbot who considered him to be 'thoroughly Roman'. F. J. Cwiekowski, *English Bishops and the Vatican Council* (Louvain 1971), pp. 52–3, 58.

13 Writing to Talbot 10 February 1863, Wiseman said, 'I have been glad that you should be pro-protector for this very reason, that the superiors are all national'. ECA, Talbot correspondence.

14 'Porzio in the Fifties', *Venerabile*, III, 270 (article based on Johnson's diary).

15 ECA, liber 821, 822.

16 In the same letter he expressed the wish that some of the men studying at the Pio might in the future become Oblates of St Charles, the association of secular priests presided over by Manning. Talbot was interested in the Oblates too, and ten years later was to be instrumental in securing the appointment of an Oblate as Rector of the English College.

17 For Wiseman's own position in 1823 see above and also Gasquet, *History*, p. 251.

18 *Venerabile*, V, 178.

19 J. Campbell, 'Louis English', *Venerabile*, V, 22–39. T. Curtis Hayward, 'Henry O'Callaghan', *Venerabile*, XVI, 215–31.

20 But Dr Goss did come out to Rome for business connected with the diocesan seminary problem in 1860.

21 ECA, Talbot Correspondence, Wiseman to Talbot, 17 November 1857.

22 ECA, Talbot Correspondence, English to Talbot, 17 July 1863.

23 For Neve see Thomas Duggan, 'Frederick Neve', *Venerabile*, V, 160–72, 274–85, 335–48.

24 For the connection of the Branchini family with the College see *supra*, p. 114, note 11.

25 ECA, Talbot Correspondence, Clifford to Talbot, 26 August 1863.

26 This was used as an argument against Neve later. Talbot is reported to have said that under Neve the College attracted more Italians than converts, who consequently went sightseeing or became Jesuits. See *The English Catholics, 1850–1950*, ed. G. A. Beck, p. 160.

27 A. Laird, 'The College Church', *Venerabile*, XXIV, 28–38; 159–73; 258–68. See also Appendix II.

28 Wiseman was firmly opposed to the revolutionary spirit, whether 1789, 1830 or 1848. In 1848 he visited Louis Philippe and his consort in exile at Claremont. He also visited Louis Napoleon in 1854, see *Venerabile*, XIX, 444–6.

29 See A. Laird, 'The College Church', *Venerabile*, XXIV, for a full account of the appeal.

30 ECA, Talbot Correspondence, quoted by A. Laird, *Venerabile*, XXIV, 165.

31 William Giles was not only Vice-Rector at the Pio but also *ripetitore* at the English College and he was to remain a superior of the College for the next 48 years.

32 For the campaign against Neve, see *Venerabile*, V, 279ff. J. Derek Holmes, 'English Ultramontanism and Clerical Education', *Clergy Review*, vol. 62, July 1977, 266–78.

33 Shortly after Neve's resignation, anxiety was felt lest the charge of anti-Newmanism should be levelled against Talbot and others. Vaughan wrote to Talbot, 30 September 1867, 'It is reported ... that you gave Dr. Neve as your reason for accepting his resignation the fact that he was a Newmanite. Please send me a line by return of post, so that the truth may be put forward. If among other reasons you alleged the above, would it not be well to express a number of the true reasons derived from his inefficiency and in a letter to the bishops. Otherwise such an expression will be used for Newman prejudiciously in some respects. Though it will not fail to let people understand what is thought of him in the Vatican.' ECA, Talbot Correspondence.

34 *Venerabile*, XVI, 218–9 and footnote references.

35 *Venerabile*, V, 283 quoting from Purcell, *Life of Manning*, II, p. 367.

36 Quoted in *Venerabile*, V, 283.

37 For a fuller account see Purcell, *Life of Manning*, II; also *Venerabile* articles in Neve's rectorship, especially *Venerabile*, V, 335–48. J. D. Holmes, 'English Ultramontanism and Clerical Education', *Clergy Review*, July 77, vol. 62, 266–78.

38 Copy of Letter in Leeds Diocesan Archives, Cornthwaite papers.

39 Quoted in *Venerabile*, V, 284.

40 ECA, Talbot Correspondence, Neve to Talbot, 23 September 1867.

41 *Venerabile*, V, 347.

42 Leeds Diocesan Archives, Cornthwaite papers, letter to Manning, 1 October.

As a supplement to this Chapter see V. Alan McClelland, 'O Felix Roma! Henry Manning, Cutts Robinson and Sacerdotal Formation 1862–1872', *RH*, 21 (1992), 180–217.

Chapter Seven

1870 and After

Talbot and Manning wanted the College to be governed with a stricter discipline and according to a constitution, and this wish was soon fulfilled. New rules were laid down by the Apostolic Visitor, Cardinal Reisach, an admirer of Manning and Protector of the College, in concert with Mgr Salvatore Nobili Vitelleschi, his assistant. Included in this decree of 29 September 1869 were regulations for the selection of alumni. The bishops were to nominate those they thought suitable for the Roman course, giving a confidential report to the Rector. The Rector, after due consideration, was to pass the list to the Protector, who made a final choice, and the Rector thereupon informed the bishops of the result. Although this meant that the chosen ones were now admitted to the course, they were not immediately alumni. For six months or so, according to the judgment of the Rector, they were in a state of probation. If at the end they were found to be suitable material, then they made a retreat and the oath of Alexander VII was administered to them.[1] Otherwise they were sent back to England. Alumni were expected to bring with them enough money to cover expenses for their return to England, which they had to deposit with the Rector on arrival. Another stipulation of these 1869 rulings was that they were not allowed to take the doctorate of theology in any Roman university without the permission of the Protector and their own bishop. There were other rulings about the convictors or commoners which made them subject to episcopal choice and examination. But, although they made a promise to observe all the rules of the house, they did not take the oath of Alexander VII.

Many of these regulations were a revival of customs operating in the previous history of the College, but they had been for so long unobserved that some of the bishops considered them new rules and feared that they were taking away some of the powers they themselves had previously enjoyed.[2]

From the students' point of view the new regime meant such things as stage plays being replaced by concerts[3] and the suppression of the Debating Society. There was a certain amount of resentment and, on a visit to Rome, Manning tried to 'settle certain disputes between the Rector and the men'.[4] There were a number of students who left the College and were transferred to other seminaries.[5]

The segregation of the students from outside influences even extended to the bishops staying at the College during the First Vatican Council. 'We can never speak to them; we see them at Benediction and now and again *in transitu*.'[6] Unlike the proceedings of the Second Vatican Council, it would appear that in 1869 an air of secrecy surrounded the discussions, at least as far as the students were concerned. Two students acted as stenographers at the Council. William Barry tells us they 'kept their secret absolutely. Allen for years after the Council would not exhibit his shorthand notes to any mortal though the contents of them were actually in print'. A similar secrecy applied to the university. Barry again says, 'In preparing for the Council, our masters of the Collegio Romano bore no insignificant although not a public, share. The year 1869 was a time of prelude; but we who attended the lectures of these famous professors heard no utterance from their lips to indicate the work they were upon.'

The main concern of the superiors of the College in those days would seem to have been to ensure a regular routine of attendance at lectures, the performance of practices of piety and periods of recreation such as the weekly visit to La Magliana and the *villeggiatura* at Monte Porzio. There was a contracting of horizons, perhaps not unrelated to the enforced, and voluntarily accepted, imprisonment of the Pope in the Vatican. Wilfred Ward, who was a student at the College for a few months in 1877–8, recalls: 'The life inside the College is much like that of any ecclesiastical college, only stricter in this respect, that *nothing* is left to your *option*. You must go out with the rest, sit with the rest at recreation, be in your room at the same time as the others for reading etc.'[7] O'Callaghan's aloofness and distance from the students did not help matters.[8] Barry went so far as to say: 'Neither, again, did the superiors of the English College in my time show the faintest personal interest in us, in our studies, or our future. Beyond a code of teasing regulations, wasted on youths who lived in a strict and almost monastic routine, we had a singular kind of liberty, following upon the perfect neglect which directed none of our reading but abandoned us to the Roman College or our own will.'

Wilfred Ward and William Barry agree as to the inadequacies of the Collegio Romano at this time. Ward remarks, 'We were taught the various philosophical positions as the "right view" and if any of us did not find those positions convincing we were accounted heterodox. Thus philosophy, which professed to prove the rational duty of accepting theism and revelation, was not really enforced by reason but by authority. Those students were best thought of who learnt best by heart.'[9] Barry complained of the way the Collegio Romano took past history for granted and proceeded in a deductive, legalistic manner. It seemed to be concerned with the abstract. Men like Franzelin were 'completely unaffected by any modern influence'. This sort of unworldliness can easily be confused with lack of concern. The professors, like the superiors at the English College, remained strangers. 'These masters of so many thousands of young men held their discipline at a distance, and no attempt outside the schools to shape life or thought, and relinquished to the College authorities what is significantly called discipline. They were not our friends.'[10]

This depressing state of affairs was to continue as far as the Collegio Romano was concerned for very many years, right into the middle of the twentieth century. But although the system changed little, the Rectors of the English College who followed O'Callaghan had more warmth than he did, and life was more tolerable.

The occupation of Rome: 1870

However, the political events of September 1870 managed to disturb the almost monastic calm, if only for a short time.[11]

On 12 September, while the students were at Monte Porzio, the sound of what was taken to be gunfire was heard. It later transpired that the papal troops were preparing for a siege and were blowing up a bridge across the Tiber. As the long threatened attack on the city by the Piedmontese now seemed imminent, the College authorities decided that the students must return to Rome. Back in the city everything was going ahead to prepare the defences and on their afternoon walks they visited the various fortifications to watch the work in progress. A very large Union Jack was hoisted over the entrance to the College. The Rector did not allow the students to join the Zouaves. This was not because he did not approve of this body of men; in fact like most Catholics of the day, he regarded these volunteer defenders of the papal power as heroes and even martyrs. In 1867 he, together with Talbot[12] and Stonor, had assisted at the obsequies in the English College of Julian Watts-Russell, who had been killed at Mentana.[13] On 19 September a party of students visited St John Lateran taking with them the College telescope, which Colonel Charette, the Commander of the troops there, asked to borrow. The Pope was at this time at the Scala Sancta, making the ascent on his bare knees, and this was the last time he was to appear in public outside the Vatican.

On the twentieth, the College was awakened at dawn by the sound of heavy gunfire and the news soon spread that the main attack on the city was in the direction of the Porta Salaria and the Porta Pia. From the College clocktower could be seen the smoke of the cannonade. When a shell fell nearby at 8.30 it was judged expedient that they should all assemble on the ground floor and as the noise grew louder they were ordered into the cellar where hot wine was provided. Anxiety was felt for the library and water buckets were got ready in case of fire, but the servant misunderstood the orders and brought water down into the cellars. It was a very brief battle and soon the white flag was hoisted over the dome of St Peter's, the Italian troops and all their camp followers entered the city and there were scenes of pillage and murder. The people rejoiced at the liberation and the results of the plebiscite, held a short time later, were overwhelmingly in favour of the new regime. The Jesuit house at Marino was sacked and the Order was once more suppressed by the civil authorities. Their escutcheon and emblems over the Collegio Romano were hacked away and hammered to pieces and the building was occupied by a detachment of the Bersaglieri.[14]

As far as the English College was concerned it was all over in ten days, for on 30 September the students were ordered back to Monte Porzio to continue the *villeggiatura* so rudely interrupted by the war.

However much the English might try and put a brave face on it or pretend that these foreign wars were of no significance to them, it was indeed the end of an era and very nearly the end of the College. The winter brought natural disasters with a very serious flooding of the Tiber.[15] There was anxiety about the College property and the cellars were flooded. Anti-clerical demonstrations became more frequent and Cardinal di Luca took refuge in the

Fig. 7.1 Julian Watts-Russell in his Zouave uniform.

College, but no one seemed to know how long it would remain a safe haven. The bishops in England were aware of the gravity of the situation and had contingency plans for the evacuation of the students.[16] Michael Dwane,[17] in a letter of 31 May 1871, exclaimed, 'To tell the truth I do not consider the English College to be now the best of places for a student to prepare for the priesthood.'

The College property and the Duke of Norfolk

No lives were lost at the English College with the taking of Rome by the Italians in 1870, but in the months that followed it became clear that, despite the initial assurances from the Italian govemment, the College would be affected when the laws concerning church property were extended to Rome.

The College possessed houses and land in the city.[18] In addition to the College and adjacent dwellings in the Via Monserrato and Via Montoro, there were properties on the Coelian, at La Magliana and near the Porta Portese. At Monte Porzio there was not only the country house but also considerable vineyards and lands, including some at Monte Compatri. In addition to this real estate, there were *canoni* (rents arising from property let on a perpetual lease) and similar sources of income from property and interest on various loans. It was estimated that the gross income was 55,146 lire which left 30,304 lire net after taxation. This was sufficient to support twenty students and superiors.[19]

Even before the new laws were passed the College began to claim exemption from the new taxes and this involved an unsuccessful law suit[20] which took them to the court of appeal and then to the court of cassation. During these two years of litigation, O'Callaghan seems to have dealt with the Roman side, and Giles, the Vice-Rector, made several visits to England. The failure to uphold their case in the Italian courts meant that the Rectors of the British colleges, that is, the English, Scots and Irish, appealed to their own government. But there was little help from that quarter. The chargé d'affaires, Sir Augustus Paget, wrote on 30 September 1872: 'I have now been instructed by Earl Granville to inform you that the subject of the circular in question has been considered in consultation with the law advisers of the crown, and that H.M. Government are unable to make any representation to the Italian Government in regard to it. It is considered that the foreign colleges have no right to claim exemption from taxes which the Italian Government may legally impose on them.'

Pl. 1 The Martyrs' Picture: the altarpiece of the College church (Durante Alberti, 1583).

Pl. 2 The fresco of the Assumption on the Martyrs' Chapel ceiling is attributed, with other ceiling frescoes, to the Jesuit artist Andrea Pozzo (1642–1709) and his school. This artist was also responsible for the frescoes in the Gesù and Sant' Ignazio.

Pl. 3 The fresco of St George on the refectory ceiling is attributed to the school of Andrea Pozzo. Illustrations of the four cardinal virtues are included in the overall scheme.

Pl. 4 A painting of St Mary Magdalen anointing the feet of Christ hangs on the far wall of the refectory: it too is attributed to Pozzo.

A | Gregorius XIII. Pont. Max. huius Anglorum Collegii fundator, ac parens
optimus Alumnos suos Christo commendat: ut, quos in Angliam ad fidei
defensionem mittit, adversus hostium insidias, atq. tormenta, divina virtute
confirmet: qua freti iam aliquot pro Catholica Romana ecclesia
fortiter occubuerunt.

B | Philippus Boncompagnus S.R.E. presb. Card. tit. S. Sixti eiusdem
Pont. Fr. Fil. Collegii Protector, et Benefactor munificentiss. idē a Deo precatur

Pl. 5 Fresco in College chapel tribune, Pope Gregory XIII praying with
College students before their mission and martyrdom.

Pl. 6 St Edmund Campion.

Pl. 7 William Cardinal Allen.

Pl. 8 The Ralph Sherwin window. Stained-glass window on the College staircase installed in 1934 to commemorate the beatification of College martyrs.

The new laws became effective in June 1873. Not only was there an increase in taxation but the income from the *canoni* was now lost. This was because the holders had been enfranchised and they became proprietors by paying to the government a nominal sum, and receiving in exchange government stock. The College gained nothing by this.[21] Moreover, the building and land not actually occupied by the community, whether in Rome or Monte Porzio, had to be sold and the proceeds of the sale had to be invested in English or Italian government stock.

All efforts were now made by O'Callaghan and the other Rectors to prevent the sale of the property; but once again no help was to be found from Britain. The situation had changed since 1848 and there was not only sympathy for the new Italian government, but the 1870 Declaration of Papal Infallibility had engendered a certain amount of coolness in the British government towards English Catholics. Paget wrote in February 1875, stating that the English College had to be considered an Italian or Roman institution and so subject to that country's laws. Its claim to be English rested solely on its having been founded for the education of English subjects. Consequently 'H.M. Government finds no justification in extending its protection to the English College as if it were a British establishment'. In August, the *giunta* appointed to carry out the laws of the suppression gave the College notice to prepare for the auction of the property.

Lord Derby was now approached by the three Rectors and it was pointed out that the British government did not seem to have taken sufficient note of the history of the establishments and their connections with Great Britain. They asked for a reconsideration of the case and they contrasted the attitude of their own government unfavourably with that of the ambassadors of France, Austria and Belgium in regard to their ecclesiastical establishments. The Duke of Norfolk[22] added his plea and indicated that the fate of the three national colleges was of great interest and concern to the Catholic laity of the British Isles. He asked the government to call upon the Italian government to adhere to the assurances it had previously given. But even this was of no avail and the final bleak word came on 2 March 1876. A letter to O'Callaghan on behalf of Lord Derby[23] expressed 'Lord Derby's regret that he sees no reason to reconsider the decision of H.M. Government, which has already been communicated to you, to the effect that the circumstances of the English, Scots and Irish Colleges do not justify H.M. Government in interfering on their behalf as British establishments'.

Meanwhile, in the autumn of 1875, the matter of the condition and finances of the English Colleges abroad had come under review by the hierarchy of England and Wales and they set up a commission to enquire into the state of things at Rome, Valladolid, San Lucar (Seville) and Lisbon. They entrusted Herbert Vaughan with the enquiry. It was pointed out that they were not undertaking a canonical visitation, nor was it intended to encroach on the authority of the ecclesiastical superiors, who, at least in the case of Rome, gave them every facility.

Our concern is with this visit in so far as it affected the College in Rome. It took place in February–March 1876, while the negotiations with the Italian and British authorities were reaching their climax. Vaughan was informed of the financial state of the College and how, as a result of the changes since 1870, the income had dropped from 30,304 lire net to 9,138. The new church was still in the process of being constructed, but with the scarcity of funds the prospect of its ever being finished was remote, unless another appeal to the Catholics of England was made. Talbot's other initiative, the Collegio Pio, was now empty of students. O'Callaghan had discouraged the practice of students passing from the English College to the Pio at the age of twenty-four. There were fewer new students of more mature age coming out of Rome and the last student had left in 1875.[24] Some of the money subsidising the Pio had been diverted to the new church fund. There were, of course, other matters disclosed – concerning the admission of students, the rules introduced by O'Callaghan, and the need for more practice in preaching and catechising – but the cloud hanging over the College was that of the expropriation of most of its property. At this point the Rector had a suggestion. In order to save the College the necessity of an 'immediate and forced sale of its property including half the buildings which make up the College quadrangle', he devised a plan whereby the real property of the College could be secured to its ecclesiastical purposes by legal transference to the name of a third party. The Duke of Norfolk had already graciously consented to act in this capacity. All that now remained was the approval of the bishops.[25] Vaughan returned to England and made his report to the Low Week meeting in April. On 4 July 1876 at 10 a.m. Via degli Incurabili no. 6, by order of the Committee for Liquidation of the Ecclesiastical State of Rome, property belonging to the German–Hungarian, English, Irish, and Scots Colleges was put up for public auction. The reserved price for the English College property was 58,200 lire, far higher than any of the other property offered that day. It was bought by the Duke of Norfolk 'for and on behalf of the English College for 59,000 lire. A later decree of 1877

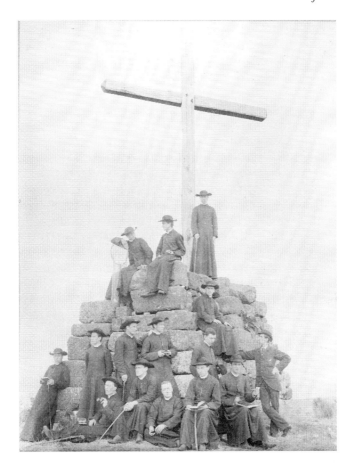

Fig 7.2 The third Tusculum Cross, erected by the
students in 1864, and destroyed by anti-clericals in 1891.
From a photograph of 1883 giving each student's name
and diocese.

ensured that the Church of St Thomas, nos 41–52 Via Monserrato
and the *casa di villeggiatura* at Monte Porzio, with its small garden,
were free from any threat of confiscation.[26]

The sequel to this purchase has to be briefly recorded.[27] On 1
May 1877, the Duke made a will in which he left this property to
the Rt Rev. James Danell of Southwark and the Rt Rev. Edward
Gilpin Bagshawe of Nottingham. On the same day he made a declaration that these purchases were 'made by me, for and on behalf of
the said College. I will that any persons who under my will or
otherwise may succeed to the ownership of the said properties ...

will and should at all times do all such acts and execute all such deeds as shall be deemed necessary for the transferring unto its name the said house and landed properties'. In 1883, on the death of Danell, a codicil was inserted nominating the Rt Rev. Robert Lacy, Bishop of Middlesborough, as legatee. When in 1904 the Duke married, a new will was drawn up and John Prior, Vice-Rector at the English College, was given power of attorney to administer the property in the city of Rome and its territory and also in the commune of Monte Porzio and Monte Compatri. This situation seems to have continued right up to the death of the Duke in 1917.

The death duties on these estates were considerable. The Duke's death was not only during the First World War, but also during a period of crisis in the English College, just before Hinsley took over. Mgr Lacy, the surviving legatee, was at the advanced age of seventy-six and there was a need for urgency in disposing of the property.[28] It was decided to sell all the property now bequeathed to Mgr Lacy (formerly belonging to Norfolk) in favour of James Redmond, the Vice-Rector. Death duties continued to be paid after this date and the College was helped in this by Mgr Amigo, the Bishop of Southwark and a great friend of the new Rector, Mgr Hinsley.[29]

As a further footnote to the 1870 laws, one must record that a document from the Ministry of Grace and Justice in 1874 recognised the rights of the foreign colleges established in Rome to receive religious instruction in the Gregorian. An annual allowance of 15,000 lire was given to the University for this purpose, thus continuing the practice of the popes as temporal rulers. But in 1885 the Italian government ceased to pay this and the Roman College was placed in considerable financial difficulties. A reply was sent to the Cardinal Vicar of Rome, to the effect that the foreign colleges were receiving theological instruction and so could not be expected to be provided for by the government and so the money was being given to the Liceo E. Q. Visconti, which now occupied the former premises of the Roman College.

Edward Howard, Herbert Vaughan and Henry O'Callaghan

The nineteenth-century connection of the Howard family with the English College had been established some time before the Duke of Norfolk came to the rescue of its affairs. Edward Howard[30] was a fellow student with Talbot at St Mary's Oscott, when Wiseman was Rector. After serving in the Life Guards[31] he was ordained priest and resided in Rome for several years. He was a member of the Congregation of Propaganda Fide in respect of the Oriental Rite[32] and a canon of S. Lorenzo in Damaso. He was a member of the reception committee for the bishops coming to Rome for the Vatican Council, presumably to concern himself with the bishops of the English-speaking world. His correspondence indicates that he was concerned with affairs in India as well as other parts of the British Empire. He was made a cardinal in 1877 and in 1878 he became Protector of the English College. In his sermon, on taking office, he not only mentioned his kinsman, Philip Howard O.P., who was also in his time the Protector, but he was at pains to dwell on both the loyalty to the Holy See and the Englishness of the College, no doubt mindful of the British government's attitude the previous year. When he was nominated Archpriest at St Peter's in 1881 he received a letter from Vaughan saying, 'Let me add my little word of congratulations upon your nomination to so high an office in St. Peter's. What grand functions they will have there! what vestments!' Evidently the Wiseman tradition still lived on in some respects in these two clerics. This same letter, apart from revealing what David Mathew called 'the easy intimacy between the Vaughan and Howard families',[33] goes on to speak of O'Callaghan and his future. 'I wonder what you are going to do for Southwark and Portsmouth. I am in favour of O'Callaghan for Southwark ... O'Callaghan is a disciplinarian and that is what is somewhat needed in Southwark ... He would get on well with H.E., a thing to be considered in a nomination to Southwark.' In the following year there was correspondence between Manning and Howard again on the subject of O'Callaghan. Manning expressed great appreciation of O'Callaghan's virtues and suggested that he be given a bishopric as all Rectors, 'except Dr. Neve and poor Dr. English who went to a better world'. But there were one or two commissions the bishops had in mind for him before that. In 1884 he was appointed co-postulator for the cause of the English and Welsh Martyrs, and the Beatification, which included many former students of the College, took place in 1886.

O'Callaghan, despite the immense difficulties that confronted him after 1870, had done much to fulfil the expectations of Manning and Vaughan. Out of the 105 students at the College during his rectorship[34] seven became bishops and many held important posts in seminaries in England and abroad, as well as positions of responsibility in their dioceses. A stricter discipline had

Fig. 7.3 Edward Cardinal Howard.

been enforced in the College and this was in keeping with the mood of ecclesiastical Rome. Even the College church was completed[35] and indeed the first ceremony in it was the consecration of the Rector as Bishop of Hexham and Newcastle in 1888, but this only took place after a month's postponement due to the Rector's nervous state. The strain seems to have been too much for him and the thought of having to leave Rome affected him. As a bishop he was not a success. His scruples became accentuated and the change of climate, from twenty years in Italy to the North of England, meant that he could never adjust, and he resigned his see in 1889. He retired to Italy, Giles, his successor as Rector, wisely refusing him rooms in the College. He died in Florence in 1904.

William Giles

In 1888 O'Callaghan was succeeded by Giles, who had already spent 36 years in Rome and was destined to live the rest of his life as Rector. We must not underestimate Giles. His very powers of survival alone make him noteworthy. He was one of the first students at the Pio, he was *ripetitore* at the English College, Vice-Rector at the Pio and, since 1865, he had been Vice-Rector at the English College. Thus he lived through the Cornthwaite, English, Neve and O'Callaghan regimes and all the changes experienced through those years. He died in 1913. He had connections with Manning long before O'Callaghan arrived. After his ordination by Wiseman at Westminster he returned to Rome to take his doctorate at the Gregorian. He was aware that, as his future probably lay at St Edmund's, he would be involved more and more with Manning's schemes and this caused him some anxiety. As a Westminster priest he followed the fortunes of the Oblates of St Charles and during one of Manning's visits to Rome he wrote to his parents:[36] 'He is of course trying here, and for me among the rest and I know from other directions that he and Mr. Vaughan have named me for one of their future staff. To decide however will of course rest with me and now I will tell you my mind as far as I know it at present. For some strong reasons and from things I have heard and know, I *dislike* the Oblates exceedingly and have no intention whatever of becoming one.' The prospect of returning to work in London did not appeal to him and he considered offering himself to Clifford, the new Bishop of Clifton, or going to Oscott to teach, but in the event he never left Rome and became a close supporter of the Oblate Rector, O'Callaghan.

Fig 7.4 Herbert Cardinal Vaughan.

Fig. 7.5 William Giles, Rector 1888–1913.

As Vice-Rector Giles was responsible for the finances; the discipline was the concern of the Rector. The undoubtedly disgraceful state of the accounts in the last days of his rectorship must not make us forget the negotiations he did on behalf of the College when the events of 1870 involved him in long stays in London on money matters.

Compared with the upheavals of O'Callaghan's years, Giles's days as Rector were relatively placid. The one big administrative decision was in 1898, when he agreed to Vaughan's scheme of re-opening the Collegio Pio as the new Beda College. Mgr Prior[37] became superior of the Beda, with the title of Vice-Rector, and most of the work of setting up the new establishment was done by him in collaboration with Merry del Val,[38] and not by Giles. Although there were provisions against repeating the circumstances that led to trouble during the Cornthwaite, English and Neve regimes and of which Giles must have been personally aware, the scheme was not entirely successful and after Giles's death the two establishments were entirely separated, to the advantage of both.

Although the Giles period was not remarkable for external material events, it had an important place in College history by reason of the mental climate encouraged by the Rector's personality. In temperament[39] he was unlike O'Callaghan and he established an easy-going relationship with the students, taking part in their Christmas concerts, accompanying them on walking tours in the hill towns near Rome, and further afield in the Appenines. He was a man of some artistic talent[40] and had a good natural singing voice, although he lacked training and had no understanding of plain-song.[41] Himself a man of great regularity and punctuality, he found it difficult to correct students or enforce the rules. As Vice-Rector he did not have to concern himself with this, as O'Callaghan was a strict disciplinarian, but when he succeeded to the rectorship the discipline suffered somewhat. He never bothered about a code of rules but just told the new students to do what the others did.[42] He was essentially conservative. He liked 'old things' and it is due to him that the College continued with the old style tricorne hats, when other clerics, after 1870, adopted the more 'modern' flat round brimmed hats. This was a reminder of old papal Rome and was a defiantly reactionary gesture. Like the 'black nobility', Giles never recognised the new 'Piedmontese' rulers of Rome.[43]

But reading through the many diaries of the period one cannot help but be struck by the friendly family atmosphere of the College.[44] There was a lively interest in current affairs, the minute book of the Debating Society is resumed and we find discussion on such topics as the advisability of allowing Catholic students to attend Protestant universities, the suitability of plainsong in church services, 'That scholastic philosophy is antiquated', and 'It would be inconsistent with the dignity of Leo XIII to accept any measures other than the total restoration of his dominions'. This latter was an extremely long debate and was held despite efforts of the superiors to have it banned by reason of the speeches against the temporal power that it might and did in fact produce.[45] The students published a satirical magazine, *The Daily Lyre*, there were regular concerts in the College and students occasionally attended concerts in the city. At least one of the students went to the 'cinematograph', sometimes twice a week.[46] Undoubtedly many of these forms of recreation were against the rules, but even officially the students were not so incommunicado as under O'Callaghan and they were allowed to show English pilgrims round Rome in 1900, during the Holy Year.

There was no rescinding of the rules instituted by O'Callaghan in 1869; the system remained the same, but it no longer prevented the students from enjoying themselves now that the College was presided over by the genial Giles. The College was affording many of them an opportunity to educate themselves by taking advantage of what Rome offered. One recalls the remarks made by Barry, in the early years of O'Callaghan's rule:[47] 'Meanwhile I was educating myself, with Rome as an object lesson beyond compare ... my time was not wasted, though it might easily have been so, except for the overmastering impulse which has always urged me to learn more and more.'

The rules were complained about, broken, but rarely questioned deeply, and only in exceptional cases was the restriction and narrowness of the life averted to. Such an exception was George Ambrose Burton, later to become Bishop of Clifton.

Burton and Roman theology

Burton came to the College after teaching at Ratcliffe and after a short time in the Rosminian House at Domodossola. He was a classical scholar and much older than the rest of the students, and in his Roman Diary we have a record of the way in which this period of College history appeared to such a one. He was constrained to follow the rules of a house intended for much younger men. He wrote in 1885, 'What pleasure I have had here has been mainly derived from my books (not Liberatore,[48] or any other of the neoscholastics), from the letters of my friends, from their interest attaching to the spots I have visited; to my companions I stand indebted to very little.' Such isolation is perhaps understandable, but it is symptomatic of the other isolation he felt from the whole Roman system. His disenchantment with the Roman theology came about by reason of its treatment of Rosmini. 'Such calumnies as these are what I am bidden by the Rector to accept in lieu of the "stains of Rosminianism". I'll be hanged for it and so may the Jesuits.'[49] 'Our professor either has never grasped or else deliberately falsifies Rosmini's statement of the question.'[50] 'Received in an open envelope a list of the 40 condemned propositions. What do I believe in now? In God, in his Christ, in Christ's Church, in Christ's vicar and in nought else – omnis homo mendax.'[51] 'I have just seen in today's *Voce* that Rosmini is on the Index now. 'Twas to be expected. It's clear that Leo means to squash and pulverise the poor Rosminians. It's devilish hard! All Jesuits' work! All!! All!!! May I live to see them let down a few pegs. Will not God take up the cause of his servants?'[52]

As he progressed on his course he began to go and see the professors and take up the defence of Rosmini. On 14 January 1890 he

Fig. 7.6 The Rector, Mgr Giles, with students in 1890–1 (Arthur Hinsley is fourth from left in the back row).

recorded a long discussion with Billot, during the course of which Billot said he 'had no great opinion of Rosmini's sanctity. From these (the propositions) it was apparent that he was not *sub influentia Spiritus Sancti* and if you looked at his political life in '48, why he walked hand in hand with Gioberti and was in the counsels of the King of Piedmont, the focus of the revolution'. Burton remarked: 'I believe Billot to be an honest and upright man, but it was evident to me that he was totally unacquainted with Rosmini's works except in so far as they are contained in the forty propositions and he has been grossly misinformed as to Rosmini's life and brief political career.' Much of the feeling against Rosmini was associated with the political stances of Catholics after 1870 and there is another passage from the diary of interest in this regard.

> 24 June 1887. Interesting talk on the temporal power with Fr. de Francis in the portico of the Lateran. He thought Providence had accomplished a great work in clearing away the rotten principalities of old Italy and in which the Church had not enjoyed free and unfettered action and in forming Italy into one nation, so as no longer to be the prey of other countries ... it might be the loss of temporal power was to be counterbalanced by an influence of another kind. And yet Fr. Francis is a hot 'papalino' and was present at Porta Pia on 20 September 1870 when he tended the wounded and the dying.

Modernism

The pain and anguish caused to Burton by the lack of understanding by the Roman theologians was not shared by many of his contemporaries at the English College, but it was a phenomenon to be repeated in the ensuing years and became a mark of Roman Catholicism during the Modernist crisis. Minocchi, in his memoirs,[53] speaks of the climate in Rome when he was a seminarian.

> Modernism had already begun, and worked secretly in the souls of each of us. So that, in spite of all the good intentions of apologetics, we gradually found it hard to reconcile present day scientific thought, even confined to the field of history and criticism, with what we were learning, or to achieve the age old harmony between science and faith, when confined to the procrustean beds of dogma, within the limitations of the theological ideas of the Fathers and the philosophy of St. Thomas.

As far as the English College is concerned, the students could not but be aware of something in the air from the negative reactions of

Fig. 7.7 Picnic at Tusculum, 1885. Bishop Giles and students enjoying the rustic life.

Rome. At the Gregorian, Billot gave a series of lectures on *L'évangile et l'église* and some of them wondered what it was all about. Hazelhurst remarked,[54] 'He seems to find it hard to restrain himself.' King[55] visited Van Laach who began to speak of Loisy. 'He said the book *L'évangile et l'église* was being translated into English, for which he was very sorry, as it was full of error. Loisy had got hold of false principles of philosophy and was applying them to matters of faith. He was working great havoc.' King also reported in his diary for 7 January 1901, 'Prior gave address on the history of the English College including a warning against Liberal Catholicism which he said would at least dull the fire of our attachment to the Vicar of Christ.' It is worth noting here that King himself (a future Bishop of Portsmouth) was recalled to England before ordination. It has been suggested that this was because of the modernist scare.

But however much the students might criticise the aridity of the Roman system and its insistence on learning by heart and on having notes dictated in class (especially philosophy class),[56] however much they might have had a sneaking regard for Loisy and others, when they returned to England they were for the most part content to adopt the official line. There were some who did not do this and who fell away, but they are forgotten and what survived was exactly what the system had calculated would remain. Richard Burke, later a canon of the Menevia Chapter, provides a good instance of this. Reminiscing several years after the events, he says:[57]

When Billot was lecturing on Loisy's *L'évangile et l'église* there was great excitement among the students and a great deal of enthusiasm but there were a few men amongst our own students who were at the time great admirers of the Abbe Loisy (he had not then been condemned) and considered Billot's arguments out of date, medieval, antiquated, and I recall now that one of those students did not remain in the College much longer and although he managed to receive ordination in a college in England he did not persevere, a *spoilt* priest in more sense than one like some of our budding modernists today. The higher criticism gripped some of the students for a time and almost unbalanced them, but no evil resulted except for the time a spirit of contempt for those who were quite content to keep to the ordinary studies. Personally, it may be because I happen to be rather dense, I failed to understand why priests preparing for the English mission should worry so much about textual criticism, especially when many of them knew they would never be appointed professors of scripture. Vanitas vanitatum. Labour thrown away in my opinion and only leading to endless questionings and doubts. Requiescat in pace.

This attitude was shared by many priests who had been trained in Rome and it is by no means dead and it leads to an important observation. An open and outgoing appreciation of many of the facets of Roman life, its antiquities, its churches and monuments, its literature, classical and modern, its politics, its wine and food, all these do not necessarily mean that one is not rigid and uncompromising when it comes to matters of orthodoxy. Conversely, those who appear to have a somewhat restricted and narrow view of doctrine and discipline are not necessarily people who do not enjoy life and what it gives. For example, Wiseman's attraction to antiquities and the classics, like the similar broad interests of the popes of the early nineteenth century, did not mean that they would be appreciative of the new liberal idea of the Risorgimento. Such a life may appear to us to contain contradictions, but they did not feel anything unusual in it, any more than those students of the 1890s felt any inconsistency between their own complaints against the system, and their enforcing of a similar system on others later. There is a distinction between life as it is lived and enjoyed in practice and the official line which always states the ideal. The Roman is able to live in these two worlds without feeling the tension, but there are a great many who are unable to bear it and break under the strain.[58]

It was on the accession of Pius X that the more intransigent line became uppermost, but the election of Cardinal Sarto had other effects on the English College, as it did on all ecclesiastical institutions in Rome. There was first of all the Decree on Church Music, which had its repercussions on the services in the colleges and the churches of the city. There was also the decision that ordinations to the priesthood should only take place at the end of fourth year theology. Other private admonitions were issued and on 7 January 1904, 'This evening the Rector mentioned that the laws of the Index were binding on us ... permission was necessary ... of course to keep such books would be a grave breach of College discipline also.'[59] A month later there was issued the Bull decreeing an Apostolic Visitation throughout Rome. The church was visited first, in November 1905, and the report occasioned by this remarks about the general need for cleanliness. In January 1906 the College was visited by T. Esser O.P., the Secretary for the Congregation of the Index. Amongst the recommendations were the need for a resident spiritual father to give conferences once a week; a *repetitio* once a week on moral theology was to be conducted, if possible in English. There was expressed the need for a competent teacher of Italian and the students were to speak among themselves on walks in Italian and Latin, to give themselves practice in those languages. There were once again, as with the visitation of the church, complaints about the dirtiness of the place; bed clothes were to be changed more often and the rooms required better flooring. *Merenda* was to be provided in the refectory, so as to avoid the students' making tea in their rooms. There was an overall stress on the importance of observing small and seemingly trifling rules, such as that of silence; these would help form character.

Despite the fact that Giles had lived for so long outside England, the links with home remained strong. He claimed to be independent of the bishops of England as to his conduct of the house, saying that he was directly responsible to the Holy Father and his representative, the Cardinal Protector. This was an attitude adopted by many Rectors in the past, but in Giles's case the situation was different in that from 1893 to 1903 Vaughan was the Cardinal Protector. This is the only case of the Archbishop of Westminster, or any English diocesan bishop, holding a post usually confined to a cardinal in Curia. This link between Westminster and the English College had begun with Wiseman and had continued throughout Manning's rule.[60] The death of Vaughan in 1903 meant that the College not only got a new Protector but a new Archbishop of Westminster. In the person of Francis Bourne, the Wiseman tradition was broken. The new Archbishop had been trained at S. Sulpice in Paris and it was not long before rumours and reports of his attitude towards the College reached the students. Hazelhurst reports, '10 May 1905 the Vice told me the reasons the Archbishop gave for wishing to close the English College. 1. It is no longer the centre of English Catholic life in Rome. 2. The bishops should have control of the money. 3. The course is too long.'

Bourne's policy departed from Vaughan's plans for a Central Seminary in England. He wanted all his diocesan students to receive their full course at St Edmund's, Ware. For this purpose he enlarged that college and built Allen Hall in 1904. He did not favour the idea of sending students to the English College, Rome, but preferred that suitable candidates should go to Rome for higher studies after ordination.

Giles became titular bishop of Philadelphia in 1904, but his last days marked a sad decline in the administration and provided other grounds for closure than those advanced by Bourne. When the negligence began is hard to determine; it may have been something to do with Mgr Prior becoming judge of the Rota in 1908 and so relinquishing College affairs. But we find that the financial matters are all in Giles's hands and accounts cease to be kept. The Libro Mastro ceases, so does the Hebdominal book. In 1907, Giles set up a trust and bought shares in London, but no one seemed to know whether it was for the English College or for the Beda. In 1911, Cardinal de Lai of the Consistorial Congregation wrote to Giles enquiring about the state of the Beda finances and how the gift of 300,000 lire from Leo XIII had been invested.

For all its failings the important things about the Giles period is that, as with O'Callaghan, men brought up in such a climate were to be influential in the future government of the Church in England. The family spirit, the interest in Italy and Rome, the loyalty to the papacy, as well as respect for authority and lack of original theological thinking were to be found in many of the products of this regime. There were, as students under him, not only bishops like Allen and Moriarty of Shrewsbury, McIntyre of Birmingham, Whiteside of Liverpool, King of Portsmouth, Burton of Clifton, Cowgill of Leeds, Keatinge, the Army bishop, but also Rectors Parkinson and Cronin at Oscott, Cullen at Lisbon, Dean at Upholland (he had been a pupil at the Beda) and many canons and diocesan officials. Above all, both Hinsley and Godfrey were pupils under Giles in the years 1890–4 and 1910–7. Both these became Rectors of the College and did much to continue the spirit of Giles, not always intentionally but often instinctively.[61]

Notes

1 This would seem to be a very similar procedure to the old arrangement, which made a distinction between students who had not yet taken the oath, 'non jurati' and those who had, 'jurati'.

2 'To consider the position of the bishops in regard to the English College at Rome. The rules lately established appear to have completely changed their position.' Item on agenda of Low Week Meeting, 1871.

3 *Venerabile*, V, 277.

4 W. Barry, *Memories and Opinions* (London 1926). Quoted in *Venerabile*, XXIII, 16.

5 According to the Liber Ruber, three left in 1868, three in 1869 and five in 1870.

6 Oscott Archives, letter of M. Dwane to Mr Creaney, 3 December 1869 (Transcript in ECA).

7 Maisie Ward, *The Wilfred Wards and the Transition, I, Nineteenth Century* (London 1934), p. 58.

8 This characteristic is mentioned by Canon Peacock, *Venerabile*, XVI, 223 and by Bishop Cowgill, *Recollections 1877–83*, ECA, scr. 84, 1.

9 Maisie Ward, *The Wilfred Wards and the Transition, I, Nineteenth Century*, p. 66.

10 *Venerabile*, XXII, 234.

11 This account is taken from the Diaries of Kirkham and Barry. See also 'The Taking of Rome, 1870', *Venerabile*, III, 321–8.

12 In the 1860s Talbot collected money from England and Ireland for the Zouaves.

13 Watts-Russell was buried at S. Lorenzo but there is a memorial to him in the College church. James Johnston, 'Julian Watts-Russell', *Venerabile*, V, 381–7.

14 For a time lectures were given in the professors' quarters of the Collegio Romano, but eventually the German College in the Palazzo Borromeo was taken over. Pius IX allowed them to use the title of Pontifical Gregorian University in 1873. J. D. Key, 'Suppression of the Roman College (1870)', *Venerabile*, VII, 314–22.

15 It was after these floods that the embankment or *lungotevere* was built thus changing the aspect of riverside Rome.

16 *Weekly Register*, 19 November 1870. 'We may add that as regards the English College in Rome, matters have been in such a critical state with its students that preparations have been made by some of the bishops for the home education of such of their subjects as are members of that institution.'

17 Oscott Archives. Transcript in Rome.

18 For these and other details of the state of the College at this time see *Report on the Condition of the English Catholic Colleges in Italy, Spain and Portugal. Printed by Order of their Lordships the Bishops of England* (Salford 1876). Bishop Herbert Vaughan was the author of the Report.

19 Because there were some outstanding debts, Talbot had decided, in 1868, that for three years the alumni should be reduced to sixteen. This was

calculated to be the best means of paying off the debt.

20 ECA, liber 1648, Tosi papers.

21 In fact, as a result of a lawsuit these tenants were now at liberty to make over to the favour of the College a certain amount as compensation. But in 1876 means had been found to delay such proceedings.

22 Henry Fitzalan Howard, 15th Duke of Norfolk, 1847–1917. He had succeeded to the title at the age of 13.

23 ECA, scr. 81, 3.

24 The last student of the Pio was ordained for the Hexham and Newcastle Diocese. The last Vice-Rector, Robert Smith, became a Cistercian and died at S. Croce in Rome.

25 An interesting observation is that after 1870, because of the loss of temporal power, there was now no question of the Cardinal Protector acting on behalf of the papacy to allow such a procedure involving the disposal of church property. It is a matter for the English bishops.

26 ECA, scr. 81, 3

27 ECA, scr. 92, 26.

28 In fact Mgr Lacy survived until 1929!

29 For the Norfolk estate see ECA, liber 619, 1145, 1152, 1162.

30 ECA, scr. 92 1–25, Howard papers.

31 He led the funeral procession of the Duke of Wellington in this capacity.

32 He left his library to the English College.

33 *The English Catholics 1850–1950*, ed. G. A. Beck (London 1950), p. 239.

34 See *Venerabile*, XVI, 225 for names and figures.

35 The mural and pavement tablets in the church were practically all due to O'Callaghan, *Venerabile*, III, 40. See also ECA, scr. 81, 2 for correspondence with T. F. Knox *re* the Latin inscriptions and the question of the identification of Persons' skull.

36 ECA, scr. 84, letter 53, Giles correspondence, 19 February 1857.

37 John Prior (1861–1926) student at the Venerabile, priest of Hexham and Newcastle diocese, became Vice-Rector to Giles in 1888. He moved to the Beda in 1898 and ten years later, when Pius X restored the Rota, he was chosen as Auditor for English speaking affairs. For a short time he was Dean of the Rota but returned to England after a breakdown in health in 1922.

38 Rafael Merry del Val (1865–1930), of Irish and Spanish stock, was born in England, educated at Ushaw, but when his father was appointed Spanish Ambassador to the Holy See he continued his studies at the Gregorian in Rome. Ordained for the diocese of Westminster he remained in Rome as a member of the Curia. He was secretary to the Papal Commission to examine the question of Anglican Orders. When his friend Cardinal Sarto became Pope Pius X, Merry del Val was appointed Secretary of State.

39 A memoir of Giles by J. Prior is to be found in *The Edmundian*, December 1913, reprinted in *Venerabile*, II, 273–91. See also A. Moriarty, 'Men of Little Showing (7) – Bishop Giles', *Clergy Review*, II, 513–20; A. Moriarty, 'The Late 80s', *Venerabile*, XII, 119–24; F. O'Farrell, 'Fifty Years Ago', *Venerabile*, X, 135–48; J. Foley, 'The passing of Mgr. Giles', *Venerabile*, XI,

230–3. Dominic Rolls, 'Rectors of the English College IX: William Giles', *Venerabile*, XXIX (1989) 41–6.

40 G. P. Dwyer, 'Bishop Giles' Watercolours', *Venerabile*, VI, 21–4. Mrs Marjorie Coughlan, 'In search of Giles', *Venerabile*, XXXI (1999), 37–44.

41 ECA, liber 829, Hazelhurst's diary, 2 February 1904, records Giles as saying, 'Why should the upstart Solesmes people claim to have the traditional method of singing Gregorian. It is sufficient just to sing the notes.'

42 ECA, liber 828, Burke's Reminiscences, 'Dicitur, traditur or whatever else will express the fact that our rules were founded on unwritten laws preserved in the archive of the Rector's brain cells that provided we occupied our time of study during the holidays in useful work we were not bound to any definite subject'.

43 Giles's attitude was vindicated by the wave of anti-clericalism that overtook Rome in 1889. It was at this time that the statue to Giordano Bruno was erected in the Campo dei Fiori and this became a rendezvous for demonstrations against the Church. Students were frequently pelted with stones and things were so bad at Whitsuntide 1890 that Giles decided that they should go to Monte Porzio. See 'A Brush with the Anti-Clericals 1890', *Venerabile*, IX, 244–6.

44 ECA, liber 824, Bishop Burton, 1884–90; ECA, liber 825–7, Bishop King, 1899–1904; ECA, liber 828, Canon Burke, 1898–1905; ECA, liber 829, Provost Hazelhurst, 1901–05.

45 See Minute Book Debating Sodety, ECA, liber 591–2.

46 ECA, liber 829, Hazelhurst's diary.

47 W. Barry, *Memories and Opinions*, p. 104.

48 Liberatore the Jesuit scholastic theologian was a target for Burton in his *Lays of Modern Rome:*
     The second year came, to my books I stuck;
     And I read the Liberator with amazing pluck.
     I talked in terms of which the sense was hid –
     Componendum, dividendum and secundum quid:
     Secundum quid was a safe remark
     And I earned the reputation of a deep-read clerk ...

49 ECA, iber 824, Ambrose Burton's Roman Diary, 20 January 1886.

50 Ibid., 22 January 1886.

51 Ibid., 17 March 1888.

52 Ibid., 19 June 1889.

53 Quoted by Michele Ranchetti, *The Catholic Modernists 1864–1907*, English trans. (London 1969), pp. 81–4.

54 ECA, liber 829, Hazelhurst's Diary, January 1904.

55 ECA, liber 825–7, King's Diary, Christmas Eve 1903.

56 This dictation of notes was characteristic of many seminaries in England also. It dates back several centuries.

57 ECA, liber 828, Burke's Diary.

58 E. E. Y. Hales, *Pio Nono* (London, 1954) pp. 261–2 remarks à propos of Dupanloup's pamphlet on the Syllabus of Errors of 1864, 'Throughout Dupanloup's pamphlet runs the distinction between the *thesis* (the ideal of

the true society) and the *hypothesis* (what is possible or just in the existing state of society). Her opponents were talking in terms of absolutes; so the Church had to make clear what were the true absolutes, or at least must deny those that were false. The great mistake was to suppose that when she condemned a proposition on the absolute plane there might not, yet, be much relative good in it, and that some measure of its practice might not often be healthy and beneficial. And when the absolute claims of a proposition were denied, it by no means followed that the contrary proposition was always valid – thus it was erroneous to say that the Catholic Church should everywhere be disestablished but it was not true to say that she should always be an Established Church.'

59 ECA, liber 829, Hazelhurst's Diary.
60 Burke wrote, ECA, 828, 'Cardinal Vaughan was most anxious to inaugurate reforms whenever he paid a visit to the College and on that account I cannot say that his presence was altogether a source of unmitigated joy.' The two tapestries that were displayed on Feast days on the lower corridor bear the arms of Vaughan.
61 Moriarty, writing of the Giles regime in the *Clergy Review*, December 1931, is not unlike Heenan writing much later his memoir of Cardinal Hinsley. As for Godfrey's views on Giles, see 'The College During the War', *Venerabile*, VI, 414.

Chapter Eight

The Hinsley Tradition

Gasquet's account of the College history comes to a virtual end in the middle of the nineteenth century with Mgr Talbot and the building of the new College church. O'Callaghan's rectorship is given a single paragraph and the same space covers Giles, McIntyre and the then Rector, Hinsley. Respect for the living and awareness of the inability to pass a detached judgment on recent events means that most historians draw the line at about fifty years previous to the time of writing. It is unfortunate that this should be so in Gasquet's case[1] since he was in a position to know, more than most, the course of events leading up to the appointment of Hinsley. Doubtless he was glad to accept the historian's excuse and so refrain from making public yet one more administrative and financial crisis in the history of the institution he loved so well.

The visitation under McIntyre

McIntyre, already a bishop, was chosen to succeed Giles in 1914[2] and one of his first acts was to refer the matter of irregularities in administration to the Cardinal Secretary of the Consistorial Congregation, after he had consulted the Protector, Vannutelli. On 3 July 1914, Pius X decided on an apostolic visitation and the short rectorship of McIntyre was spent in facilitating this. The visitation report had praise for the character of the Rector, but it expressed doubt whether he was the one to set things right and prevent a recurrence of the recent negligencies. He was not a good administrator and his age, 61, was against him.

Fig. 8.1 The College roofline after 1911.

The visitors were confronted with three big problems.[3] Firstly, there was the need for the two establishments of the English College and the Beda to be made completely separate. The successful disentanglement of the finances was effected. The formal separation was dated 1 January 1918 and the new constitutions of both colleges were published in the *Acta Apostolicae Sedis*, vol. X n. 5, 1 May 1918. The Beda moved to new premises.

Secondly, in the English College there was a lack of internal organisation and this was attributed to the disregard of the Constitution of 1818. In particular, the power of the Cardinal Protector was ineffectual and the Rector was exercising uncontrolled and absolute authority. The Cardinal Protector, Vannutelli, who was in poor health, resigned and was succeeded by Gasquet, who took office on 10 September 1915. The visitation report says, 'The Cardinal Protector stands in the same relation to the College as a bishop to his own seminary.' The Rector was to be nominated by the Protector, after consultation with the bishops. But McIntyre, in his correspondence on this matter during the visitation, pointed out that in reality the Holy See reserved to itself the right to appoint a Rector; he himself had been nominated by the Consistorial Congregation.[4] The report also expressed the need for better legislation concerning the appointment of the other superiors. There had to be greater supervision of students in the College and even more so on *villeggiatura*. The visitors were shocked at the fact that there were no prefects. They were told: 'They do not have them in English seminaries.' At Monte Porzio a senior student often acted as superior; this they called a 'grave irregularity'. There was a lack of spiritual direction, since there was no resident spiritual director. The moral, religious and intellectual formation of the students had to be brought into relationship with the necessities of the country in which they were to exercise their priesthood. This meant that relations with the English and Welsh hierarchy needed to be attended to, and the bishops should have more say in the discipline of the house, since it was their subjects who were being educated in the College. It was recommended that a committee of the four archbishops (Westminster, Birmingham, Liverpool, Cardiff) should periodically examine the administration. Gasquet himself was in favour of the powers of the Protector being reduced in order to give a greater say to the English bishops.[5] Dimissorial letters should be given by the bishops and not by the Cardinal Protector. Gasquet favoured the idea of the Rector being appointed for a definite term, say ten years.

The third point for complaint was the bad administrative system,

and here we are on familiar ground. But some of the recommendations of the visitation are of particular interest. It was suggested that
nuns be introduced to look after the domestic arrangements, as was
now the case at the Lateran seminary. Monte Porzio and La
Magliana should be sold as they were unsuitable and unhealthy. A
new villa should be purchased.

The visitation was completed on 15 July 1916 and the visitor was
appointed Apostolic Administrator, so that the College was now
under the direct control of the Holy See.[6] In the following January
the Congregation of Seminaries nominated deputies to serve under
the Cardinal Protector. Mgr Stanley[7] and Mgr Serafini were
appointed for disciplinary matters, and Philip Langdon, a
Benedictine and Gasquet's secretary, and Raffaele di San Giuseppe,
the Carmelite who had conducted the visitation, were nominated
deputies for the economy. On 7 February 1917 there was a meeting
of Cardinal Bisletti, the Prefect of the Congregation of Seminaries,
Gasquet the Protector, Bishop Giacomo Tinbaldi, the Secretary of
the Congregation, the four deputies, and the Rector, McIntyre. A
full report was given of the visitation. The Apostolic Administrator
was entrusted with the carrying out of the decrees, and it was
decided that they would report back in a year's time. During these
twelve months there was a thorough examination of the accounts.
These had been very much neglected and the Libro Mastro was
resumed as from 1917. The visitor disagreed with the calculations
of the College *essatore* as to the assets; he reckoned that the College
was worse off financially than it realised. But by 15 October it was
possible to draw up a statement of the *situazione patrimoniale*.[8]

Hinsley's appointment

Even during the visitation the search had begun for a new Rector.
It was also necessary to replace John Foley as Vice-Rector. At the
age of 26, he was considered too young and inexperienced, just as
McIntyre was too old at 61.[9] Hinsley's name seems to have been
first mooted in 1916 and, in a letter to his friend Sheehan, he gave
his reasons for not wanting the job in Rome.[10] When McIntyre was
reappointed as Auxiliary in Birmingham the way was now clear for
a new appointment. Hinsley's name had also figured on McIntyre's
list and Gasquet supported his candidature. But there was opposition to Hinsley from several members of the hierarchy, on the
grounds that he lacked the requirements of courage and determi-
nation necessary for such a post. His years as a priest had been a

series of false starts, promise leading to nothing; he could not persevere in any one job.[11] In the end, Hinsley's name was on the *terna* for Rector of the Beda and the three nominated for the English College were Kavanagh, O'Farrell and Moriarty. But it was Hinsley who was appointed on 28 October 1917, less than two weeks after the financial accounts of the College were finally settled. He wrote a letter of acceptance to Gasquet on 8 November and arrived at the College at the end of that month, but he did not take up his post fully until the work of the Apostolic Administrator was completed at the agreed date in February 1918. So it is that his first report on affairs of the College, as Rector, is for the year March 1918 to March 1919.

The 'congregation' consisting of the Cardinal Protector and the deputies, which had administered the College, met regularly after February 1918, but it was only on 26 June 1919 that the Rector began to be present at these proceedings.[12] This state of affairs, set up as a result of the visitation, was not fully understood by former students of the College resident in England. They attributed it to a seizure of power by Gasquet and the Benedictines. In some 'Notes for Mgr Hinsley', the Roman Association stated,[13] 'The entire control of the finances of the English College appear to have been taken over by S. Callisto in February 1917 ... the Reverend Philip Langdon took full control of the College accounts. He took entire possession of the *computisteria*. The key of this office was in his keeping and he kept all the accounts with the assistance of one, Domenico.[14] The college staff had no access to this office. Even the salaries of the Rector and Mgr George (of the Beda) were paid by Rev. P. Langdon.' The facts are true, but the crisis that brought about this situation was not appreciated by those who had been students under Mgr Giles.[15]

Hinsley soon realised that his powers as Rector were restricted but this did at least ensure that he was not alone and had support for the considerable tasks that confronted him. The material state of the building, especially the kitchens, was one of disrepair. The roof was leaking and there was only one bathroom. The departure of the Beda meant that there were vacant rooms, which could be adapted to College use, but the number of students was very small. At the outbreak of the 1914 war there had been thirty-three students at the English College; during the war years this had fallen and when Hinsley arrived there were only fifteen and there were no students at all in the first two years of philosophy. But there was at least a policy and in his first annual report he staunchly defended the new Constitution against criticisms that a totally different and

Fig. 8.2 Arthur Hinsley, Rector 1913–29.

alien system of government and discipline had been imposed.[16] A series of letters testifies to his frequent recourse to Gasquet and the support he received from that quarter.[17] One of the four deputies set up by the new Constitution was Mgr Stanley, who throughout his life gave generous financial aid to the College.

Hinsley was aware that he had powerful friends in Rome, but from England he had to win supporters. Both Gasquet and McIntyre had written to the Roman Association in 1916 asking for help and for contributions towards the restoration of the buildings in Rome and at Monte Porzio. The suggestion that bursary funds should be used for this purpose was rejected by the Association. Now the Association was, for the most part, made up of men who had been brought up under the Giles regime and they did not welcome the changes being made at the College and the implied criticism of Giles. They found fault with Gasquet's plans for a reorganisation of the library, with the contractor he had employed to carry out repairs and even with the bank in which he was now depositing the College money.[18] However, before Hinsley was appointed, Gasquet had persuaded the bishops to issue a joint pastoral letter and this was read out in all the churches on the last

Fig. 8.3 Francis Cardinal Gasquet.

Sunday of October in 1917 and a collection was taken up for the English College. The appeal realised £5,181 10s. 6d., a remarkable sum for wartime England. But the Roman Association, who had undertaken the organisation of the collection, was unwilling to send the money out to Rome unless it had some indication of how it was to be used. 'The Association would not trust anyone except itself with the spending of the money that had been collected.'[19] The majority of the bishops were against this attitude and Gasquet found a warm supporter in Amigo of Southwark. But it was not until Gasquet secured the intervention of Bisletti, at the Congregation of Seminaries, that the Association released the money.[20] It was this situation that confronted Hinsley on his arrival in Rome and in his first annual report he protested against the action of the Association and expressed gratitude and admiration for the untiring interest and energy which the Cardinal Protector had shown in striving to place the College on a proper foundation and in an honourable position.

Hinsley is often remembered for the introduction of the sisters to look after the domestic side and for the purchase of Palazzola as a summer villa. In both of these acts he was carrying out the wishes of the visitation,[21] but special credit is due to him for the rapidity with which he acted and the way he seized opportunities. This had been a characteristic of his days at Bradford and at Ushaw.[22] Permission to sell Monte Porzio had been obtained in 1917 and in 1918, for the first time for many decades, there was no *villeggiatura* there. The summer was spent at Montopoli,[23] a property north of Rome, rented for the occasion. It proved to be an eventful summer, in that the holiday was extended because of 'Spanish 'flu' in Rome, and it was here that they had news of and celebrated the armistice at the end of World War I. By 30 March 1920 the contract for the purchase of Palazzola had been signed.[24] But the new villa did present some difficulties, in that it would lie empty for nine months of the year, and when the Roman Association met in Rome in 1922, Hinsley asked for their ideas on the possible utilisation of the property when the College was not in residence there.[25]

The coming of the nuns to the College was connected with the leaving of Monte Porzio. During the summer of 1918 the villa at Monte Porzio was not entirely empty, since it housed a community of sisters, who were refugees from the war. They had come from the North of Italy. Hinsley managed to persuade them to stay on and look after the College in Rome. The affair was wound up so rapidly that when the students returned from Montopoli, in November 1918, the nuns were already installed[26] and were able to cater for the celebrations on 18 December to mark the centenary of the restoration of the College after the French occupation.

The other problems confronting Hinsley were tackled in an efficient way. By August 1923 he had secured the services of Fr Joseph Moss as resident spiritual director. A visit to England in the summer of 1919 produced twenty new students and by 1921 the number of students had grown from fifteen to sixty-two. Efforts to enlist a tutor or *ripetitore* were not so successful. Mgr Petroccia had been in this post for over twelve years and now with the increased numbers it meant that he was giving twelve to fourteen lectures a week. He was a professor rather than a tutor, and had other commitments at the Lateran. There was need for a younger man and, as Hinsley said in his annual report for 1918–1919, 'It would be a great gain to have a ripetitore who understands the mentality of Englishmen and who would elicit knowledge instead of lecturing.' In correspondence with Gasquet on this point the name of William Godfrey was mentioned.

The work of modernisation continued. The bottom corridor was made more impressive, central heating was installed, new quarters

Fig 8.4 An aerial view of Palazzola, the College summer residence purchased in 1920.

Fig 8.5 Palazzola, the cortile with the wall of the church on the left: the cortile has been glazed in recent years.

Fig. 8.6 Palazzola, the façade of the Church of Our Lady of the Snows.

were built at Palazzola for the nuns, the rooms near the Rector's apartments were reconstructed and the present-day *salone* emerged. The students' common room was enlarged, a new organ was acquired for the church and a swimming tank installed in the garden. The number of students in the year 1926–7 was up to seventy-six, of whom eleven were on burses provided by Mgr Stanley.

In 1925, as part of Mussolini's schemes for the improvement of Rome, a plan was disclosed for the erection of a covered market in the Via dei Cappellari.[27] This would mean the demolition of part of the College and the loss of the already exiguous garden. Just before Christmas 1925, Hinsley had a letter published in *The Universe*, but in the new year the case for the College was taken up by *The Times*. There was a leader and a special article entitled 'A threatened Foundation'. From *The Times* the news spread to the Italian press, *Tribuna*, *Piccolo* and *Il Giornale d'Italia*. In February *The Times* carried pictures of the threatened wing of the College (the third library and the *guardaroba*) and of the martyrs' chapel, which would also be affected. The *Lancashire Daily Post* gave publicity to the story and the *South Wales News* dwelt on the College's 'cymric associa-

Fig. 8.7 The College garden and *guardaroba*, part of the college threatened with demolition in 1925.

tions'. In those days the views of *The Times* counted for much, even in Italy, and eventually the plan was changed, although it was not until February 1929 (just after the Lateran Treaty between Italy and the Vatican was signed) that the Governor of Rome finally approved of the modification and the English College was saved. This mobilisation of public opinion was due to Hinsley's prompt action and we can also be sure that he entered into negotiations in the private field as well.[28]

The Hinsley spirit

As was the case with Giles, Hinsley was able to impress his version of the Roman spirit on the house. In many ways his task was harder as he had to cope with the newer outlook of the post-war generation and at a time when the visitation had called for a tightening up in discipline and administration. In 1926 he could say, 'The spirit of our men is excellent. There is a healthy public opinion and a tradition of earnestness, loyalty, regularity.'[29] Something of that spirit can be gained from a perusal of the College magazine, *The Venerabile*, which was started in 1922. There was a social life in which the Rector, superiors and students all took part; there were regular plays and concerts; the tradition of Gilbert and Sullivan operas began; debates and societies flourished and, in the magazine itself, a high standard of articles on historical, literary and travel themes was achieved. Much of this had been a feature of life at the College before the war, but it now took on added vigour and continued right through the period in England and lasted well into the early 1960s, in almost unchanged form. It was a very English sort of existence. There was an air of imperial self-consciousness which received a boost from such things as the visit to Rome in 1923 of King George V and Queen Mary, and which was nourished by periodic visits from members of the Royal Navy on leave in Rome, and cricket matches against a British Embassy XI. A feeling of super- iority towards foreigners was tempered by an affection for Italy.[30] But this was not specifically Catholic, as these sentiments were shared by people like E. M. Forster and Norman Douglas. The isolation from England, in the days before easy air travel, tended to give the common room an air of an officers' mess on the North West Frontier, and during vacation the reading in the refectory of such books as *South with Scott* and *The Worst Journey in the World* helped to inspire a more secular heroism than that of their sixteenth-century forebears. This was hardly to be wondered at, since the Constitution and Rules forced members of the College into each other's company, and contact with the city was strictly ecclesiastical and even this was restricted and supervised. That the tension did not become unbearable and that many were able to enjoy and profit from their Roman days was due in no small measure to the increased numbers at the College and the varied experience and talents of those who were students. It was only in the 1960s that the centripetal forces became less marked and with increasing contacts outside the College community, the pattern of social life changed.

Studies

As under the Giles regime, there was still a marked divide between life as it was lived and what was taught at the University. When the Gregorian is mentioned it is often a question of successes in examinations, from the statistical point of view. There seems to be little relationship between the learning imparted at the University and the students' day-to-day interests. There is evidence of interest in the history and archeology of Rome, the history of the College and the tradition of the Martyrs, but there is little sign of the deeper theological issues that were bubbling up beneath the surface. But

Fig. 8.8–10 Modernisation: *top*, main corridor; *centre*, common room; *bottom*, swimming pool, with remnants of the original Hospice in the far wall.

after all, perhaps Rome is the last place to look for such awareness when the whole purpose of the course was to initiate into the received viewpoint. One might suggest that a contributory factor in this inability to assimilate the official learning with their own interests, was the failure to obtain any lasting and satisfactory arrangement about a *ripetitore* in theology. In his report for 1925/6 Hinsley stated:

> The superiors of the College have not the time nor the qualifications to act as tutors. Young adult minds are required for the work, men fresh from their studies and in close touch with the University ... Italian *ripetitores* have invariably proved unsuitable for our students.

He goes on to ask for two English priests as tutors. But the very next year we find that there are two men from the German College acting in this capacity and so the same request is repeated in 1927/8. However, it is worth noting that in the year 1925/6 Fr Martin D'Arcy SJ acted as *ripetitore* in philosophy. Not unconnected with this state of affairs was the regret expressed that more and more students were taking the minor course in theology.

> In some cases at least, a student who is not up to standard in theological studies might derive greater benefit from a seminary course in England ... Rome of course is an education in itself, but the Rector must report according to the measurable standard of University studies.

The desire was that students should conform to the standards of the Gregorian. How far the Gregorian was itself suitable, either for the Church at large or for the needs of England, was never questioned, except doubtless in the minds of the students themselves, who nevertheless continued their outward attempt to conform. That theology proved little intellectual stimulus to students can be gleaned from remarks such as, 'The majority of Romans don't look upon the Gregorian as alma mater.'[31] Matters did improve to the extent that in 1930/1, by the time Godfrey became Rector, there were no students in the College who were not following the higher course that led to the D.D. The Gregorian itself improved its standards after the decree *Deus Scientiarum Dominus* (1935). Although this reform was welcomed, there is little evidence of any critical assessment of the studies. But perhaps it would be too much to expect such an assessment, as comparisons were not available. A course of theology at a British university was not then open to Catholics, nor would such a course have been considered either

Fig. 8.11–12 The College library comprised three rooms: *above*, the second room with the first room visible through the open door; *below*, the third room which alone remained as refurbished in the 1920s until 2004.

sufficiently orthodox or appropriate for future priests.

A sidelight on the studies in Rome during their period is given by the correspondence about the re-organisation of the College library.[32] In the papers about this there are a series of memoranda from members of the College as to the purpose of such a library. Some called it a 'white elephant' since, of the 20,000 volumes, not more than a third would be required by the students during their residence in the College. Very few outsiders consulted the library, and it was pointed out that the Scots College found adequate a room 'less in size than any of ours'.[33] It was suggested that the oriental section should be packed away out of sight; it was never used now and should not receive any additions. The literary section should be transferred to Palazzola and all that was needed was a very small room. Hinsley however, consulted competent scholars both in Rome and in England and the library was catalogued and remained in one piece.[34] The catalogue was completed by Dr Reinthaler in 1930. By October 1932, *The Venerabile* could report that the work was finished and that little red patches were attached to those books that were prohibited.[35] These doubts about the advisability of a library on a large scale are worth recording, since they reflect the prevailing opinion that the College was catering mainly for a first degree course, which demanded the reading of set books and not research.

However, in 1925, Hinsley had envisaged students staying on to do further studies in Rome, either at the Gregorian, the Apollinare, the Biblical Institute or even a course in paleography or diplomacy at the Vatican. But despite this, the value of the Roman course was misleading, since without any further studies, until *Deus Scientiarum Dominus,* students were able to get the doctorate. This was very much an inflated degree, as the length of time spent in study was only one year more than the normal seminary course in England.

Yet Rome had a strong position, since it was only there that it was possible to gain a Catholic theological degree and attend an English seminary. There were English seminaries at Valladolid and Lisbon but there were no equivalent theological degrees given. There were theological degrees given at Louvain and Fribourg, but there was no English house of residence there. In 1923 Cardinal Bourne announced, at the National Catholic Congress in Birmingham, his desire of setting up a Catholic theological faculty in England. He was not satisfied with the Gregorian course and had a scheme to acquire the Leys school at Cambridge. This plan came to nothing, since the Bishop of the Diocese, Cary-Elwes, was not informed of the negotiations and when he did discover what was going on, he took umbrage. This announcement of Bourne at Birmingham, in August, created a certain amount of panic in Roman circles and on 29 September Bishop Casartelli of Salford wrote to Gasquet[36] saying that the scheme had to be opposed, as such a Catholic faculty of theology and philosophy would be damaging to the English College in Rome.

Hinsley's own theological position was strictly orthodox. He had taught at Ushaw where his philosophy was in the spirit of the Thomistic revival of Leo XIII. In 1896–97 he had engaged in public debate in *The Tablet*, attacking St George Mivart and Fr David Fleming OFM for their favourable reception of Fr Zahm's view of evolution.[37] Later, he taught Church history at Wonersh and he was specially vigilant of any hint of modernism in his students. In this he drew close to the views of Bishop Amigo, who had to deal with Tyrrell and Maud Petre.

This tendency to play safe theologically may seem to be excessively cautious to later ages, but in the early part of the twentieth century it could not be otherwise in the Rector of a seminary in Rome, so much in the ascendancy were the anti-modernists and those loyal to the absolute claims of the papacy. His administrative gifts and his ability to inspire confidence and love in his students and encourage their initiative compensate for many of his other deficiencies. Among the Gasquet papers[38] there is a petition to make Hinsley a bishop and the reasons adduced are, 'La chiesa cattolica in Inghilterra ha bisogno dello spirito di Romanita.' His name was mentioned when Hexham fell vacant, but it was considered unwise to remove him from the work he was doing at the College. It was, in fact, as a recognition of the work that he had done for the College during the last nine years that he was nominated titular bishop of Sebastopolis in August 1926. He was consecrated in November of that year by Cardinal Merry del Val with Palica, the Viceregent, and Amigo of Southwark as assistants.

The Hinsley regime is of more than domestic interest, since under him were formed spiritually, theologically and culturally the churchmen who were to mould English Catholic thought right into the 1970s. Cardinal Heenan's memoir of Hinsley gives a good idea of what many of the students thought of 'the Boss'. There were many English College bishops before Hinsley and there are later ones not formed by him, but it is doubtful if the extent of the influence of the College on the hierarchy can be equalled in any other such limited number of years. Griffin, Heenan, Masterson, Grimshaw, Dwyer, Rudderham, Restieaux, Ellis, Tickle, Halsall and Pearson were all students under Hinsley, at one time or another, and thus seven dioceses were indirectly under his influence.[39] How they actually became bishops is, of course, another matter. In fact it seems to have been the policy in Rome to appoint Roman trained priests and this applies also to countries other than England. The North American College, for example, was regarded as a nursery for future bishops.

There can be little doubt that the days in Rome, as a student under Hinsley, were looked back on with great gratitude and not a little nostalgia.[40] But Hinsley's own life was not to be bounded by the English College and in 1927 he was appointed Apostolic Visitor to Africa. This visit occupied him greatly and he seems to have soon forgotten the trivia of the Via Monserrato, without losing the affection he had for his friends there. As R. L. Smith puts it,[41] 'When he came back [from Africa] after two years, the Venerabile was too small for him.'

The end of Hinsley's rule

The African commitment lasted much longer than the six to nine months originally expected. Hinsley certainly enjoyed it and his letters back to Rome were largely an account of his travels. He easily shook off the work of College administration, confident that he need have no fears for the day-to-day running of the College, which was in the hands of the Vice-Rector Mgr Redmond. The annual reports were presented by the Vice-Rector, after they had been examined by the *deputati* for the College administration, Mgr Cicognani and Mgr Heard, and by the Cardinal Protector. 'While the College cannot but feel the absence of its head, at the same time it is felt that when he departed, he left the whole machinery in full and regular working order.'[42] But changes were on the way. Mgr Stanley, a great benefactor, died. Dr Moss, the spiritual director, became Vice-Rector of the Beda, which meant that the Vice-Rector of the English College was now the sole superior. Cardinal Gasquet died in 1929 and a new protector, Merry del Val, was appointed. Like Gasquet he was sympathetic to Hinsley and, although never a student at the English College, he had been indirectly concerned with its affairs for many years.[43] But twelve months later he was dead and Hinsley was no longer Rector. Hinsley's work in Africa took on a more permanent basis when he was made Archbishop of Sardis and Apostolic Delegate, which meant that he would have to resign the rectorship.

There was considerable delay in appointing a successor. Consultations were going on, but the new Protector, Lepicier, had

Fig. 8.13 View of the new Gregorian University. It was not to be completed until the 1920s.

only just taken office and he was in fact installed during the inter-regnum. Hinsley himself was in the dark, but he was aware that there were attempts being made to have a 'non- Roman' appointed, perhaps a Bourne nominee. In the senior student's diary[44] for 19 May 1930, we read 'The old boss tells us the new Rector is to be decided upon tomorrow. God grant we may be saved from some whose names we have heard.' The next day Hinsley is reported as saying that he was 'fighting for a Roman'. But still no news came. Hinsley left Rome without knowing anything and wrote to Redmond, the Vice-Rector, on 10 June:

> The delay in appointing a Rector is very trying. I know nothing. To you this delay must be most annoying. I think you deserve more consideration! You know exactly what was the situation when I left. If I thought I could have done more, I would have stopped on till somebody had been definitely decided.[45]

He adds a little later on, 'I saw His Eminence of Westminster yester-day. Very pleasant, but not a word about the Venerabile.' It was not until 26 June that Redmond was able to announce to the students that Dr Godfrey of Ushaw had been appointed. There was a general sigh of relief. 'He is at least one of our own.'[46] Godfrey arrived at Palazzola on 4 August and almost immediately made his presence felt by a strict enforcement of the rules.

The rectorship of William Godfrey

William Godfrey, ordained in 1916, at the end of McIntyre's rectorship, had a brilliant career as a student. He was the first Englishman to be chosen for the solemn public act in theology since Wiseman's days. A contemporary writes: 'an exemplary student and very popular ... an impersonator of no mean ability ... very amusing at the piano ... a most efficient choir master'.[47] On his return from Rome he spent some months as a curate in Liverpool and then went to Ushaw as classics master in 1919, and was later professor of philosophy and theology. His name had been mentioned as a possible superior in Rome as early as 1917.[48] In 1928, and again in 1929, Mgr Redmond, acting as Rector in Hinsley's absence in Africa, had approached Archbishop Downey, his bishop, and the authorities at Ushaw, to release Godfrey to enable him to become *ripetitore* in Rome. This reputation was justified, during his years as Rector in Rome, in as much as he worked in conjunction with Mgr Ruffini,[49] Secretary to the Congregation of Seminaries and Studies on the Decree *Deus Scientiarum Dominus*, that was to do so much to reform the standards of theology in seminaries and bring Catholic universities into line with their secular counterparts on the continent. Godfrey's rectorship coincided with what many regard as the high point in teaching and learning at the Gregorian, when the colleges in Rome produced their best scholarship.[50] However, the style and the system were quite different from those of a British university and Godfrey himself could sometimes scarcely conceal a contempt for English university life and learning, which he considered to be superficial and flippant.

Godfrey succeeded to a difficult domestic situation. Hinsley's mission to Africa meant that there was, practically speaking, no Rector from November 1927 until August 1930. Some of the students, who had begun their studies during those years, scarcely knew the Rector and yet his presence and influence were there, but, with such a long absence, a 'myth' had begun to grow up. Godfrey had need not only to stress his own authority but to return to the older fidelity to the rules. In his first annual report he was able to say, 'The observance of the rules is generally satisfactory, and markedly improving. This is all the more creditable when the difficulties of last year are borne in mind, and want of adequate supervision by the superiors.'

The value that was placed on restrictions in themselves (arbitrary rules) was that they helped to form character, and there is an implied connection between the hardship and suffering caused by the rules and the suffering of the martyrs.[51] Godfrey was not alone in this persuasion. Life in the College, from the 1920s right up to 1940 and beyond, bears the same imprint. If one looks through the notes Hinsley, Godfrey and his successor, Macmillan, made use of in addressing the students on various occasions during the year, it is at times difficult to tell which Rector is speaking, were it not for the different handwriting and dates. The similarity has to do with the observance and purpose of the rules. If Godfrey differed from the others, it was in the fact that he was never afraid of unpopularity and never compromised his principles.

But such an insistence on routine meant at times an inability to cope with the untoward. An instance of this is seen in October 1931.[52]

> The Rector informed the senior student that he heard today from a new student who is already on his way to the College. The Rector has never had any application from this person from Nottingham. Perhaps things have been overlooked owing to the bishop's death. The Rector could not turn him back as he is coming by sea. The following plan was proposed to the senior student. He should take a room on the superiors' corridor and the new man take the (senior) student's present one, n. 67, over the garden. This was practically settled. The senior student informed the lads indirectly through one who passed the word around and there was a slight uproar, it was proposed on the spur of the moment that Mr. Luke (3rd year philosophy) who just missed leaving the 'slums' on Via Monserrato should go to the senior student's room and the new student get on the Monserra'. The senior student saw the Rector. He objected that once a man was in a room tradition said he could remain there for the remainder of his course and in the present case of Mr. Luke this tradition would create difficulty. With regard to the new man he would automatically leave n. 67 next year and take his choice in turn. The Rector has now one or two schemes which may fructify.

This incident is a good illustration of the way in which an attitude to the rule can add to the complications of a life already plagued by customs and traditions. Fortunately, the student in question was able to become a normal member of the house, and indeed a future Vice-Rector, vicar general of Nottingham and Bishop of Shrewsbury.

But the strictness of the Godfrey regime has to be seen in the context of the conditions under which all clerics who lived in Rome were supervised in the 1930s. The Rectors were under considerable pressure from the Congregation of Seminaries and Studies and, for the most part, they had no alternative but to yield to it and, consequently, draw on themselves the unpopularity and opprobrium of the students. There would appear to be a constriction in those years that one had not experienced before.[53] Perhaps it was the strain the Church was feeling from the Fascist government in Italy. There is certainly a contrast between the euphoria and laissez-faire of the 1920s and the fears of the 1930s. Godfrey, writing later in his preface to the Liber Ruber, reflects:

> While fingering the pages of our own Liber Ruber we did not think that other books of the same kind were being made and that the day would come when the simple word 'martyr factus est' might be written alongside the names of men with whom we conversed in the halls of the Gregorian University and whom we saw with books under their arms treading the Roman streets or walking on the Pincio in the evening sunshine. Yet so it was. Other colleges were training their own sons for an ordeal which, in the early years of the century, seemed not to threaten.[54]

But life from the disciplinary point of view became more difficult and tensions began to show themselves. There is the entry for 16 April 1931 in the senior student's diary, 'Rector put up notice about Protestant Bibles. No one should buy or retain same in the College. All centres of Protestant Propaganda in Rome must be avoided. This he had had from the Congregation. Doubtful whether we should destroy books that we already have.' As an example of the notes that issued from the Congregation, we have one from Ruffini in July 1938, informing the Rector that the Plenary Congregation of the Cardinals had made provisions concerning the summer–autumn holidays of students of the ecclesiastical colleges in Rome, to the effect that the itinerary of journeys must be made known to the Rector and cannot be modified without permission. They must always use the ecclesiastical dress of the countries in which they are. They are not to travel alone, but in company and under the vigilance of a suitable person. They are to present themselves to the diocesan authorities and be in continual contact during their stay. Their lodgings must be chosen according to the suggestion of the local ordinary. Even outside Rome, students ought to observe, during their travels, rules analogous to those given by the vicariate concerning amusements and public places. The Rector is to ask the ecclesiastical authorities of the places visited for a report on his students' conduct. All this, one must note, concerns the students on vacation.

The seriousness with which Godfrey applied these rules meant that he was given assignments of trust, which helped to test his loyalty still further and brought him more and more into the

Curia's way of looking at things. Hinsley had been sent on a mission to Africa and had acquitted himself well. Godfrey accompanied a mission to Malta in 1936, was part of Pizzardo's[55] suite in the papal mission to England for the coronation of King George VI and then in 1938 he was made Apostolic Visitor to the seminaries in Great Britain and Malta. This was an important mission and indicates that his direction of the English College[56] was officially recognised. But of course the College itself did not escape this general visitation of seminaries that Pius XI had set in motion. This took place while Godfrey was absent visiting other seminaries. The report on the English College had a mild reproof for the Rector. 'The Rector is asked to act a little more kindly with students especially those who are sick or in poor health. There should be more light in the chapel and common room.'

Considering the murmurings of the students and the complaints they had about the Rector, and also considering the way in which certain quarters in Rome looked somewhat askance at the behaviour of the English with their swimming tank and system of discipline, the final outcome of the visitation was mild. But the accusation that the Rector lacked kindness and humanity, especially with the sick, caused a certain amount of pain and embarrassment to the students. Godfrey had not been popular and the senior student's diary testifies to this on many occasions and evidently some students had not hesitated to make their complaints to the Visitor.

The Munich crisis of August 1938 brought anxiety about the future of the College and what would happen in the event of war. But the minutiae of College life sometimes seemed to be of equal importance. Just after recording the Munich crisis the senior student wrote;

> 3 October. Talk from the Rector. Some person in the House has been cutting lace off corporals and palls. Who he is or why he did it are major mysteries. He probably did it because he objects to the rococco style of much of our altar linen. Also the Rector's lace alb was missing for a month and found rolled into a ball in the oil cupboard. The Rector feels very strongly about it all, saying that such a person had no right to be in the College at all.

But the Rector saved up the news about the official report on the visitation. On 21 November rumours began to circulate in the Italian press that the Vatican and the British government had agreed to have a representative of the Vatican in London and Mgr Godfrey was to be the new delegate. Confirmation came in the

Osservatore Romano of 23 November and the students were 'pleased for more reasons than one', and in the common room that evening the Rector was presented with a set of episcopal robes, from the stage property men. It was with this news in the air that he announced the result of the visitation and the criticism it contained of his rule. There was a wave of sympathy for him, but this receded a little in the ensuing days.

The secrecy that surrounded Godfrey's appointment as Rector was to be surpassed by the nomination of his successor, which reduced the whole procedure to absurdity. On 27 January 1939, news arrived in a private letter to one of the students from Upholland that Dr Macmillan was to be the new Rector. Upholland had a day off to celebrate the appointment. When the senior student went to Archbishop Godfrey, still acting as Rector, he was given the reply that as there had been no official notification, there was nothing to be said. The following day newspaper cuttings from the English press began to arrive, carrying articles about the new Rector. Godfrey still refused to say anything, or to drink the new Rector's health, as nothing official had yet arrived. On 30 January, another private letter arrived with the news from Upholland that the new Rector would be arriving in Rome the following Sunday. On 2 February the old Rector and the senior student presented the College candle to the Pope, as was customary at Candlemas, but there was no mention of the new Rector. Then on 4 February, the eve of Dr Macmillan's arrival, the old Rector finally agreed to drink his health. He said that he still did not know officially of the appointment, but he thought no harm could be done. 'It seems that a week or two ago he had a circular from the Vatican complaining that some appointment or other had not been kept secret. This made him very cautious.' So the new Rector arrived on the Sunday afternoon and there was a concert in his honour in the evening. But the morning was a day of recollection, it being the regular first Sunday of the month. Godfrey departed three days later.[57]

Notes

1 Francis Aidan Gasquet, a Benedictine monk of Downside, had devoted himself to historical research after a breakdown in health in 1885. He played an important part in the Roman rejection of the validity of Anglican Orders. He was close to Cardinal Vaughan and his name was on the *terna* for the succession to Westminster, as was that of Rafael Merry del Val, another close friend. Already a frequent visitor to Rome when he was created Cardinal in 1914, he took up permanent residence in Rome at the

Palazzo S. Callisto in Trastevere. See Shane Leslie, *Cardinal Gasquet* (London 1953).

2 He was auxiliary bishop in Birmingham when he was appointed to Rome and after his brief term in office he returned to assist Bishop Ilsley in Birmingham and eventually succeeded him as Archbishop. For an appreciation of McIntyre see A. Villiers, *Venerabile*, VII, 86–93.

3 The ensuing account relies on the documents in ECA, scr. 100, 1 and the document of the Congregation of Seminaries and Studies issued 2 January 1917 giving the official report.

4 This may, of course, have been because McIntyre was already a bishop when he was appointed Rector.

5 Downside Archives, 888 and 888.8, Gasquet papers.

6 ECA, Liber 618, 2. This was a similar situation to that obtaining under Corsini.

7 Algernon Charles Stanley, fourth and youngest son of the second Lord Stanley of Alderly, took Anglican Orders but was received into the Catholic Church in 1879: he studied for a year in Rome at the Accademia and was ordained priest in 1880. After a period at Spanish Place, London, he settled in Rome in 1893. Cardinal Vaughan appointed him as his auxiliary in Westminster in 1902, but on the death of Vaughan, Stanley returned to Rome where he spent the last years of his life, dying there in 1928.

8 The College *essatore* calculated that the College was in credit of 5053.50 lire but the visitor's accountant reckoned it to be only 2251.38 lire.

9 In the light of future events it is interesting to note that in a letter of Archbishop Whiteside of Liverpool to Gasquet in 1917, it is suggested that there was a newly ordained priest who at some future date would make a good superior of the English College. His name, William Godfrey. Downside Archives, 888, 3.

10 Downside Archives, 888, 3.

11 Ibid.

12 For details as to how the administration was placed in the hands of Gasquet, see ECA, liber 618 and scr. 86, 1 and 2.

13 ECA, scr. 86, I. See also Dominic Rolls, 'A Troubled Transition. The Roman Association of the English College 1913–1922', *Venerabile*, 1988, 59–63.

14 Domenico Romualdi was cameriere to Cardinal Vives y Tuto, but entered service at the English College in October 1913. Apart from the years of exile, he remained in service until his retirement in 1951. He died in 1954.

15 J. C. Heenan in his *Cardinal Hinsley* (London 1944), says (p. 41) 'It was this which caused the abrupt dissolution of the triumvirate which Cardinal Gasquet had appointed at the English College'. It was not a Gasquet appointment, it was not a triumvirate, there were four deputies, and it was not abruptly dissolved. In fact it continued until 1924, the meetings becoming gradually less frequent.

16 ECA, scr. 100, 1.

17 Downside Archives, 888, 4, English College correspondence. There is included here a 14-page document to Gasquet which gives Hinsley's account of the condition of the College October 1919–August 1920.

18 ECA, scr. 86 1 and 2.

19 Downside Archives, 888, the Bishop of Nottingham to Gasquet, 3 June 1918. For Moriarty's account of the collection (he was president of the Association 1916–1919) see *Venerabile*, XII, 122.

20 They had in the meantime invested the money. But they deducted expenses and handed over the remainder to the Rector.

21 In an article in the *Venerabile*, III, 105–113 by R. L. Smith on 'The Rector's Consecration', the author tells us about Hinsley's speech to the students where he gave credit to others for the improvements in the College and he comments 'as an expression of affection the Rector's speech must have reddened innumerable ears, as an exercise in truth it was lamentable'. History might rewrite that last remark.

22 Cf. J. C. Heenan, *Cardinal Hinsley*, p. 41.

23 For Montopoli see J. Scarr and R. Meagher in *Venerabile*, VI, 277–93; also J. Prior, *Venerabile*, XX, 295–301.

24 R. Meagher, 'Early Days at Palazzola', *Venerabile*, IX, 28–35, tells us that during the winter of 1919–20 the Rector made all the students pray that a suitable property might come on the market. For the background to the purchase see 'Carlo Arnaldi and the Purchase of Palazzola', *Venerabile*, II, 65–7.

25 This meeting was held in Rome as a belated celebration of the centenary of the restoration of the College under Gradwell in 1818. Gasquet had thought up the idea but he was unable to win the support of the Association to come out to Rome in 1918 as originally intended.

26 See *Venerabile*, XXIV, 188 for an account by the nuns of their first days at the English College.

27 J. Garvin, 'The Piano Regolatore', *Venerabile*, IV, 236–8.

28 De Cupis, who had bought the upper villa at Palazzola from the College, was not only a friend of Hinsley but had friends amongst the Fascist Party, including Count Ciano.

29 ECA, Rector's Report for 1925–6.

30 A reference to the lending list of books at Palazzola indicates an interest in Italian culture that was fostered during the summer vacation.

31 *Venerabile*, II, 71. See also the editor E. H. A. on Gregorian life, *Venerabile*, II, 197–8.

32 *Venerabile*, II, 249.

33 R. L. Smith, *Venerabile*, X, 243 when speaking of time wasted in a library is simply repeating what he said as a student during the Hinsley regime; cf. ECA, scr. 86.6.

34 In 1921 the Rector discovered, during the course of the summer, in a disused cupboard opposite the entrance to the clock tower, 87 books of the 16th–18th centuries, including Henry VIII's *Assertio*. It was also during Hinsley's time that the library acquired Mgr Prior's library of over 500 volumes; ECA, liber 837.

35 ECA, liber 835, *Index Librorum Prohibitorum Bibliothecae Ven. Col. Anglorum de Urbe*, is interesting reading. Compiled originally at the time of the new catalogue it includes Arsdekin, *Theologia tripartita* which seems to have been

used as a text book in the eighteenth century, as well as such classics as T. Brown, *Urn Burial*. Most of the prohibited books were in Room III.

36 Downside Archives, 888, 5, English College correspondence.

37 Hinsley's first letter occasioned the remark, 'Who is this Hinsley who is seeking to obtain some cheap renown regardless of the harm he does.' Mivart to Fleming, 8 December 1896, David Fleming Papers, OFM Archives. I am indebted to Fr Justin McLoughlin OFM for this reference. For this period in Hinsley's life see also J. C. Heenan, *Cardinal Hinsley*, p. 38; St George Kieran Hyland, 'Arthur Hinsley parish priest', *Venerabile*, XIII, 25–9; S. Leslie, *Cardinal Gasquet*, p. 197; J. Derek Holmes, 'Some notes on liberal Catholicism and Catholic modernism', *Irish Theological Quarterly*, vol. 38, 348–57.

38 Downside Archives, Gasquet Papers 993; also Shane Leslie, *Cardinal Gasquet*, p. 257.

39 Many English College men taught in the seminaries in England. This was hardly surprising since there was no theological education at degree level open to Catholics in England. Priests who studied at British Universities did not read theology but either Arts or Sciences.

40 J. C. Heenan, 'A Roman's first Impressions [of the parish]', *Venerabile*, VI, 147–52. He remarks, 'one misses the common room horribly'. G. P. Dwyer, 'Wine', *Venerabile*, XII, 7. B. Wrighton, 'The Philosopher on Pindo', *Venerabile*, VI, 13–20. J. B. Hawkins, 'Fuimus Troes', *Venerabile*, VI, 179–83. For another reaction to College life, see Paul Roche, *0 Pale Galilean* (1954). J. C. Heenan, *Not the Whole Truth* (London 1971), pp. 47–64, gives mature reflections on his Roman days in the light of Vatican II.

41 *Venerabile*, XI, 114.

42 Report, 1927/8.

43 For Merry del Val see M. C. Buehrle (with foreword by J. C. Heenan), *Rafael Cardinal Merry del Val* (London, 1957); Alfonso de Zulueta, 'Reminiscences of Cardinal Merry del Val', *Ushaw Magazine* 244, December 74, 33; J. D. Holmes, 'Cardinal Merry del Val an uncompromising ultramontane', *Catholic History Review* 60 (1974), 55–64.

44 ECA, liber 831.

45 ECA, scr. 86, 10.

46 ECA, liber 831.

47 L. Charlier, *Venerabile*, XXII, 81.

48 Downside Archives, 888.3; also ECA, scr. 86.

49 Later Cardinal Archbishop of Palermo and active contributor to the debates at the Second Vatican Council.

50 It was at this time that the Gregorian University moved to its new buildings in the Piazza Pilotta.

51 'Sherwin, Walpole, Morse, Hart, Buxton, Lewis and all the rest of the gallant company seem to me to live again in those young men who were my fellow students, or who, in the days when I was Rector, were given to me to be led to the same sacred priesthood and to the same altar and sacrifice.' Godfrey's preface to the Liber Ruber published in 1940 (CRS, vol. 37).

52 ECA, Senior student's diary.

53 The Cardinal Protector at this time was the Servite, Alexis Lepicier, who had not only been an upholder of the neo-scholastic revival under Leo XIII, but also shared many of Godfrey's views on the spiritual formation of clerical students.

54 This was published in 1940.

55 Cardinal Pizzardo's friendship with the College lasted into the post-war years when he was Secretary of the Congregation of Seminaries. He was also one of the prime movers of 'Catholic Action' in the 1930s and this movement was to create certain tensions in the House as the senior student's diaries testify.

56 One must not fail to record Godfrey's work for the fabric of the College, especially the building of a new wing at Palazzola to take the increased student numbers. With financial help from Mgr Smith, the Vice-Rector, the Villa chapel was restored to its gothic origins.

57 For a further consideration of Godfrey, see M. E. Williams, 'Seminaries and Priestly Formation' in *From Without the Flaminian Gate*, ed. V. A. McClelland and M. Hodgetts (London 1999), pp. 78–80.

Chapter Nine

The War, the Exile and the Return to Rome

The rise of Mussolini and the emergence of Fascism were noted with that rather detached interest that greeted most aspects of Italian politics. The March on Rome was recorded and its unexpectedly orderly progress was remarked on.[1] The discipline that the new regime gave to Italian life brought it a certain respect from the English, who were inclined to mock the Italians for their inefficiency. At first anti-British feelings were not obvious. Indeed, it was only after the outbreak of war with Germany that they began to grow and even then they were not shared by the majority of the Italian people with whom the College came into contact. In the 1930s the value of the pound sterling plummeted in Italy[2] and this meant that economies had to be made in expenditure, including food. This was due to England's leaving the gold standard while the Italian lira remained tied to gold. Sanctions against Italy, because of the war in Abyssinia, did not affect the College to any large extent. The hierarchy continued with their support and the number of students remained well over seventy. Apart from the help given by the burses in the custody of the Roman Association, the bishops had to find all the money for the students' upkeep; the old idea of the College providing for the complete board, lodging and education of the alumni had now gone forever.

During these years, English Catholic opinion was firmly on the right politically.[3] The fortunes of the Nationalists in the Spanish civil war were eagerly followed. This meant that English Catholics failed to find a sympathetic ear in circles connected with the press, universities or government, all of whom were largely supporters of

Fig. 9.1 During the Second World War the
College was used as a hospital by the Knights of
Malta.

the Republican cause. In Rome, however, the climate was more
congenial and the victories in the last months of that war, the fall of
Barcelona and the fall of Madrid were not only celebrated with flags
in the city, but by extra wine at the English College.[4]

The patriotism of the English Catholics could not be doubted.[5] As
far as the rule permitted[6] the interests of England were closely
followed and feelings against Hitler's Germany were strong. So
when Pius XI pointedly left Rome during Hitler's visit in 1938, the
English College students felt encouraged.[7] If there was any tension
between their feelings as loyal Englishmen and their political and
religious sympathies with Spain and Italy, it was no more serious
than the long-standing tug of loyalties between the Crown which
was Protestant, and their religion which was Catholic.

It was in these conditions that John Macmillan became Rector. Strict, but less decisive than Godfrey, his reasonable and generous approach to the rules was welcomed by the students.[8] Early in 1939, Pius XI died and there was all the excitement of the Conclave and the election and coronation of Cardinal Pacelli as Pope Pius XII. But during the spring and summer the political crisis developed and in August the Rector left Palazzola to spend several days in Rome where he made preparations for the safety of the College in the now inevitable war. Money was transferred to the Vatican Bank. The Martyrs' picture, relics, chalices and silver plate, as well as the College archives, were taken to the Vatican for safe keeping. At the Villa the students followed the events; the invasion of Poland, the British note to Germany, the declaration of war and the King's speech to the Empire. Not only the fate of the College but their own personal future became precarious with the prospect of a general mobilisation. But before long it became clear that Italy was not going to war yet. The 'Rex' and 'Conte di Savoia', pride of the Italian mercantile fleet, resumed their sailings across the Atlantic. There now ensued the seven or eight months of what became known as the 'phoney war' when there was little military action at all between Germany and Britain and France. Life in Rome continued as usual. There were reminders of the war in such things as the College church bereft of its altarpiece. The Beda had not returned and were now in an English home at Upholland. There were some scarcities of food and on occasion it was necessary to curtail or cancel days out. Early on, the Italian government had promised that in case of war all clerics would be given facilities for leaving the country. From the British point of view, the students in Rome had registered with the consul and that was all that was required for the present.

The exodus

It was in May 1940, with the invasion of the Low Countries, that the situation changed dramatically. On Whitsun eve (11 May), Rome was placarded everywhere with anti-British posters. Two of the students tore some of these down and were followed back to the College by one of the *carabinieri*. No action was taken, but the Vice-Rector had a few words to say to the house that evening about self control. On Whit Sunday it was announced that there would be no day out tomorrow, but that preparations were to be made for departure, and the students were asked to be as secretive as possible about their probable going home. Monday, Tuesday and Wednesday were days of great activity. Passport photographs had to be obtained and provisions collected for the journey. So as not to arouse too much suspicion, some students were designated to attend lectures at the University as usual The subdeacons were recalled from their retreat at the Jesuit *casa*. The stage-property men managed to fit out everybody in civilian clothes, a formidable task since at Rome and the Villa the cassock was the only dress known. The final decision to leave was made by the Vice-Rector, as Macmillan had been in England since the beginning of March. At 9 a.m. on 15 May, the Rector arrived back and after an early rise the next morning, there was Mass, breakfast and then a fleet of taxis to take everybody to the station. The English and Scots students had a reserved carriage and they were seen off at the station by the two Rectors and one or two friends, including two from the German College, thereby returning the compliment of 1915 when it was the English who said goodbye to the Germans who had to leave Rome. At 8.25 a.m. the train pulled out of Roma Termini and the English College went into exile.[9]

The overland journey took them through an Italy preparing for war and a France that was already invaded. At Paris it was realised that the channel ports were about to fall, so the party proceeded to Le Havre, where they secured places on the last boat for England. In London they were greeted by Cardinal Hinsley and after Mass at Westminster Cathedral, they departed to their various homes. Within a month the College had reassembled at Ambleside.

Ambleside

A move to England had been visualised from the beginning of Macmillan's rectorship and the actual departure from Rome was, in the event, carried out by the Vice-Rector Mgr Smith. There was always concern that the College should remain in existence as a community, to preserve the spirit and traditions of Rome. There was an unspoken resolve that the dispersal, which followed the French occupation of Rome in 1798, should not be repeated. That the College found in England the home that it did is again largely due to Mgr Smith. It was he who noticed the advertisement in a newspaper advertising Croft Lodge, and, as a former Stonyhurst boy, he was instrumental in the College taking up a more permanent abode at St Mary's Hall.

The senior student's diary describes Croft Lodge, Ambleside:

A fair-sized house owned by a Protestant lady, Miss Cobbe, who let it to a body called the Catholic Holiday Guild, for the summer as a hostel. We were the first 'guests' of a Miss Davison, the manageress. Miss Cobbe reserved the use of the dining room on the ground floor and all the first floor except the drawing room which was used as a chapel. We squeezed into the two remaining floors as bedrooms or domitories, and seven second year philosophy slept in an outhouse. The Vice-Rector and Fr. Ekbery shared a room. The Rector on his visits stayed with the *parroco*, the Rev. G. Atkinson. A large sized garden looked on to the river Brathay and there was a boathouse with a rowing boat. Mr. Firth hired another.

The six weeks spent at Ambleside consisted of lectures, examinations and a routine similar to that at the Villa. In retrospect, one of the more significant things this brief period in College history reveals is the challenge it made to certain assumptions about clerical training. These assumptions were, perhaps, more secure in Rome than elsewhere, but they were not confined to the Venerabile. What was unexpectedly new about the changed circumstances was not the presence of England rather than Rome, but the fact that much of the housework had to be done by the students themselves. In Rome there were servants, but now the students had to make their own beds and help in the kitchen. It is best summed up in a motion passed at a public meeting, 'That this house repudiates potato peeling and looks upon it as a purely voluntary effort'. We read in the senior student's diary that: 'This motion was reached after much discussion on what is and is not in the programme of a seminary. Either the Vice must get maids or a mechanical potato peeler.' Moreover the students now had to deal with women, in the person of the manageress. Previously the rule had protected them. In Rome, the girls who worked in the kitchen were under the strict surveillance of the nuns. The nuns themselves were only spoken to at the serving hatch and, because of the difficulty in remembering English names, they only knew the students by their laundry numbers.[10] But now a more personal relationship had to be established. There were complaints that the staff 'should call people Mr', that 'the manageress should remember that we are not her employees, but in her hotel as her guests'. One only wonders whether former ordained students were able to adjust more painlessly to the life style of the presbytery.

This domestication of the students continued during the first year at St Mary's Hall. But the old order began to re-establish itself when nuns were introduced, and on the return to Rome, for a time at least, things went back to what they were before. Ambleside was prophetic of the future and the conditions that would obtain in the 1970s, although in the 1970s they did have a mechanical potato peeler.

St Mary's Hall

That the College was able to survive the war was due, in no small measure, to her former Rectors as well as her present superiors. Hinsley was Archbishop of Westminster and Godfrey was Apostolic Delegate and both proved of great help to Macmillan. The obtaining of St Mary's Hall, Stonyhurst, was due to characteristically swift moves by Hinsley. Prompted by Mgr Smith, the Jesuits made an offer of Stonyhurst. Upholland had offered hospitality to the Beda and some sort of Jesuit connection was appropriate, not only on historical grounds but because the link with the Gregorian would have to be preserved, if at all possible. But a great deal of prudence and caution were necessary. St Mary's Hall was originally the house of study for the philosophers, but when Heythrop was founded in 1926, the building was left desolate and, apart from two years when it was used as a junior school, it was empty up to the outbreak of war. It was then taken over by the army. However, Hinsley was able to negotiate with the War Office in 1940 and the army evacuated it in favour of the English College.[11]

Thus the College now had a roof over its head and the use of a suitable building, one that had already been used as a college and which possessed a chapel and kitchens. But it had yet to be furnished. Cardinal Hinsley persuaded priests to lend or give books.[12] Furniture and books came from the diocesan seminary of Leeds, which had recently closed (as a result of Godfrey's visitation, or so it was said) and the Rector of that establishment was Mgr Dinn, a former student of the College. After a few troubled months and many fruitless letters, the Rector at last secured the services of a community of nuns to look after the kitchens, and the Sisters of St Joseph of Peace served the College faithfully until the return to Rome.[13]

It was desirable that the course of studies begun in Rome should be continued and that new students coming to the College should be started on a course that could be completed at the Gregorian when they eventually returned to Rome. To this end a competent teaching staff had to be gathered and the courses and professors would have to be approved by the Gregorian. This was eventually accomplished, with the result that the degree of Licentiate in theol-

Fig. 9.2 St Mary's Hall, Stonyhurst, home to the College during the Second World War: front and gardens.

ogy was conferred after successful examination at the end of the theology course. In addition to this, one student who had presented his doctorate dissertation at the Gregorian before the exodus was allowed to give the *experimentum* and defend his thesis before a panel of examiners at St Mary's Hall in 1943.[14] To provide this suitable staff, Macmillan secured the support of the Jesuit Provincial who responded to the call, although he had problems of his own. Fellow exile, Fr Robert Dyson, who had taught at the Biblicum, took charge of Scripture until his services were required back in Rome. Fr Bernard Leeming, who had taught at the Gregorian, took Dogmatic Theology and when he was needed at Heythrop, other members of the Society were released to come and spend time teaching particular treatises. It was only in the last year that the Jesuits were unable to provide staff, and then three former members of the College, who had the degree of DD,[15] became members of staff, joining Dr Butterfield, who taught moral theology, and Fr Ekbery, the *ripetitore*, who was in charge of the philosophy. The Rector and Vice-Rector lent a hand in teaching and so a competent staff was assembled, in very adverse circumstances. The vicinity of Stonyhurst meant that there was never any shortage of confessors or priests to give talks and conferences.

Behind this outward appearance of success there were moments of anxiety. Ecclesiastical superiors, such as the Provincial of the

Fig. 9.3 Corpus Christi procession in 1944, Stonyhurst.

Society or individual bishops, from time to time were in need of priests and either withdrew men from the staff or refused to allow them to take up posts at the College. The local ordinary, Bishop Marshall of Salford, was very warm in his welcome of the College to his diocese and gave the Rector every facility and permission to invite other bishops if he so desired, to give conferences and hold ordinations. Because of the demand of military service and to gain exemption from conscription, the entire house was tonsured in October 1941, except for one student, who was only 16 years old. The Roman Association decided that the burses and scholarships intended for study in Rome should also apply for study at the College in England.

The way of life during those years was marked by wartime restrictions with which the new Vice-Rector, Fr Grasar, had to cope. These became worse as the war progressed. There were the material constraints, the blackout as part of the air-raid precautions, rationing of food and clothing, the occasional air raid.[16] Travel restrictions affected the number of visitors who were able to come and give retreats and talks. There were other effects of war. The number of new students dropped because of the call-up, and there were some who left to join the forces.[17] These difficulties affected all ecclesiastical establishments and seminaries in England, but for the English College there was the feeling that it was not just the war

Fig. 9.4 The walk between lectures at St Mary's Hall, Stonyhurst.

that made things abnormal, it was also the idea of studying in England. The belief that the College was 'in exile in England', shows how much things had changed since the early days of the foundation. For William Allen to study in Rome for work in England was abnormal and only a *faute de mieux*. But now the lack of the Roman experience was felt and lamented. Movements, at various times, to go home for Christmas (the College went home on 30 December after the feast of St Thomas of Canterbury) and at Easter were either voted down at public meetings or refused by the Rector.

But a seminary is a living and changing thing and as the years passed the number of those who knew Rome diminished and the others who took their places had been sent by their bishops, not for the sake of St Mary's Hall but in the hope that the course would be completed in Rome. Their picture of College life in Rome was formed from what their elders said and tricks of memory distorted the reality. What was preserved was a series of Roman customs and rules that had been modified for English usage. There was an identity crisis in some minds, those who asked how exactly St Mary's Hall was different from any other seminary in England.[18] There were now lectures in the house and they were not always in Latin. Undoubtedly there were peculiar customs: singing the 'Salve Regina' on the stairs after night prayers; Wiseman's conversion of England prayers before lunch; the divine praises and hymns in

Italian at Benediction. But other colleges had their traditions and peculiarities as well. The English College was only Roman in memory or in hope; it did not live in the present. But I suppose that this is true of most people in wartime. It was not a particularly inspiring age, the Rector's health was not good and there were long periods when he was absent. There were the usual troughs and peaks of student life.

The College property in Rome

Despite the war, news trickled in from Rome. The departure had left the administration of the College buildings in the hands of the *computista,* Commendatore Bruno Freddi, and the architect, Filippo Sneider. Both the British Legation to the Holy See and the Congregation of Studies kept a watch on its interests. In January 1941, Archbishop Godfrey learnt from Sir D'Arcy Osborne at the Legation, that the responsibility for the College property lay with the ecclesiastical authorities, and this was shared by Cardinal Pizzardo of the Congregation of Studies and the Nuncio to Italy.[19] Towards the end of the same month, Mgr Montini[20] of the Secretariat of State wrote to Godfrey telling him that the Knights of Malta were taking over the College buildings for use as a hospital. This arrangement was principally due to the efforts of Cardinal Pizzardo. On the other hand, the Nuncio to Italy was receiving enquiries from the Italian authorities as to the legal status of the College. It was pointed out that it was a Pontifical College and so there could be no question of its being sequestered. Correspondence of a more personal nature came from Mgr Heard of the Rota, who was now a prisoner in the Vatican, but he had little knowledge of what condition the College was in. Then, after four years, came the news of the liberation of Rome and hopes of an early return soared.

The liberation of Rome

When Rev. R. P. Redmond, chaplain to the forces and a former student, entered Rome with the victorious Allies, in June 1944, he wrote to the Rector to say that he had visited the College, that it was being used for civilian casualties and was 'beautifully kept'. 'The sisters are quite undisturbed and carry on with the cooking and laundry.' The rooms were being used as wards, and part of the church was a store. But Palazzola was less fortunate. The Germans had occupied it for about three months. Much of the bedroom furniture had been used as firewood and a mortar bomb had hit the roof of the cloister, but the damage was not as bad as it might have been. He reported that the place was now being tidied up by the caretaker and his wife. The refectory walls had been covered with 'surprisingly good designs'. Other former students, now with the forces, visited the College and wrote giving information and impressions.[21]

Archbishop Griffin, who was now Archbishop of Westminster, was one of the first civilians to get to Rome after the liberation and he wrote to the Rector on 2 September 1944, 'While in Rome I took the opportunity of looking round the Venerabile. I also spoke to Prince Chigi. As far as the Red Cross [*sic*] people go, they will leave the College provided they get a week or so's notice. The Congregation of Seminaries and Studies would be glad for you to return, and so would the Rector of the Gregorian.' With regard to the means of return, a hospital ship was suggested, and then he went on to list the points in favour of return. It would be good for the men to get back to the Roman atmosphere and it would be good to have English people in Rome, to inform the Holy See about English matters. On the other hand, there were great difficulties about food and fuel for heating. Transport was lacking and even if they got as far as Naples by sea, there were no trains and no civilian transport to Rome.

Two more years were to pass before the students returned. Sometime in 1944 the hospital found new premises and left, taking with them a lift they had installed in the stairwell. Work went ahead preparing the building for its reoccupation, but with the departure of the Knights of Malta, the rent they had been paying ceased and there was the problem now of providing for the nuns and the College servants. The Rector acceded to a request by Cardinal Pizzardo that some of the rooms should be used to house lay Italian university students and part of the College was also occupied by Mgr Carroll-Abbing's relief work for the needy of Rome. At the end of January 1946, the Rector went to Rome to see if it were possible for the College to return in October. He was there for the Consistory and the creation of thirty-two cardinals in February,[22] where he acted as host at the English College to Archbishop Griffin, who stayed for part of his time in Rome at the College. It was there that he and the other two 'Empire Cardinals', McGuigan of Toronto and Gilroy of Sydney, received the *biglietto*.[23] Later in the day the three cardinals received the customary congratulatory messages or *visite di calore* in the *salone*. The College was still occu-

Fig. 9.5 Arthur Cardinal Hinsley.

pied by the university students and the relief work offices, but these would vacate the place by July. The Rector was able to see for himself what the state of the College was and he thanked all those who had looked after the interests of the establishment during the war years: Cardinal Pizzardo of the Congregation of Seminaries and Studies, Cardinal Canali, who was in charge of the Vatican relief work, Cardinal Caccia Dominioni the Cardinal Protector, and Commendatore Freddi the accountant, who had never ceased to concern himself with College affairs, no matter what the risk or inconvenience.[24] The Italian officials and friends of the College played no less a part in its survival than did their counterparts in that other absence from Rome at the beginning of the nineteenth century.

The Rector returned to England in April with a report and recommendation to the bishops, for their Low Week meeting, that the College should reopen. He had the words of Cardinal Pizzardo still ringing in his ears, 'Venga, venga, la Santa Sede vi aiuterà'. To give some indication of the cost of living he compiled for the students a price list of essential articles; razor blades, umbrellas, alarm clocks, cigarettes and wine. And to celebrate, the toast 'To

Fig. 9.6 Bernard Cardinal Griffin.

Rome' was drunk at St Mary's Hall in Strega brought back from the Eternal City.

The return

The summer term at St Mary's Hall was spent in preparing for the return. Borrowed property was sent back, visas and passports had to be prepared, arrangements about transfer of money to be made and extra clothing coupons to be obtained. Most of this work, which continued through the vacation, fell on the Vice-Rector, Fr Grasar, and the senior student and his aides. In October the College returned in four parties of about seventeen people in each group, by train across France and Italy. The thirty-three remaining students at the Hall were now augmented by seven postgraduates and twenty-six in first year. Continuity had been preserved, since those who joined the College during the first year in England were now going out for their last year in Rome. But there was another continuity as well. Despite the war, the way

VEN·COLLEGII·ANGLORVM·DE·VRBE
IOANNES·MACMILLAN·RECTOR
MODERATORES·ET·ALVMNI
SALVA·BELLI·FORTVNA·AD·AVLAM·S·MARIAE·EXSVLANTES
PATRVM·SOCIETATIS·IESV·APVD·STONYHVRST
SEX·PER·ANNOS
HOSPITIO·SOLACIISQ·COMITER·SVSTENTATI
ROMAM·FAVSTE·TANDEM·REDVCTI
LAETI·LIBENTES·POS·D·S
ANNO·SAL·MCMXLVI

Fig. 9.7 Commemorative plaque at St Mary's Hall, Stonyhurst.

of life of the clerical student in Rome had changed little, if at all. There was the same traditional dress, cassock and 'wings', with the eighteenth-century beaver hat, the same rules and regulations about *camerata*.[25]

The aftermath of war meant that there were allied military personnel in the city still, and there was war damage to be repaired. Palazzola put in a claim for 973,000 lire.[26] Then there came the Italian parliamentary elections of the spring of 1947. These caused a certain amount of anxiety and there was a real fear of a Communist victory and the possibility of yet another exile. However new and exciting these days were to those who lived through them, they were nothing really new in the long history of Rome and the College; another war, another peace, another kind of government. When Holy Year came in 1950, the Rector 'did not want a repetition of 1925'. Like his predecessors, he feared that the great number of pilgrims would unsettle the students and upset their routine.

The days of St Mary's Hall receded into the distance, but not before it had been put on record with two inscriptions – one in the College in Rome, situated on the bottom corridor, along with the other marble slabs recording important events in the College history. The other was a bronze memorial tablet, bronze being regarded as more suitable for the English climate at St Mary's Hall, which reads:

VEN COLLEGII ANGLORUM DE URBE
IOANNES MACMILLAN RECTOR
MODERATORES ET ALUMNI
SAEVA BELLI FORTUNA AD AULAM S MARIAE
EXSULANTES
PATRUM SOCIETATIS IESU APUD STONYHURST
SEX PER ANNOS
HOSPITIO SOLACIISQ COMITER SUSTENTATI
ROMAM FAUSTE TANDEM REDUCTI
LAETI LIBENTES POS D S
ANNO SAL MCMXLVI

It is a pity that no allusion could have been made to the historical link between Stonyhurst and Liège, with whose affairs the College in Rome was at one time closely tied.

Despite indifferent health, Macmillan continued as Rector until the first year to have done the full Roman course since the war were approaching ordination. He managed to secure early ordination for ten of that year and, at the same time, 18 November, made known his intention to resign the rectorship. The sole reason for this was his health. The Vice-Rector, Mgr Tickle, became Rector on 19 December 1952 and the next day the ordinations took place. Macmillan left Rome in the New Year. It was a fitting moment to lay down the burden and the College owes very much to John Macmillan for piloting it through very difficult seas.

Notes

1 *Venerabile*, I, 167. Also *Venerabile*, I, 367 where it is recorded that the motion was debated 'That Fascism would benefit England'. It was defeated 21–12.
2 In September 1931 there were 90 lire to the pound; in November of the same year it had dropped to 63. ECA, Liber 886, Senior Student's Diary.
3 For this theme see A. Hastings, 'Some Reflections on the English Catholics of the late 1930s', in *Bishops and Writers* (London 1977) pp. 107–25.
4 ECA, Senior Student's Diary, 28 March 1939.
5 There was some trouble during the Silver Jubilee celebrations of George V, but this was attributed to an Irish element.
6 There was not free access to radio or to newspapers in these days.
7 See College Diary, *Venerabile*, IX, 76.
8 ECA, Senior Student's Diary, e.g. 20 November 1939.
9 A. Clark, 'Exodus 1940', *Venerabile*, IX, 292–404. H. Lavery, 'The Ambleside Episode', *Venerabile*, IX, 405–13. J. Macmillan, 'The Venerabile

in Crisis', *Venerabile*, X, 3–14. R. L. Smith, 'The When and Wherefore of the Exodus', *Venerabile*, X, 15–34. A. Hulme, 'Jubilee of the Exodus', *Venerabile*, XXV, 201–3. In a series of articles in Vol. XXXI (1997) *The Venerabile* celebrated the Golden Jubilee of the return to Rome.

10 This was true even after the war and when the nuns began to attend concerts given by the students in the College, a special play bill was drawn up with numbers in place of the names of the cast and performers.

11 The full story is told by J. Macmillan, 'The Venerabile comes to St. Mary's Hall', *Venerabile*, X, 209–17.

12 ECA, scr. 86, 14, letters to P. W. O'Gorman and E. Ellis.

13 ECA, scr. 86, 14.

14 This was J. Cunningham who was later to become Bishop of Hexham and Newcastle, see *Venerabile*, XI, 51–4 and XII, 57.

15 Revs James Rea (Clifton), Thomas Lynch (Portsmouth), R. Patrick Redmond (Hexham and Newcastle).

16 On Friday 20 December 1940, at the end of Stations of the Cross, two land-mines were dropped near the Lower Hodder Bridge. It was the front of the House that suffered chiefly and there was need to replace many panes of glass.

17 Five former students were killed on active service. Peter Firth and Gerard Nesbitt met their deaths as army chaplains in Normandy and Sub-Lieutenant J. R. T. Walker, RNVR, Sergeant Observer R. Rawcliffe, RAF, and Rear Navigator Neville Carlile, RAF, were also killed.

18 This was well expressed by R. L. Smith, 'Romanita', *Venerabile*, X, 237–46.

19 ECA, scr. 86, 13.

20 Later Pope Paul VI.

21 For information on this, see *Venerabile* especially vol. XI (insert at beginning), vol. XII, 536, 154–6, 240a, 240b, 280–90.

22 This was the largest creation of cardinals at one time since 1517.

23 The *biglietto* was the official letter telling the recipient that the Holy Father had decided to make him a cardinal.

24 An appreciation of Commendatore Bruno Freddi by R. L. Smith is to be found in *Venerabile*, XIX, 394–5.

25 It was not until Easter 1964 that the *ferraiuolo* was replaced by a sash. 'Hats and wings' were discontinued in May 1966 when permission for 'clergyman' was received.

26 ECA, scr 86, 17.

Chapter Ten

From Post-War to Post-Conciliar Rome

When the College returned from St Mary's Hall, Stonyhurst in October 1946 it was to a Rome scarred by war. The Allied Military Government was still in position and it was only after the elections in April 1947 that the recently established Italian Republic assumed full control. The united left-wing Front was defeated at the polls by the Christian Democrats and a period of stability and growth under the leadership of Alcide de Gasperi began. This was to lead to a boom in the Italian financial situation that contrasted with the sluggish revival in post-war Britain. Although there were stories at home of starving Europe, the reality was much more bearable than had been forecast. There were food shortages, polenta instead of bread at some meals, and a severe lack of transport, public as well as private. But there was an overriding sense of urgency and the repair of the war damage was being achieved by the hard manual labour of the Italians, who at this time possessed few of the mechanical aids that emerged later on in the century. The College property had been badly affected, especially at Palazzola which was severely damaged in the fighting on the outskirts of Rome. The superiors had the responsibility of seeing that the students were properly housed and fed. Relief was obtained from the Vatican through the newly appointed Cardinal Protector, Nicola Canali. There were almost as many new students in first year as in the rest of the house put together, but despite the disproportion there was quickly established a good *esprit de corps*. Although scarcely noticeable at the time, there were contrasting reactions to the situation. On the one hand there was the desire to rebuild and construct a new and better

Fig. 10.1 Visiting St Peter's during the Jubilee on 12 December 1950.

world; on the other there was the idea of a quick return to normal
after the upset of war. This latter was the prevailing mood in the
seminary. There were very few changes in the daily timetable from
what took place before the war. As a result of the allied occupation
the English language was more commonly heard spoken in Rome
but the lectures at the Gregorian were still in Latin and this was the
language in which any business with the secretariat was conducted.
The regulations about *camerata*, the restrictions on smoking, the
need for permission to depart from the fixed regulations, all
remained as before the war, notwithstanding the number of ex-
service men and former university graduates and the relaxation of
some of the formalities of life that had been brought about by wartime conditions. In retrospect it is remarkable how easily the house
conformed. This situation was to continue to the close of Pius XII's
pontificate and it applied to more than seminary life. There were
signs of change under the surface, but it was only afterwards that
their significance became apparent when the Decrees of the Second
Vatican Council made copious footnote references to previous
statements of Pius XII. At the Gregorian the same text books as
were used in the 1930s were still standard. In 1947 there was a clar-
ification from the Holy See as to what exactly was the matter and
form of the sacrament of orders: it was the imposition of hands, not
the handing over of the sacred instruments. In the Holy Year of
1950 the Assumption of Our Lady was defined, and this had the
effect of overshadowing the appearance of the encyclical *Humani*

Fig. 10.2–3 The *camerata* system and clerical street attire continued into the 1960s.

Generis and its warning about 'the new theology'. Forthcoming events were casting their shadows before, but in the bright sunshine of the resurgence of a new democratic Europe they were little heeded by most zealous seminarians.

It was in 1952, with the ordination of the first generation of post-war students, that John Macmillan resigned the rectorship. He had been in ill health for much of his rectorate and he now felt he could depart, having guided the College through the years of exile and at last been able to provide for students to enjoy the full Roman course of seven years. He was succeeded by his Vice-Rector, Gerard W. Tickle, and the *ripetitore*, Dr Alan Clark, became the new Vice-Rector.

This was a smooth transition. 'Jock' Tickle had been a chaplain to the Forces during the war and since 1946 he had assisted Macmillan in re-establishing the college in the early years back in Rome. He was eminently suited to this task as he possessed the qualities necessary for a superior in the circumstances. There was his 'man management' and ability to secure the support of students and personnel of the College as well as his capacity to deal with Italian officialdom and observe the requirements of protocol in relations with the British Embassy and consulate. This he did in a measured, polite but determined way. His practical skills as a

Fig. 10.4 Cardinal Godfrey visits Pope John XXIII with the College in attendance: the front group to the left includes Mgr Tickle, the Rector, Mgr Worlock, the Cardinal's secretary and Alan Clark, the Vice-Rector.

former theatrical producer were also allowed full scope. First as Vice-Rector and then as Rector, he supervised much-needed refurbishment: the College property at Palazzola was repaired, the swimming pool restored and new tennis courts and the famous steps up to the Sforza built. In Rome he acquired secondhand furniture to equip additional rooms for students and visitors as well as being able to put his hand to odd jobs of plumbing and electrical wiring in the College and in some of the adjacent property. In the later period of his rectorship his social skills and ready hospitality assumed an even greater importance.

On the death of Pius XII and the accession of John XXIII things began to change and the announcement of a General Council of the Church to be held in Rome marked the beginning of enormous changes in the Church. At this point it was not foreseen how much the training of priests would be caught up in the development to come.[1] In the meantime, the first impact on the College was of a more practical kind. There was an increase in important visitors and residents in the College.

At first it was a matter of receiving individual bishops from England who were engaged in the preparatory work of the Council. Later when the Council opened in 1962, almost the whole of the English hierarchy was resident in the College while the Council was in session. This entailed the fitting out of further guest rooms and a readiness to entertain and provide for the needs of visitors during their stay in Rome. Although this made great demands on all in the College, students as well as staff, in the long run it had its rewards in so far as the hierarchy became aware at first hand of some of the problems of running a college abroad and also felt a certain indebtedness to the Rector and the College for the treatment they had received during the exhilarating but exhausting sessions of the Council. This is not the place to attempt an assessment of the effects of the Council on the Church throughout the world. Indeed, even after nearly forty years we are scarcely yet in a position to do this with any degree of confidence. But the experience of those who were in the College at this time was something very special. It was profound and it engaged a whole generation with the ideas and spirit of the Council. It engendered a mood of dynamic optimism and commitment to a renewed vision of the Church. They were heady days. Many of the theologians who were drafting the documents for the Council Fathers were the students, teachers and professors at the Gregorian and so there was a sense of participation in events, a first-hand experience quite different from a mere reading of the published *Acta* and *Decreta* or listening to entertain-

Fig 10.5 Vatican II: Council Session in St Peter's.

ing anecdotes of what happened inside and outside the council chamber.

Other noteworthy events occurred during these years. In 1961 there was the visit of the Queen and Duke of Edinburgh to Rome. Cardinal Heard was nominated Protector of the College in succession to Canali. In 1962 there were celebrations for the sixth centenary of the foundation of the Hospice in Rome. Pope John XXIII died in 1963 and, two months after his election, his successor, Pope Paul VI, paid an informal visit to Palazzola on 22 August 1963. On this 'friendly visit from a neighbour' the Pope spoke of 'the strategic point in the life of the Church' held by England by reason of her language. Tickle's rectorship came to an end in 1964 when he was appointed Bishop in Ordinary to Her Majesty's Forces.

Life after the Council

It fell to Tickle's successor, Leo Alston, and his Vice-Rector, John Brewer, to introduce the conciliar spirit of *aggiornamento* into the College. The most urgent demands that confronted the new team in 1964 were the building and finances at the material level, and the human and spiritual welfare of the College community in the aftermath of the Council. In the expectation of increased numbers of aspirants to the clerical and religious life, a number of Roman colleges had decided to leave their premises in the city centre and provide modern accommodation outside the walls. Both the Beda and Scots Colleges followed this development and erected new buildings on the outskirts of Rome. The English College having only recently celebrated the sixth centenary of the foundation of the old English Hospice, decided to remain on the original site hallowed by so many centuries of the history of Rome and of England. This did not mean rejecting the need to modernise, it only made it a little more difficult.

A wholesale regeneration of the property was undertaken. The kitchens were refitted, the nuns' quarters brought up to date, students' rooms refurbished. The first library was made into a reading room and new stacks and shelves provided in the adjoining room. As a token of gratitude for their stay in the College during the Council the hierarchy paid for the re-equipment of the refectory with new tables and chairs and wood panelling. Because of the age of parts of the building extreme care and delicacy was needed in some of this work of reconstruction. Money had to be raised. The

Fig 10.6 The College photographed with Council Fathers: the English Bishops.

Fig. 10.7 William Cardinal Godfrey, former Rector.

College was registered in England as a charitable trust and trustees were appointed. Pensions (students' fees) were increased following the rise in the standard of living. The upper villa at Palazzola was sold, arrangements being made that the new owners would not allow anything to take place that would be detrimental to the College. Subsequent devaluations and fluctuations in currency meant that financial crises arose from time to time, as they did in the life of other institutions.[2] But all these physical transformations were symbolic of even more significant changes that took place in the life of the seminary. An impetus towards modernisation brings its traumas and can be very unsettling in a community. As the editor of the 1972 *Venerabile* magazine put it:

> Only those who studied at the college during the past seven or eight years can fully appreciate the difficulties which were undergone and the real and positive changes which were brought about in the college in the time of Mgrs Alston and Brewer. They were in office during a time of general ferment in the Church and consequently in the seminary as well. The concept of authority was undergoing radical and powerful revision.

Fig. 10.8 William Cardinal Heard, the last Cardinal-Protector.

Alston himself, both as Rector[3] and afterwards[4] was quietly and restrainedly informative about some of these changes. Following the practice of other colleges in Rome those in major orders now dressed as 'clergymen' in the street. Cassocks, hats and wings and *camerata* became a thing of the past. There was no longer a daily obligatory walk in the afternoon. In the refectory during meals 'long reading' was allowed to die out. Rules were lightened and there was less need for 'permissions'. The bell was silent. Liturgical changes began with the 'dialogue mass' where everyone made the responses in Latin. Then the use of the vernacular became more frequent. Concelebration was introduced and prayer groups began to be formed among the students.[5] Similar developments were taking place in the other colleges in Rome. At the Gregorian there were changes. Fr Hervé Carrier, who became Rector in the 1960s, introduced student representation on University committees. The need for some sort of practical pastoral experience before ordination to the priesthood began to be seen as of value and there were visits made by the students to the sick and lonely. During the summer vacation some students worked with the local youth at Sermoneta.[6] All these projects began to be operative in the years immediately following the Council and they had an effect on the style of life in the College. Less need was felt for the homegrown entertainment that had been such a feature of life for very many years. The traditional production of a Gilbert and Sullivan operetta ceased. *Chi Lo Sa?*, the comic magazine, stopped publication and even the *Venerabile* magazine appeared less regularly and sometimes not at all.

The visit of Archbishop Ramsey of Canterbury and his stay in the College in March 1966 deserves special mention. It was one of the first practical manifestations of the spirit of the Council and had a deep impact on the students and their attitude towards ecumenism. In the summer of 1966 the College magazine had as its frontispiece the photograph of the Archbishop standing below the portrait of Cardinal Pole and the caption 'Reginald and Michael Cantuar', sending out a challenge to the future as well as a flashback to the last days of the Hospice and the beginnings of the College. In 1970 there took place in Rome the canonisation of the 40 English martyrs – ten of whom were former students at the College – and in 1987, 85 martyrs were beatified and these included nine former students. Such visits and events in the life of the College are part of the benefit of living in Rome. Indeed, balancing them against the daily rhythms of prayer and study presents its difficulties but these are of the same order as those confronting many priests in a parish.

There was also the matter of the *villeggiatura*. A great deal of work had been done to bring back Palazzola to its former state and also to take it forward to the future. But what exactly was that future? With the financial situation of the College as it was, how could it afford to maintain Palazzola, which lay unused for nine months of the year? Some of the other Roman colleges, having moved out of the polluted atmosphere of central Rome and profiting from the easier conditions of travel between Rome and their homelands, were beginning to consider disposing of their summer villas. The opening up of seminary life to the demands of the wider world of the parish and neighbourhood had begun to erode the strong bonds of community that had manifested itself at *villeggiatura* time. In 1968 the author of the College Journal wrote:

> It is a sad fact but true that most people this year ... are ... not looking forward to the villa.[7]

They were perhaps even dreading it. There were many reasons, primarily due to the general disappointment that the Rector's suggestion of a six weeks' holiday in England for everybody had not materialised. But it was to be the case that second year theology

Fig. 10.9 Pope Paul VI visits Palazzola, 22 August 1963, welcomed by Rector
Gerard Tickle.

Fig. 10.10 Pope Paul VI with the students at Palazzola during the informal visit of 22 August 1963.

Fig. 10.11 Archbishop Ramsey of Canterbury visits the College, in March 1966, welcomed by Rector Leo Alston.

were to spend the entire summer at home. Some of this time would be spent in gaining pastoral experience.

Dissatisfaction with the villa was regarded by many Old Romans as the ultimate apostasy. It is not easy to see beyond the horizon and in those days the horizon was set by the limitations afforded by the difficulties of travel between England and Italy and the regulations imposed on seminarians forbidding participation in life outside the College. Once these were removed then there was released the attraction of work in England. It is here that the real future lies and the reason why the College was founded in the first place. The last full *villeggiatura* was in 1969 and from 1970 onwards three or four weeks only were spent at Palazzola; the rest of the time all the students were in England.[8] In 1970 the college diarist remarked:

> So with only a few days of *villeggiatura* left, and everyone looking forward to August 9th, your weary diarist leaves the conclusion to someone else. A venerable canon is quoted as saying on his departure, 'After fifty weeks in England, this fortnight has been really wonderful, though I feel ready to go back tomorrow.' His feelings are shared by us all. It has been an interesting and at times exciting villa, but England, my England.[9]

Where did that leave Palazzola? It would be under the next Rector that a way was to be found of making the villa a viable proposition in the new situation and also a benefit to the Church in England.

After seven years Leo Alston came to the end of his term as Rector and he returned to England. This was to set a precedent in so far as for many years Rectors had been given an indefinite appointment. Now it became a set term. This had indeed been the practice in the seventeenth and eighteenth centuries when the Jesuits administered the college. The change in superiors was further signified by making the Vice-Rector, John Brewer, Auxiliary Bishop in Shrewsbury. Successive Rectors (Cormac Murphy-O'Connor 1971, George Hay 1978, John Kennedy 1984, Adrian Toffolo 1991, Patrick Kilgarriff 1999 and Nicholas Hudson 2004) have each been called to take the College a further step into a future that has never ceased to provide something unexpected. With the passage of time the Second Vatican Council never grows stale but continues to show its effects throughout the Church. But the general pattern of development remains the same. The need for *aggiornamento* is still there. It is to be seen in the 1973 Report to the Bishops' Low Week Conference and the setting up of the Bishops' Committee and also in the re-ordering of the College church and its dedication on 1 December 1981.[10] In 1995, after 75 years' service to the College, the Elisabettine Sisters had to withdraw for lack of vocations.[11] This was a severe loss felt on all sides. However, it had been anticipated for some years and was in keeping with general trends in the Church. The decline in vocations applied to the religious as well as the diocesan clergy and it pointed to a re-assessment of what kind of apostolate was appropriate to contemporary society.[12]

Meanwhile, since 1972 the Gregorian has been revising the studies, and the course after philosophy has now widened into two cycles. The first one consists of three years general theological studies followed by the second, two years of specialisation leading to the Licentiate.[13] Moreover, study at other universities in Rome is now possible and some students attend the Angelicum where there are more courses taught in English. Some also attend the Liturgical Institute of S. Anselmo and the Patristic School at the Augustinianum.

As for Palazzola, beginning with some former students bringing out parish groups to spend a short time there in the summer, it has now developed into an all year round retreat, conference and holiday centre. The cortile has been glazed in and central heating installed. There is a resident director and the Sisters of Mercy look after the administration until 2004.

The College enters the twenty-first century better known and with more friends and visitors from among the laity. The history of the last fifty years dissuades any forecast of what the future may hold. However there remains the same urgency as was there in the beginning to 'bring fire to the earth' and to do it 'today rather than tomorrow'.

Notes

1 *Ruby Thoughts, Reflections of a 'Year'* by Gerald Creasey (2001) tells the story of the last class of students to have received the whole of their training in the College in the pre-Conciliar days. It contains a series of individual reflections on how they now look upon their college days in the light of 40 years of experience of the post-Conciliar Church

2 The fullest account of the post-war situation of the College is to be found in 'Aspects of the Financing and Administration of the College', Peter Coughlan, *Venerabile*, 1980, 22–65.

3 'Innovation – Renovation', *Venerabile*, XXIV 73–6.

4 'Thoughts from Abroad', *Venerabile*, XXV, 227–30.

5 *Venerabile*, 1978, 29–32.

6　*Venerabile*, XXIII, 162–5.

7　*Venerabile*, XXIV, 295.

8　An account of the last full villa is to be found in *Venerabile*, XXV, 145–52.

9　*Venerabile*, XXV, 200.

10　*Venerabile*, 1982, 9–28.

11　*Venerabile*, 1996, 33–4.

12　It led to the re-organisation of the nuns' quarters and the foundation of Sherwin House, a residence for clerics working or studying in Rome that was distinct from but part of the College, until 2004. 'A House of Variety', Varghese Puthussery, *Venerabile*, 1996, 22–3.

13　*Venerabile*, XXV, 91–108, XXVI, 19–23, 1978, 41–5.

Appendix I

The Buildings of the Venerable English College: An Historical Account

Jerome Bertram

I. The site in antiquity

The site of the College in ancient times formed part of the low-lying Campus Martius, in the bend of the river, which, being always unhealthy and liable to flood, was not inhabited until the Dark Ages, when the loss of the aqueducts drove the population from the high ground in search of water. The Campus was laid out, for the greater part, as sports-grounds and pleasure gardens. It appears that a road crossed it, roughly on the line of the present Via di Monserrato; if the existing street line were straightened from the Via Capo di Ferro, through the Via dei Venti to the Via dei Banchi Vecchi, the resulting alignment would cut off the curve in the Via di Monserrato, and run across the back wall of the College church, precisely where a small patch of ancient street paving was exposed in the nineteenth century. The other ancient buildings on the site should therefore be related to this road.

At the northern end of the site is a small columbarium, discovered and described in the *Venerabile* in 1964.[1] This must antedate the extension of the Pomerium by Claudius in 49 AD, which probably included the College site.[2] The adjoining well and 'thermopolium' were believed to be ancient when first discovered, but are probably both contemporary with Cardinal Howard's palace.

The major ancient building on the site is tentatively identified with the barracks of the 'Factio Veneta', built by Vitellius in 69 AD.[3] During the seventeenth-century rebuilding of the College, an inscription, since lost, was found, reading:

IMP (caesare Domitiano) AVG GERMANICO XV/M
COCCEIO NERVA II COS THALLUS AGITATOR
L AVILLI PLANTAE SER/DOMINVM SILVANVM
DE SVO POSVIT ITEM DEDICAVIT[4]

This is interpreted to refer to a shrine of Silvanus built in the neighbourhood of the barracks in 90 AD. The inscription would have been mutilated
in 96 AD, when Domitian fell from grace.

Excavations in 1964 revealed traces of a large facade wall, running
under the present kitchen parallel to the Roman street, and about twenty
metres back from it. In front of this wall was a drain which received water
from downpipes in the thickness of the wall. The drain produced coins
from the late first and early second century AD, consonant with the wall
being part of Vitellius' barracks.[5]

Beyond this, one can only speculate on the ancient site. It is probable that
there was a colonnade between the barracks and the street, in which case the
travertine capitals and bases used for the mediaeval church, and now in the
garden, may be survivals from it. Other fragments, now in the garden and
built into the walls around the back of the swimming tank, are probably not
from this site but brought in from College property near the Catacombs,
though it is tempting to read the fragment *EVENE* as *e factionE VENEta*.

After the fall of the Empire we have no further information on the site
until the fourteenth century, though it can be presumed that, in common
with the rest of the Campus Martius, it was built over and divided into a
number of small tenements, each with its well and garden. There is no
evidence for a church on the site before the foundation of the Hospice.

2. The English Hospice 1362–1577

When the 'University of Poor English' bought the first house on the site,
from John Peters alias John the Shepherd, in 1362, the area now occupied
by the College was divided into at least nine tenements. Between 1362 and
1406 all the properties between the Swedish Hospice and the Prison of the
Corte Savella had been bought either for the Hospital of St Thomas, or for
that of St Chrysogonus, later St Edmund, in Trastevere. The three houses
nearest the Corte Savella belonged to the latter Hospice, until the union of
the two houses in 1464.

The first mention of a chapel for the Hospice is in 1363 when Cardinal
Morone's account, written c. 1556–77, states that a chapel was erected with
several altars.[6] There is, however, no contemporary evidence for this, and
the first certain reference is in 1376, when a title deed was drawn up 'in
capella hospitalis'. In 1377 Gregory XI wrote from Avignon to approve the
foundation of both Hospice and chapel, and granted faculties for the sacraments to be administered in the chapel.[7] In 1383 John Palmer requested in
his will that he be buried in the Hospice chapel, though faculties for burial
were not yet granted.[8]

In 1374 the Hospice seems to have let a house next door to the Hospice proper to Gilbert Newman, and reclaimed it two years later, paying Newman 80 florins for improvements done during that time; presumably the house was virtually rebuilt.[9]

In 1412 the Royal Arms were erected over the door of the Hospice, with an inscription to emphasise English claims to the Crown of France, signed by Lawrence Cache. This may have led Robert Gradwell, in his history of the College, to assert that the Hospice was then rebuilt,[10] as is often repeated, though there is no other evidence for it. The royal connection with the Hospice was earlier attested by the gift of a painting, which has been shown to have been a companion piece to the Wilton Diptych. Presumably it was given in about 1400; it depicted Richard II and Anne of Bohemia, with the Madonna and other saints.[11]

The next we hear of the chapel is in 1445, when Eugenius IV granted a Bull conferring faculties and privileges to the Hospice chapel, including the right to establish a cemetery.[12] This was first exercised in 1446, when Richard Hason was buried under an inscription stating he was the first to be buried in the chapel after its consecration; part of the original inscription survives in the new church.

We have no indication of the size or design of this chapel, but since the accounts for the rebuilding of the chapel in 1497 indicate that much of the original building was incorporated, it is clear that it was on the same site, probably the same length but narrower than the 1497 chapel. It is probable that the Gothic window, now in the garden, and the small fragment of another window or doorway in the same style, bearing the Royal Arms, may belong to this stage of the chapel. If so, it would seem likely that the 1445 Bull indicates that the chapel was first built soon after that date, replacing an oratory constructed out of one of the old houses incorporated into the Hospice. The Gothic fragments are similar to the windows in the octagon of the Hospital of S. Spirito in Sassia, which date from the third quarter of the fifteenth century. They probably come from the south wall above the high altar, which would have survived the 1497 rebuilding. They may have been walled up, since the Hospice buildings of 1450 would have blocked the light from them, and have survived until the nineteenth century, when, for the first time, there would have been sufficient interest in them to preserve them. Other fragments of this first chapel, which may have been re-used in 1497 and so survived, are the four carved beam-ends, possibly off a hammerbeam roof, one of which bears the Royal Arms.

The remainder of the Hospice buildings, we must presume, were unaltered until 1449. The various private houses would have been used as they were, with a certain amount of alteration, and connections between them. We hear of the existence of 'porches' or 'cloisters', which were doubtless the columned porticoes that stood in front of most Roman houses, until they were forbidden in 1475. Probably, like others in the city, they were pillared with classical columns, possibly from the old Barracks of the Blues.

In 1449 plans were drawn up and an agreement was made between the Warden, William Stanley, John Lax, Master of Works, and Walter

Sandwych LLD, and Thomas Calbudower LLD, both Camerarii, on the one side, and Master Salvatus, son of Andrew, on the other side, on 26 January 1449. By this agreement Mr Salvatus was to construct a new building in tufa, with doorways, window-frames, beams etc. in chestnut. Materials from the demolished buildings were to go to the builder. The works were carried out, accounts presented and the bill delivered on 11 June 1453, and it was paid eleven days later, coming to 1,918 ducats, 10 bolandini.[13] Presumably, in the course of this work, much of the Hospice was rebuilt, and we may provisionally attribute the cortile between the church and the Swedish Hospice to this time. Unfortunately it has not proved possible to make sense of the detailed measurements of the new building, recorded in 1452,[14] since they were designed to show the quantity of material used, not the plan to be followed.

The cortile was entered from the street, through the present back entrance; on left and right were ranges of buildings extending to the back wall of the property. Those on the left are still standing; those on the right, which included the stables, are mostly gone. In the centre of the cortile was a tank or cistern. A second cortile lay behind the church, and beside this was a third range of buildings, possibly the remains of one of the original houses, including the sacristy. It is probable that the cross-range, containing the present kitchens and refectory, was not added until the end of the sixteenth century.

In 1496–7, at the initiative of Robert Sherborne, King's Orator, the church was substantially rebuilt. The work was done by Master Leo de Roncha and cost a thousand ducats. It is described in Liber 17:[15] the church was to be of brick throughout, and stuccoed all over. Two new walls were to be built the length of the nave (presumably adding aisles to the original church) and a crypt was to underlie the whole length of the church, but probably only for the width of one aisle. Over the aisle away from the street was to be a library. Nave and library were to have wooden ceilings; probably the aisles had brick vaults. Across the back of the nave was to be a choir loft. The nave was separated from the aisles by brick columns with capitals and bases of travertine. There were to be stone steps to the high altar.

The work was finished in December 1497, but it was not consecrated until 26 September 1501.[16] This church remained standing until the end of the eighteenth century, and, from the plans and drawings surviving, it is possible to form a very reasonable estimate of its appearance. The building was rectangular, measuring 13.53 by 17.10 metres. On the street side was a single door with a step, and on the other side two doors. The central nave was 6.50 metres wide, flanked by arcades of six arches. The capitals and bases of the columns were undoubtedly those now in the garden, and were rather mediocre examples of Ionic style. The sanctuary extended the whole width of the nave and was railed about, taking in one bay of the arcades. The altar stood against the wall. The ceiling of the nave was of carved wood with heavy carved beam-ends or corbels; four of these survive, having been brought in from the garden in 1962.

The street-side aisle had three windows, which were rectangular with stone frames. It had a brick vaulted ceiling, and a lean-to roof, allowing a clerestorey with three or four windows to the nave. On the further side from the street was a similar aisle, but with the library built above it. Access to the choir-loft across the end of the nave was probably through the library. The number of side altars in the aisles seems to have varied, but for most of the time that the church was in use, there were four.

The sacristy adjoined the church on the side away from the street, precisely where the present sacristy is, and possibly some part of the fabric survives. Inventories of its furnishings, and those of the church, survive from various dates in the sixteenth, seventeenth and eighteenth centuries. The church was sacked in 1527 and most of the plate and valuables stolen, but by a Bull of 3 March 1530 Clement VII granted indulgences to all who would contribute to making good the loss.[17]

Burials in the church were frequent during the late fifteenth and early sixteenth centuries. The majority of the monuments were probably simple incised inscriptions let into the floor, though a fine incised slab with effigy survives for John Wednesbury, Prior of Worcester, 1518, and we know that at least one other effigial slab has been destroyed.[18] Archbishop Bainbridge, 1514, was buried under a large relief effigy in white marble. An eighteenth-century drawing, now hanging in the Birmingham Oratory, shows that there was originally a plain rectangular tomb-chest supporting the surviving slab. This was formerly in front of the high altar, from which it was ordered to be moved in 1576, following Cesare Spetiano's visitation.[19]

The only alterations later made to the church, apart from continued burials and repairs, were the installation over the high altar of the great painting of the Trinity by Durante Alberti in 1580, following a recommendation by Spetiano in 1576, and the famous series of paintings of English martyrs by Niccolo Circignani, finished in 1583, probably covering the aisle walls.

3. The college 1577–1680

The only immediate effect on the buildings from the transformation of Hospice into College was the taking over of the house next door, between the old Hospice and the Swedish Hospice, which was occupied by the first students, and a connection made between the two buildings.[20] A few years later, in 1581, the College bought the garden and adjacent buildings from behind the old Hospice building. This had been leased from the de Valle brothers since 1574, but following a gift of 2,000 scudi from the Pope the College was able to buy it outright on 13 October 1581.[21] The new property consisted of a garden, a 'domuncula' and wine cellar. In December 1581 the Pope 'constructed some rooms at his own expense'.[22] Probably the buildings concerned were the range containing the present kitchen and refectory, and the garden range which then consisted of an open loggia on the ground floor and second floor, and one great room on the first floor, the present 'third library'. How much of these buildings was already standing when the College bought them, and how much was rebuilt during the last few years of the sixteenth century is unclear. Certainly the ceiling of the then refectory, now the main kitchen, which was destroyed in 1967, was dated to the last quarter of the sixteenth century.

Apart from minor works such as replastering the church in 1599[23] and rebuilding the garden wall in 1607[24] the buildings were to remain unchanged until the end of the seventeenth century. There are several accounts of the state of the College during this century, of which the most detailed is that drawn up in 1630 by Orazio Torriani, architect, to accompany the general visitation.[25] The plans drawn for this occasion show all the buildings already described, with detailed measurements, and occasionally notes on the use of the upper floors. In the cortile behind the church stood a clock tower, which contained three bells in 1661. Two of these survive; the third existing bell is dated 1704 and may be a recasting.

A major addition to the College in the seventeenth century was the acquisition of the old prison of the Corte Savella, which stood at the northern end of the block of College property. In about 1650 the College petitioned the Pope concerning the nuisance which the screams of tortured prisoners caused to members of the College who wanted to recite their breviaries in the garden.[26] The Pope's reply was to give the College permission (effectively a command) to buy the property, as a new prison was to be built in the Via Giulia and the old one was no longer required. This permission had to be given three times before the College finally bought the place on 17 September 1654.[27] The buildings were then beyond repair, and were virtually demolished and rebuilt as a 'palazzo' in 1658 at a cost of 6,697 scudi, 62 bajocchi. Detailed accounts for every part of the building survive, signed by Paolo Picchetti, architect, and a plan of the finished Palazzo was added to the 1630 survey.[28] The Palazzo was never intended to be part of the College but was a property to let; it was leased to Antonio Veneto of the Holy Rota in 1675 for 280 scudi,[29] from whom it passed to Cardinal Howard of Norfolk who was in residence before 1682.

4. The college rebuilt

By 1680 it was clear that the old Hospice buildings were inadequate for the needs of the College, and would need to be replaced. A description of the College made between 1660 and 1680[30] describes it as 'old, with neither convenience nor architectural merit, with narrow and inconvenient stairs; only ten rooms serve to accommodate the scholars, each with its private library, and a few others for the Rector, the other ministers and officials'. In 1682 therefore a number of alternative plans were produced for a new building on the site of the old Hospice, but in the same year the more radical decision was taken to demolish the four properties between the College and the new Palazzo, and build a new College there. Meanwhile Cardinal Howard was planning to extend the Palazzo over the nearest of these houses. On 21 January 1682 this house was with some difficulty recovered from its tenant,[31] since the new building had been begun, to extend the College and the Palazzo, which were to be made adjacent over the site of the said house. Since this house stood back from the street line of the Palazzo and other properties, licence was acquired on 13 November 1682 to take in the area of street necessary to straighten the line.[32] The licence mentions Francesco Massari as architect, who may therefore have been responsible for the new buildings. The popular ascription to Carlo Fontana seems groundless for want of evidence or stylistic likelihood.

The building works continued off and on from 1681 to 1689, though the major expenses are recorded from 1682 to 1685, by which time it may be presumed that the fabric was substantially complete. The total cost to the end of 1689 was 21,463 scudi, 87 bajocchi.[33] This sum was met in part by the sale of some country property in 1685,[34] but the College was put to considerable financial strain, and eventually had to reduce the number of alumni after the visitation of 1737–9.[35] The builder's accounts show that the foreman of works was one Giovanni Jacometti throughout the time of building.[36] During excavations for the foundations in 1682 were found a statue of a faun, and the dedicatory inscription to Silvanus already cited.[37]

Cardinal Howard, as Protector of the College, lent his name and prestige to the project but does not appear to have contributed financially in any way. Indeed the College had some difficulty in extracting the rent for the Palazzo from him,[38] and after his death in 1694 had more trouble in recovering the Palazzo itself from the Dominicans, who considered themselves to have inherited it from Howard.[39]

The new building comprised the present entrance corridor and the whole cortile on the northern side, as well as the main staircase and clock tower and the refectory and rooms above it. The old refectory, now becoming the kitchen, and the garden wing were not altered, nor were any of the old Hospice buildings between the church and the former Swedish Hospice. Cardinal Howard extended his Palazzo to meet the new College buildings, but there was no communication between them, and there may well have been a wall dividing the cortiles of the two buildings, completing the square of blind arcading in the College cortile.[40]

It is clear that it was intended to demolish and replace the church at the same time. The corner of the new building adjoining the church was left unfinished, as it remains to this day, with a rough edge ready for the church wall to be bonded in, and access to the top floor on the street side was by a temporary gantry, which remained in use until 1968.[41]

Drawings and plans survive for a church attributed to Andrea Pozzo.[42] The design was for an oval church with a double dome, six side chapels and sacristies behind. It seems that, had it been built, the present clock tower would have appeared to stand centrally behind it, when seen from the Piazza Sta Caterina, which explains the height of the tower.

The new buildings stood to the second floor throughout, and had a third floor on the street side only. It does not appear that they have been substantially altered since.

In 1685 the library was transferred to the new building from its old site above the church,[43] although the main cortile was not yet quite finished. By 1689 the new buildings were in full use, and the old Hospice building let to tenants.[44] Cardinal Howard was paying 390 scudi a year for his Palazzo, and five shops underneath it brought in additional rents.

The interior decoration continued more slowly. In 1701 the College paid Andrea Pozzo 22 scudi for work done on the fresco in the domestic chapel, and 40 scudi for a picture to go over the altar.[45] The fresco of the Assumption is generally considered to have been designed by Pozzo, but nearly all executed by assistants, which explains the comparatively small sum paid for the master's work in touching it up.[46] The fresco of St George in the refectory cannot be attributed to Pozzo, but there is a reference to payment for a gilder to gild the frame of 'the great picture by Fr Pozzo in the refectory' in 1700, which may refer to the Pharisee's Supper painting still there.[47]

During the eighteenth century nothing was done to the College apart from repairs. In 1705, 806.93 scudi were spent on repairs to the Palazzo which was then rented by Mgr Scotti of the Rota.[48] Later in the century Cardinal Caprara complained about alterations to the garden wall and referred to the perspective painting which was designed to be seen from the main corridor.[49] (Wiseman considered that this painting was by Pozzo, but it seems unlikely.[50])

In 1737–9 the College was visited and repairs were recommended to the church roof,[51] and wooden altars were to be replaced in stone or brick.[52] In 1773 work was in progress on the first floor[53] and in 1774 the church roof was again in need of repair.[54] In 1778 Martha Swinburne was buried in the church, but very shortly afterwards it seems to have been abandoned as unsafe.[55] By 1789 the Sodality Chapel was used for all functions, and licences were granted at intervals to celebrate the feasts and indulgences attached to the now unused church.[56]

A description of the College buildings in the last years of the Italian secular regime can be gathered from the Diaries of John Kirk.[57] The two notorious prisons were the space above the vault of the sacristy of the Sodality Chapel, and the room at the end of the second floor of the garden wing (later the nuns' chapel).[58] The corridor overlooking the garden on the second floor, above the library, was the 'Divines' Gallery', mentioned by Kirk,[59] and the second floor of the garden wing was an open loggia. It was at the far end of this loggia, thus totally isolated from the College, that Ricci, General of the Jesuits, was imprisoned in 1773.

In February 1798 the armies of the French Republic entered Rome, and the few remaining students fled to England. A last mass was said in the Sodality Chapel on Saturday, 4 April 1798.[60] During the short-lived Roman Republic much of the College property, including all the paintings and plate, were sold, and the buildings probably let to tenants.

During the twenty years before the College could re-open, the fabric was kept in repair with the exception of the church.[61] It appears that the church had been declared unsafe and unroofed before 1818, and the timber from the roof used to repair other parts of the College.[62] There is no certain evidence for deliberate desecration of the church, but it seems that one or two graves had been opened in search of lead, and all the fittings and altars were removed. Mass obligations, which had lapsed since 1798, were farmed out to neighbouring churches in 1803.[63]

5. The college restored: 1818–1978

When the College reopened in 1818 an architect's report was prepared on the state of the buildings. All were sound except for the church, which was flooded and causing weakening to the foundations of surrounding buildings.[64] Servi, the architect, produced a scheme on 10 June 1819 for a new building on the site, comprising an octagonal structure to include storerooms, sacristies and a small cemetery.[65]

The Congregation approved this scheme, though urging that expenses be kept down, and by 19 May 1820 Servi was able to report that work was well advanced on the new building, and it seems to have been finished that year.[65] William Kavanagh, a student of the College, died on 19 September 1820 and, according to the Liber Ruber, was buried in the chapel,[67] but as the Liber Ruber was not written up until about 1850 the source is suspect.

A description of the College in about 1820[68] makes it clear that the old Sodality Chapel was used for most functions, and was equipped with an English organ by Bevingtons.[69] Another chapel was constructed on the second floor 'at the end of the playroom', dedicated to the Blessed Virgin. This chapel is mentioned at intervals during the nineteenth century; it was decorated with murals by Charles Weld, and a stained-glass window which survives behind the present stage.[70] This chapel probably ceased to be used after the new church was opened; it was knocked into the common room in 1922, but the frescoes survived until 1948. The three big rooms overlooking the garden were used as a lecture room, library and *guardaroba* respectively. By 1824 a new clock had been installed.[71] In 1827–8 some repairs were done in the range overlooking the garden, as timbers bearing that date were found during the rebuilding in 1967.[72] In 1834, according to an inscription in the front hall, Nicholas Wiseman collected up the remains of the monuments from the old church and placed most of them in the room at the end of the corridor to the left of the main entrance. The monuments seem to have suffered considerable damage during the fifty years or so since the old church had been abandoned, and some restoration was necessary, especially to the Bainbridge monument. It was at this time that two ancient stone lions, which had originally formed part of a fountain in the cortile of Cardinal Howard's Palazzo,[73] were appropriated as supports for the monument.

Considerable damage was done to the clock tower in 1849, when it was

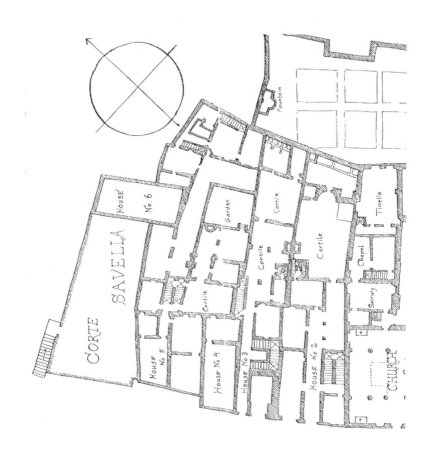

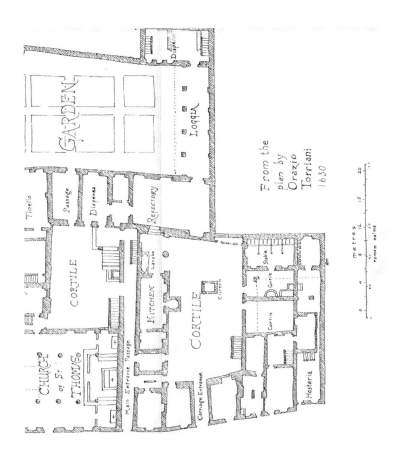

1630 plan by Oratio Torriani.

struck by a French cannon ball during the retaking of Rome for the Pope.[74] In 1853 the newly founded Collegio Pio came to share the English College buildings, and some alterations were made to accommodate them. The open loggia on the second floor of the garden wing was enclosed to form rooms, and the ground floor loggia was probably enclosed at the same time. The Pio seem to have used the whole of the garden wing, and the rooms over the present second library on the second floor. Bricks found in this area during works in 1967 bore the date stamp 1854.[75] Plans for most of these alterations survive in the archives. A sketch of the garden, made in 1860 by Francis Goldie, shows the garden wing with both loggias walled up, though the arches still show on the second floor.[76] It was probably at this time that the ante-room with wash-basins, at the entrance to the refectory, was abolished.

The largest project of the nineteenth century was the rebuilding of the College church. Plans were first drawn up in about 1854, the intention being to combine the College chapel with a parish church for the English community in Rome. Consequently there would have been a very large building occupying the site, not only of the mediaeval church but extending along the street as far as the end of the College property. This would, incidentally, have involved demolishing virtually all that remained of the mediaeval Hospice. Four rival plans were produced; the first, commissioned in 1864, was an elaborate neo-Gothic affair by E.W. Pugin, and was rejected as being out of keeping with the city. Of the second only a ground plan without attribution survives; it was centrally planned and probably Baroque. The third, in the 'Roman Mediaeval Style' was signed R.P.S. and dated August 1865. The final design, accepted in 1866, was by Conte Vergilio Vespignani. It comprised an aisled basilica with triumphal arch separating nave from chancel, which terminated, like the aisles, in an apse. The chancel would have been the College chapel, and the nave the parish church. A large sacristy would have been attached to the left chancel aisle.

Work began in 1865, and the foundation stone was laid, 35 feet below ground, by Pius IX on 6 February 1866. The nave was built first, and by 1869 was substantially complete, though the tribunes were still lacking. In order to keep the rents flowing as long as possible, the houses on the site of the apse were left standing, and the foundations of the apse actually appear to have been laid underneath the sitting tenants.

The scheme was cut short in 1869 when Mgr George Talbot was removed to an asylum: it had been conceived and backed by him, and was dependent on subscriptions from England, which were not forthcoming. Moreover the Manningite Rector, O'Callaghan, disapproved of the scheme of uniting the College chapel with a parish church, and the fall of Rome in 1870 dealt the death blow to the original scheme. The apse and sacristy were abandoned, and the house on the site (No. 48) was hastily patched up and relet to tenants. The nave was finished off as cheaply as possible. It was apparently first used on 18 January 1888, though the interior decoration was not completed for a few more years. The majority of the surviving monuments from the old church were placed in the new one, and in 1883 new inscriptions were cut to replace those destroyed; some of these contain fragments of the originals. The windows were supplied by Hardman of Birmingham. The paintings in the tribune were copied from engravings of the martyrs' paintings in the old church by one Capparoni, who also executed four lunettes at the back of the church in 1893.[77]

Of other works in the College, little was done save essential repairs following the loss of virtually all College property in 1870. The Collegio Pio was allowed to die out by the Rector in 1875 – it had been severely damaged by shelling in 1870[78] and was again damaged when the fort of Monte Verde blew up in 1891,[79] though it was by then abandoned. In 1897 Leo XIII refounded the Collegio Pio as the Beda, and on the recommendation of Mgr Merry del Val, a number of rooms were built on the top floor overlooking the garden and along the garden wing, thus completing the third floor. These rooms seem to have been ready by 1899.[80] The old Sodality Chapel was made over to the Beda, who used virtually all the garden wing as well as the top floor.

After the First World War the College's financial situation improved under Rector Hinsley, and much needed repairs could be carried out. In 1917 the house next to the church, No. 48 (the old Hospice) had to be substantially repaired, as it had been weakened by the attempt to build the church under it.[81] In 1918 the Beda was moved out, and the English College rapidly expanded to fill their rooms, and eventually to take over much of Cardinal Howard's old Palazzo.

Changes since 1921 are chronicled in the *Venerabile*. In 1922 the common room was extended into the old Madonna Chapel.[82] In 1923 central heating was installed.[83] In 1924 part of No. 48 was taken over as rooms, into which the nuns moved in 1927.[84] The 'Salone' was constructed by turning the first floor rooms on the street side into one long room, and dividing the former corridor into the Rector's rooms.[85] In 1925 the swimming tank was finished,[86] and the organ installed in the church; the College had previously made do with the old organ from the Sodality Chapel.[87] In 1927, when the nuns moved out of the second floor of the garden wing, it was redesigned to provide music rooms and an infirmary.[88] In 1931 part of the top floor of the old Palazzo was taken over as student rooms, and the remainder was occupied in 1937, forming the 'North-West passage'.[89] In 1933 the old Sodality Chapel, which had been empty since the Beda moved out, was refurnished, the tribune demolished, and the old 'dungeon' above the sacristy turned into a side chapel.[90] The only substantial new building in the twentieth century was the bath block with sacristies and lavatories, which was inserted into the old chapel cortile in 1936–7, and known as the 'Queen Mary'.[91]

After the war no repairs were immediately necessary. A wooden floor was inserted into the chapel in 1948,[92] the garden was refurbished in 1954[93] and the swimming tank altered in 1959.[94] Between 1959 and 1968, however, much of the College was found to be in need of radical rebuilding. Work began on the garden side, over the libraries, culminating in the summer of 1967, when the floor and ceiling of the second library were

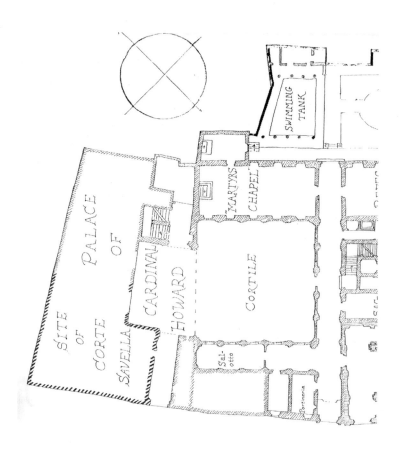

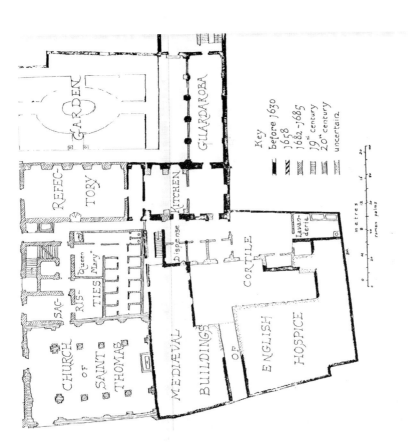

Plan of College buildings with construction dates.

removed, leaving the whole wing perilously unsupported until the new steel girders could be inserted. To relieve the weight on the walls the concrete vaults over all three library rooms were removed, and in the process the first two libraries were refurnished.[95] The refectory was refurnished and the ceiling fresco cleaned after Vatican II, the cost being met by a donation from the Council Fathers.[96] On the other side of the building the first floor of the old Palazzo was taken over as accommodation for the Council Fathers in 1962[97] and the second floor as student accommodation in 1966.[98] The top floor was virtually demolished and rebuilt in lighter materials, lightening but not removing the vaulted ceilings below, in 1968.[99] Most of the top floor of the Palazzo was abandoned since it was considered unsafe, but in 1976 it was converted into a flat and let to tenants, as were the former bishops' apartments on the first floor.

The final phase of the restoration was the repainting of the outside of the buildings and the restoration of the clock tower, which was finished in November 1976.

Since 1978 several alterations have been made. The departure of the nuns led to the conversion of their roons into graduate accommodation, including major alterations in the old *guardaroba* area, revealing a couple of ancient columns.

Notes

1 *Venerabile*, XXIII, 175.
2 The cippus recording this extension, now at the corner of the Via dei Banchi Vecchi, was moved from the Cancelleria in 1509. (Guida Rionale di Roma, Rione VII Regola Parte II, p. 14, by Carlo Pietrangeli.) A direct line from the Cancelleria to the river would include the college site within the Pomerium.
3 Tacitus *Historiae*, II 94.
4 C.I.L. vi 62i.
5 *Venerabile*, XXIII, 27 sqq.
6 *Venerabile*, XXI, 50.
7 Reg. Vat. 284 f 56v.
8 M 115, 29 May 1383. (The relevant part of the ms is destroyed by a hole in the parchment, but the Index Chron. of 1774 quotes it: Liber 1597 f 754.)
9 M 75 21 Sept. 1374. M 87, 8 April 1376.
10 Liber 1292 f 65.
11 John Harver, 'The Wilton Diptych, a Re-examination', *Proc. Soc. Ant.* 1961 (Liber 1656).
12 M 200 23 Mar. 1445.
13 Liber 17 f 11, 11v.
14 Ibid., f 9v–10v.
15 Ibid., f 20v.
16 Ibid., f 41v.
17 M 259, 3 Mar. 1530.

18 Thomas Metcalf, 1503, had a 'figura incise', Scr. 82.2. See J. Bertram, 'Incised Slabs in the English College, Rome' in *Transactions of the Monumental Brass Society* XII, part 4 (1979), 278–83, and XVI, part I (1992), 79–82.

19 *Venerabile*, XX, 7.

20 *Venerabile*, XX, 98.

21 M 313.

22 Index Archivi ad loc. Liber 1594 f 168.

23 Liber 6 p. 224.

24 Liber 1598 f 299.

25 Libri 246–9.

26 Scr. 8.3d.

27 Liber 10 ff 77–82, 100–4.

28 Liber 971 'Muratore 1658'. Liber 249 f 13.

29 Liber 11 f 64.

30 Scr 31.5.1.

31 Liber 11 f 199.

32 M 401.

33 Libro Mastro KK (Liber 72) f 528.

34 Scr. 31.5.6. and 8.1.1b.

35 Liber 324.

36 Liber 975 'Muratore'.

37 Scr. 86.3 (Letter to Hinsley from A. Edith Hewett).

38 Liber 11 f 270 sqq (three years back rent paid in 1688, 1170 scudi).

39 Scr. 7.13.

40 References are ambiguous, e.g. Scr. 8.1.1d.

41 See print *c.*1700 in Graphische Sammlung, Vienna, reproduced *Venerabile,* XXV, 46.

42 Bernhard Kerber, *Ein Kirchenprojekt des Andrea Pozzo als Vorstufe für Weltenberg?* Architectura 1972 (Liber 1579).

43 Scr. 31.5.6.

44 Scr. 31.6.1.

45 Libro Mastro LL (liber 73) f 435.

46 Opinion of Fr H. Pfeiffer, S.J.

47 Liber 978 'Doratore 1700'.

48 Scr. 8.6.

49 Scr. 8.2.

50 *Recollections of the last Four Popes*, Chapter 1.

51 Scr. 43.42.

52 Liber 324 f 125.

53 Liber 1593 f 72.

54 Scr. 43.4I.

55 Scr. 43.37.

56 e.g. Scr. 49.7; 49.27 etc.

57 Birmingham Archdiocesan Archives C 693. Transcript VEC archives Liber 815.

58 *Venerabile*, III, 162.

59 See *Venerabile*, XX, 205.
60 Liber 660.
61 Liber 1067 'Filza 1808'.
62 Scr. 56.1.3.
63 Liber 661 sqq.
64 Liber 549 f 4v.
65 Scr. 56.1.3.
66 Liber 616 f 11v.
67 Liber 1630 f 6o.
68 *Venerabile*, VI, 159.
69 Liber 1644 pt 6 'Inventario 1849'.
70 Ibid.
71 Liber 550 f 1.
72 *Venerabile*, XXIV, f 178.
73 Scr. 8.1.2. f 7.
74 *Venerabile*, IV, 253.
75 *Venerabile*, XXIV, 178.
76 Liber 644 frontispiece (vignette).
77 See Anthony Laird *The College Church*, *Venerabile*, XXIV 159–73, 258–68.
78 *Venerabile*, III, 327.
79 *Venerabile*, X, 142.
80 H. K. Mann, *History of the Beda*, 1918.
81 Liber 1144.
82 *Venerabile*, 166.
83 Liber 1165a.
84 *Venerabile*, II, 83.
85 *Venerabile*, II, 83.
86 *Venerabile*, II, 284.
87 *Venerabile*, II, 179 of XXIV, 265.
88 *Venerabile*, III, 383.
89 *Venerabile*, V, 25; VII, 243.
90 *Venerabile*, VI, 425; VII, 146.
91 *Venerabile*, VII, 84.
92 *Venerabile*, XIII, 272.
93 *Venerabile*, XVII, 119.
94 *Venerabile*, XIX, 468.
95 *Venerabile*, XXIV, 176–8.
96 *Venerabile*, XXIII, 305.
97 *Venerabile*, XXIII, 305.
98 *Venerabile*, XXIV, 600, 176.
99 *Venerabile*, XXV, 66.

References to items in the VEC archives were according to the threefold division introduced in 1773 as indexed 1977.

Liber: a numbered book in the Libri series which now incorporates the former 'Z' books and other material formerly uncatalogued.

M: a numbered membrane in the Membranae series as listed in 1962 and sequence completed 1977.

Scr.:   Reference number to the Scritture series, in volumes with up to three successive subdivisions, as catalogued at successive dates to 1977.

Appendix II

The Bull *Quoniam Divinae Bonitati* on the Foundation of the English College at Rome in 1579

Summary

Gregory, Bishop, Servant of the Servants of God, to be remembered for ever! Since God in His Goodness has appointed Us as Pope during this time when the Church is troubled with heresies and schisms, We have decided that the best way to defend the Church is to establish national Colleges in Rome to train young men in theology to work as missionaries in Protestant countries. In the case of England we have already noticed many young men who have come to Rome to train as priests for work in England, and accordingly We are now Establishing an English College in the buildings of the former English Hospice where these young men have already established themselves. The College is to consist of a Rector, staff and at least fifty scholars from all parts of England and Wales, and shall teach Theology and Philosophy, and Greek and Hebrew where appropriate. They shall also study spirituality, Church music and liturgy as arranged by the College staff. For this purpose We grant an annual income of 3,000 Crowns.

We make over absolutely the buildings and all the property of the former English Hospice to this new College, which property the Rector may take possession of immediately. However if the College should ever be closed, the property should revert to the English Hospice which would then be re-established. None of the former chaplains and governors of the former Hospice shall have any further rights over the property of the College. Moreover the College and all its property is directly under Papal authority, and totally exempt from all interference by the civil administration of Rome, and from all taxation. The Rector, staff and students shall have all the privileges and rights enjoyed by the Rector and Doctors of Rome University, and We forbid all civil and ecclesiastical authorities from interfering with them.

The Superiors of the College, with the Protector's consent, may grant degrees of Bachelor, Licence, Doctor and Master in Arts or Theology and even other faculties, which degrees shall have exactly the same status and rights as those of Rome University. Students may be ordained after an examination but dispensed from canonical intervals, dimissorial letters and irregularities by these Letters. They may exercise their ministries freely within the College.

For the administration of the College We appoint Cardinal Morone as Protector: he shall have overall authority in all temporal matters, right of arbitration in all disputes within the College, and complete freedom to make regulations and statutes. He shall be responsible for the admission of students. New students should be examined by his deputies before they come to Rome, and if judged satisfactory should be admitted for up to six months' probation. If they still seem acceptable, they should take an oath to return to England to work as priests as soon as they are commanded to do so.

The Rector or Spiritual Director shall have faculties to absolve the students from all sins and ecclesiastical penalties, except for certain reserved sins, and to dispense from most impediments to ordination. No civil or ecclesiastical authority may contradict this on any pretext.

Anything to the contrary notwithstanding.

We grant a Plenary Indulgence to all Rectors, staff and students at the moment of entering the College, and if they should die while at the College, at the moment of death.

Let no man contradict or oppose this decree.

St. Peter's, Rome, 1 May 1579.
(Registered 9 January 1580)

Full text of Bull of Foundation of the Venerable English College in the City: 1 May 1579

Gregory, Bishop, Servant of the Servants of God, to be remembered for ever! Since God in His goodness has deigned to raise Us, poor as We are, to the highest summit of the Universal Church, in this age when Christendom is so troubled, and He has entrusted to Us the burden of administering the inheritance, which He won by His precious Blood, it has been Our constant concern dutifully to consider how We may not only shew Our gratitude to God from Whose mercy we have received so much, but also ensure that Our efforts are beneficial for the Church, in so far as We are able with the help of God in his kindness.

i)   Day by day We observe, and We are much saddened by it, that the Spotless Bride of Our Lord Jesus Christ is assaulted by a conspiracy of different enemies, violently attacking her on several fronts. To the Jews and Turks, our ancient foes, are added heretics as well as schismatics, who are steeped in every sort of crime and wickedness and bring destruction on our Holy Mother Church prompted by the emissaries of our Enemy. Because of this Our duty calls Us to oppose all these assaults with the powers granted to Us by the Lord, wherever We see the need to be greatest, and to come to the aid of the peoples whom God in His kindness has entrusted to Us in Our weakness, preparing safeguards against the assault of our foes. No better safeguard nor more certain remedy can be devised than that the young people of those regions oppressed by this plague be well instructed in Catholic doctrine while their minds are open to be easily formed in virtue, and accordingly since the beginning of Our Pontificate we have taken steps at Our own expense to establish Colleges in this City for different nations, to be Seminaries for solid formation in Catholic Doctrine.

ii)   While We were thus employed, We turned Our loving attention to the Kingdom of England: this once flourished with great wealth and concern for the Catholic Faith, but it is now devastated by the dreadful taint of heresy which has seized almost the whole Kingdom. We took pity on this calamity, as We have often in other cases, and We remembered that the English people have always excelled in faithfulness, reverence and obedience towards the Roman Pontiffs and the Holy Apostolic See ever since they were brought to the Faith of Christ by Blessed Pope Gregory. Even in the darkness of Our times she has shone in the lives of distinguished and renowned men who have not hesitated to pour out their life's blood for the authority of this See and the truth of the orthodox Faith. Moreover there appear frequently before Our eyes young men who have fled hither from that wretched Kingdom, and have been led by the Holy Spirit to abandon their country, their families and their possessions, and have sorrowfully offered themselves to Us to be instructed in the Catholic religion in which they were born, with the aim primarily of assuring their own salvation, but also so that once instructed in the knowledge of theology they might return to England to enlighten others who had fallen away from the way of truth.

iii) We therefore desire to imitate the kindness of Gregory I towards the English, and his beneficence towards them, so that they may rejoice in the Lord that We have called them back from error just as they rejoiced at his first benefits to them. We appreciate the sincere loyalty of the aforementioned young men towards the Holy See, and their eagerness to learn Catholic doctrine, and therefore on Our Own initiative and fully informed, in the Fullness of our Apostolic Power, to the Praise of Almighty God and the Increase of the Catholic Faith, and for the Benefit and Profit of the English Nation, so dear to Us, *We do Establish and Institute for ever in the Buildings of the English Hospice in Rome, a College to be called the ENGLISH COLLEGE* in which shall be housed not less than fifty scholars, of all nations and languages within the Kingdom of England, to have their own Rector and Staff, and wherein they shall study Philosophy and Theology, and moreover Greek and Hebrew as far as each is able, and they shall strive to reach whatever standard shall seem adequate.

iv) They shall all apply themselves to such studies as their superiors shall direct, and shall also take pains in piety and devotion, Church music, liturgy and the sacred rites as the superiors shall think fit. To support all this We institute an Annual Grant of three thousand gold Crowns, to be paid freely and in full by the Apostolic Camera or the Datary, in gold, in equal monthly instalments, until they can be assured of a similar annual income from other sources provided by Us or Our Successors.

v) Moreover We do Grant and Assign for ever, for their Abode and Use, the aforesaid Buildings in which the English chaplains once lived, though already the said students live there by Our command, together with two houses adjoining the said Hospital at the left side towards the Church of St. Bridget of Sweden, and the adjacent property. Moreover, for the support of divine worship in the English Church of the Most Holy Trinity and St. Thomas the Martyr, not to mention the stipend of the said College, and the support of the said Rector, Students and Staff, We do altogether separate from the said Hospital and attach to the said College all and every other house, tavern or shop, stable, inn, garden, park, land, rent, produce and all and several other mobile and immobile goods and chattels, as well as all property, rights and privileges of the said Hospital, both in this City and elsewhere, wheresoever they be, and of whatever quality, species, nature, value, quantity, and annual income they may consist, all of which, their situations, definitions, confines and boundaries are to belong expressly to the College as if they had been named and described in detail in these present letters. And that the buildings and other things that can be marked should be so marked externally with the arms and emblems of the said College as soon as possible, that they may be recognised by others. Therefore the Rector and Scholars aforesaid may freely on their own authority take corporal possession of all these goods, in their own person or by an agent or agents, and they may retain them for ever, and may examine, require and receive all their produce, returns and income, rights, duties and emoluments, and may freely and licitly apply them to the common use of themselves and the said College, without any need for a licence from the Urban Vicar or anyone else. The Bursar and other staff and servants of the said College shall be subject to the Rector, and shall obey absolutely his commands and orders, nor shall they do or attempt anything against his will. The Bursar shall be bound to render an account either to the current Protector of the College or to the Rector himself if he wishes and requires it, or to any deputies they may appoint, twice in the year or as often as he or they shall think fit. Moreover if at any time it be decided to dissolve the aforesaid College for any reason, the Buildings, Church, houses, rents and all aforesaid shall belong to the foresaid Hospital as if the Foundation of the College and other provisions had never been made, as We hereby restore in that event the same Hospital with regard to all these matters.

vi)   At the same time We do strictly forbid the aforesaid chaplains, as well as the governors and administrators of the said Hospital, of whatever rank and title, henceforth to intervene in the aforesaid buildings, church, houses, shops, rents, produce and other property, rights and privileges, neither directly nor indirectly on any pretext whatsoever. Nor shall they presume to molest or disturb the College, its Rector, Students and Staff now and subsequently. And We do decree that anything that may be attempted contrary to any measures already made or contained in these presents, either on the part of the said chaplains or of any others, knowingly or unknowingly, shall be null and void.

vii)   Moreover We do take under Our protection and that of Blessed Peter and this See, this College, its Rectors, Students and Staff for ever, and the foresaid and all other goods and chattels of whatever quality or quantity both within and without the said City and in whatever other place they may be. We do place them directly under Our authority and that of this See, exempting them entirely in all matters general and particular from any jurisdiction, correction, visitation, dominion, authority and power of any one that shall be at any time Vicar, Governor, Senator, Consuls, Conservators, or Reformators of the said City, General Auditor of Cases in the Curial Apostolic Camera, as well as the general Rector of Studies, or any other whatsoever Tribunal, Judge or Official, even the local Ordinaries, Rectors of parish churches, or any other authority both in the said City and elsewhere.

viii)   Moreover We do exempt and fully release for ever the entire property and possessions of the College from payment or exaction of any sort of dues, tolls, direct taxation or stamp duty, even for wine from Ripa and Ripetta, as well as grain, oil, cloth of any kind, and any other sort of goods, and also tithes and any other sort of tax, both ordinary and extraordinary, imposed or to be imposed for any reason whatsoever.

ix)   Moreover We do grant and proclaim to the same College and Students, Rectors and Governors, that they may use, possess and enjoy all and every privilege, exemption, liberty, faculty and indult which the Studium Generale of the same City and its Rector and the Doctors living therein do now use, possess or enjoy, or shall in the future use, possess and enjoy, not merely in comparable measure but in precisely the same and equal measure.

x)   We do Admonish and Forbid the Vicar, Governor, Auditor, Senator, Consuls, Conservators, Reformators, Rector, judges, Officials and Others aforesaid, not to mention the Camerarius of the Holy Roman Church, the Presidents and Clerks of the Apostolic Camera, and any sort of Commissioners for collecting taxes, customs or tithes and other aforesaid dues currently appointed, both individual and general, from impeding or molesting the College, Students, Rector, Staff and Governors aforesaid or any one of them, on the pretext or at the occasion of any faculties, privileges and letters whatsoever, granted for any duration or form, even for the benefit and revenue of the aforesaid Officials and for other such reasons, nor shall they suffer them to be so impeded or molested.

xi)   Moreover We do grant to the Superiors of the said College, with the consent of the said Protector, licence to put forward those whom they shall consider to have studied for the requisite time in the said College or elsewhere, and to be suitable in knowledge and conduct, for the Degrees of Baccalaureat, Licenciat, Doctorate or Magistrate in the aforesaid Faculties of Theology and Arts, following the norms of the council of Vienne, and for other degrees according to the usage of Rome University, and to grant them the customary insignia of these Degrees. Moreover those who have graduated thus in the aforesaid faculties may interpret, teach and dispute in these subjects, and exercise the functions proper to such a degree or degrees, both publicly and privately, in all Universities of general studies, and they may and should use, possess and enjoy all privileges, graces and favours, prerogatives, and Indults that are used, possessed or enjoyed or may in the future be used, possessed or enjoyed, by right or custom, by graduates in the aforesaid or other Universities or elsewhere, according to the Customs and Practice of that and other such Universities, just as if they had obtained the foresaid degrees in that same University according to the Statutes, Customs and Practice thereof.

xii) Finally, since it is expedient that the scholars trained in this College should join the ranks of the priesthood, as the time and occasion demands, after long studies, whether completed or not, so that they may become accustomed to the sacred ministries and functions, and preside at the services in the said Church of the Most Holy Trinity or may be sent out as workers, these Students may be advanced to holy Orders up to the priesthood, by licence of the Protector and by the consent of the Rector of the said College and after an examination, even if outside the canonical times and without observing the intervals laid down by the Council of Trent, and even without dimissorial letters from their own Ordinaries, and without any benefice or patrimonial title, taking no account of any irregularity of birth, for which and the like we do grant dispensation by these presents. And We grant that they and any other priests living in the said College after they shall have been ordained may exercise their ministry even at the altar, and may freely and licitly receive Penance and the Eucharist (even on great feastdays) and the Sacrament of Extreme Unction, from the Spiritual Director or any other priest of the same College, as arranged by the Rector.

xiii) Moreover, in order that proper care may be taken for the maintenance and good ordering of the said College, not only in the actual formation and discipline of the students but also in their feeding, clothing and other necessities, and that they may be readily and efficiently looked after, We do constitute and deputise Our venerable brother John, Bishop of Ostia, namely Cardinal Morone, as Protector and Defender of the said College. His concern and responsibility shall be not only the aforementioned matters but also everything relating to the admission, maintenance and dismissal of the scholars of the said College. We grant to him and his successors in the office of Protector of the said College, full faculty and authority to appoint, remove or replace bursars, solicitors and accountants, so that the College may be well administered, with regard to the direction of the students, and the goods, chattels and rights of the College, both spiritual and temporal; as well as the right to decide, define, judge and arbitrate over all differences, lawsuits and controversies among any members of the College, Students and Staff, Lay and Cleric (though not priests) without right of appeal, but summarily and straightforwardly without ostentation or delay. Moreover he may make and promulgate, and repeal if need be, rules and statutes, as long as they be lawful and honourable, conformable to Canon Law and the foresaid Council of Trent: he may change and correct them, or establish new ones, which once made and promulgated, or repealed, changed or corrected, shall thenceforth be held and obeyed as if they were approved and confirmed by Our Apostolic Authority, as We do command all the Scholars of the said College to hold them and obey them inviolably!

xiv)   As for the correct method and form of admitting the said Scholars, We do ordain and decree that those who are to be admitted be examined in France, Belgium or elsewhere by examiners appointed or to be appointed by the said Protector, as he may think best, according to the form to be appointed by him. Once they have passed this examination, if the Protector decide on the evidence of the aforesaid examiners (in person or by letter) that they be intellectually capable, morally satisfactory and such as ought to be received, he may then admit them.

xv)   However once they are admitted to the College they shall not be at once enrolled among the Scholars of the College, but their conduct shall be tested during four to six months, shorter or longer as the College Authorities shall think fit. If they then seem acceptable for the College, they shall take an oath that they will persevere in the ecclesiastical life, and will be prepared at all times to return to their native country at their superiors' bidding, and work for the care of souls as far as they be able in the Lord.

xvi)   Moreover We do grant free faculties to the current Father Rector of the said College freely and licitly to grant dispensations (in his own person or through a suitable Confessor whom he shall choose and appoint) to any of the said scholars, from any excommunication, suspension or interdict, or other sentence, censure or ecclesiastical penalty, which they may have at any time incurred on any grounds or for any reason. He may absolve them from any sins, excesses and delicts, however grave or serious, even in the cases contained in the letters customarily read on Maundy Thursday (excepting only conspiracy against the person or States of the Roman Pontiff, forgery of Apostolic letters or documents, sale of arms or any other contraband to infidel countries, and laying of violent hands on prelates). He may impose a suitable penance on them for sins committed, and moreover dispense from any irregularity they may have contracted saving only voluntary homicide, bigamy and heresy.

xvii) We do decree that all the aforesaid shall stand in perpetuity, and that judgment and decision must always be made accordingly on all and single such matters, by any judges ordinary or delegate, even the Auditors of Cases of the Apostolic Palace, and the Cardinals of the Holy Roman Church, in any cause or matter, notwithstanding any faculty or authority any of them may have in judging or interpreting otherwise, and that anything that may be attempted on the part of anyone of whatever authority, knowingly or unknowingly, shall be null and void.

xviii) Notwithstanding Our Own policy of not abrogating laws, and making clear the true value of revenues, setting up a commission for this sort of corporation, and summonsing those concerned, Not to mention the recent Lateran Council's law, and other Apostolic Constitutions, and the Statutes and Customs of the aforementioned Hospital at Rome and the Camera, though confirmed by whatever Oath, Apostolic decree or authority. And the privileges, indults and letters Apostolic granted, approved or renewed to them and the same Senator, Consuls, Reformators, Camerarius, Universities and their Colleges, Rectors and other persons aforesaid, not to mention the Roman people, tax collectors, contractors and others, though granted for whatever duration and force or whatever clauses in favour of such Hospitals; And all these aforesaid We hereby expressly and particularly do abrogate, in this case only, considering their effect to be sufficiently described in these presents, Which effect shall in all other cases remain. Anything to the contrary notwithstanding.

xix) Moreover, to add spiritual endowments to these temporal benefits, in order that the devotion of the faithful may be fortified by them and so grow and increase, We do grant in perpetuity, relying on the mercy of Almighty God and the authority of the Blessed Apostles Peter and Paul, to all Students, Rectors and Staffmembers who shall be received into this College, at the time of their arrival, and moreover any who shall happen to die in this College, at the moment of death, if they be truly penitent and contrite, a Plenary Indulgence and Remission of all their Sins.

And it shall not be lawful for any man to infringe or dare presumptuously to contradict this Our decree of Erection Institution Assignation Will Separation Translation Restitution Inhibition Susception Subjection Exemption Liberation Communication Precept Interdict Dispensation Indult Constitution Deputation Donation Command Statute Ordination Tribute Decretal Concession and Derogation. And if anyone shall presume to attempt this let him know that he will incur the indignation of God Almighty and the Blessed Apostles Peter and Paul.

Given at Rome at St. Peter's, in the Year of the Incarnation One Thousand Five Hundred and Seventy Nine, on the First Day of May, in the Sixth Year of Our Pontificate.

M. Datarius.
Cae. Glorierius.

A. de Alexis ...

On the Ninth of January 1580 the present letters Apostolic were presented in the Camera Apostolic and by decree there made were admitted and registered in their books, To wit in the Fourth Volume of Signiaturae of different Popes, page 44. By me the undersigned Notary of the said Camera: Tideus de Marchis.

versio anglica
22 Maii 1978
Jerome Bertram

Appendix III

Statutes, Constitutions and Rules of the Venerable English College

1. The original statutes of the English College, Rome are those of 12 June 1579 and they are printed in A. O. Meyer, *England and the Catholic Church under Elizabeth,* English translation, London, 1916, pp. 481–5. The rules are given under the following headings: Quod pertinet ad ingressum, Quod pertinet ad pietatem, De eo quod pertinet ad studia, Quod pertinet ad domesticam disciplinam, Quod pertinet ad valetudinem.

2. The Report of Cardinal Sega's first visitation in 1585 (Meyer, *op. cit.,* 492–519) includes a section Constitutiones Collegii Anglicani which begins 'Omnis Reipublicae Status ...' and contains sections headed: De admittendis, De instruendis, Observanda ab omnibus circa pietatem, Circa Studia, Circa domesticam disciplinam, Institutio sodalitatis Bmae Virginis in Collegio Anglicano, Sodalitatis Bmae Virginis in Collegio Anglicano leges et institute, Regulae pro praefectis cubiculorum, Ordo domus, De alumno parocho, Attestatio medici. This account of the Constitutions is substantially the same as that found at the beginning of the Liber Ruber *(CRS,* 37).

3. In 1600 a fuller form of Constitution, also beginning 'Omnis Reipublicae Status' was drawn up and this was identical for the colleges in Rome, Seville and Valladolid. This can be found in the *CRS* volume on the English College, Valladolid *(CRS,* 30). It is very similar to the 1585 version but there is no section on the Sodality. The Douai Constitutions of 1600 also begin in the same way, but they then differ somewhat in wording and content.

4. It seems that the 1600 Constitutions remained unaltered until the suppression of the College in 1798. Visitations did take place in the seventeenth and eighteenth centuries but no substantial modifications were made. For example, in the 1657 Visitation (Liber 228)

there is a section headed 'Della domestica disciplina di questo Collegio Inglese' which gives details about the daily timetable, food, clothing, recreation and exercises of piety. At the end of the report there are 'Ordinationes et declarationes' of the Protector, Francis Barberini, which consist of small additions to some of the sections of the existing Constitutions and a questionnaire to be answered by those seeking entrance to the College. In the 1739 Visitation report (Liber 324) there is an order to the effect that the Constitutions 'de domestica alumnorum disciplina' are to be read every month in the refectory. Although based on previous documents the text is worded somewhat differently and is more detailed than the 1600 Constitutions.

5.   These documents reveal that in this early period of the College's history there was a continuity and consistency in the day to day life of the students. A three-year philosophy course was followed by four years' theology. Students attended the Roman College for lectures each day and in the afternoon or evening there were 'repetitions' or supplementary lectures by tutors at home. There was a resident spiritual director. The day began with half an hour mental prayer (often in one's room according to the Jesuit practice). This was followed by Mass. There was a visit to the Blessed Sacrament after lunch and in the evening devotions in church (litanies) with examination of conscience. Retreats were held during the year. On feast days there was sung Mass and Vespers. Monthly communion and confession were the norm, but on greater feasts all communicated. The programme was similar to other seminaries in Rome and fidelity to this rule of life was the test of the candidate's suitability for the life of a priest whether in England or elsewhere. The rules of the house imposed silence at certain times, forbade visiting of other people's rooms, restricted associations within the community to those in the same *camerata*, examined incoming and outgoing mail and discouraged any peculiarities in food, dress and furnishings of rooms. There were of course customs and traditions that were characteristic of the College in Rome, but the general rule of life was common to all seminaries of the day and there was the accepted belief that by obedience to these rules and regulations one was opening oneself to God's grace and preparing for a future life as a priest. References that occur, from time to time, of tightening up of rules are largely a matter of securing a better observance of the laws that already exist.

6.   In 1818 with the restoration of the College, a new Constitution was drawn up. This was of a much simpler form than that of 1600 and it contains specific requirements demanded by the circumstances of the time. A free translation is here appended (Scr. 6, 1).

Constitutions of the English College, Rome
11 June 1818

The English College was established by His Holiness Gregory XIII on 1 May 1579 for the education of young Englishmen in the sacred sciences so that after their training and formation they would return to England to instruct others in the Catholic religion.

Bearing this in mind, no one is to be admitted as an alumnus of this College unless he is English and a Catholic. However, young Catholic men born in other regions can be accepted if their father was English.

Those who are to be admitted should have already studied humanities and know the Latin language, so that they can immediately begin the study of logic.

The greatest care is to be exercised in selecting students and this is to be the method adopted: Each year the Rector is to inform the Cardinal Protector, who has the power of election, what places will be available for the following year. He will write to the Vicars Apostolic of England for them to select and examine new students according to the form prescribed by the Decree of Cardinal Barberini.

Those youths chosen by the Vicars Apostolic will be sent letters of nomination, signed by the Protector and with his seal. They will come to Rome in the autumn and be admitted to the College. But before becoming alumni they are to be placed on probation for four or six months during which time the Rector and the Ecclesiastical Deputies will form a judgment as to their manners, disposition, intelligence, health and vocation. If anyone is found to be unsuitable he shall, with the approval of the Protector, be sent back to England.

After this period of probation they will be accepted as alumni. They are to make a three day retreat and at the end of this they are to take the oath of Alexander VII in the presence of the Rector. The oath will be signed and forwarded by the Protector to the Congregation of Propaganda Fide where it will be lodged.

Students who have completed their studies in Rome and have been ordained priest are to be examined by examiners designated by the Protector, before they leave for the mission in England. This is to be done in the presence of the Rector and the Ecclesiastical Deputy and is for the purpose of ascertaining their suitability for the role of missioner. They will receive letters of commendation from the Protector to the Vicars Apostolic and they will proceed to England by a designated route and provided with travelling expenses of forty scudi. Alumni thus sent to England must not wander into other countries nor be deflected from their sworn vocation even under the pretext of good. They are to go directly to the mission and present themselves to the Vicars Apostolic and obey their commands.

Although in the Apostolic Letters of Foundation fifty is prescribed as the number of alumni, the present income of the College is not sufficient to provide for so many. For the present there are to be eight alumni, the number to be increased when the income allows for this.

Other young men, whose pension is paid from other sources, may be admitted as commoners up to a number approved by the Cardinal Protector. Men from Scotland and Ireland may be admitted as long as the Scots and Irish colleges are not yet reopened in Rome.

No one may be admitted unless he deposits with the Rector money to cover travelling expenses back home and he has also to pay three months pension in advance. He must promise to conform to the way of life of the other students in food, clothing and discipline, but he will not be obliged to the missionary oath. He will be required to meet the same standards as the alumni.

No one is to be received as a guest. This is forbidden both because of the shortage of accommodation and because of the abuses which can result.

Apart from the eight alumni, there will live and be fed at the College's expense: Rector, Confessor, Ripetitore, Prefect, Room servant, Clothing servant, Cook and his assistant, Doorkeeper.

Annual Stipends.

	scudi
Rector	120
Confessor	36
Ripetitore	48
Prefect	30
Room servant	24
Clothing servant and assistant	48
Cook and assistant	48
Doorkeeper	18

The ministers of the College shall do their duties faithfully according to the rules set out for each.

Food for Rector, alumni, confessor, ripetitore and prefect.

Breakfast Tea with milk and bread. On Sundays and Thursdays butter may be added.

Dinner Wine, soup, main dish and then cheese and fruit. On Sundays and Thursdays there is an additional dish.

Supper Salad, one dish, cheese and fruit. On fast days the dish omitted at supper may be added to dinner.

Food for the others.
> Dinner   Wine, soup and one dish.
> Supper   Salad and one dish.

Each person is entitled to twenty ounces of bread, five measures of wine, three ounces of cheese.

All are to be subject to the Rector. There are two Deputies chosen by the Protector and they are to be regularly consulted.

Every month there is to be a meeting (*congregatio*) in the house of the Protector or at the College according to the convenience of the Protector. At this meeting, which is to discuss College business, there shall be present the Rector and the two Deputies and such other ministers as may be invited. At the meeting there will be given an account of all that pertains to piety, study, discipline and administration. Bills, money orders etc are to be made in the name of the Rector.

The horarium is to be set up by the Rector with the Protector's approval. The choice of all ministers is to be made by the Protector. [There then follow sixteen pages of rules in which are prescribed the duties of Rector, Confessor, Ripetitore, Prefect and the servants. Rules for the alumni come under three heads: De pietate, De studiis, De domestica disciplina and they are very similar to those obtaining before the interregnum.]

7.   Details of the horarium set up by the Rector can be gained from Gradwell's Journal, now in the Westminster Archives. Students rose at 5.30, meditation at 6.00, Mass at 6.30 and the rest of the day followed a pattern very similar to earlier days. In the list he gives of books that were read publicly in church, and in the refectory, we can detect the influence of Douai and the English secular clergy. The works include Challoner's *Meditations* and his *Memoirs of Missionary Priests*, various works of John Gother, Butler's *Lives of the Saints*, Eustace's *Tour Through Italy*, Wilson's *British Martyrology* and Dodd's *Church History*. At least the latter would hardly have been read during the time the Jesuits were superiors of the College.

8.   In 1869, as a result of the visitation by Cardinal Reisach, the Protector, and his assistant Archbishop Vitelleschi, new Constitutions and Rules were drawn up. These were considerably longer and more detailed than any previous document and are an example of the nineteenth-century legislation that governed seminaries up to the Second Vatican Council. There follows a brief resume of this sixty page document.

It begins with the preface *Omnis Reipublicae Status* taken from the earliest Constitution. Chapter one, *De admittendis*, lays down the requirements for admission to the College and covers much of the same ground as the 1818 Constitution. Chapter two, *Circa Pietatem,* gives detailed instructions as to spiritual duties. There are nineteen paragraphs concerning such matters as prayer on rising, half an hour meditation in chapel, that has been prepared the night before, daily Mass, examination of conscience, spiritual reading, visit to the Blessed Sacrament, a visit before the afternoon walk, five decades of the rosary each day, choir practice and office in choir on Sundays and feast days, fortnightly confession, retreats in the autumn and in Holy Week, singing the Salve Regina before retiring at night.

The third chapter deals with study and includes rules about silence and keeping to rooms and no visiting during study time. Chapter four, *De Disciplina et Moribus,* stresses the need to respect the Rector, Vice-Rector and other superiors and stipulates that the students be divided into *camerata* as is the custom with all Colleges in Rome. One is only allowed to talk to those of the same *camerata,* although the Rector may allow various *camerate* to take recreation together. Particular friendships were warned against. Rules about dress are followed by minute regulations about rooms – no private property, never lock the door, no food or drink to be kept, no singing or reading aloud so as to disturb others. There is to be no smoking, and letters, books and parcels can only be received with permission of the Rector. One is not allowed to keep firearms. There is to be no standing in corridors, no talking to the servants, no admission to the kitchen, and no windows are to be opened without the permission of the Rector. There are special rules to be observed in the refectory and also in the library. No one is to go out of the College without the permission and companion allotted by the Rector. In walking to the schools and for recreation the rules of *camerata* are to be observed. There is to be no visiting of cafes or *trattorie,* on pain of expulsion from the College. The prefects of *camerata* are to determine where the afternoon walks should go, but crowds have to be avoided and so the Corso and the Pincio are not to be frequented in the afternoon. Churches should be visited and, on entering any church, the Blessed Sacrament chapel should be visited first. The prefect will give a sign when they are to terminate this visit; then they go to the Lady Chapel, the shrine of the Saint whose feast it is, and then they can look around the church. There are also rules about avoiding the quarters of the Collegio Pio and it is forbidden to speak to the students of this other College. When they visit the Villa every fortnight for lunch, there is to be no smoking and they are not to indulge in games or gossip unfitted for clerics. Chapter five has special rules for the prefects and chapter six concerns the rules to be followed during the autumn *villeggiatura.* Chapter seven concerns ordinations and the return to England.

Although there was yet another set of Constitutions in 1917, the 1869 Rules contain many of the norms that were followed in the College until recent times and subsequent editions of the Rules (for example the booklet produced by Godfrey in 1934) are extracts from this comprehensive document that appeared when O'Callaghan was Rector.

9. The 1917 Constitution, which Hinsley had to apply, is very general in character and contains no details concerning internal discipline. A full translation of the document is given here.

Constitutions of the English College Rome
29 December 1917
(Acta Apostolicae Sedis X, pp. 201–3)

I   The purpose of the English College Rome is to see that those English students who reside there and are the hope of the Church, are instructed in good living and the virtues appropriate to those in sacred orders.

II   The College is immediately subject to the Sacred Congregation of Seminaries and Studies.

III   There shall be a Cardinal Protector (Patronus).

IV   The Cardinal Protector, by the authority of the Holy See, exercises those rights and duties which are proper to the Bishops of England and which they themselves cannot undertake, subject to the rules and prescriptions of these present Constitutions.

V   The Cardinal Protector shall be over all those who dwell in the College, the superiors as well as their subjects. He shall decide on matters pertaining to recruitment, correction and dismissal of the students. He shall decide who are to be granted burses. He will receive the oath which students have to tender according to the Constitutions. He shall decide on all matters that are deemed necessary and opportune for the direction, progress and administration of the Institution.

VI   The Bishops of England will consult the Protector about the admission of students to the College.

VII   The Protector will issue testimonial letters for Orders, but each bishop will give his own dimissorial letters.

VIII There will be two bodies of Deputies, one for discipline, the other for the administration of temporal goods. Each body will be made up of two priests nominated by the Congregation of Seminaries and Studies for a period of six years. The Protector will make use of the Deputies in important matters.

IX   The Rector is to be chosen by the Pope and he performs his office at the behest of the Holy See. He directs the College, he provides for its needs, but on matters of importance he has to consult the Protector. All have to give their assistance and cooperation to the Rector.

X   The Rector, or his delegate, is the parish priest of those resident in the College.

XI   Each year the Rector is to make a report about the state of the College; the piety, discipline, studies and domestic affairs, to the Congregation of Seminaries and Studies and also to the Bishops of England.

XII   To assist the Rector there is a Vice-Rector nominated by the Protector after consultation with the Vicar of Rome, the Rector and the Deputies for discipline. The Vice-Rector acts when the Rector is absent or impeded and he has to see that everything is carried out well in the College.

XIII A Spiritual Director, chosen by the Pope, lives in the College whose task it is to form the souls of the students. In addition there are to be two confessors, approved by the Vicar, designated by the Protector after consultation with the Rector.

XIV   A Bursar nominated by the Protector after consultation with the Vicar, Rector, and administrative Deputies, looks after the household but dependently on the Protector and Rector. There is nothing to prevent the Vice-Rector fulfilling the role of Bursar.

XV   The Rector is to designate a prefect to each *camerata*.

XVI   The Constitution of Gregory XIII, *Quoniam Divinae Bonitati,* is confirmed in matters relating to the possession and dominion over temporal goods both movable and immovable.

XVII Studies are to be pursued by the students according to the requirements of the law. Academic titles and degrees are to be accepted from faculties or universities instituted by the Holy See.

XVIII Alumni are to proceed to Orders according to the common law, any contrary privilege is hereby taken away.

XVIX In cases of the dismissal of students, the Cardinal Protector is to make the decision after consulting the Rector and the Deputies for discipline. The Ordinary is to be informed immediately, unless circumstances should advise otherwise.

XX   Where these Constitutions do not decree otherwise the common law is to be observed and the Bull of Erection of the College, *Quoniam Divinae Bonitati,* remains in full force.

The Fathers of the Congregation of Seminaries and Studies met in full council on 18 December and approved these Constitutions. The next day Benedict XV, in audience to the Secretary, ratified and confirmed it and ordered the Constitution to be kept for ever, notwithstanding the contrary.

Rome, from the Secretariate of the Sacred Congregation of Seminaries and Studies on the Feast of St Thomas of Canterbury, Bishop and Martyr.

29 December 1917
Caietanus Card. Bisletti Prefect
Jacobus Sinibaldi Ep.Tiberien Secretary

10. Thus we may conclude that the pattern of life, as to study and piety, was unchanged for many centuries, no matter what upheavals went on outside in Rome or in England. It was only at the time of the Second Vatican Council that substantial modifications began to be made in a way of life and discipline that dated from the time of the martyrs.

11. For the sake of completeness there is herewith appended the original text of the oath that was taken by every alumnus up to very recent times.

Forma iuramenti quod ab alumnis Collegiorum ac Seminariorum Anglicanae nationis in sua admissione suscipiendum est.

Ego N. N. Collegii Anglorum de Urbe alumnus, considerans divina erga me beneficia et illud in primis, quo me ex patria haeresi laborante, eduxit, et Ecclesiae suae Catholicae membrum effecit; cupiensque tantae Dei misericordiae non penitus me ingratus praebere, statui totum me divino ejus famulatui, in quantum possum, pro fine hujus Collegii exequendo, offerre; et promitto, iuroque Omnipotenti Deo, me paratum esse animo, ac futurum semper, quantum sanctissima ejus gratia me adjuverit, ut, suo tempore, sacros ordines suscipiam, et in Angliam ad proximorum animas lucrandas revertar, quandocumque Superiori hujus Collegii, pro sui instituti ratione, illud mihi praecipere visum fuerit in domino. Interim vero dum hic vivo promitto me quiete et pacifice victurum, et Collegii constitutiones, regulasque pro meo virili observaturum Romae.

The College Martyrs and Year of Martydom

Saint Ralph Sherwin	1581
Luke Kirby	1582
Polydore Plasden	1591
Eustace White	1591
Henry Walpole SJ	1595
Robert Southwell SJ	1595
John Almond	1612
Henry Morse SJ	1645
David Lewis SJ	1679
John Wall OFM	1679
Blessed John Shert	1582
Thomas Cottam	1582
William Lacey	1582
William Hart	1583
Thomas Hemerford	1584
John Munden	1584
George Haydock	1584
John Lowe	1586
Robert Morton	1588
Richard Leigh	1588
Edward James	1588
Christopher Buxton	1588
Edmund Duke	1590
Christopher Bales	1590
Thomas Pormont	1592
Joseph Lambton	1592
John Cornelius SJ	1594
Edward Thwing	1594

John Ingram	1594
Robert Middleton	1601
Robert Watkinson	1602
Edward Oldcorne	1606
Richard Smith	1612
John Thules	1616
John Lockwood	1642
John Woodcock OFM	1646
Anthony Turner SJ	1679
Venerable Thomas Tichborne	1602
Edward Morgan	1642
Brian Tansfield SJ	1643
Edward Mico SJ	1679

In addition to the 41 listed above, three had their causes deferred in the 1886 Beatifications.

1. William Chaplain who died in prison in 1583. There is a doubt whether he was ever a student at the College. A certain Roche Chaplain was a student. Are they the same person?
2. James Lomax, a former student, died in chains in 1584.
3. Martin Sherson (or Sherton) died in chains in 1587, but there is some doubt whether he was a student at the College.

Robert Johnson, an English student at the German College, was martyred on 28 May 1582 and was almost certainly counted among the forty-four (Anstruther I, 191 and see *Venerabile*, 1988, 24).

Appendix V

Cardinals Protector of the Venerable English College

Giovanni Morone	Already Protector of England when the Hospice became a college. Died 1 Dec 1580.
Filippo Buoncompagni	31 Dec 1580–9 June 1586. Nephew of Pope Gregory XIII.
Enrico Caetani	30 June 1586–13 Dec 1599. During this protectorate Cardinal Ippolito Aldobrandini (later Pope Clement VII) acted as Vice-Protector between Oct 1586 and Jan 1592. During the visitation of 1585 Cardinal Filippo Sega was Vice-Protector and in 1596 Cardinal Francesco Toleto was Vice-Protector. He was succeeded as Vice-Protector by Camillo Borghese who continued in this office under the next Protector until 1605 when he became Pope Paul V.
Oduardo Farnese	Late 1599 or early 1600–21 Feb 1626.
Francesco Barberini	2 March 1626–10 Dec 1679. Nephew of Pope Urban VIII. In 1629 Giovanni Garcia Mellini was Vice-Protector. From 5 Feb 1646–7 April 1659 Aloysio Capponio was Co-Protector.
Philip Thomas Howard OP	By June 1680–17 June 1694. The first Protector of English nationality.
Sede Vacante	17 June 1694–2 Sept 1706.
Alessandro Caprara	2 Sept 1706–7 June 1711.
Sede Vacante	7 June 1711–Dec 1717.
Filippo Antonio Gualterio	Dec 1717–21 April 1728.

Gianantonio deVia	May 1728–12 Jan 1740.
Luigi Pico de Mirandola	Sept 1741–9 Aug 1743.
Federigo Marcello Lante	By Oct 1743–3 March 1773.
Andrea Corsini	13 March 1773–18 Jan 1795. Nephew of Pope Clement XII.
Filippo Campanelli	27 Jan 1795–18 Feb 1795.
Romualdo Braschi	27 Feb 1795–April 1817. Nephew of Pope Pius VI. During Braschi's last illness Cardinal Pietro Francesco Galeffi acted as Vice-Protector.
Ercole Consalvi	Early 1818–24 Jan 1824. His early days in the Roman Curia were under the protection of Henry Stuart, Cardinal York. As well as Protector of the College he was also Secretary of State to Pope Pius VII.
Placido Zurla OSB	May 1824–20 Oct 1834. Appointed Vicar of Rome by Pope Leo XII, Prefect of the Congregation of Studies and friend and confessor to Pope Gregory XVI.
Thomas Weld	25 Dec 1834–19 April 1837. Member of old English Catholic family who gave Stonyhurst to the Society of Jesus. He advised the Pope on matters relating to England.
Giacomo Giustiniani	1837–1843. His mother was British. He resigned in favour of Cardinal Acton.
Charles Januarius Acton	5 Aug 1843–23 June 1847. Born in Naples where his family had lived for many years. Educated in England and Rome. Advisor to the Pope on matters concerning England.
Gabriele Ferretti	26 July 1847–Jan 1869. Cousin of Pope Pius IX. From 25 Aug 1860–Jan 1869 Mgr George Talbot was Pro-Protector Delegatus.
Karl August von Reisach	29 Jan 1869. Former Prefect of Studies at College of Propaganda Fide. Archbishop of Munich and Freising, but living in Rome because of conflict with the Bavarian government. A friend of Cardinal Manning. Salvatore Vitelleschi took possession 'ad assistere et coadjuvare' 19 Feb 1869.
Annibale Capalti	9 Feb 1870–
Edward Henry Howard	24 March 1878–16 Sept 1892. Born and educated in England. Entered papal diplomatic service. Archpriest of St Peter's.

Herbert Vaughan	1893–19 June 1903. Archbishop of Westminster. The only English Ordinary ever to be Cardinal Protector.
Vincenzo Vannutelli	1903–19 Aug 1915. Resigned in favour of Cardinal Gasquet.
Francis Aidan Gasquet	10 Sept 1915–5 April 1929. Monk of Downside, member OSB of Commission on Anglican Orders, Vatican Librarian and Archivist.
Rafael Merry del Val	6 May 1929–2 Feb 1930. Born in England of Irish and Spanish stock. Secretary of Commission on Anglican Orders. Close friend and Secretary of State to Pope St Pius X.
Alexis Henri Marie Lepicier OSB	22 March 1930–20 May 1936. Had lived many years in England as student and master of novices in the Servite Order. Taught Dogmatic Theology at College of Propaganda Fide.
Camillo Caccia Dominioni	Nov 1936–12 Nov 1946.
Nicola Canali	1 Feb 1947–3 Aug 1961. A former secretary to Cardinal Merry del Val. In charge of relief work in Vatican and distribution of funds in post-war Europe.
William Theodore Heard	20 Dec 1961–16 Sept 1973. A Scot by birth. Former Dean of the Rota. First and only former student to be Protector.

The office of Cardinal Protector no longer exists.

Appendix VI

Rectors of the Venerable English College

1578	Morus Clynnog custos of the Hospice was the first Rector, but by the time the Bull of Foundation reached the College he had resigned in favour of:
1579	Alfonso Agazzari. He and all the succeeding Rectors up to the Suppression of the Society were Jesuits.
1586	William Holt
1588	Robert Persons
1589	Joseph Cresswell
1592	Mutio Vitelleschi. Future General of the Order 1615–45.
1594	Girolomo Fioravanti
1596	Alfonso Agazzari. The first Rector to serve for a second term.
1597	Mutio Vitelleschi
1598	Robert Persons. The first Rector to die in office.
1610	Thomas Owen
1618	Thomas Fitzherbert
1639	Thomas Leedes (alias Courtney). A former student.
1644	Robert Stafford
1647	Joseph Simon (alias Emmanual Lobb). A former student.
1650	Thomas Babthorpe
1653	Edward Leedes (alias Courtney)
1655	John Manners (alias Simcocks)
1658	John Stephens (alias Poyntz)
1664	Christopher Anderton
1667	Edward Leedes (alias Courtney)
1671	John Clarke
1673	Christopher Anderton
1683	William Morgan
1686	Charles Campion (alias Wigmore)

1687   Christopher Anderton
1687   Anthony Lucas
1693   Ralph Postgate. A former student.
1699   Robert Mansfield
1704   Ralph Postgate
1707   Francis Powell
1712   Richard Plowden
1716   Thomas Eberson
1724   Levinius Brown. A former student.
1731   Percy Plowden
1734   Joseph Marshall
1737   Henry Sheldon
1744   Christopher Maire
1750   Henry Sheldon
1756   Nathaniel Elliott
1762   Charles Booth
1766   William Hothersall. The last Jesuit Rector.
1773   Cardinal Corsini assumed full powers and the Italian secular priest, Giovanni Giovannucci, was Vice-Rector. He was succeeded by:
1784   Marco Magnani. Sometimes referred to as Rector.
1787   Stefano Felici. Rector, who ruled until the College was suppressed by the French in 1798.

In 1818 the College re-opened and Robert Gradwell, an English secular priest, was the first Rector. Since this time the Rectors have always been members of the English secular clergy. In 1828 Gradwell was made Coadjutor Bishop for the London District.

1828   Nicholas Wiseman. Became Coadjutor for the Midland District in 1840 and eventually Cardinal Archbishop of Westminster.
1840   Charles Michael Baggs. Became Bishop of the Western District in 1844.
1844   Thomas Grant. Became first Bishop of Southwark in 1851.
1851   Robert Cornthwaite. Eventually Bishop of Beverley and later Leeds.
1857   Louis English. Died in office.
1863   Frederick Neve
1867   Henry O'Callaghan. Oblate of St Charles. Became Bishop of Hexham and Newcastle in 1888.
1888   William Giles. Made titular Bishop of Philadelphia in *partibus* 1903.
1913   John McIntyre. Auxiliary Bishop and eventually Archbishop of Birmingham.
1917   Arthur Hinsley. Made titular Bishop of Sebastopolis in 1926. Eventually Cardinal Archbishop of Westminster.
1929   William Godfrey. Apostolic Delegate to Great Britain in 1938. Eventually Cardinal Archbishop of Westminster.

1939   John Macmillan

1952   Gerard Tickle. Became Bishop of Bela and Bishop in Ordinary to the Armed Forces in 1964.

1964   Joseph Leo Alston

1971   Cormac Murphy-O'Connor. Became Bishop of Arundel and Brighton 1977. Eventually Cardinal Archbishop of Westminster.

1978   George Hay

1984   John Kennedy

1991   Adrian Toffolo

1999   Patrick Kilgarriff

2004   Nicholas Hudson

Episcopal Appointments of Former Students since 1818

In this list of former students raised to the Episcopate since the 1818 restoration, some names appear more than once, since some were transferred from one see to another. The dates refer to the year of appointment.

1828   Robert Gradwell. Educated at Crook Hall. Never a student at the Venerabile but was the first secular priest to be Rector since Clynnog. Bishop of Lydda and Coadjutor to the London District.

1840   Nicholas Wiseman. Bishop of Melipotamus and Coadjutor to the Central District.

1843   James Sharples. Bishop of Samaria and Coadjutor to the Lancashire District.

1844   William Riddell. Bishop of Longona and Coadjutor to the Northern District.

1844   Charles Baggs. Bishop of Pella and Vicar Apostolic of the Western District.

1847   Nicholas Wiseman. Pro-Vicar Apostolic of the London District.

1847   William Riddell. Vicar Apostolic of the Northern District.

1847   Nicholas Wiseman. First Archbishop of Westminster. Cardinal.

1851   William Turner. First Bishop of Salford.

1851   George Errington. First Bishop of Plymouth.

1852   Thomas Grant. First Bishop of Southwark.

1853   Richard Roskell. Bishop of Nottingham.

1855   Alexander Goss. Bishop of Martyropolis and Coadjutor to Liverpool.

1855   George Errington. Archbishop of Trebizond *in partibus*.

1855   William Vaughan. Bishop of Plymouth.

1856   Alexander Goss. Bishop of Liverpool.

1860   Ferdinand English. Archbishop of Port of Spain, Trinidad.

1861	Robert Cornthwaite. Bishop of Beverley.
1869	Charles Eyre. Archbishop of Anazarba and Administrator Apostolic of the Western District of Scotland.
1878	Robert Cornthwaite. First Bishop of Leeds.
1878	Charles Eyre. First Archbishop of Glasgow.
1879	Richard Lacy. First Bishop of Middlesbrough.
1882	John Vertue. First Bishop of Portsmouth.
1894	Thomas Whiteside. Bishop of Liverpool. First Archbishop of Liverpool 1911.
1897	Samuel Allen. Bishop of Shrewsbury.
1902	George Ambrose Burton. Bishop of Clifton.
1903	William Giles. Bishop of Philadelphia *in partibus*.
1905	Joseph Robert Cowgill. Bishop of Olenus and Coajutor to Leeds.
1906	William Anthony Johnson. Bishop of Arindela and Auxiliary in Westminster.
1909	John Vaughan. Bishop of Sebastopolis and Auxiliary in Salford.
1911	Joseph Robert Cowgill. Bishop of Leeds.
1912	John McIntyre. Bishop of Lamus and Auxiliary in Birmingham.
1917	John McIntyre. Archbishop of Oxyrynchus and Auxiliary in Birmingham.
1917	William Keatinge. Bishop of Metellopolis and Bishop to the Armed Forces.
1921	John McIntyre. Archbishop of Birmingham.
1926	Arthur Hinsley. Bishop of Sebastopolis *in partibus*.
1929	John McIntyre. Archbishop of Odessa *in partibus*.
1930	Arthur Hinsley. Archbishop of Sardis. Apostolic Delegate to Africa.
1932	Ambrose Moriarty. Bishop of Miletopolis and Coadjutor to Shrewsbury.
1934	Ambrose Moriarty. Bishop of Shrewsbury.
1935	Arthur Hinsley. Archbishop of Westminster. Cardinal 1937.
1938	Bernard Griffin. Bishop of Abya and Auxiliary in Birmingham.
1938	William Godfrey. Archbishop of Cius. Apostolic Delegate to Great Britain.
1938	John Henry King. Bishop of Opus and Auxiliary in Portsmouth.
1941	John Henry King. Bishop of Portsmouth. Archbishop *ad personam* 1954.
1943	Bernard Griffin. Archbishop of Westminster. Cardinal 1946.
1944	Edward Ellis. Bishop of Nottingham.
1945	Joseph Halsall. Bishop of Zabi and Auxiliary in Liverpool.
1947	Joseph Masterson. Archbishop of Birmingham.
1947	Francis Grimshaw. Bishop of Plymouth.
1949	Joseph Rudderham. Bishop of Clifton.
1949	Thomas Bernard Pearson. Bishop of Sinda and Auxiliary in Lancaster.
1951	John Carmel Heenan. Bishop of Leeds.
1953	William Godfrey. Archbishop of Liverpool.
1954	Francis Grimshaw. Archbishop of Birmingham.

1955	Cyril Edward Restieaux. Bishop of Plymouth.
1956	William Godfrey. Archbishop of Westminster. Cardinal 1958.
1957	John Carmel Heenan. Archbishop of Liverpool.
1957	George Patrick Dwyer. Bishop of Leeds.
1957	James Cunningham. Bishop of Jos and Auxiliary in Hexham and Newcastle.
1958	David Cashman. Bishop of Cantano and Auxiliary in Westminster.
1958	James Cunningham. Bishop of Hexham and Newcastle.
1962	William Theodore Heard. Titular Archbishop of Feradi Maggiore *pro hac vice* (had been a Cardinal since 1959).
1962	William Eric Grasar. Bishop of Shrewsbury.
1962	Brian Charles Foley. Bishop of Lancaster.
1963	John Carmel Heenan. Archbishop of Westminster. Cardinal 1965.
1963	Gerard William Tickle. Bishop of Bela and Bishop in Ordinary to the Armed Forces.
1965	George Patrick Dwyer. Archbishop of Birmingham.
1965	David Cashman. First Bishop of Arundel and Brighton.
1969	Alan Charles Clark. Bishop of Elmham and Auxiliary in Northampton.
1970	Michael Bowen. Bishop of Lamsorti and Coadjutor to Arundel and Brighton.
1971	John Brewer. Bishop of Britonia and Auxiliary in Shrewsbury.
1971	Michael Bowen. Bishop of Arundel and Brighton.
1972	Mervyn Alexander. Bishop of Pinhel and Auxiliary in Clifton.
1974	Mervyn Alexander. Bishop of Clifton.
1976	Alan Charles Clark. First Bishop of East Anglia.
1977	Owen Swindlehurst. Bishop of Chester-le-Street and Auxiliary in Hexham and Newcastle.
1977	Michael Bowen. Archbishop of Southwark.
1977	Cormac Murphy-O'Connor. Bishop of Arundel and Brighton.
1982	Francis Thomas. Bishop of Northampton.
1984	Patrick Kelly. Bishop of Salford.
1985	Hugh Christopher Budd. Bishop of Plymouth.
1985	John Brewer. Bishop of Lancaster.
1987	Crispian Hollis. Bishop of Cincari and Auxiliary in Birmingham.
1989	Crispian Hollis. Bishop of Portsmouth.
1991	Vincent Nichols. Bishop of Othona and Auxiliary in Westminster.
1996	Patrick Kelly. Archbishop of Liverpool.
2000	Cormac Murphy-O'Connor. Archbishop of Westminster. Cardinal 2001.
2000	Vincent Nichols. Archbishop of Birmingham.
2001	Kevin McDonald. Bishop of Northampton.
2001	Kieran Conry. Bishop of Arundel and Brighton.
2001	John Hine. Bishop of Beverley *in partibus* and Auxiliary in Southwark.
2002	Arthur Roche. Bishop of Rusticiana and Co-adjutor of Leeds.
2003	Bernard Longley, Bishop of Zarna, Auxiliary in Westminster.

2004   Paul Gallagher, Bishop of Hodelm, Apostolic Nuncio to Burundi.
2004   Kevin McDonald, Archbisop of Southwark.
2004   Arthur Roche, Bishop of Leeds.
2005   Paul Hendricks, Bishop of Rosemarkie, Auxiliary in Southwark.
2005   David McGough, Bishop of Cunavia, Auxiliary in Birmingham.
2006   John Arnold, Bishop of Lindisfarne, Auxiliary in Westminster.

Appendix VIII

The Venerable English College Archives: a General Description and Summary Catalogue

Introduction

The College has been fortunate in preserving, in its archives, a remarkably complete collection illustrating six hundred years of the history of the College and Hospice, of the Church in England, and even of the world-wide Church. The present arrangement of the archives dates from 1773, when Cardinal Corsini had the whole collection sorted and catalogued, so that the newly completed catalogue follows the original in its three great divisions of *Membrane* or scrolls, *Libri* or bound books and *Scritture* or unbound papers. In addition, there are now sections of photographs and drawings, and the papers of Vatican II.

The oldest material is in the *Membrane* section. This consists of nearly five hundred parchment scrolls, of which the earliest is dated 1280. The vast majority are mediaeval property deeds relating to the original Hospice buildings and property: among these are the deeds by which the first house was bought for the Hospice in 1362. Papal Bulls and briefs are more common in the sixteenth and seventeenth centuries, and among these is the Bull *Quoniam Divinae Bonitati* by which Gregory XIII founded the College in 1579, and other Bulls by which he and his successors endowed and favoured it. In the last two centuries most of the scrolls refer to individual characters in College history.

The *Libri* series was originally intended to include only bound manu-script books, relating to College finances and administration. Pride of place among these belongs to the famous Red Book (Liber Ruber) or regis-ter of students which, now in its sixth volume, is an unbroken series of the greatest interest, beginning with the first students in 1579, including many martyrs and confessors, and continuing to the present day. The account books form another unbroken series from even before the Hospice became a College, and the various cashbooks, ledgers, petty accounts, bills, receipts and the like, relate not only to the College and its property in Rome, but also to the old Villa property at Monte Porzio, and the Abbey of S. Savino in Piacenza. In addition, there is a considerable collection of miscellaneous manuscript material; much of it relates directly to the College and its activities, such as scripts for plays and concerts from the early seventeenth century on, minute books of College societies, diaries of staff and students, photograph albums and the infamous satirical magazine *Chi-lo-sa?*. Other manuscripts are of less relevance to the College, though of far greater value: they include some transferred from the Library, such as a fifteenth-century collection of the poems of John Lydgate, and three early sixteenth-century Greek manuscripts with the only known text of two sermons of St John Chrysostom. Other manuscripts are recusant works, such as the autobiographies of William Alabaster and Anthony Tyrrell and some of Christopher Green's collections on English Martyrs. A later manuscript is the autograph of Wiseman's *Recollections of the Last Four Popes*. Printed books are also included, some directly relating to the College and its history, others transferred from the Library for safekeeping. It is a motley collection, containing items of great value, side by side with others of purely domestic interest.

The *Scritture* is now a single series of some 130 'volumes', including unbound letters and papers of all sorts. In the first 80 'volumes' (catalogued separately) are the pre-1800 papers, still substantially arranged as they were in 1773. The bulk of them are legal documents concerning the ceaseless lawsuits over College property, but there are many miscellaneous letters, including some from St Charles Borromeo, St Robert Bellarmine, Cardinal Pole, and other great figures of the Counter-Reformation. From within the College there are many documents on the troubled management of the students during the early years, as well as the official 'Response' or questionnaires filled in by each student from 1598 to 1686. In the later part of the series, the nineteenth- and twentieth-century material, there is still a large proportion of legal documents, but the great part consists of letters. The most valuable are those from English bishops to the Rectors of the College during the early nineteenth century, when the Rectors acted as agents for English Church affairs; these are well indexed and provide an important source for the history of the years leading up to the restoration of the hierarchy. The personal letters and papers of several individuals are filed here, including those of Cardinal Edward Howard, Archbishop Stonor and Monsignor George Talbot. The letters include sixteen from Cardinal Newman, several autographs from Pius IX, and others of interest.

The new series of photographs, plans, printed maps, prints and the like, designated series 'P', includes a large collection of photographs of people and places, some dating from the 1860s. There are also a number of plans and drawings of the College and its property, some dating from the sixteenth century, and many beautifully drawn as part of a survey of property in 1630. There are three drawings by Andrea Pozzo for a new church in about 1700, and a large collection of drawings and plans for the church that was eventually built in the nineteenth century. Also kept in the 'P' section are miscellaneous antiquities, including a number of coins and medals and a curious paper scroll bearing a detailed genealogy of the kings of England, written towards the end of the reign of Henry VIII.

The section of Vatican II documents includes the working papers of the Council, the draft schemata, and other officially produced documents, much liturgical material, and the unofficial documentation and circulars, particularly those from the bishops of England and Wales.

The archives are at present run by students of the College, and cannot provide professional facilities for research. However they are open to serious scholars by written appointment, and photocopies or microfilms can be made of most of the material. Some of the more recent collections cannot be made available yet.

Summary Catalogue

MEMBRANE

1–154	13th and 14th centuries.
155–223	15th century.
224–333	16th century.
334–405	17th century.
406–412	18th century.
413–430	19th century.
431–445	20th century.

LIBRI

1–12	Instrumenta: copies of deeds from Membrane.
13–36	Account books etc from the Hospice.
37–215	Account books of the College, 1579–1850.
216–325	Miscellaneous College books, registers, property accounts etc.
326–400	Mass registers, 1696–1787.
411–439	Monte Porzio account books.
440–485	Mission fund account books.
486–512	Piacenza property accounts etc.
513–565	Miscellaneous accounts and other books.
566–584	Hebdom's books.
585–650	Miscellaneous books, mostly 19th and 20th centuries.
651–797	Mass registers, 1788–1967.
798–898	Miscellaneous books, 19th and 20th centuries.
899–966	*Chi-lo-sa?* 1921–1968.
967–1058	Bundles of accounts, bills, receipts etc, 1565–1798.
1059–1204	19th- and 20th-century account books, files and bundles.
1205–1476	Miscellaneous manuscript and printed books (indudes most of the former series of 'Z' books).
1477–1498	Bundles of *scritture* of Monte Porzio and Piacenza, 1229–1798.
1499–1673	Miscellaneous manuscript and printed books.

SCRITTURE

1	Pre-1800 general and legal papers, arranged alphabetically, Abiati–Angeluccius.
2	The Archpriest and Chalcedon Controversies.
3–12	General and legal, Aqua–Inventorio.
13–14	General and legal matters, out of order.
15–22	General and legal, Luramentum to Scholares.
23–28	Scholares: includes the Responsa.
29–31	General and legal, Scholares–Status Collegii.
32	Robert Persons' controversial works.
33	Latin plays.
34	Paper documents, bulls etc.
35	English plays and poems.
36	Miscellaneous, includes Martyrs' collections.
37–39	General and legal, Stillington–Zurla.
40	Vineyard accounts.
41	English religious affairs, and miscellaneous.
42	Liège College and Mission fund.
43–44	18th-century property and accounts.
45–46	Late 18th century; suppression of Jesuits.
47–48	18th-century accounts.
49–50	Italian Secular Regime letters and papers.

SCRITTURE (PART II)

51–53	Interregnum (1798–1818).
54–55	Letters from Bishops' agency, Gradwell's period.
56–62	Gradwell: letters and papers.
63	The Canadian bishops' agency.
64–67	English Bishops' agency etc, Gradwell period.
68	Early 19th-century College finance.
69	Baltimore and Philadelphia Bishops' agency.
70–74	English Bishops' agency, Gradwell and Wiseman period.
75	Wiseman's letters and papers.
76	Letters from Bishop G. Brown and Cardinal Newman.
77–78	Rectorships of Baggs, Grant and Cornthwaite.
79	Papers of Louis English.
80	Rectorships of English, Neve and O'Callaghan.
81	New Church: rectorships of O'Callaghan and Giles.
82	The New Church.
83	Miscellaneous early 19th century.
84	Rectorships of Giles and McIntyre.
85	*Ecclesiastical Polity* and Pius IX.
86	Rectorships of Hinsley, Godfrey and Macmillan.
87	Rectorships of Tickle and Alston.
88	St Mary's Hall and the 'Exile'.
89	Archivists' correspondence.
90	Relic certificates.

91	The Martyrs' Association.
92	Letters and Papers: Cardinal Edward Howard.
93	19th-century miscellaneous.
94	Archivists' notes and transcripts.
95	The Gregorian University.
96	Rectorship of Tickle, miscellaneous.
97	Palazzola and 20th-century property papers.
98	Canonization of the Forty Martyrs, 1970.
99	Letters and Papers: Cardinal William Theodore Heard.
100	The College: mid-20th century.
101	Students' certificates, 20th century.
102	Vatican II incidental papers.
103–105	The College: students and domestic matters, 20th century.
106	Correspondence with dioceses (reserved).
107	Vocations, strategy and planning.
108	College guests and public relations.
109	Appeal and development, 1960–70.
110	Church affairs, 20th century.
111	Interregnum, 1798–1818.
112–114	Late 18th-century accounts.
115	Leo XIII.
116	Stocks and securities, 20th century.
117	Archivists' notes and transcripts.
118	Miscellaneous displaced material.
119	Epitaphs and monuments.
120	Library, Infirmary and Bodgers.
121	Articles and offprints, 20th century.
122	Letters and Papers: Richard Brown, Mgr Prior, Bp Stanley, Sr Brook; Fr Pears.
123	Letters and Papers: Abp Edmund Stonor.
124	The *Venerabile* magazine.
125	20th-century Bishops' agency (reserved).
126	19th-century financial papers.
127–130	19th-century property papers, Monte Porzio and Rome.

VATICAN II

A. *books:* the printed and bound documents issued by the Council.

1	Preparatory and general matters.
2	The liturgy of the Council.
3	The Decrees (arranged as in the official Vatican edition and coded by the initial letters of the Latin titles of the documents).

B. *papers:* loose sheets and the like, filed in boxes.

1–2	Semi-official information bulletins, and press releases.
3–4	Preparatory and general matters.
5–11	The Decrees arranged as above.

'P'

1–7	Photographs of topographical interest.
8	Coins and medals.
9–13	Photographs of people, College groups etc.
14	Photographs of items from the archives.
15	Small drawings, prints etc.
16	Miscellaneous 'museum' material.
17–20	Folders of large photographs.
21–23	Folders of large plans and drawings, College buildings and property.
24	Printed maps.
25	Prints and engravings, large.
26	Printed posters.
27	Newspapers.
28	An imaginary reference number for the loose framed pictures etc hanging up around the archives room.
29	Photocopies, printing blocks and microfilms.
30	Negatives.

OBSOLETE REFERENCE SYSTEMS

Many items are still marked with pre-1773 shelfmarks: these cannot now be collated. Of more recent shelfmarks, which have become obsolete, a series was at one time in use of 'scritture' with initial letters (e.g. Scr. A101; J145 etc). These letters were used to refer to decades from 1790 to 1969, by the letters A to S (omitting O): of these papers all have been recatalogued: the following only can still be identified:
Scr. J110–J145 now Scr. 92.1–26 (Cardinal Edward Howard).
Scr. R106–R108 now Scr. 90.1–3.

The former Martyrs Association files M i to M xv are now divided as follows:
M i–M xiii now Scr. 36.4–15.
M xiv–M xv now Scr. 91.4.

The old series of 'Z' books was dispersed, many returned to the library, and others recatalogued as *Libri,* nearly all of them with numbers between 1205 and 1476.

ADDENDUM

Over recent years there has been an increasing number of enquiries relating to the contents of the College Archives and there is a clear need for a printed catalogue of the archives which can be made available to scholars everywhere. The College is keenly aware of the necessity of a new catalogue and is consulting widely as to what this will entail. It will be some time before the publication of such a list will be possible and so scholars are still reliant on the current typescript catalogue of 1978 and its indexes. This in itself represents a huge input of work over the years by the College archivists. To give some idea of the riches of the collection we append a detailed description of a small part of the catalogue, viz. Libri 1–1058. This appeared in various editions of *Venerabile*, vols XXII–XXVI.

CATALOGUE OF LIBRI 1–1058

No.	Size (cms)	Title	Period and Contents
1	42.5 × 28.5	Liber Primus Instrumentorum	(1) 1504–08 pilgrim lists, rentals, inventories. (2) Sixteenth-century instrumenta.
2	43 × 27.5	Liber Secundus Instrumentorum	Seventeenth-century instrumenta.
3	33.5 × 23.5	Libro d'Istromenti del Ven. Collegio Inglesi dall'Anno 1726–83	
4–12	33.5 × 22.5	Chronologia monumentorum variorum ab anno 1145–1775	Nine volumes of bound deeds, the earliest being copies.
13	29 × 22		1504–21 annual accounts of the Hospice, with rentals, pilgrim lists, inventories, etc. Bound by John Clerk, Bishop of Bath and Wells, 1524.
14	33.5 × 21.5	Summarium Secundum Instrumentorum	1510–1647 abbreviated versions of property deeds.
15	Missing		
16	30 × 21.5	Liber acquittanciarum de Anglia et fratrum receptorum in Roma 1446	Lists of *confratres* of the Hospice, arranged under their English dioceses. Three *firma Angliae* receipts.
17	39.5 × 25	Res diversae 1450–1510	1450–1514 – mainly constitutional documents, elections to office in the Hospice, admission to the Confraternity and relations with the Crown and royal envoys.
18	30 × 21.5		Annual accounts, rentals and pilgrim lists, 1479–84.
19	Missing		
20	30 × 21.5		Daily expenditure in the Hospice, 1/11/1534–30/10/1535.
21	23.5 × 16		Daily expenditure, 1543.
21A	(provisional)	Expenses, 1543.	
22	34.5 × 24	Liber Rationarius Hospitalis	Expenditure, annual accounts and rentals, 1523–48. This book was bought by John Clerk.
23	35.5 × 24	Liber Rationarius	Expenditure, annual accounts and rentals 1548–59. This book was bought by Cardinal Pole.

No.	Size (cms)	Title	Period and Contents
24	30 × 21		Daily expenditure, Nov. 1533–Oct. 1534.
25	30 × 21		Daily expenditure, Nov. 1535–Oct. 1536.
26	30 × 21		Daily expenditure, Nov. 1536–Oct. 1537.
27	28.5 × 20		Daily expenditure, May 1547–April 1548 (Thomas Goldwell's Computus).
28	29 × 21		Daily expenditure, May 1548–Oct. 1549.
29	29 × 21		Daily expenditure, Nov. 1550–April 1552.
30		Liber Rationarius Hospitalis	1/4/1559–30/4/1562. Annual accounts, with rental.
31		Commensalium Liber	1/5/1559–1/5/1570
32		Expensae extraordinariae	1555–75 (excluding 1559 and 1560).
33	34–5 × 24	Inventarium Rerum Hospitalis	1445, 1496, 1515 (copies); 1525, 1538, 1543, 1544, 1546, 1548, 1551, 1553, 1561, then yearly till 1578. This book was bought by John Clerk.
34			Alphabetical index of church and sacristy contents. Also directions for the sacristan on great feasts, 1585.
35			Sale book of wine and vinegar from the College's Summer villa at Monte Porzio, 1746–63.
36		Cassa della Madonna delle Grazie	Two entries only.

Libri 37–85: 'Libri Mastri Del Collegio' – containing daily expenditure, annual accounts and rentals from the year 1579 to 1850.

No.	Size (cms)	Period
37 (A)	44.5 × 30	28 March 1579–83
38 (B)	44.5 × 30	1584–87
39 (C)	43 × 28	1588–89
40 (D)	43 × 28	1590–91
41 (E)	43.5 × 28	1592–95
42 (F)	34.5 × 23	1596
43 (G)	44 × 30	1597
44 (H)	44 × 28.5	1598
45 (I)	43 × 28.5	1599
46 (K)	45 × 32	1600
47 (L)	45 × 32	1601
48 (M)	45 × 32	1602 and, from p. 83, 1611

49 (N)	45 × 32	1603 and, from p. 93, 1610
50 (O)	45 × 32	1604 and, from p. 83, 1609
51 (P)	45 × 32	1605 and, from p. 89, 1608
52 (Q)	45 × 32	1606–7

For nos 53, 54, 55 and 56, see nos 51, 50, 49 and 48 respectively. There are no separate books corresponding to these nos.

No.	Size	Period
57 (R)	45 × 32	1612–13
58 (S)	45 × 32	1614–15
59 (T)	45 × 32	1616–17
60 (U)	44 × 28	1618–19
61 (X)	44 × 28	1620–22
62 (Z)	44 × 28	1623–27
63 (AA)	43 × 28	1628–30
64 (BB)	43 × 28	1631–34
65 (CC)	43 × 28	1635–39
66 (DD)	43 × 28	1640–44
67 (EE)	43 × 28	1645–48
68 (FF)	43 × 28	1649–54
69 (GG)	43 × 28	1655–64
70 (HH)	43 × 28	1665–71
71 (II)	43 × 28	1672–80
72 (KK)	43 × 28	1681–90
73 (LL)	52 × 39	1691–1703
74 (MM)	43 × 28	1704–15
75 (NN)	43 × 28	1716–24
76 (OO)	41 × 28	1725–31
77 (PP)	43 × 28	1732–38
78 (A)	55 × 38	1739–45
79 (B)	55 × 38	1746–53
80 (C)	55 × 38	1754–62
81 (D)	55 × 38	1763–77
82 (E)	55 × 38	1778–88
83 (F)	53 × 38	1789–95
84 (G)	53 × 38	1805–20
85 (H)	56 × 40	1821–50

Libri 91–105 appear to be accountancy journals or day books from which the *Libri Mastri* or ledgers (*libri* 37–65) were written up until 1637. In 1590 and 1613 two other series of account books begin ('libri della cassa o sia di uscita', cf. *libri* 106, 12, 111, 113; and 'libri di entrata o sia dell'esattore', cf. *libri* 107–8, 110, 112, 114–5), the exact nature of which has not yet been determined. Both series then combine until 1698 (*libri* 116–119), after which there is another division: into 'libri di entrata e uscita dell'Esattore' 1699–1793 (*libri* 126–136), and 'libri del Rettore di entrata ed uscita del Collegio' 1699–1787 (*libri* 145–150 and 155, 143–4).

Bank transactions are recorded in *libri* 137–141. *Libro* 152 is the cash journal for approximately the same period. Apart from summaries, the remaining books consist of the names of College debtors (*libro* 142), registers of Mass stipends (*libri* 153–4) and the accounts for one year of a College-owned farm (*libro* 156).

No.	Size (cms)	Title	Period and Contents
86–90	Missing		
91 (A)	43.5 × 29	Libro di entrata e uscita	28 March 1579–83
92 (B)	43.5 × 28.5	ditto	1584–87
93 (C)	43 × 28	ditto	1588–89
94 (D)	43 × 28	ditto	1590–91
95 (E)	43.5 × 28.5	ditto	1592–28 February 1596
96 (F)	34 × 23.5	Libro di entrata e uscita	1596
97 (G)	34 × 22.5	ditto	1597–99
98 (K)	35 × 24	ditto	1600–03
99 (O)	35 × 23	ditto	1604–07
100 (P)	35.5 × 24	ditto	1608–11
101	35 × 23.5	ditto	1612–18
102	35 × 23	ditto	1619–24
103	35 × 22	ditto	1625–29
104	35 × 23	ditto	1630–34
105	34.5 × 22.5	ditto	1635–37
106	31.5 × 22	Libro della cassa o sia di uscita	1590–1624, cash expenditure
107	29 × 20.5	Libro di entrata o sia dell'Esattore administrator's receipts	1613–24; property and payments
108	28 × 21	as No. 107	1625–34
109	24.5 × 17	Ristretto di entrata e uscita	1630–37, 1644–46, 1653–67, summary of income and expenditure
110	28.5 × 21	as No. 107	1635–43
111	34 × 22.5	as No. 106	1637–49
112	28.5 × 21	as No. 107	1643–49
113	34 × 22.5	as No. 106	1649–71
114	29 × 21	as No. 107	1650–57
115	29 × 21.5	as No. 107	1657–69
116	34.5 × 22.5	Libro di entrata e uscita	{ 1669–79 income 1672–79 expenditure
117	34.5 × 22.5	ditto	1680–88 income and expenditure
118	34.5 × 23	ditto	1688–90
119	34.5 × 23	ditto	1691–98
120–121	Missing		
122	43 × 28.5	Ristretto del libro mastro	1690–1714; summary of the ledger
123	34.5 × 22	as No. 106	1625–34
124–125	Missing		
126	35.5 × 22.5	Libro di entrata e uscita dell'Esattore	1699–1705; property administrator's cash book
127	35.5 × 24	ditto	1706–16
128	35.5 × 23	ditto	1717–23
129	35.5 × 24	ditto	1724–30
130	35.5 × 24.5	as No. 126	1731–38
131	36 × 24.5	ditto	1739–47

No.	Size (cms)	Title	Period and Contents
132	35.5 × 24.5	as No. 126	1748–62
133	35.5 × 24.5	ditto	1763–75
134	35.5 × 23.5	ditto	1776–83
135	37 × 24	ditto	1783–88
136	35.5 × 24	ditto	1789–93
137	36 × 23.5	Registro de' Mandati, che si spediscono al Sagro Monte della Pietà	1779–98; payments instructions to the bank
138	16 × 11	Libro de' Depositi, fatti al Sagro Monte della Pietà a Favore del Collegio	1773–78; sums deposited at the bank
139	23 × 17	Libro de' Depositi fatti and al Sagro Monte della Pietá in Credito del Collegio Inglese di Roma, e degli ordini spediti al S. Monte	1773–83; sums deposited payments instructions
140	21 × 14.5	Registro de' depositi ...	1779–83
141	20 × 13.5	(as No. 139) Libro de' depositi fatti al Sagro Monte della Pietà per il Venerabile Collegio Inglese	1783–93
142	30.5 × 21	Nomi de' debitori del Collegio	1775–86; debtors
143	29.5 × 22	Libro del Rettore di entrata ed uscita del Collegio	1774–76; receipts and payments relating to the College itself
144	36 × 24.5	ditto	1776–87
145	35 × 24	ditto	1699–1707
146	34–5 × 23.5	ditto	1708–12
147	34.5 × 23.5	ditto	1712–27
148	35.5 × 24	ditto	1728–39
149	35 × 24	ditto	1740–54
150	35.5 × 24.5	ditto	1754–75
151	Missing		
152	31 × 21	Giornale d'ingresso ed uscita a denaro dell'almo Collegio Inglese	1783–97; cash journal
153	29 × 21.5	Registrum Causarum Ven. Collegii Anglorum Urbis	1747–50; Mass stipend register (in Latin)
154	28.5 x 20	ditto	1755–82
155	35 × 12.5	as No. 143	1754–75
156	29 × 11	Conto del Pizzicarolo	1786; accounts of a vineyard property

There are no *Libri* 157–65. *Libri* 166–215 comprise the section 'Libro dello Spenditore' (1591–1796). These are lists of the daily expenditure on the daily running of the College, on such items as food, laundry, etc.

No.	Size	Period
166	34 × 22.5	1591–93
167	33 × 22	1594–96
168	34 × 22	1597–1600
169	34.5 × 22.5	1601–July 1607
170	30.5 × 21.5	Aug 1607–Aug 1609 (also contains a list of visitors to hospice property 1553–63)
171	35 × 23	Sep 1609–13
172	27.5 × 20.5	1614–18
173	34.5 × 23	1619–Sep 1620
174	27.5 × 20	Apr 1620–Feb 1622
175	27 × 19.5	Mar 1622–Feb 1624
176	28.5 × 19.5	Mar 1624–Jul 1626
177	28 × 21	Aug 1626–Dec 1628
178	27 × 21	Jan 1629–Aug 1631
179	28 × 21	Sep 1631–Apr 1634
180	28 × 21	May 1634–Dec 1635
181	28 × 19	1636–37
182	29 × 20	1638–39
183–184	Missing	
185	29 × 22	1644–Jul 1646
186	30 × 21	Aug 1646–Dec 1648
187	30 × 21	1649–Aug 1652
188	34 × 22	Sep 1652–Aug 1654
189	33 × 22	Sep 1654–Jul 1656
190	34 × 23	Aug 1656–58
191	34 × 23	1659–61
192	23 × 16	1662–May 1663
193	27 × 21	Jun 1663–Jan 1666
194–195	Missing	
196	34 × 23	May 1670–Jan 1672
197	35 × 23	Feb 1672–Apr 1676
198	35 × 23	May 1676–Dec 1681
199	34 × 23	Jan 1682–Apr 1688
200–202	Missing	
203	30 × 22	Jul 1710–Jul 1716
204	35 × 24	Aug 1716–Dec 1721
205–206	Missing	
207	36 × 24	1729–34
208	35 × 24	1735–41
209	36 × 24	1742–48
210	36 × 25	1749–58
211	36 × 25	1759–Jun 1771
212	35 × 24	Jul 1771–Aug 1779
213	35 × 24	Sep 1779–Dec 1786
214	37 × 24	1787–92
215	37 × 24	Jan 1793–Jun 1796

The next section, *Libri* 216–326, contain the miscellaneous books. In the 'Inventario' of 1774 this section began at no. 223 and the contents were arranged in alphabetical order, with many numbers left blank. In the course of time most of these have been occupied, and although generally there has been an attempt to preserve this order, it has frequently proved impossible. The majority of these books deal with administrative affairs from the foundation of the College until the dissolution in 1798.

No.	Size	Title	Period and Contents
216	21 × 14	Obblighi di Messa	*c.*1730 Biography of Benefactors
217	28 × 20	Libro delle Congregazioni	Financial reports 1773–88
218	28 × 22	ditto	ditto 1773–97
218a	28 × 22	ditto	ditto 1789–97
219	29 × 20 (unbound)	ditto	ditto 1747–95
220	29 × 21 (unbound)	ditto	ditto 1778–94
221	Missing		
222	27 × 20	Libro di Locazioni	ditto 1738–97
223	25 × 23	Libro di Entrata e Uscita del Cardinale Alano	1587–94: Cardinal Allen's accounts
224	Blank		
225	29 × 22	Libro di Esazione di Giacomo d'Albone	1609–29
226	31 × 21		1569, 1594: Lawsuits involving College property at Piacenza
227	29 × 20	Libro di Entrata di Rogerio Baines	1623–30: Baines' income
228	27 × 20	Relationi dello Stato del Collegio Inglese	1657: report presented to Card. Barberini (formerly Scr. 47:5)
229	28 × 21	Crediti e Debiti di Girolamo Baffi	1612
230	34 × 23	Altri di conti del med.o col Card. Borromeo	1605–21: Borromeo's account with Baffi
231	35 × 25	Altro di Instromenti appartenti al Med.o	1614: other accounts with Baffi
232	29 × 22	Liber locationum (Case) domorum hospitalis	1406–1517: rents from hospice property
234	35 × 22	Liber receptorum pensionum Domorum	1524–50: ditto
236	30 × 21	ditto	1525–26
238	29 × 21	ditto	1526–35
240	44 × 29	ditto	1551–57
242	29 × 21	Liber Visitationis Domorum Hospitalis	1553, 1602: Inspection of hospice property (also copies of bulls concerning College 1579–1636)
244	8 × 21	Libro di Esazioni delle	1562–73: rents

233–245 odd numbers are blank

No.	Size	Title	Period and Contents
246	33 × 23	Descrizione delle Case con le piante	1630: College property in districts of Regola and Ponte

No.	Size	Title	Period and Contents
247	33 × 23	ditto	ditto for Parione and S. Eustachio
248	33 × 23	ditto	ditto for S. Angiolo, Trastevere, Borgo and Ripa
249	47 × 37	Libro delle piante delle case	Maps of above mentioned property
250	Blank		
251	47 × 17	as Liber 244	1693–1703
252	28 × 21	Istoria delle Case	1772: notes on property
253	32 × 21	Libro di memorie appartenenti all'eredita di Carlo Cassiani	1613: report on bequest
254–255 Blank			
256	35 × 22	Libro di Entrata ed Uscita del Collegio di Liegi	1675–1721: Rome account of English College, Liège
257	Blank		
258	35 × 24	as 256	1713–23
259	35 × 24	Entrata ed Uscita del Beni nel Ducato di Parma e Piacenza	1787–91: College property at Parma and Piacenza
260	35 × 26	as 256, *but* Collegio di Rems	1588–93: as 256, but for Rheims
261	Blank		
262	28 × 11	as 260	1588–1620
263	22 × 14	ditto	1622–29
264	26 × 18	Libro di Comestibili	1629: list of food purchases
265	23 × 15	Libro della Congregazione belle Beata Vergine	1581: Our Lady sodality
266	36 × 25	Libro di Conti del Collegio	1772–92: accounts
267	28 × 20		1733–73: accounts of Liège
268	30 × 22	Libro delle Spese del Retore	1618–92: Rector's account
269	30 × 22	(formerly Scr 26: I)	1777: Lawsuit with S. Girolamo
270	35 × 24	Libro dei Debitori del Collegio	1689: College debtors
271	36 × 25	ditto	1739
272	29 × 23	Libro di Entrata ed Uscita di S. Edmondo	1445–66: accounts of hospice of St Edmund
273	29 × 23	ditto	1615–28
274	27 × 20		1626: poems on death of Card Farnese
275	20 × 13	Libro del Fomaro	1608–12: accounts of College baker
276	28 × 11	The account of Fra Giacinto	1683–4: list of menus (also contains accounts 1587–8 and 1608–9)
277	35 × 15	Index Archivii Collegii	1630: index of College archives
278	Blank		
279	35 × 24	Mandati al Monte del Collegio	1773–91: instructions to College bank
280	35 × 24	Libri di Monti dei Particolari	1614–17: private accounts

No.	Size	Title	Period and Contents
281	27 × 21	Orationes ab alumnis havitae	1581–1642: prayers for students
282	34 × 12	Liber in quo adnotantur qui excepti fuerunt in Collegio titulo hospitii	1580–1656: list of guests (Pilgrim Book)
283	20 × 14		1654–1732 ditto
284	33 × 23	Libro Mastro dell'eredità di Bernardino Pippi	1644–50: nos. 284–7 concern Pippi's property which was bequeathed to the college
285	32 × 23	Giornale della medesima	
286	28 × 21	Istromenti	
287	34 × 18	ditto	
288	28 × 21		17th-century medical receipts
290	Blank		ditto
289	19 × 13		
291	24 × 21	Ricevute di alcuni salarati del Collegio	1637–52: wages paid to College employees
292	20 × 14		1733–71: as no. 282
293	29 × 22	Libro di Ricordi dei Rettori	1613–76: Rector's accounts and memoranda
294	Blank		
295	23 × 18	ditto	1672–78
296	Blank		
297	33 × 23	ditto	1708–31
298	Blank		
299	21 × 14	Libro di Memorie di Valerio Salvatori	1692–93
300	Blank		
301	31 × 23	Liber Censualis Bonorum Abbatiae S. Savini	16th century: accounts of Abbey
302	53 × 39	ditto	1693: inventory of Abbey
303	35 × 25	Scholares in Collegium recepti (*includes* Constitutiones Collegii)	1579–1783: list of students (Liber Ruber)
303 *bis*	35 × 25	ditto	1787–96
304	20 × 14		1579: Students' complaints and demands for Jesuit superiors
305	29 × 23	Libro dei Scholari	1610–15: scholars' pensions
306	22 × 14	ditto	1616–24
307	24 × 18	ditto	1619–22
308	34 × 25	ditto (*includes* Giornale del Ven. Collegio Inglese di Remis in Francia)	1619–45
309	27 × 20	ditto	1624–33
310	29 × 22	ditto	1628–34
311	27 × 21	ditto	1634–41
312	28 × 21	ditto	1635–41
313	28 × 21	ditto	1642–46

No.	Size	Title	Period and Contents
314	28 × 21	ditto	1648–55
315	27 × 21	ditto	1670–86
316	32 × 24	ditto	1686–1729
317	Blank		
318	21 × 14	Exemplum authenticum Regularum Collegii	1600: College rules
319	Missing		
320	21 × 14	Regulae Studiorum Collegii	1642–1739: rules for study and repetitore's notes
321	35 × 23	Thomas Morus: Tragoediae	1612: Latin play
322	22 × 17	Soccite di Capre	1614–19: accounts of goat herd at Monte Porzio
323	33 × 23	Stato del Collegio	1703: report on College for Apostolic Visitor
324	33 × 22	Acta S. Visitationis Apostolicae	1739: official report of visitation
325	31 × 22	Inventario delle scritture del sacro Collegio Inglese in Piacenza	1612: college property at Piacenza
326	Blank		

The next section comprises the 'Libri degli Obblighi delle Messe' 1696–1787. When the Archives were catalogued at the start of the Italian secular regime, the books then completed ended at no. 396 (1773), and space was left for future volumes before the beginning of the next section at no. 411. This space had been filled by 1787, and the enumeration for the next decade before the dissolution duplicated nos. 411–20. The nineteenth-century volumes were later added to these in a new section beginning at no. 651. These Mass obligation books contain a list of the Masses for benefactors which were to be said annually, and the signatures of the priests by whom they were celebrated.

327	40 × 15	1696–1704
328	34 × 12	1705
329	34 × 12	1706
330	35 × 12	1707
331	45 × 17	1708
332	45 × 17	1709
333	45 × 17	1710
334	45 × 17	1711 (also contains an additional unsigned duplicate list of Masses to be celebrated)

335–376 inclusive contain an annual volume for the years 1712–53.
377–383 are blank.
384–410 inclusive contain an annual volume for the years 1761–87.

Libri 411–439; Libri di Monte Porzio. The account books concerned with the administration of the college villa and its surrounding property.

No.	Size	Title	Period and Contents
411	Missing		
412	22 × 17	*Obscured.*	College debtors 1611–85, reverse also contains general accounts for 1623 and 1684
413	28 × 20	Memorandum of old accounts from 1625–35	1685 1611–90

(The contents of this and the following volumes contain lists of accounts in Italian, unless otherwise stated.)

No.	Size	Title	Period and Contents
414	28 × 20	(Volume recently rebound)	1621–24
415	28 × 20	Memorandums of old accounts of Creditori and Debitori from 1630–45	1632–45
416	31 × 21	Libro dei Censuali	From 1637. Reverse contains accounts 1611–15, and title 'Memorandum of old accounts'
417	26 × 20	Libretto di Entrata e Uscita	1647–76
418	45 × 17		1649–60
419	24 × 17	Excerpta ex libris Patris Tunstalli	1615–17, 1650–68
420	34 × 21	Giornale	1671–80
421	27 × 21	Entrate a Monte Porzio	1675–78
422	27 × 22	ditto	1679–92
423	27 × 21		1681–93
424	34 × 21	Giornale	1635–1721, and in reverse 1691–1720
425	33 × 22		1693–1721
426	29 × 21		1706–38
427	28 × 24	Uscita di Casa	1706–31
428	36 × 25	Entrata e Uscita	1739–47
429	29 × 21	Collegio di Liège	1708–51: accounts concerning holdings at Monte Porzio for benefit of English College, Liège
430	Missing		
431	28 × 21	Capitali di Monte Portio (*sic*)	1682–96
432	21 × 15		1708–74: many pages cancelled from 1721
433	35 × 23	Libro di Diversi Debitori	from 1721
434	28 × 22	Memorandums for posterity of what here in Rome may concern our College in Liège	1694–1759: reverse contains other accounts 1752–81
435	35 × 25	Entrata e Uscita	1748–69
436	24 × 18	*obscured*	1752–82
437	41 × 28	Debitori diversi	1782–92
438	36 × 24	Entrata ed Uscita	1793–97
439	36 × 24	ditto	ditto

Libri 440–444: 'Libri Instrumentorum Missionis': these volumes contain notes and commentaries in Latin, concerning the responsibilities of the college authorities for the financial aspects of the mission, and records of business transactions (no accounts). Nos. 445–6 were left blank in the 1774 *inventario* for additions to this series, but one of these was later filled by a volume from the previous section, and the other by an account book of the mission.

440	34 × 25	A	1611–73
441	30 × 21	B	1609–21, 1661
442	35 × 24	D *(sic)*	1614, 1634, 1674–1708
443	35 × 24	C *(sic)*	1617–22, 1662–1716
444	34 × 25	Missione	1719–46
445	36 × 25	Spese ed Entrate del Mentano di Monte Porzio	1776–98
446	28 × 21	Padre provinciale et altri	1744–73: account book of expenses for the mission

Libri 447–485: 'Libri della Missione', dealing with the accounts of the mission funds, particularly property at Monte Porzio and Magliana, administered by the college authorities.

447	20 × 14	Saldo de Conti della Veneble *(sic)* Missione Inglese di Roma	1772–92
448	13 × 10	Missione Inglese 1773	1773–78: account at Monte di Pietà
449	20 × 14	Rincontro de Depositi al Monte	1773–83: ditto but more complete
450	33 × 23	L. Mastro	1622–24
451	ditto	A	1625–26
452	ditto	B	1627–29
453	ditto	C	1630–32
454	ditto	D	1633–36
455	ditto	E	1637–39
456	ditto	F	1640–42
457	ditto	G	1643–45
458	ditto	H	1646–49
459	ditto	I	1648–49
460	44 × 29	K	1649–52
461	29 × 22	Entrata e Uscita	1773–84
462	29 × 23	ditto	1774–75: only three pages used
463	20 × 14	Depositi al Sagro Monte della Pietà, etc.	1783–93: as no. 448
464	37 × 26	Entrata ed Uscita *etc* in potere del Rdo Sre D. Marco Magnani Vice Prefetto	1784–87: few pages used
465	34 × 23	M	1668–74
466	34 × 23		1668–93
467	34 × 23		1694–1706
468	36 × 24	Missione Inglese	1707–21

No.	Size	Title	Period and Contents
469	36 × 24	ditto	1722–38
470	37 × 25	ditto	1739–50
471	36 × 24	ditto	1751–78
472	27 × 19	Uscita	1649–67
473	46 × 33	Libro Mastro A	1744–61
474	46 × 32	Libro Mastro B	1761–82
475	44 × 29	Debitori diversi Dell' Entrata di Monte Porzio	1744–81
476	36 × 24	Entrata ed Uscita	1778–83
477	36 × 24	as 464, *but* nelle mani di Marcantonio Bargigli Esattore	1783–93
478	29 × 21	Libro Mastro di L. di Monti	1609–13: as 449
479	27 × 22	Capitali di Roma e della Magliana	*c.*1662: notes on yields of farm at Magliana and other properties for the benefit of the mission. (Reverse contains accounts of 1625–26.)
480	28 × 21	Magliana	1617–22. Reverse 1616–22
481	29 × 21	Uscita del 1623	1623–28
482	29 × 22	Uscita della Magliana	1702–24
483	36 × 24	ditto	1725–48
484	35 × 23	Giornale della Magliana	1749–72
485	35 × 25	ditto	1773–77

Libri 486–512: The various account books dealing with the college possessions in the Duchy of Piacenza, granted by Pope Gregory XIII in 1581–82 (cf. Liber 242, p. 80). These properties, comprising the Abbey of San Savino, the Priory of Santa Vittoria, and their dependencies, were confiscated when the Jesuits were suppressed in Piacenza, later recovered by Cardinal Corsini, and finally lost after the French invasion of Italy.

No.	Size		Period and Contents
486	30 × 20		1464 seq
487	31 × 21		1517 seq
488	31 × 21		1551 seq
489	31 × 21		1567 seq
490	37 × 24		1570–94
491	31 × 22		1574 seq
492	35 × 24		1581 seq
493	30 × 21		1583–90
494	31 × 22		1591 seq
495	36 × 24		1596 seq
496	32 × 21		1602–12
497	32 × 21		1612–18
498	39 × 25		1618–33
499	41 × 28		1653 seq
500	32 × 23		1677–93
501	36 × 25		1618–39
502	34 × 24		1693–1703

No.	Size	Title	Period and Contents
503	43 × 29		1693–1751
504	44 × 30		1694–1769
505	36 × 24		1701–19
506	36 × 24		1701–48
507	35 × 24		1720–63
508	37 × 25		1746–52
509	37 × 24		1748–67
510	36 × 24		1764–67
511	31 × 22		1768 *Inventario*
512	50 × 39		1781–89

Libri 513–548 comprise another series of account books, added to the enumeration system after this was established in 1773–4. This series has two sections, one being concerned with various administration accounts, and the other, from 522–537, containing the *'Entrata ed Uscita'* books of the Rector and *Esattore*.

513	50 × 39	Libro Mastro della Ven. Missione Inglese dall' anno 1783. 1783 1795 (inventory of expenses).
514	36 × 25	Registro de Mandari par la Ven. Missione Inglese di Roma. August 4, 1773–November 19, 1797.
515	36 × 25	Entrata ed uscita della V. Missione Inglese nelle mani del Sig. Giuseppe Cini. 1793–98 (accounts).
516	36 × 25	Entrata ed uscita di Caffa dei Beni della Ven. Missione Inglese di Roma per uso della Amministratore di Monre. 1782–99 (incomplete).
517	36 × 25	Entrata ed uscita Inpotere del R.S.D. Stefano Felici, Viceprefetto della Ven. Missione Inglese di Roma. 1787–98.
518	36 × 25	– 1792–97. Accounts (various Latin MSS., period 1785–97; Puzzolana and Magliana property affairs).
519	36 × 25	Entrata ed uscita del V. Collegio Inglese nelle mani del Sig. Giuseppe Cini Esattore. 1793–98.
520	36 × 24	Saldo dei Contia e Debbitoria Spettanti al Ven. Collegio Inglese di Roma. 1794–1800.
521	27.5 × 20.5	Registro dei Depositi del Sagro Monte della Pietà di Roma in Credito del Collegio e Missione Inglese a libera Dispozione dell Em.o e Rino Sig. Cardinale Andrea Corsini Prottetore. 1783–95.
522–537		Entrata ed Uscita. 1787–1877 (not in perfect chronological order).
538	47 × 35	Libro Mastro Provisorio del Collegio e Missione Inglese. (Also contains Rubricella Nov. 1799–1805).
539	36 × 25.5	Saldo dei Conti delli debitori appartenenti alla Ven. Missione Inglese di Roma. 1787–1800 (also contains Rubricella della Missione).

No.	Size	Title Period and Contents

540,541 43 × 31   Debitori diversi dell'Entrate in Monteporzio spettanti alle Ven.
Missione Inglese di Roma.
1792–1800.

542   35.5 × 25   Libro dell'Istromenti del Collegio e Missione Inglese di Roma.
1799–1815.

543   35.5 × 25   Rincontro del Sagro Monte della Pietà di Roma spettante al
Ven. Collegio Inglese di Roma.
1776–97 (two vols).

544   35 × 26   Registro de'Mandati del Collegio e Missione Inglese di Roma.
1801–16.

545   28 × 20   Bilanci degli anni 1798 e 1799 del Ritratto a Spesa della Vigna
alla Magliana di pertinenza del Ven. Coll. Inglese
amministrata del Sig. Giuseppe Cini.
1798–99.

546   29 × 20   Ricente Diverse che appartengono all'Entrata ed Esito del
Sig. Cini, 19.11.1799–21.4.1801.
1799–1801 (numbered 1–252).

547   29 × 20   Ricente ed altri documenti appartenenti al Conto di Cassa
inpotere del Sig. Cini, e due giustificazioni del Sig. Camillo
Branchini, Esattore.
1801 (numbered 104–105).

548   29 × 20   Ricente ed altri documenti appartenenti al Conto di Cassa
del Sig. Cini. Depositano dal 1.1.1802–31.12.1802.
1802.

549   32 × 23   Accounts of College Property. Descriptions of same.
1818–28.

550   33. × 523.5   Storici e stato patrimoniale del Ven. Collegio Inglese.
1824.

551   31.5 × 21.5   Status et Nomina Superiorum et Alumnorum.
1923–24.

552   38 × 26   Alumni (post First World War).

554   38 × 20   Register of Students at St Mary's Hall, Stonyhurst.
1940.

555, 557 Missing

558, 559 28 × 19.5   Liber Iuramentorum.
1837–1913.

560   Missing

561   35 × 23.5   Ven. Collegio e Missione di San Tommaso dell'Inglese in
Roma. Registro dell'Istrumenti stipolati dall' anno 1817.

562   24 × 18   Document granting Giles' Doctorate.
1857 (with seal).

563   24 × 18   Document granting Howard's Doctorate.
1858 (with seal).

564   27.5 × 21   Accounts of Joseph Humble, Francis Azzopardi, Edmund
Sower, James Bond, Henry Davey, Walter Buckle, John Wise,
Alfred Pigott, John Fitzgerald, Joseph Bans, Thomas Roskell,
Thomas Bennet, Stephen Perry, Thomas Drinkwater, William
Talbot, and Charles Graham.
1844–55.

No.	Size	Title Period and Contents
565	28 × 21.5	Address by Cardinal Acton on becoming Protector of the College, April 10th, 1842.
566–575		Libellus de Missis Solemnibus. 1821–1907.
576	Missing	
577	38 × 25	Sacrae Functiones Ven. Collegio Anglorum. 1926–39.
578–582		Liber Hebdomadarius. 1939–40, 1940–60 (Rome), 1932–39, 1947–54 (Palazzola).
583–586	Missing	
587–592		Minute Books of the Debating Society. 1841–1901 (including the Blue Book of the Society).
593–597		Minute Book of the Grant Debating Society (1922–50) and of the Grant Literary Society (1925–39). (The books are interdispersed.)
598–599	21 × 16	Literary Society Minute Book. 1945–47.
600	20 × 16	Diary of Master of Ceremonies. April 1942.
600–602	Missing	
603	20 × 15	Sacristan's Guide.
604	23 × 18	Second Sacristan's Guide.
605	21 × 16	Diary of M.C. 1939–40, 1946–50.
606–608	Missing	
609–610	16 × 10	Copy of the Will of Samuel Giles.
611	Missing	
612–614	30 × 22	Libro della Congregazione del Ven. Collegio Inglese e Missione Inglese di Roma. 1810–11, 1814–23.
615–617		College Register. 1820, 1824–41, 1869–70.
618	31 × 21	Ven. Collegio Inglese Verbale della Adunanze dei Deputati alla Disciplina e alla Economia. 1917–24.
619	32 × 22	Diary of the 'Consiglio di Amministrazione' of V.E.C. 1918.
620	28.5 × 20.5	Report on the first session of the Lawsuit Mons. Gulielmo Giles v Signore Eugenio Bennicelli ed altri. 1897.
621	35 × 23	Rincontro del Monte del Ven. Collegio e Missione di S. Tommaso delg'Inglesi di Roma. 1817–34.
622	Missing	
623, 624	36 × 24	Registro degli Ordini. 1817–49.
625	29.5 × 21	'Coppialettere'. 1848–51.
626	28.5 × 21	Dichiarazione delle Patanti dei Luoghi di Monte.

No.SizeTitle Period and Contents

627   22 × 17   MS Rules of the Oblates of St Charles.
628   40 × 27.5   Colletti per la Erezione della nuova Chiesa di S Tommaso di Canterbori and other accounts.
1864–81.
629   38 × 27   Mass obligations.
1918–19.
630   28 × 19.5   Collections of the Sermons preached on St Stephen's Days.
c.1840–70.
631   27 × 19.5   1. Copy of Gregory XIII's Institution of the V.E.C.
2. Observations on College Rules by N. Wiseman.
1837.
3. Rules of V.E.C.
1818.
632   27.5 × 21   1. Notes on College procedure, ordinations etc.
c.1850.
2. Notes on students, clothes list.
633   20 × 14   Journal.
1843 (and later notes, 1858, 1860, 1862, 1867).
634   29 × 23   Obit book of V.E.C.
(Original copy, with additions made in 1920s).
635, 636 Missing
637   27.5 × 21.5   Library Rules as modified by the General Meetings of November 1855 and February 1864, and other documents concerned with the Library.
638, 639 18.5 × 21   Accounts of the Students' Library.
1819–68.
640   24.5 × 20   Students' Pensions, English College.
1911–17.
641   22.5 × 17.5   List of meals served in College.
1887–89.
642   22 × 16   Meditations.
1838.
643   10 × 11   Sketches (1893–1902) and Sketches by J. J. Hally (1902).
(a & b)
643   15.5 × 13   Stonyhurst Gita Book.
1940–46.
644   23 × 19   Memoriae Romanae et Coll. Angl. by Francis Goldie, S.J.
1860.
645, 646   Sketches (including Giles' sketch book).
647   20 × 14   Document granting Dominico Maria Savignono the right to teach.
1720.
648   22 × 16   Visitors' Book (1860) on Wiseman's visit to Rome.
649, 650 28 × 21   Transcripts of Bishops' Agency Papers, and of Papers relating to the refoundation of the College.
1812–22.
651–654 48 × 19   Pro Ecclesiae S Thomae Nationis Anglicane.
1788–91.
655   Missing

No.	Size	Title Period and Contents
656–660	48 × 19	Pro Ecclesiae S Thomae Nationis Anglicanae. 1793–95, 1797–98.
665–678	34.5 × 12	Mass intentions. 1803–09.
679	Missing	
680–694	34.5 × 12	Mass intentions. 1810–18.
695	42 × 15	Pro Ecclesiae S Thomae Nationis Anglicane. 1818–50.
696–727	34 × 15	Mass intentions. 1819–50.
728	Missing	
729–780	34 × 15	Mass intentions. 1852–1904.
781–874	Missing	
785–790	35 × 15	Mass intentions. 1913–917.
791	Missing	
792–797	34 × 15	Mass intentions. 1920–67.
798	31.5 × 22	Registro delle Rette dei Convittori del Collegio Inglese. 1865–70.
799	30.5 × 23	Registro, riscossioni e pagamenti dal'anno 1.6.1869 al 31.12.1894, Rettore O'Callaghan.
800	32.5 × 23	Conti delle Vigne di Monte Porzio Coltivate per Conto del Collegio Inglese, dall'Ottobre, 1888 al 1885, dopo l'afatto col Sig. Enrico Butti.
801	31 × 22	Registro Vigna della Magliano dall'anno 1878 al 1892.
802	38.5 × 27	Registro dei Censi Carroni ed altri Assegni fissi rislossi dall'anno 1876 al 1903.
803	38.5 × 26.5	Registro delle corrisposte pagate dagli inquilini delle case dall'anno 1876 al 1903.
804	27.5 × 19.5	London Joint Stock Bank. 1865–1912.
805	14 × 9.5	Offreuves pour l'Eglise de St Thomas de Canterbury a Rome. 1864.
806	17 × 11	Account of Monies received and expended on behalf of the Church of St Thomas of Canterbury: H. O'Callaghan, Treasurer. 1867–88.
807	18 × 11.5	Subscriptions for the rebuilding of the Church of St Thomas of Canterbury, Rome.
808	12 × 8	Visitors' Book. c.1880.
809–812	22 × 17	Wiseman Society summaries of Papers. 1928–58.
813	20.5 × 15	Student's Diary, 1770, with transcript by H. E. G. Rope.
814	20 × 14	Diary of Casemore May–Oct. 1771.

No.	Size	Title Period and Contents
815	18.5 × 12	E. Heppenstall's Book. 1821–28.
816	20.5 × 17	Diary of Revd John Kirk.
817–820		Talbot's Diary. June 1845–Sept. 1850; Sept. 1846–Aug. 1847; Nov. 1855–Dec. 1855; July 1852–Dec. 1852.
821–822	23.5 × 19	Diary of G. Johnson. Aug. 1851–Jan. 1852; Jan. 1853–Jan. 1854.
823	16 × 9.5	Diary of A. C. Stanley. 1855.
824	18 × 11.5	Roman Diary (Bishop Burton). 1884–90.
825–827	22 × 18	John King's Dairy. 1899–1904.
828	18 × 11.5	Reminiscence and excerpts from the Diary of Canon Burke. 1898–1905.
829	15 × 9.5	Diary of A. E. Hazlehurst. 1901–05.
830	27.5 × 22	Diary of Luke Sherrin. Jan–Feb. 1902.
831–833		Senior student's Diary. 1930–44; 1949–56.
834	30 × 20.4	Senior Student's Vade Mecum.
835	16 × 10	Index Librorum Prohibitorum Bibliothecae Ven. Collegii Anglorum de Urbe.
836	36 × 24	Library Stock List.
837	32 × 22.5	Accessions Register of Library. July 1917–March 1968.
838	28 × 21	Notes on diverse topics. 19th Cent.
839	28 × 21	Panegyric on St Winifred.
840	19.5 × 14.5	De Divina Gratia ad Primam Secunda D. Thomae. Latin MS.
841	40 × 29	Stock list of third Library (shelves 50–91). Pre First World War.
842	23 × 19	Notebook on Edward Howard. St Mary's College. 1845.
843	26 × 19	Notebook of theological Theses.
844	23.5 × 19	Sick Book of St George's district and Theological Notes. 1848 and after.
845	22 × 17	Notebook, theology and philosophy, and diary. *c.*1850.
846	23 × 18	Notes on Retreats given at V.E.C. 1889–95.
847	9.5 × 15	Notebook – episcopal functions at High Mass, notes for conferences etc. 1900.
848	20 × 15.5	Apostleship of Prayer Register of Associates (1892–1925) and accounts and observances.

No.	Size	Title Period and Contents
849	17.5 × 11.5	Concert Wine Logbook: accounts of wine for functions in the Common Room. 1947–56.
850, 851		Visitors' Book. 1876–83, 1893–1902.
852	31.5 × 21.5	Visitors' Register. Card. Bourne. 1911–21.
853	32.5 × 23.5	College Song Book. 1955–58.
854	32 × 22.5	Grant Debating Society Minute Book. 1962–65.
855	28 × 22.5	Epitaphs of English Clergy and Laity in Rome.
856	17 × 12	Regulae Venerabilis Collegii Anglorum de Urbe. 1934.
857	20.5 × 16	Letters from Frederick Neve to Ullathorne, copied from documents at Edgbaston Oratory.
858	30 × 21	The Address to William Giles on his appointment as Domestic Prelate. Sept. 1891.
859	26.5 × 19.5	1925 Jubilee – a glimpse. Sr Mary Clare.
860	30.5 × 20	MSS entitled Historical Collections respecting the Veto. 1812.
861–862	30 × 23	Ecclesiae Anglicanae Trophiae. 1584.
863	25 × 16.5	Expression of loyalty to Hinsley. Nov. 1926.
864	20.5 × 15	Diary of H. Martindale.
865	35 × 26	Scrapbook of Death of Bp. Giles (1913).
866	19 × 14	Infirmarians' Book. 1958.
867	27 × 21	Visit of Pope Paul VI to Palazzola, 22 Aug. 1963.
868–870		Minutes of Public Meetings. Feb. 1925–July 1956.
871	30.5 × 25	News Cuttings. 1896–1901.
872	28 × 23	Scrapbook (1908–19).
872a	25.5 × 19	Public Meetings. 1934–43.
873	25.5 × 19	Miscellanea copied from the *Venerabile*.
874	20 × 15	Index to Minute Book of Public Meetings.
875	20.5 × 16	Minute Book of the Literary Society. 1957–65.
876	20.5 × 13	Copy of the Obit Book. *c.*1920.
877	31 × 25	Scrapbook for 1909–19. H. Rope.
877a	22 × 14	Diary for 1918 (June lst–6th).
878	30.5 × 20.5	Hebdom's Book. Oct. 1960–May 1968.

No.	Size	Title Period and Contents
879	27 × 20	Wiseman Society. Jan. 1950–March 1961.
880	20 × 14	Italian MS about Death, Purgatory, Heaven and Hell.
881, 882	20.5 × 15	Senior Student's Diary. 1939–war.
883	20.5 × 15.5	Students' Public Fund Accounts. 1915–30.
884	32.5 × 23	College Song Book. 1924–29.
885	26.5 × 19.5	Public Purse Accounts. 1952–55.
886	26.5 × 19.5	Senior Student's Diary. 1926–32.
887	20.5 × 15	*Venerabile* Minute Book. 1923–39.
888	21 × 15	*Venerabile* Magazine Subscribers. 1922–26.
889	24.5 × 18.5	*Venerabile* Magazine list of contributions and advertisements. 1922–28.
890	16 × 10	Initial expenses fund of the *Venerabile*, and Secretaries' Diary. 1931.
891	28 × 20.5	Address Book of the Association of the Venerable English College of St Thomas *de Urbe*.
892	33 × 21	Senior Student's Diary. 1944–49.
893, 894	30 × 22	*Venerabile* Subscribers (1926–40) and Advertisements (1933–40).
895–897	27 × 20.5	Gross receipts and expenses of the *Venerabile*, 1922–43.
898	21 × 17	Notes on Christmas Productions. 1949–57.
899		*Chi lo sa?* (internal College magazine). 1921–68.
950–964		*Chi lo sa?* The Inner History (editor's notes): 950 Vol. 4, 1927. 951 a & b Vol. 6, 1929 (not identical), 952 Vols. 13, 14; 1936, 1937. 953 not allocated. 954–56 Vols. 17–45, 1939–63.
965		Typed editorial notes for *Chi lo sa?* 1959–62, 1965, 1967.
966	Missing	
967–1058	26 × 20	Six series of bound papers in brown paper wrappings. First series, 967 992: Conti e obblighi artisti e bottegari. 1565–1772. Second series, 993–1018: Receipts. 1599–1762. Third series, 1019–1025: Missione e giustificazione. 1744–97.

No.	Size	Title Period and Contents
		Fourth series, 1026–1028: Collegio giustificazione. 1744–97.
		Fifth series, 1029–1040: Rettore – giustificazione diverse. 1773–97.
		Sixth series, 1040– 1058: General accounts. 1739–92.

Select Bibliography and Reading List

A. PREVIOUS HISTORIES OF THE COLLEGE

Official visitation reports often included a short history of the foundation. Lawsuits concerning property called for historical documentation. Disputes concerning the direction of the College led both seculars and Jesuits to put forward their version of past events. As examples of the latter we have:

William Allen. *An Apologie and True Declaration of the Institution and Endeavours of the two English Colleges* (1581).
Robert Persons. *Initia et progressus Collegii Anglicani de Urbe ab Anno Domini 1578 (quo primum institutum est) ad annum 1587.*
J. H. Pollen (ed.) *Memoirs of Robert Persons S.J.* CRS 2.

There also exist early accounts of the College from hostile sources. The most notable of these are:

Anthony Munday. *The English Romayne Life.* London 1582.
Lewis Owen. *The Running Register recording a true relation of the state of the English colleges, seminaries and cloisters in all foreign parts.* London 1626. Pages 15–51 deal with the College in Rome.

In the early nineteenth century Robert Gradwell made several attempts to write a history and the most complete of these is to be found in Liber 1292 of the English College Rome Archives.

General histories of the Catholic Church in England often devoted some space to the history of the College. Many of them rely on the not unbiassed M. A. Tierney (ed.) *Dodd's Church History of England.* 5 vols (1829–1843).

T. F. Knox in his historical introduction to *The First and Second Diaries of the*

English College Douai (1878) has a few pages on the beginnings of the College in Rome.

H. Foley in his *Records of the English Province of the Society of Jesus* dedicated the whole of volume VI (1880) to the English College and although by no means complete and not entirely accurate it did provide the first printed documentation about the College.

Forty years later in 1920 Gasquet published *A History of the Venerable English College Rome* which has been up to now the standard work.

Gasquet also wrote *The Obit Book of the Venerable English College Rome* (1929) which contains interesting material about former students. Since then there has been the short pamphlet *The Schola Saxonum, The Hospice and The English College in Rome* (1951) by H. E. G. Rope who was for many years archivist at the College. There have also appeared several illustrated brochures which include a brief history of the establishment (1967, 1978 and 1999).

B. MANUSCRIPT SOURCES

There is a great wealth of archive material waiting to be explored.

In England
Diocesan Archives, Archives of the Religious Orders (especially the Jesuits at Stonyhurst and Farm Street), College Archives at Ushaw and Oscott, the County Records Office in Preston where the Dicconson Papers are now lodged, the Stuart Papers at Windsor and the Public Record Office.

In Rome
The Vatican Library, Propaganda Fide, Archivio di Stato and private collections such as the Corsini library.

For the present work however only four archives have been directly consulted.
1. The Archives of the Venerable English College, Rome. A description of these is to be found in Appendix VIII and in the text these archives are referred to according to Libri or scritture (scr.).
2. Archives of the Archbishop of Westminster. These have been consulted for Gradwell's Journal and the Roman Agency Papers of Smelt and Macpherson. In the text these are often referred to as Westminster.
3. Leeds Diocesan Archives. Many papers from the old Northern District are to be found here and particular use has been made of the extensive Briggs Correspondence. Referred to in the text as Briggs or Leeds.
4. Archives of the English Benedictines kept at St Gregory's Downside. Here are to be found the papers of Cardinal Gasquet. Referred to as Downside.

C. PRINTED MATERIALS

The volumes of the Catholic Record Society contain much that is relevant to the English College Rome. These are referred to as CRS with the corresponding volume number. Four of the series deal explicitly with the College.

The Liber Ruber of the English College Rome 1. Nomina Alumnorum 1579–1630 ed. W. Kelly CRS 37.
The Liber Ruber of the English College Rome. 1. Nomina Alumnorum 1631–1783 ed. W. Kelly CRS 40.
The Responsa Scholarum of the English College Rome 1598–1621 ed. A. Kenny CRS 54.
The Responsa Scholarum of the English College Rome 1622–1685 ed. A. Kenny CRS 55.

One should also note CRS 2 Miscellania II The Memoirs of Father Robert Persons.

Recusant History (formerly *Biographical Studies*): *a Journal of Research in Post Reformation Catholic History in the British Isles 1957*, published by the Catholic Record Society, contains many articles of interest for the College.
Deserving of special mention is:
Laird A. *The English College in Rome under Italian Secular Administration* RH 14 pp. 127–147.

The Venerabile, the College Magazine, contains printed source material and historical articles as well as providing a record of College life since 1922. The magazine appeared twice a year between 1922 and 1968. Four issues (2 years) made up one volume with continuous pagination. From 1969 there was only one issue a year but the volumes continued to be reckoned as comprising four issues. References are given according to volume and page. There were no publications in 1973, 1975, 1976, 1977. When the magazine resumed in 1978 as an annual publication the old method of reckoning four issues for a volume was continued, but each issue was paginated separately. Hence all references from 1978 are given according to year not volume.
   Of the many articles cited in the notes the following are worthy of special attention.

Anstruther G. *The Sega Report* Ven XX pp. 208–223.
Anstruther G. *Owen Lewis* Ven XXI pp. 274–294.
Duggan T. *College Rectors VII–Frederick Neve 1863–1867* Ven V pp. 160–172; 274–285; 335–348.
Kenny A. J. *The Inglorious Revolution 1594–1597* Ven XVI pp. 240–258; XVII pp. 7–25; 77–94; 136–155.
Kenny A. J. *From Hospice to College 1559–1579* Ven XXI pp. 218–273.
Laird A. *The College Church* Ven XXIV pp. 28–38; 159–173; 258–268.

Of the many other articles cited in the text the following have a specific College interest:

Gossett S. 'Drama in the English College Rome 1591–1660' in *The English Literary Renaissance* 1973 pp. 60–93.
Hicks L. 'The English College Rome and Vocations to the Society of Jesus. March 1579–July 1595'. *Archivium Historicum Soc. Jesu III* (1934) 1–36.
Pollen J. H. 'The Restoration of the English Jesuits 1803–1817'. *The Month* CXV 585– 597. 'The recognition of the Jesuits in England'. *The Month* CXVI 23–36.

D. SELECTED BACKGROUND READING

Anstruther G. *The Seminary Priests. A Dictionary of the Secular Clergy of England and Wales 1558–1800* 4 vols. 1968–1977.
Aveling H. *The Handle and the Axe.* 1976.
Beck G. A. (ed.) *The English Catholics. 1850–1950.* 1950.
Bossy J. *The English Catholic Community. 1570–1850.* 1975.
Brady W. H. *The Episcopal Succession.* 3 vols Rome 1877.
Chadwick H. *St. Omers to Stonyhurst.* 1962.
Champ, J. *The English Pilgrimage to Rome,* Gracewing 2000.
Challoner R. *Memoirs of Missionary Priests.* 1924 edn.
Cwiekowski F. J. *English Bishops and the Vatican Council.* 1971.
Daw, C. *et al. The Forty Four,* 2000.
Delumeau J. *Catholicism Between Luther and Voltaire.* 1977.
Dillon A. *The Construction of Martyrdom in the English Catholic Community 1535–1603.* 2002.
Edwards F. *Robert Persons. The Biography of an Elizabethan Jesuit 1546–1610.* n.d.
Foley H. *Records of the English Province of the Society of Jesus.* 7 vols 1875–83.
Gillow J. *A Bibliographical Dictionary of English Catholics.* 5 vols 1885.
Guilday P. *The English Catholic Refugees on the Continent.* 1914.
Haile M. *An Elizabethan Cardinal. William Allen.* 1914.
Hales E. E. Y. *Pio Nono.* 1954.
Hales E. E. Y. *Revolution and Papacy.* 1960.
Harvey, M. *England, Rome and the Papacy,* 1993.
Harvey, M. *The English in Rome 1362–1420.* 1999.
Heenan J. C. *Cardinal Hinsley.* 1944.
Kirk J. *Biographies of English Catholics* (eds J. H. Pollen and E. Burton). 1909.
McClelland V. A. 'O Felix Roma, Henry Manning, Cutts Robinson and Sacerdotal Formation 1867–1872'. *Recusant History* 21 180–217.
McCoog, T. M. *The Reckoned Expense: Edmund Campion and the Early English Jesuits.* 1996.
Meyer A. O. *England and the Catholic Church under Elizabeth I* (English translation). 1916.
Metzler J. (ed.) *Sacrae Congregationis de Propaganda Fidei Memoria Rerum 1622–1972.* 1971– (referred to as SCPF).

Pastor L. von. *The History of the Popes.* English edition vols XIX–XL. 1930–1953.

Questier M. C. *Conversion, Politics and Religion in England 1580–1625.* 1996.

Schofield, N. (ed.) *A Roman Miscellany,* Gracewing 2002.

Shell A. *Catholicism, Controversy and the English Literary Imagination 1558–1660.* 1999.

Vaughan H. *Report on the Conditions of the English Catholic Colleges in Italy, Spain and Portugal.* 1876.

Vickers, M. *St Eustace White,* 2002

Villoslada R. G. *Storia del Collegio Romano* (Analecta Gregoriana LX–VI). 1954.

Walsham A. *Church Papists.* 1993.

Ward B. *The Dawn of the Catholic Revival in England 1781–1803.* 2 vols 1909.

Ward B. *The Eve of Catholic Emancipation.* 3 vols 1911–1912.

Ward B. *The Sequel to Catholic Emancipation.* 2 vols 1915.

Ward M. *The Wilfrid Wards and the Transition. 1. Nineteenth Century.* 1934.

Ward. M. *The Wilfrid Wards and the Transition. 2. Insurrection versus Resurrection.* 1937.

Wiseman N. *Recollections of the Last Four Popes.* 1858.

Note to be added to the Wiseman books:

(Have been reprinted in three small volumes, with historical notes added by Richard Whinder, Fisher Press, 2005–6.)

Index

Acquaviva, Claudio 33, 49
Acton, Cardinal Charles 132, 141,
    155, 293
Agazzari, Alfonso 8, 12, 21, 24, 27, 295
Alabaster, William 47, 58, 303
Alberry, Richard 107, 109
Alberti, Durante 12, 30
Albornoz, Gil De 1, 29
Aldobrandini, Ippolito *see also*
    Clement VII 292
Alexander VII 53, 165
Alexander, Mervyn 300
Alfred (King) xvii
Aliciati, Terence 79
Allen, William 5, 11–13, 15, 24,
    29–30, 39, 44, 52, 62, 71, 75, 228
Allen, Samuel 166, 187, 299
Almond, John 290
Alston, Joseph Leo 242–5, 249–50,
    297
Ambleside 223–4
Amigo, Peter 174, 198, 208
Anderton, Christopher 295
Anne of Bohemia 255
Apollinare (Seminary) 112, 127, 140,
    142, 207
Aquinas, St Thomas 79
Arnold, John 301
Arsdekin (or Archdeacon), Richard 79
Askew, John 7
Avancinus 146

Babthorpe, Thomas 295
Baggs, Charles 122, 129, 133, 139,
    143, 296, 298

Bagshaw, Christopher 39
Bagshaw, Edward Gilpin 173
Bainbridge, Christopher 1, 257
Baines, Peter 123, 129
Baines, Roger 37, 52–3, 59, 84
Bales, Christopher 290
Baltimore *see also* Carroll, Dr 99, 107
Bamber, John 151
Banns, Joseph 145
Barberi, Dominic 138
Barberini, Francesco (The Elder) 43,
    47, 49, 54, 62, 292
Barberini, Francesco (The Younger)
    69
Barberini, Maffeo *see* Urban VIII
Baronius, Caesar 12, 37
Barrett, Richard 12
Barry, William 166, 167
Bell, Thomas 7
Beda College, *see also* Collegio Pio
    179, 187, 194, 196, 209, 222,
    242, 265
Bellarmine, Robert 37, 55, 303
Benedict XIV 76, 79
Berthier (General) 92
Bianchetti (Cardinal) 56
Billot, Louis 183–5
Bishop, William 86
Bisletti, Gaetano 195, 198, 288
Blacklo, Thomas 57, 73
Blackwell, George 28
Blond 108
Blount, Thomas 80–1
Bonaparte, Napoleon 65, 92, 95
Booth, Charles 296

Borghesi, Camillo *see also* Paul V 28, 292
Bornham 62
Borromeo, St Charles 3, 5, 29–30, 127, 303
Boscovitch, Roger 47
Bourne, Francis 186, 207–8, 210
Bowen, Michael 300
Branchini (family) 114, 123, 163
Braschi, Duke of 94
Braschi, Romualdo 81, 94–5, 100, 103, 293
Brewer, John 242–5, 250, 300
Briggs, John 125, 131–3, 135, 139, 143–5, 155
British College 71, 106
Brown, Levinus 132, 296
Brownson, Orestes 129
Bruno, Giordano 49
Bull of Foundation (of College) 8, 26, 29, 41, 47, 74
Budd, Hugh Christopher 300
Buoncompagni, Filippo 292
Burke, Richard 184
Burton, George Ambrose 181, 187, 299
Butterfield, William 226
Buxton, Christopher 290

Caetani, Enrico 74, 292
Caccia-Dominioni, Camillo 231, 294
Cache, Lawrence 255
Calbudower, Thomas 256
Campanelli, Filippo 293
Campion, Charles (alias Wigmore) 295
Campion, Edmund 11, 45
Cancellieri 119
Canada 99, 107
Canali, Niccola 231, 236, 294
Canisius, Peter 55, 79
Canova 65
Capalti, Annibale 293
Capparoni 265
Capponio, Aloysio 292
Caprara, Alessandro 75, 292
Carrier, Hervé 245

Carlile, Neville 235
Carne, Sir Edward 3
Carroll, Dr 99
Carroll-Abbing, John 230
Cary-Elwes, Dudley Charles 207
Casartelli, Louis Charles 208
Cashman, David 300
Castlereagh, Lord 101
Catherine of Braganza 62
Challoner, Richard 73, 76, 80, 83, 89
Chaplain, Roche 291
Chaplain, William 291
Charette (Colonel) 168
Charles II 62, 86
Charles V 3
Charles Edward (The Young Pretender) 63, 65, 86
Charnock, Robert 33
Chigi, Prince 230
Cicognani, Amleto 209
Ciano (Count) 217
Cini, Vincenzo (Citizen) 93, 114
Circignani, Niccolo (Pomarancio) 12, 30, 257
Cisalpine Club 99
Clark, Alan 238–9, 300
Clarke, John 295
Claxton, Henry (alias Morse) 89
Clement, Cesar 56
Clement VII 257, 292
Clement VIII 39, 74–5
Clement XI 69, 88
Clement XII 76, 80, 293
Clifford, William Joseph 153, 161, 177
Clynnog, Morus 3–5, 7–8, 17, 19, 29, 60, 295
Colet, John 1
Collegio Pio 143–5, 147, 150–1, 153, 157, 159, 161–4, 172, 177, 179, 264–5, 286
Collegio Romano 9, 19, 25, 38–9, 40–4, 46, 79, 83, 109–12, 127, 142, 166–8
Como, Thomas Galli, Cardinal of 13
Connel, James 85
Conry, Kieran 300
Consalvi, Ercole 95, 99, 100, 103–10,

112, 114–15, 149, 293
Cope, Alan 37
Cornthwaite, Robert 122, 142–7, 149, 153, 157, 161, 177, 179, 296, 299
Cornelius, John 290
Corsini, Andrea 53, 77, 80–5, 90, 102, 108, 110, 293, 296, 302
Cottam, Thomas 290
Courtney, Edward (alias Leedes) 295
Courtney, Thomas (alias Leedes) 295
Cowgill, Joseph Robert 187, 299
Cox, Edward 123
Coxe Hippisley, Sir John 105–6, 116
Crashaw, Richard 43
Cresswell, Joseph 295
Cronin, Charles 187
Crosby, Richard 107
Crookall, John 151
Cullen, John 187
Cunningham, James 235, 300

Danell, James 173–4
D'Arcy, Martin 205
Dean, Joseph 187
de Cupis 217
de Francis, Fr 183
de Gaspari, Alcide 236
de Lai, G. 187
de Lisle, Ambrose Philips 138
de Roncha, Leo 256
de Valle 257
de Via, Gianantonio 293
Derby, Lord 171
Dereham, Sir Thomas 62, 144
di Luca, Antonio 162, 168
Di San giuseppe, Raffaele 195
Dicconson, Edward 88, 331
Dinn, John 225
Dollinger, Johann 119
Dominioni, Camillo Caccia 231, 294
Douai College 5, 7, 11–13, 15, 21, 28, 30–2, 34, 37–42, 44, 62, 73–5, 82, 89, 98, 101, 104, 110, 111, 120, 281, 285
Douglas, Norman 203
Douglass, James 93, 100, 113
Drinkwater, Thomas 151, 153

Duke, Edmond 290
Dupanloup, Felix 190–1
Duphot (General) 92
Dwane, Michael 170
Dwyer, George Patrick 190, 208, 218, 300
Dyson, Robert 266

Eberson, Thomas 296
Edinburgh, Philip Duke of 242
Ekbery, George 226
Elizabeth I 3, 5, 16
Elizabeth II 242
Ellis, Edward 208, 299
Ellis, Philip Michael 62
Elliott, Nathaniel 296
English, Ferdinand 145, 298
English, Isabella 145
English, Louis 137, 144–6, 149–50, 157, 163, 179, 296
Errington, George 112, 123, 132, 135, 138, 163, 298
Esser, T. 186
Eugenius IV 255
Evelyn, John 43
Eyre, Charles 132, 299

Fagan, Mr 93
Farnese, Odoardo 45, 75
Fea, Carlo 119
Felici, Stefano 83–5, 92–3, 296
Feria, Duke of 45
Ferretti, Gabriele 142, 146, 293
Fioravanti, Girolamo 295
Firth, Peter 235
Fisher, St John 37
Fitzherbert, Thomas 37, 45, 47, 49, 51, 53, 71, 108, 295
Fitzherbert-Brockholes (family) 104
Fleetwood, James 107
Fleming, David 208, 218
Foggini, Pier Francesco 81–2
Foley, Brian Charles 300
Foley, John 195
Fontana, Carlo 67, 259
Fornari, Cardinal 143
Forster, E. M. 203

Fransoni, Luigi 139
Franzelin, John Baptist 167
Freddi, Bruno 229, 231
French College 150

Galeffi, Pietro 95, 115, 293
Galileo 45
Gallagher, Paul 301
Galli, Thomas (Cardinal of Como) 13
Gandolphy, Peter 101, 105-7, 115
Garnet, Henry 108
Gasquet, Aidan 19, 42, 71, 192-9,
    208-9, 215-18, 294
Gavazzi, Alessandro 138
George III 65
George IV 114
George V 203, 234
George VI 214
George, Mgr 196
German College, Rome 9, 19, 28, 33,
    37, 79, 140, 172, 188
Gibson, Matthew 104-5
Giffard, Bonaventure 71
Giles, William 153, 170, 177, 179-82,
    184, 186-7, 189-92, 196-7,
    202-3, 296, 299
Gilroy, Norman 230
Gillow, Henry 107
Gioberti, Vincenzo 183
Giovannucci, Giovanni 82, 296
Girolamo, Benedetto 108
Giustiniani Giacomo 129, 132, 141, 293
Godden, Thomas 73
Godfrey, William 155, 187, 199, 205,
    210-19, 225, 229, 239, 244, 296,
    299, 300
Goldie, Francis 264
Goldwell, Thomas 3, 15, 17
Gordon Riots 100
Goss, Alexander 163, 298
Gother, John 73
Gower, John 7, 285
Gradwell, Robert 42, 74, 94-7, 101,
    103-17, 125, 149, 151, 217, 255,
    285, 296, 298
Granada, Luis de 43
Grant, Alexander 139

Grant, Thomas 122-3, 125, 129,
    131-3, 135, 137, 139, 142-3, 145,
    147, 151, 155, 161, 163, 296, 298
Granville, Earl of 170
Grasar, Eric 227, 232, 300
Grassi, John Anthony 103, 106
Graziosi 163
Green, Christopher 303
Green, Stephen 91
Gregorian University *see also* Roman
    College 174, 177, 184, 188, 203,
    205, 207, 210-11, 213, 225-6,
    230, 237, 240, 245, 251, 306
Gregory I 274
Gregory XI 254
Gregory XIII 5, 8, 9, 12-13, 15,
    17-18, 25, 32, 38, 272, 283, 288,
    292, 302
Gregory XIV 32, 75
Gregory XVI 118, 122, 125, 133,
    138-9, 293
Griffin, Bernard 208, 230, 232, 299
Griffiths, Thomas 132
Grimshaw, Francis 208, 299
Gruffydd, Robert 3, 29
Gualterio, Filippo Antonio 292

Hart, William 290
Hason, Richard 255
Hall 26
Halsall, Joseph 208, 299
Hay, George 250, 297
Haydock, George 290
Hazelhurst, Henry 187
Heard, William Theodore 29, 209,
    229, 242, 245, 294, 300
Heenan, John Carmel 208, 299, 300
Hemerford, Thomas 290
Hendricks, Paul 301
Henry VII 1
Henry VIII 3, 217, 304
Henry (Stuart), Cardinal York 63-5,
    86-8, 100, 102, 293
Henshaw, Henry 7
Heptonstall, George 107
Hine, John 300
Hinsley, Arthur 74, 174, 182, 187,

192, 195–9, 201–12, 216–18, 223, 225, 231, 265, 287, 296, 299
Hodgson, Joseph 107
Holt, William 37, 52, 295
Hothersall, William 81, 296
Howard, Edward 141, 162, 174, 293, 303
Howard, Philip 49, 53, 55, 60–3, 65, 67, 72, 75, 86, 175, 258–60, 292
Hollis, Crispian 300
Huddleston, John 86
Hudson, Nicholas 250, 297
Husenbeth, Frederick Charles 104

Ingram, John 291
Innocent VI 1
Innocent XIII 76
Irish College, Rome 16, 31, 47, 71, 93, 169, 172

Jacometti, Giovanni 259
James I 86
James II 55, 62, 67, 86
James III (the Old Pretender) 62–3, 71
James, Edward 290
John XXIII 239, 240, 242
Johnson, G. 146
Johnson, Robert 291
Johnson, William Anthony 299

Kavanagh, Bernard 196
Kavanagh, William 107, 109, 261
Kearns, John 107
Keats, John 121
Kelly, Patrick 300
Kennedy, John 250, 297
Keatinge, William 187, 299
Kellison, Matthew 44
King, John Henry 184, 187, 299
Kirby, Luke 17, 290
Kirk, John 76, 81, 89–91, 260
Kilgarriff, Patrick 250, 297
Knights of Malta *see* Malta, Kinghts of

Lacey, William 290
Lacordaire, Jean Baptiste Henri 119

Lacy, R. 174, 189, 299
Lambruschini 132
Lambton, Joseph 290
Lamennais, Hugues Félicité Robert de 119
Langdon, Philip 195, 196
Lante, Federigo Marcello 293
Lax, John 255
Leedes, Edward (alias Courtney) 295
Leedes, Thomas (alias Courtney) 295
Leeds Seminary 225
Leeming, Bernard 226
Legenda, Carlo 67
Leigh, Richard 290
Leo XII 112, 118, 293
Leo XIII 180–1, 187, 208, 219, 265, 306
Lepicier, Alexis 209, 219, 294
Lessius, Leonard 37
Lewis, David 290
Lewis, Owen 5, 7–8, 17, 24, 27–30, 37
Liberatore, Matteo 143
Liber Ruber 22, 29, 49, 60, 213, 218, 261, 281, 316, 332
Liège (English College) 51–3, 55, 58, 71, 84–5, 98, 234, 305
Lily, William 1
Linacre, Thomas 1
Lingard, John 103–6, 108
Lisbon (English College) 16, 35, 42, 73, 110–11, 172, 187
Litta, Lorenzo 101, 103–5
Lobb, Emmanuel (alias Joseph Simon) 43, 86, 295
Locke, John 80
Lockwood, John 291
Loisy, Alfred 184–5
Lomax, James 291
Lombard College 150
Longley, Bernard 300
Louvain, Jesuit College at 52
Lowe, William 7, 290
Luca, Antonio Di 162, 168
Lucas, Anthony 296
Ludovisi, Ludovico 47
Lydgate, John 303
Lynch, Thomas 235

McDonald, Kevin 300
Macmillan, John 212, 215, 222–34, 238, 297
Macpherson, Paul 92, 99, 102–6, 113, 115
McGough, David 301
McGuigan, James 230
McIntyre, John 187, 192, 194–5, 211, 216, 296, 299
Macaulay, Lord 121
Magliana, La 53, 59, 84, 166, 170, 195, 319
Magnani, Marco 83, 90–1, 296, 319
Mai, Angelo 119
Maire, Christopher 47, 296
Malta, Knights of 221, 229–30
Manners, John (alias Simcocks) 295
Manning, Henry Edward 118, 122, 127, 132–3, 137, 143, 147, 152–5, 157–8, 161–6, 175, 177, 186, 293
Mansfield, Robert 296
Maria Clementina 63, 70
Martin, Gregory 7, 29
Marsh, Walter 17
Marshall, Henry Vincent 227
Marshall, Joseph 296
Mary I 3
Mary of Modena 71
Mary of Teck 203
Maryvale (Old Oscott) 98
Mathew, Tobie 53, 59
Mattei, Cardinal 119
Maronite College, Rome 9, 19
Masterson, Joseph 208, 299
Massari, Francesco 259
Mayes, Lawrence 88
Mellini, Giovanni 47, 89, 292
Merry del Val, Rafael 179, 189, 208–9, 215, 218, 265, 294
Meyer 19
Mezzofanti, Giuseppe 119, 138
Mico, Edward 291
Middleton, Robert 291
Milner, John 101, 103, 105–7
Milton, John 43
Minocchi 183

Mivart, St George 208, 218
Monti, Cardinal 76
Montini, John-Baptist (Paul VI) 229
Montopoli 199, 217
Morgan, Edward 291
Morgan, William 295
Moriarty, Ambrose 187, 191, 196, 217, 299
Morone, Giovanni 4, 7, 8, 60, 254, 273, 278, 292
Morton, Dr 4, 5
Morton, Robert 290
Morris, John 143, 146, 154–5, 163
Morse, Henry 79, 89, 290
Moss, Joseph 199, 209
Murphy-O'Connor, Cormac 250, 297, 300
Munday, Anthony 16–17, 330
Munden, John 290
Murat 109
Mush, John 7
Mussolini, Benito 201, 220

Neri, St Philip 12, 127
Nesbitt, Gerard 235
Neve, Frederick 146, 150–3, 157, 159, 161–4, 175, 177, 179, 296
Newman, Gilbert 255
Newman, John Henry 121, 127, 129, 133–4, 153, 156, 303
Nichols, Vincent 300
Nicolai, Mgr 110
Norfolk (Fifteenth) Duke of 170–4, 189
North American College, Rome 150, 209

Oates, Titus 62
Oblates of St Charles 127, 157, 163, 177
O'Callaghan, Henry 131, 152, 154–5, 157, 161–2, 166–7, 170–2, 175, 177, 179–81, 187, 189, 192, 264, 287, 294, 296, 305, 325
Odescalchi, Carlo 125
O'Farrell 196
O'Handley 106, 116

Oldcorne, Edward 291
Old Hall (St Edmund's College) 98, 107, 112, 114, 126
Old Oscott 98
Osborne, Sir D'Arcy 229
Oscott (St Mary's College) 106, 123, 126, 132, 138, 141, 162, 175, 177, 187
Owen, Jane 57
Owen, Thomas 49, 51, 295

Paget, Augustus 170–1
Palazzo Muti 63, 66
Palazzola 198, 201, 207, 210, 217, 219, 222, 229, 230, 233, 236, 240, 242, 244, 246–51
Palica, Giuseppe 208
Pallotti, Vincent 139
Palmer, John 254
Palmerston, Lord 135
Pamfilj (gardens) 77
Panzani, Gregorio 55, 57
Parisotti (Procurator) 95
Parkinson, Henry 187
Parma, Duke of 76
Passaglia, Carlo 129, 143
Paul III 3
Paul V 28, 74, 292
Paul VI 235, 242, 247–8
Pearson, Thomas Bernard 208, 299
Perrone, Giovanni 143
Perry, Philip 80
Persons, Robert 11, 13, 21, 24, 27–9, 32–3, 35, 37, 41–2, 45, 49, 56, 59, 71, 75, 295, 305, 330, 332
Peters, John (otherwise John the Shepherd) 254
Petre, Maud 208
Petre, Vicar Apostolic 88
Petroccia, Mgr 199
Philip II 7
Piacenza (Abbey of S. Sabino) 9, 32, 53–4, 59, 76, 82, 303
Picchetti, Paolo 258
Pico de Mirandola, Luigi 293
Pilgrim Book 9
Pippi, Bernardino 87

Pius VI 84–5, 94, 293
Pius VII 65, 94, 99, 100, 104, 112, 118, 149, 293
Pius IX 130, 133, 137, 140–2, 144, 146, 150–3, 159, 168, 264, 293, 303, 305
Pius X 185, 192
Pius XI 214, 221–2
Pius XII 222, 237, 240
Pizzardo, Giuseppe 214, 219, 229–30
Plasden, Polydore 290
Plowden, Charles 106
Plowden, Percy 296
Plowden, Richard 107, 296
Plunkett, Oliver 89
Pole, Reginald 2–4, 30, 108, 246, 303
Pomarancio, *see* Circignani, Niccolo
Pormont, Thomas 290
Porter, Nicholas 94
Porzio, Monte 53, 59, 77, 84, 100, 109, 113, 119, 125–6, 145, 151, 159, 161, 166–8, 170–1, 173–4, 194–5, 190, 197, 199, 303
Postgate, Ralph 62, 296
Powell, Francis 296
Poynter, William 101, 103–6, 110–11, 125
Poyntz, John (alias Stephens) 295
Pozzo, Andrea 67, 87–8, 259–60, 303
Prior, John 174, 179, 184, 187, 189
Prior Park 123
Propaganda Fide 41–2, 47, 55, 57, 59–60, 62, 65, 71, 73, 76, 84, 99, 101–2, 105, 125, 127, 133, 149, 153, 175
Pugin, Edward Welby 148, 151, 264

Quarantotti (Secretary of Propaganda) 99, 115

Ramsey, Michael 246, 249
Rawcliffe, Richard 235
Rea James 235
Redmond, James 174, 209–11
Redmond, Raymond Patrick 229, 235
Reisach, Karl August von 285, 293
Restieaux, Cyril 208, 300

Rheims (English College) 7, 37, 52, 110
Ricci, Lorenzo 82, 260
Richard II 255
Riddell, William 298
Rienzo, Cola di 1
Roche, Arthur 300, 301
Rock, Daniel 107, 123, 132, 139
Roman Association 152, 196–9, 220, 227
Roman College *see* Collegio Romano
Romualdi, Domenico 196, 216
Rope, Henry Edward George 57, 162
Roskell, Richard 161, 298
Rosmini, Anthony 181, 183
Rudderham, Joseph 208, 299
Ruffini, Ernesto 211, 213

St Mary's (Stonyhurst) 223–8
St Omer (English College) 43, 55, 71, 76–7, 82, 88, 90
St John, Ambrose 134, 153
Salvatus, Master 256
San Lucar (Seville College) 88, 172
Sandwych, Walter 256
Sapienza University 118
Sargeant, John 73
Sarto, Cardinal 185, 189
Savella (Corte Savella prison) 49, 65, 254, 258
Schola Saxonum 144
Scotti, Mgr 260
Scots College (Rome) 63, 71, 92–3, 105, 170–2, 207, 242
Scots College (Royal Scots College Valladolid) 114
Sedgley Park 98
Sega, Filippo 26–7, 32, 35, 37, 39, 43, 55, 281, 292
Serafini, Mgr 195
Servi 261
Seville 88, 118–9, 137, 172
Sharples, James 107, 298
Sheehan 195
Sheldon, Henry 296
Shelley, Sir Richard 4
Sheprey, William 37

Sherborne, Robert 256
Sherson (or Sherton), Martin 291
Shert, John 7, 17, 29, 290
Sherwin, Ralph 11, 12, 14, 22, 290
Simcocks, John (alias Manners) 295
Simon, Joseph (alias Emmanuel Lobb) 295
Sixtus V 17, 19, 23, 32
Smelt, Robert 84, 93–4, 100, 102, 113
Smith, Richard 291
Smith, Richard (vicar apostolic) 32, 39, 55, 60, 76, 86, 89
Smith, Richard L. 209, 217, 219, 222–3, 225, 235
Smith, Robert 159, 189
Sneider, Filippo 229
Sobieski *see* Maria Clementina
Sodality of the Blessed Virgin Mary 19, 21, 23, 32, 260, 261, 281, 315
South American College 150
Southwell, Robert 290
Spada, Cardinal 53
Spencer, Ignatius 123, 138
Spetiano, Cesare 5, 29, 257
Squarcione, Acarizio 28
Stafford, Robert 295
Standon Lordship 98
Stanley, Algernon 195, 197, 201, 209, 216
Stanley, William 255
Stendhal 121
Stephens, John (alias Poyntz) 295
Stone, Marmaduke 85
Stonor, Christopher 102
Stonor, Edmund 141, 150, 153, 159, 162, 168, 303, 306
Stonor, John Talbot 77, 81, 84, 87–90
Stonyhurst 85, 98, 103–7, 115, 223, 225–34
Strickland, William 84, 87
Swinburne, Martha 260
Swindlehurst, Owen 300

Talbot, George 123, 141–2, 144–7, 150–5, 157, 159, 161–4, 165, 168, 172, 175, 188, 264, 293, 303
Talbot, James 83, 90

Tansfield, Brian 291
Taparelli, D'Azeglio Aloysio 143
Tempest 26
Thomas, Francis 300
Thorpe, John 80, 90
Thules, John 291
Thwing, Edward 290
Tichborne, Thomas 291
Tickle, Gerard William 208, 234,
    238–42, 247, 297, 300
Tinbaldi, Giacomo 195
Toffolo, Adrian 250, 297
Toleto, Francesco 27–8, 33, 292
Tosti (Sig.) 110
Torriani, Horatio 258
Trent, Council of 13
Turner, Anthony 291
Turner, William 298
Tyrrell, Anthony 302
Tyrrell, George 208

Ullathorne, William Bernard 133,
    147, 153, 157
Upholland 187, 215
Urban VIII 45, 49, 57, 76, 292
Ushaw College 98, 104, 107, 112,
    114–6, 118–9, 131–2, 135, 142,
    189, 199, 208, 210, 211

Valladolid (English College) 16, 31,
    35, 56, 80, 88, 90, 110, 172, 207
Vanderville, John 39
Vatican I 137, 166, 175
Vatican II 166, 237, 240, 241–3, 250,
    285, 289
Vaughan, Herbert 118, 122, 127,
    164, 172, 174–5, 177–9, 186–8,
    191, 216, 294
Veneto, Antonio 258
Vertue, John 299
Vespignani, Vergilio 151, 264
Visitations
    1585 17–23
    1596 26–8, 35
    1623 41
    1630 43, 47
    1645 53

1657 54
1671 54
1702 69
1739 71–7
1869 165
1906 186–7
1916 192–5
1958 214–15
Vitelleschi, Mutio 295
Vitelleschi, Salvatore 165, 285, 293

Wadding, Luke 37
Walker, John R. T. 235
Wall, John 290
Walmesley, Charles 80, 99
Walpole, Henry 290
Walsh, Thomas 104
Ward, Barbara 47
Ward, Mary 47–8, 58
Ward, W. G. 127
Ward, Wilfrid 166, 167
Warham, William 1
Watkinson, Robert 291
Watts-Russell, Julian 168–9, 188
Wednesbury, John 257
Weedal, Henry 132
Weld, Charles 85, 261
Weld, Thomas 125, 128, 141, 293
Weston, Dr 47
White, Eustace 290
White, William 112
Whiteside, Thomas 187, 216, 299
Wigmore (alias Campion) 295
Wilton Diptych 255
Wiseman, Nicholas 107–9, 112–14,
    118–41, 143–4, 146–7, 149–53,
    155, 162–4, 175, 177, 185–6,
    260–1, 296, 298, 303
Witham, Robert 31, 71
Wonersh, St John's College 208
Woodcock, John 291
Worlock, Mgr 239
Worthington, Dr 12, 47

Zahm, Fr 208
Zurla, Placido 85, 113, 117, 293